D0889871

Native American
Place-Names
of Indiana

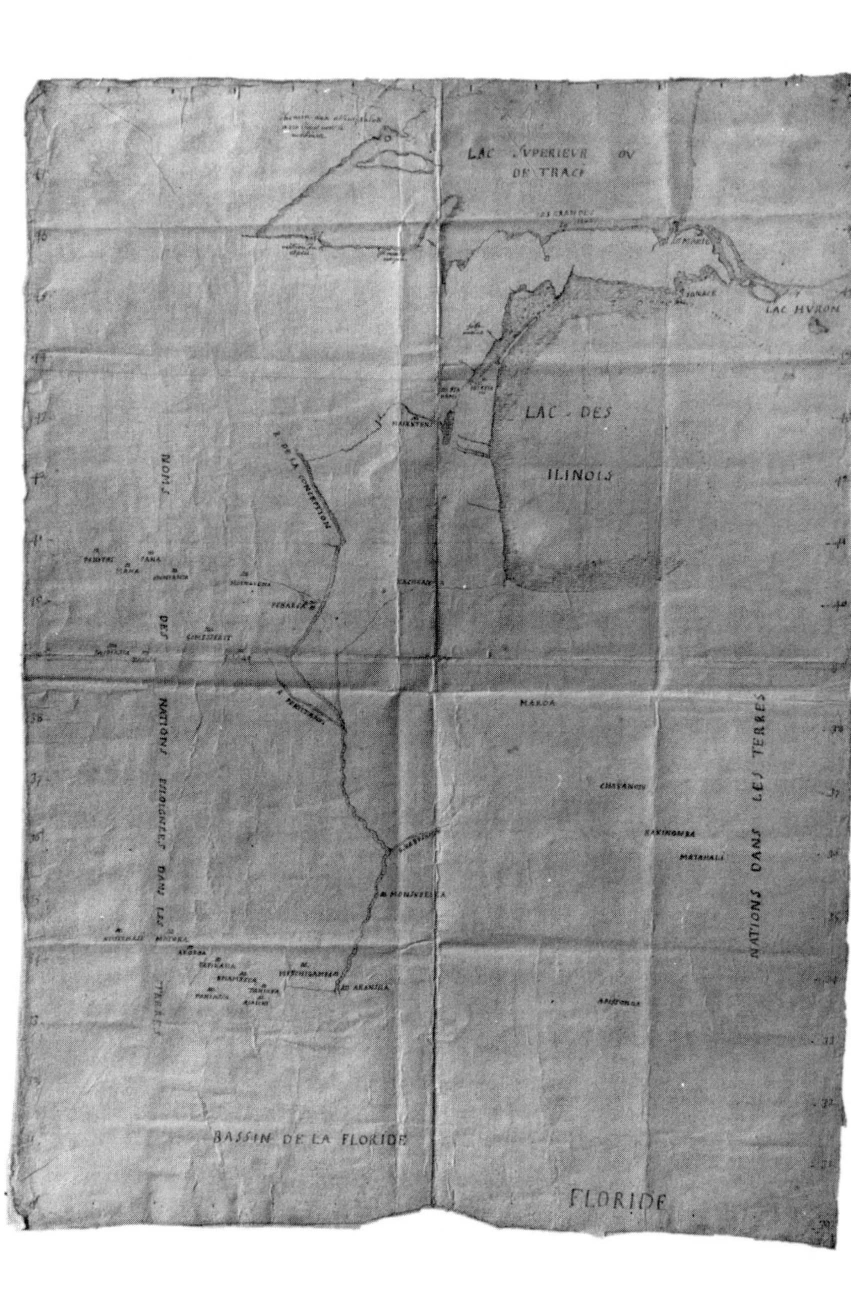

LAC SVPERIEVR OV
DE TRACY
LAC HVRON
LAC DES
ILINOIS
NOMS DES NATIONS ELOIGNÉES DANS LES TERRES
NATIONS DANS LES TERRES
MAROA
BASSIN DE LA FLORIDE
FLORIDE

Native American Place-Names of Indiana

MICHAEL McCAFFERTY

UNIVERSITY OF ILLINOIS PRESS
Urbana and Chicago

BOWLING GREEN STATE
UNIVERSITY LIBRARIES

Frontispiece: Jacques Marquette, (Carte du Missisipi), 1673–74. Archives de la Société de Jésus Canada Français. Recueil 196.

© 2008 by Michael McCafferty
All rights reserved
Manufactured in the United States of America

C 5 4 3 2

♾ This book is printed on acid-free paper.

Library of Congress Cataloging-in-Publication Data

McCafferty, Michael
Native American place-names of Indiana /
Michael McCafferty.
p. cm.
Includes bibliographical references and index.
ISBN 13: 978-0-252-03268-4 (cloth : alk. paper)
ISBN 10: 0-252-03268-3
1. Names, Indian—Indiana.
2. Names, Geographical—Indiana.
3. Indiana.—History, Local.
I. Title.
F524.M33 2008
977.2—dc22 2007035938

For those who created these names

"... gathering the beauty that streamed away
from them back to their own faces again."

—Rainer Maria Rilke, *Duino Elegies,* second elegy

Contents

Preface

The intent of this book is to present a historically clear and linguistically clean picture of the place-names in Indiana created and used by local historic American Indians. These are the oldest names on record for this land.

A "historically clear picture" will show who created the names, as well as when, where, how, and why they were used, and a "linguistically clean picture" will provide the appropriate native language forms, morphological analyses, and the correct translations for them.

Indiana is well endowed with historically attested Native American place-names, in large part because of the region's pivotal position in history. Still, in the late 1600s and early 1700s, France's royal mapmaker, Jean-Baptiste Louis Franquelin, sitting at his drawing board in Québec, advocated doing away with all native place-names in formulating the European geography of North America. It was his practical wish that this land bear exclusively French-language place-names, so as to dispel, in his opinion, the confusion created among his compatriots by mobile aboriginal bands using different names for the countless rivers and places of the North American interior (Delanglez, "Franquelin, Mapmaker," 40). Nonetheless, as the reader will see, the everyday usefulness of indigenous place-names for the French-speaking people who actually lived and worked here carved out a future place for many of them. Then, as English-speaking people moved north and west into what is now Indiana, these newcomers interacted for many years with already established American Indian and French-speaking communities and individuals. Trade and treaties necessitated the use of names that had universal familiarity, and it was these practical interactions that created the very continuity in Indiana's oldest place-name inventory of which everyone today is the beneficiary—not only because of the names' historical value but also for their unique perspectives and beauty.

A glance at a map of Indiana will show that European languages, especially English, are represented in the names of the majority of the state's cities, towns, villages, unincorporated areas, counties, townships, streets, parks, geological landmarks, and even streams and lakes. Nevertheless, Native American place-names are plentiful throughout the state. In fact, in any direction one turns in Indiana, a native place-name beckons from very close by.

Acknowledgments

The author is indebted to the following people for the help they generously offered towards the creation of this book: Daryl Baldwin, Bridgie Brelsford, Lucille Brennan, Laura Buszard-Welcher, R. Joe Campbell, Wallace Chafe, Donald Cochran, Isabelle Contant, David Costa, Duane Esarey, Yaïves Ferland, Chuck Fiero, Ives Goddard, Noel Justice, Robert Karrow, Franz Koks, John Koontz, John Langley, Carmen Laroche, Jiyoung Lee, Philip Lesourd, Thomas Mason, Brian McCafferty, David McCafferty, Margaret McCafferty, Robert McCullough, Gunther Michelson, John Nichols, John O'Meara, David Pentland, Stewart Rafert, Robert Rankin, James Rementer, Richard Rhodes, Blair Rudes, Walter Salts, Richard Schmal, Suzanne Sommerville, Randolph Valentine, Robert Vézina, Paul Voorhis, Mark Walczynski, and Ray Writnour. A Clio grant from the Indiana Historical Society helped with much of the research.

I would like to have given this book to several folks no longer with us: Glenn Black, Lucy Blalock, Bill Bright, Lucien Campeau, Jean Delanglez, Jacob Piatt Dunn, Floyd Lounsbury, Gabriel Godfroy, Eli Lilly, Robert Taylor, Virgil Vogel, and my grandparents.

Technical Considerations

The linguistic nature of *Native American Place-Names of Indiana* requires the use of various technical terms. The definitions for most of these items are in the glossary.

The historical recordings of American Indian words will appear between single angled brackets, as in, for example, <Soosoocpahaloc>. Phonemic transcriptions of native words will be written in italic script, for example, Miami-Illinois *kihčikami(i)wi,* "big-water." The initial characters of phonemic spellings are never capitalized—even in proper names. For example, Potawatomi *wabmimi,* "white passenger pigeon," is the proper phonemic spelling of the name of the historic Potawatomi leader known in English as White Pigeon. French terms are also naturally italicized, for example, *la rivière des Illinois.* A parenthetical letter in a phonemic spelling indicates unknown but possible length, as in Miami-Illinois *waapaahši(i)ki,* "it shines white." An asterisk placed before a phonemic spelling will indicate either an undocumented yet expected form or a reconstructed form in the case of Proto-Algonquian or Proto-Iroquoian, for example, PI **õ·tariʔ,* "lake." Two asterisks will mark an impossible or ungrammatical form, for example, ***meehčikaminki.* Linguists write schwa, the sound of the unstressed initial vowel of English "adopt," in different ways. All recordings of schwa in this book will be written *ə,* as in Potawatomi *nbəs,* "lake."

Phonetic transcriptions, which represent the actual pronunciation of underlying phonemic forms, will be written in single brackets, for example, phonetic Miami [pèehsiúŋgi] for phonemic *apeehsionki,* "at the fawn." Glosses will appear within double quotation marks, and a comma will separate a native term from its translation: *meenkahsenahkiki,* "it is big stone country." In the bibliography and notes, double quotation marks will also identify the titles of historic maps.

Vowel length is an essential aspect (i.e., a phonemic characteristic) of most of the Native American languages discussed in this book. Incorrect vowel length in a term can change the meaning of the intended word or render the expression confusing to the native speaker. For example, in Miami-Illinois, *niipi,* "my arrow" with a long vowel in the first syllable sounds different from the word *nipi,* "water." Consonant length is also an essential aspect of Unami, one of the languages that figure in this book. According to the spelling conventions adopted for the different native languages that appear in this volume, vowels and consonants will be marked for length with either a raised dot, as in Southern Unami *ɔ·p·-,* "white" or by the doubling of a linguistic symbol (gemination), as in Kickapoo *metemooha,* "old woman." Though not a problem for linguists, gemination can lead to pronunciation mistakes by English-speaking nonlinguists. For example, one might erroneously conclude that Miami-Illinois long *ee* represents the sound of the ee in English "meet," whereas it actually approximates the vowel sound in the word "mail." Therefore, if unsure, the reader should check the list at the end of this section to see what sound a particular symbol represents.

Essentially, only four prosodic marks will occur in this work. The acute accent (´) will indicate primary stress, as in Miami-Illinois phonetic [eehsípana], "raccoon." The grave accent (`) will mark secondary stress, as in Munsee *kwə̀nə́moxkw,* "otter," but will show middle pitch in Wyandot, as in *uhyì·žuh,* "big-river." The breve accent (˘)will mark a very short unstressed vowel, as in Munsee *wá·sə̆le·w,* "it shines." The tilde (˜) will indicate nasalization, as in phonetic Miami-Illinois [hsènaamĩ́ži], "sugar maple tree."

The historic recordings of local Indian place-names often differ, sometimes dramatically, from their linguistic spellings. These dissimilarities generally derive from the fact that not only do the sounds of Native American languages often differ from those of European languages but also the historical spellings of terms in the local Native languages were the work of French-, English-, or occasionally German-speaking nonlinguists employing writing systems that were inadequately equipped for making good recordings.

That said, in the Potawatomi language, whose speakers first entered the Indiana area in the early 1700s, an extensive vowel shift has occurred in roughly the last century and a half. By the end of the 1800s, most Potawatomi short vowels except *o* had become *ə.* Then, by about 1930, unstressed short vowels were deleted altogether in nonfinal odd-numbered syllables. Hence, as the reader will see, strictly in terms of vowels, the Potawatomi recorded by the earliest chroniclers looks quite different from the modern language. In fact, the early recordings of Potawatomi somewhat resemble Ojibwa, which is understandable since Potawatomi can be described as an Algonquian language composed of an Ojibweyan substrate and a Sauk-Fox-Kickapoo-Mascouten superstrate. However, older Potawatomi and modern Potawatomi also look different in terms of consonants. Specifically, the original contrast between preaspirated consonants and nonpreaspirated consonants in Algonquian first showed up in Potawatomi and Ojibwa as a contrast between "fortis"/geminate consonants and "lenis"/plain consonants respectively, with the latter only randomly voiced. When the lenis consonants were not voiced, almost all early historical recorders, such as Father Friedrich Baraga in the 1800s, would write the lenis and fortis consonants the same way—as k, t, s, and so on. Charles Hockett, an Algonquianist who worked with Potawatomi in the 1900s, typically wrote the contrast in that language as *kk* and *k*, respectively, for example. But in the twentieth century, in both Potawatomi and Ojibwa, the lenis obstruents started to become voiced more and more often. Chuck Fiero, an Ojibweyanist and a consultant for the present volume who has worked with Ojibwa speakers in northwest Ontario, was the first person to begin writing this contrast systematically with voiceless versus voiced letters. In other words, Fiero wrote *kk* as "k," and *k* as "g." This practice was later adopted by the Ojibwa scholars John Nichols and Richard Rhodes, and is now fairly standard, except for certain northernmost dialects of Ojibwa where preaspiration still exists. According to Costa, who has done some fieldwork with modern Potawatomi, the geminate/plain contrast in that language is not easy to hear, and plain obstruents are not always very clearly voiced. Moreover, he notes that, in Potawatomi, it is not at all just a simple question of a voiced/voiceless contrast. The fortis consonants are geminated, that is, pronounced with a somewhat stronger articulation, and always voiceless; the lenis consonants are nongeminated, and pronounced somewhat softer—and sometimes voiced and sometimes not.[1] For Potawatomi, this book will generally cast interpretations of historical recordings in modern Potawatomi, and will thereby have forms that reflect the contrast between fortis and lenis consonants. However, it will also include historical phonemic forms that show no voicing. Overall, I have adapted Laura Buszard-Welcher's practical orthography for modern Potawatomi to standard Algonquian transcription, hers being a modest reworking of the spelling convention employed by the Wisconsin Native Language Project.[2]

Entries in the Miami-Illinois language, which was spoken in Indiana starting in at least 1679, generally follow David Costa.[3] However, in the present volume *č* replaces Costa's *c* for representing the sound characteristically written ch in English, as in "child." Kickapoo etyma appearing herein will be written according to the spelling system developed for that language by Paul Voorhis. In addition, Voorhis's *c* will also appear as *č*.[4] Kickapoo was spoken in Indiana at least by the early 1700s. Shawnee language forms are transcribed according to the technical spelling convention worked out for that language by Charles Voegelin.[5] Shawnee and the other Algonquian languages mentioned above are classified as "Eastern Great Lakes Algonquian languages" or "Central Algonquian languages."

On the other hand, Unami, commonly known as a "Delaware Indian" language, is an Eastern Algonquian language. Northern Unami is the name of an extinct dialect of this language once spoken south of Raritan Valley and the Delaware Water Gap in what is today central New Jersey, and in adjacent areas of eastern Pennsylvania. Northern Unami was later spoken in the Indiana area in the early 1800s. Southern Unami is another dialect of this same language once spoken in New Jersey below the Trenton falls, in the adjacent area of eastern Pennsylvania, and along the Delaware coast.[6] Near the turn of the nineteenth century speakers of Southern Unami were living in the central and southern Indiana area. Words in Unami in this book appear in the technical orthography created for this language by Charles Voegelin.[7] However, the low back rounded vowels, which Voegelin writes *o* and *o·*, are herein written *ɔ* and *ɔ·*, and his long mid-back rounded vowel *u·*, following Ives Goddard, will be written *o·*. Munsee, another Delaware Indian language, closely related to Unami, was spoken in prehistoric and early historic times in what is today northern New Jersey along the upper Delaware River and southern New York along the lower Hudson. It was also spoken in Indiana around the turn of the nineteenth century. In this book Munsee terms are written in the technical orthography developed for this language by Ives Goddard.[8]

Iroquoian words will appear in the orthographic system formulated by Floyd Lounsbury and Wallace Chafe.[9] However, I follow Blair Rudes in writing the affricate *č*, which some Iroquoianists write *ts*. In transcribing certain vowels, I also follow Rudes.[10] In keeping with the general practice of modern Iroquoian linguistics, Iroquoian citations will in most cases include their morphophonemic, segmented forms. For example, for the Huron-Wyandot phrase "standing rock," |t-ka-hrε̃ʔn-ot-eʔ| is the morphophonemic form of phonemic *kahrε̃ʔnú·teʔ*, while [kahrẽʔndú·teʔ] is the phonetic (surface) form of this term. As I am not an Iroquoianist, I am indebted to Blair Rudes, Gunther Michelson, and Wally Chafe for the help they provided with the Iroquoian material appearing in this volume.

The following is the technical alphabet used in this book along with the nearest equivalent sounds in English, with the exception of the sound *x*, which is not a sound native to English:

p	"pat"
b	"bat"
t	"tag"
d	"dog"
k	"cat"
g	"get"
ʔ	"button" (glottal stop represented here by orthographic -tt-)
h	"hand"
č	"chip"
ǰ	"jar"
θ	"think"
s	"sit"
z	"zero"
š	"shall"
ž	"measure" (represented here in English by orthographic s)
x	"Bach" (orthographic -ch pronounced as in German)
r	(presumably a tap in Old Miami–Illinois and Huron-Wyandot)
l	"lap"
m	"map"
n	"nap"
ŋ	"sing" (represented in English by orthographic ng)
w	"win"
y	"yore"
a	"altitude"
æ	"at"
α	"father"
e	"ate"
ε	"set"
ə	"another"
ʌ	"up"

i	"eat"
I	"it"
o	"boat"
ɔ	"ought"
u	"boot"
ã	as in Parisian French *sans*
ẽ	as in Parisian French *saint*
ɛ̃	an Iroquoian nasal vowel pronounced with the tongue lower than in the case of French ẽ
õ	as in Parisian French *son*

The reader will also occasionally see the symbol 8. This is actually a digraph composed of a circle surmounted by a crescent. It is very common in early historical French Jesuit documents. Hurried missionaries and later printers simplified this letter for convenience sake by writing it in the shape of an eight (8), as I shall do in this book. See chapter 2 for a detailed description of how this symbol was used by Jesuit missionaries who recorded the Miami-Illinois language. In addition, the linguist Albert Gatschet, whose recordings of Miami-Illinois place-names appear herein, used this symbol for short *o*.

Many of the recordings of French terms in the primary sources often lack the accent marks typical of modern French spelling. In this book historical French spellings will be reproduced exactly as their seventeenth- and eighteenth-century scribes penned or printed them. Therefore, such spellings may not necessarily reflect the modern orthographic standards for that language that readers are familiar with.

Finally, English phonetic transcriptions are generally written for standard nonregional American English. The reader should note that the English phonetic transcriptions herein appear in a broad transcription style and do not portray dialect-specific diphthongs.

Abbreviations

C	consonant
Fr.	French
AI	animate intransitive verb
II	inanimate intransitive verb
lit.	literally
PA	Proto-Algonquian
PI	Proto-Iroquoian
pl.	plural
sg.	singular
V	vowel

Introduction

The primary-source documents that preserve Native American place-names for Indiana are the maps, itineraries, letters, and reports composed by French missionaries, explorers, soldiers, traders, cartographers, and travelers in the seventeenth and eighteenth centuries, as well as English language maps, military reports, trade ledgers, treaties, surveys, settler records, and travel diaries from the eighteenth and early nineteenth centuries. German missionaries working for a short time near the turn of the nineteenth century in what is now central Indiana also saved a few important local place-names from the Delaware languages. Finally, primary-source place-name data for Indiana were still being collected in the early 1900s from native speakers of Miami-Illinois and Potawatomi. The single richest primary sources of American Indian place-names for Indiana are the works of Jacob Piatt Dunn (1855–1924) and Albert Gatschet (1832–1907).

In the late 1800s and early 1900s, Dunn, an Indiana historian and librarian, collected local Native American place-names. His principal place-name consultants for the Miami-Illinois language were *waapanahkikapwa,* a well-known and highly respected Indiana-based Miami tribal leader whose European name was Gabriel Godfroy; *wiikapimiša,* a Wea woman whose European name was Sarah Wadsworth; and *kiilhsohkwa,* a granddaughter of the famous Eel River Miami warrior *mihšihkinaahkwa,* known historically to English speakers as Little Turtle.[1] Dunn's work, however, has some shortcomings. He often did not indicate which individuals supplied which names, and he often failed to supply complete place-names, leaving out terms for "river" and "creek" in the case of some hydronyms.[2] In a couple of instances, Dunn's Indian place-names appear to be his own inventions.

Albert Gatschet, a Swiss-born linguist who immigrated to the United States in 1868 and worked for the U.S. Bureau of American Ethnology, also recorded important local Miami-Illinois language place-names, most of which Dunn did not get. About the turn of the twentieth century Gatschet traveled to Oklahoma to record the language of native speakers of Miami-Illinois, a couple of whom in their youth had lived east of the Mississippi. His principal informant for Indiana place-names was the Wea woman *wiikapimiša.*

Both Dunn's and Gatschet's recordings hold significance for Algonquian linguistics. For example, without them we would neither have a sense of the full grammatical range of Miami-Illinois place-name morphology nor be aware of the anomalous grammatical nature of Miami-Illinois "noun + noun" place-names within Algonquian. In addition to Dunn's published works on American Indian place-names, a limited amount of additional onomastic material collected by him is located in the Indiana State Library in Indianapolis and in the National Anthropological Archives (NAA) in Suitland, Maryland. Gatschet's Miami-Illinois language material is also at the NAA. For the NAA data collected by Dunn and Gatschet, as well as for the small amount of place-name material collected by another early linguist, Truman Michelson, I have used the files of David Costa, the world's authority on the Miami-Illinois language, and of Daryl Baldwin, director of the Myaamia Project at Miami University of Ohio.

A curious mix of primary- and secondary-source data describes the works of Daniel Hough (1827–1880) and Hiram W. Beckwith (1833–1903). Hough was an Indiana Quaker known for his rather extensive book collection, which is now housed at Earlham College in Richmond, Indiana.[3] The map he drew, titled "Indian Names of Lakes, Rivers, Towns, Forts of Indiana," is an invaluable contribution to our knowledge of local native place-names. Exactly when Hough made his map is unknown. It was published after his death by Beckwith, a historian and a contemporary of Hough, who added some material to it and then included it in his 1882 article "Indian Names of Water Courses in the State of Indiana."[4] Beckwith, the first president of the Illinois Historical Society, wrote extensively on the Wabash Valley and was particularly interested in the river's aboriginal past. In the course of his historical research he collected a number of Native American place-names and discussed them not only in the Indiana county histories he authored but also in his 1884 book *The Illinois and Indiana Indians.*[5] It has been impossible to determine exactly where Hough and Beckwith obtained most of their Indian place-names. Dunn states that Hough consulted the Miami themselves. Beckwith exchanged letters with Mary Ann Baptiste, a longtime resident of the Wabash Valley Wea community and later the wife of the famous Peoria leader "Batticy" Baptiste. Beckwith even visited her in Paola, Kansas, on November 30, 1878, for the expressed purpose of obtaining Indian place-name information for the Wabash Valley.[6]

Like Dunn's work, Hough's and Beckwith's have their shortcomings. Both occasionally ascribed place-names to the wrong languages or supplied faulty translations.[7] In addition, Hough's map contains some egregious copy errors, which Dunn attributed to Hough's engraver. In this, Dunn appears to be correct. For example, Hough's map has "Pemsquahawa" for what was surely originally *Tensquatawa, the name of the famous Shawnee Prophet commonly written Tenskwatawa. Since this American Indian leader's name was as well known as that of any indigenous person in Indiana in the first half of the nineteenth century, it is inconceivable that the well-read Hough was the source of this error.

Useful secondary-source documents that contain locally created American Indian place-names include county and state histories, all from the eighteenth, nineteenth, and early twentieth centuries,[8] as well as a map designed by E. Y. Guernsey (1883–1975).[9] An important figure in the early days of Indiana archaeology, Guernsey brought together information from old maps, books, and sometimes, it surely seems, from his own imagination in order to design a map in 1932 that, among other things, includes historic Native American and French hydronyms and toponyms in Indiana. His chart has enjoyed widespread dissemination in Indiana through the state's Department of Natural Resources. However, one should approach Guernsey's map with a great deal of caution because of the mediocre quality of its linguistics as well as its numerous ethnographic inaccuracies. Furthermore, nearly the entirety of Guernsey's place-name inventory is undocumented, and several of his so-called Delaware language place-names are of questionable authenticity. That said, the complex grammatical nature of some of the native names he collected indicates that they are genuine and could not be his own creations.

The Value

What's in a place-name? What value can we find in analyzing these utterances that human beings use to organize their external world?

In truth, place-names are a repository of meaning that can offer a view of a people's relationship with the world. In some cases, place-names can even provide a glimpse of the symbolic or spiritual realities of those who created the names. Place-names can thus help us understand what is important and meaningful to a particular culture, what some of its values are.

Certainly, in Indiana, European American place-names reflect discrete cultural priorities: religion, exemplified by the hagionyms Maria Creek, St. Joseph River, St. Mary's River, and St. Leon; history, represented by the toponyms Lafayette, Vincennes, Alamo, and Monroe County; Old World memories, embodied in the names of towns and villages such as Vevay, Otterbein, and Leopold; Greco-Roman cultural roots, expressed by such names as Argos, Arcadia, Attica, and Mount Etna; whimsy and humor, as seen in the names of places such as Carefree, Birdseye, and Stone Head; and, finally, exotica, found in the names of a host of localities, including Peru, Cuba, Angola, Montezuma, Morocco, and Buddha, to name just a few.

In contrast, locally created American Indian place-names in Indiana generally fall into four main categories: (1) those that refer to a physical and/or spiritual attribute of the phenomenon in question, be it a river, lake, or site; (2) those that refer to whatever particularly noteworthy plant or aquatic animal lived in such a place; (3) those that refer to the location of a tribe; and (4) in rare cases, those that include the personal names of historically important residents.

Most Native American place-names in Indiana tend to be descriptive expressions related to the immediate physical environment, labels created by hunting-gathering-farming peoples specifically for practical geolocational purposes within a complex natural world. In fact, the penchant that such names possess for communicating direct, meaningful, and typically very useful information, most often geophysical, biological, or ethnonymic in nature, is their most common characteristic. In this light, one should never underestimate the significance of place-names for these indigenous societies. For instance, *kiteepihkwanwa*, the Miami-Illinois word for buffalo fish (*Ictiobus cyprinellus* and *Ictiobus bubalus*) and the origin of the word "Tippecanoe," the name of a major Indiana river, indicated an abundance of these animals in this particular stream. Therefore, this river's Miami-Illinois name served the function of defining this waterway as a source of a particular kind of food. In Indian America, examples of such information-laden place-names are legion.

A native group's knowledge of its local geography organized by place-names was vital for its survival, but its geographical understanding often extended far beyond its own neighborhood. Kari and Fall remind us of the awareness that Native Americans have had of places that lay even at great distances from their homes. They write about Shem Pete, a hunter who spoke Dena'ina, an Athapascan language of northwestern Canada and Alaska, and who knew six hundred localities by name in an area of roughly thirteen thousand square miles—territory more than a third the size of Indiana.[10] Likewise, surviving historical aboriginal maps as well as numerous historical accounts in French or English of the complex system of trails, rivers, and portages throughout eastern North America amply support the notion that native peoples of the seventeenth and eighteenth centuries in this part of North America routinely possessed comparable geographic and place-name knowledge. In 1703, in speaking of the Indians living in the land known today as the northeastern United States and Canada, La Hontan observed that "they draw the most exact Maps imaginable of the Countries they are acquainted with."[11] Of course, this really should come as no surprise, since such competency is precisely what one expects of seminomadic peoples.

In general, knowledge of the early historical natural environment can often help explain a place-name's meaning or establish its authenticity as well as reveal its significance for the original inhabitants. In a physical sense the land now called Indiana has been radically altered since the early 1800s, so much so that in many instances the referents for native place-names no longer exist. In fact, were prehistoric or historic Indians to return to Indiana today, they would feel as if they had arrived on another planet or stumbled into a dream. Many aspects of their former world would be irrevocably lost. It is for this reason that accurate and successful research of local indigenous place-names requires an understanding of the historical natural realities in which the native peoples lived and in which they conceived these names. Moreover, one must also be able from time to time to shed personal prejudices about how those realities were defined. In so doing, one allays the shock that may come from discovering, for example, that in the minds of many prehistoric and early historic Indians the Wabash and the lower Ohio below the mouth of the Wabash were the same river, while for others the Ohio and the lower Mississippi were one and the same.

The Work

When dealing with Native American place-names, as with other historical phenomena, one needs to avoid hasty explanations and, in fact, bristle with questions at every turn. Lacking this essential attitude, the researcher will invariably (1) go astray in the wilderness of copy errors and misspellings committed by less than meticulous scribes and map makers down through the ages, (2) get hopelessly lost amid the fantasies fabricated by old settlers, (3) fall prey to whimsical folk etymologies spun by pioneers or even by American Indians lacking an adequate command of their language(s), or (4) believe that certain native place-names are genuine when in truth they are just earlier guesses that became established in the literature as truth. In other words, Indian place-names have been piquing the American popular imagination for a long time, and strange things have happened to some of them along the way. One can hope to deal effectively with the multilayered challenge they present only by taking into account the precepts laid down by the great Iroquoian language scholar Floyd G. Lounsbury, which correctly place the emphasis in this type of work on its *linguistic* aspect.[12]

Lounsbury pointed out that one must first know the original language from which a particular place-name comes in order to determine if the name as recorded is a real native utterance, if it observes the grammar and word-formation rules of the native language. Second, it is essential to determine the time period in which people created and used the name. Third, it is necessary to ascertain the term's actual meaning and its original native language form, not a historical European language version of it. Fourth, one must figure out if the translation—French, German, or English as in the case of Indiana's native place-names—has escaped tampering by those who would cast it in a conveniently constructed European language phrase. Fifth, it is important to have the name verified, ideally by a native speaker of the language, or at least by the best scholars who have worked with native speakers. However, in the case of this book, it was not possible to consult native speakers of Miami-Illinois or Huron-Wyandot, since there are none remaining from those languages.

Even so, in these and all cases, one must equip oneself with the very best information on the language in question and then consult as carefully as possible the historical record, all the while keeping in mind the age of the source, the ability of the person who recorded the place-name, and the recorder's native language. In Indiana a number of so-called Indian place-names fail to comply with one or more of the basic criteria outlined above. However, only by trying to satisfy all of these requirements can the researcher hope to analyze a place-name successfully as well as position it in the proper historical context. Indeed, it is the question of context that contributes to making this book not a gazetteer, an informal coffee-table-book inventory of Indian place-names and their translations, but a historical study.

The reader will notice that on rare occasions in this volume I have ventured into the realm of the speculative. I do not view such speculations lightly, but they do arise naturally during research. The reader should note, then, that the few that appear herein are offered only in view of the fact that knowledge is a transpersonal affair. My intent is simply to present my research into these place-names and hopefully guide other scholars who also might choose to grapple with them. Finally, I hasten to add that the responsibility for all the native language forms and their translations appearing in this book, as well as all theoretical considerations, is mine alone.

The Names

A plethora of ancient names, spun from many different languages, has blanketed this land known today as Indiana since humans first saw it near the end of the last ice age. In fact, an untold number of place-name realms fashioned by a host of ancient societies spanning the millennia preceded those recorded by the first Europeans in this area.[13] Thus the Native American place-names in the state that have survived to the present day represent merely the last layer of aboriginal names to cover an area where, in late prehistory, the place-name matrices of at least Algonquian, Iroquoian, and Siouan language groups overlapped.[14]

Indiana's oldest place-names are at least three hundred years old, and most come from an Algonquian language known as Miami-Illinois. Speakers of this language are known to have arrived in the area around 1679. However, the ancestors of these people probably lived just to the north and/or northeast of what is now Indiana prior to the mid-1600s and probably hunted all the way to the Ohio River.[15] One Miami-Illinois place-name—for the Ohio River itself—is verifiably prehistoric. In this connection, the important and revelatory work on the Miami-Illinois language done by David Costa in the past twenty years now affords the researcher new perspectives and opportunities for an analysis of Miami-Illinois language terms that was not possible earlier. Indeed, this book could not have been done without Costa's work.

Hydronyms, the names of bodies of water, are the most commonly occurring Native American place-names in Indiana. They have survived in impressive numbers because Indiana's many lakes and streams were vital to the aboriginal inhabitants as sources of food, delineators of the natural world, and containers of spiritual presence. In addition, these streams and lakes served as highways—travel ways, trade routes, and warpaths. In the seventeenth century, with the arrival of the Frenchman, whose name in many Algonquian languages translates to "wooden-boat person," these waters became the fundamental connective tissue of the Indian-French relationship.[16] In fact, the use of American Indian river names was an everyday experience in the lives of *all* the native peoples and of *all* the French military personnel, traders, and missionaries. The Miami-Illinois name for the Wabash River, for example, was as well known in the eighteenth century as the moniker "Interstate 65" is today. Later, in the late eighteenth and on into the nineteenth century, local interactions of every sort involving local Indians and a host of newly arriving Europeans, all of whom used these lakes and rivers for similar purposes, assured the useful continuity of a great many American Indian hydronyms. Thus, in view of their universal importance throughout Indiana's prehistory and early history, it is little wonder that the names for streams and other bodies of water comprise the majority of the state's surviving indigenous place-names.

Across the Indiana landscape, eponyms derived from European languages are almost exclusively patronymic in character, most commonly family names of important historic figures, such as we see in the names Mooresville, Montgomery County, and Logansport. But local place-names referring to flora and fauna are far more commonly American Indian in origin or reference, and they are commonly translations of personal names of local historic Indians, not references to actual plants or animals, as in the case of Wolf Creek and Flowers Creek, where the former refers to a man known as Black Wolf and the latter to a man named One-Flower.

In this connection, the reader may notice throughout the book the absence of several well-known and indisputably *Indian-related* place-names, including such notables as Squirrel Creek, Flowers Creek, Metocina Creek, Washonis Creek, and Weasaw Creek. Even though these place-names and many others like them refer to local historic American Indians, they do not appear in this book since there is no known documentation that supports their being indigenous creations. It is impossible to determine, for lack of documentation, if the area's historic Indians actually created these particular place-names and used native language forms of them or if these place-names were simply the inventions of early American militia, traders and settlers who used them to indicate the locations of Indians familiar to them. The perennial problem in dealing with place-names of this nature does not lie in recognizing them as living memories of the underlying Indian-woven cultural fabric but in proving that they are actually part of the aboriginal weave.

That said, most genuine local Indian place-names are still in use today, as either transcriptions of the original Native American language terms or as translations into English. Indeed, the most defining features of the land of Indiana bear the names with the deepest roots in time—and these roots are, naturally, Native American.

In providing references for the material in this book, I have cited the most easily available published documents whenever possible. Nevertheless, in some cases, citations of original French manuscripts or of published editions in French have been necessary because of either the lack of English editions or translations, or the lack of satisfactory English translations.[17]

Native American Place-Names of Indiana will be successful if it brings to a halt the litany of errors that has plagued the interpretation of local indigenous place-names for nearly two centuries. Hopefully, it also will open a small window onto the vast original namescape.

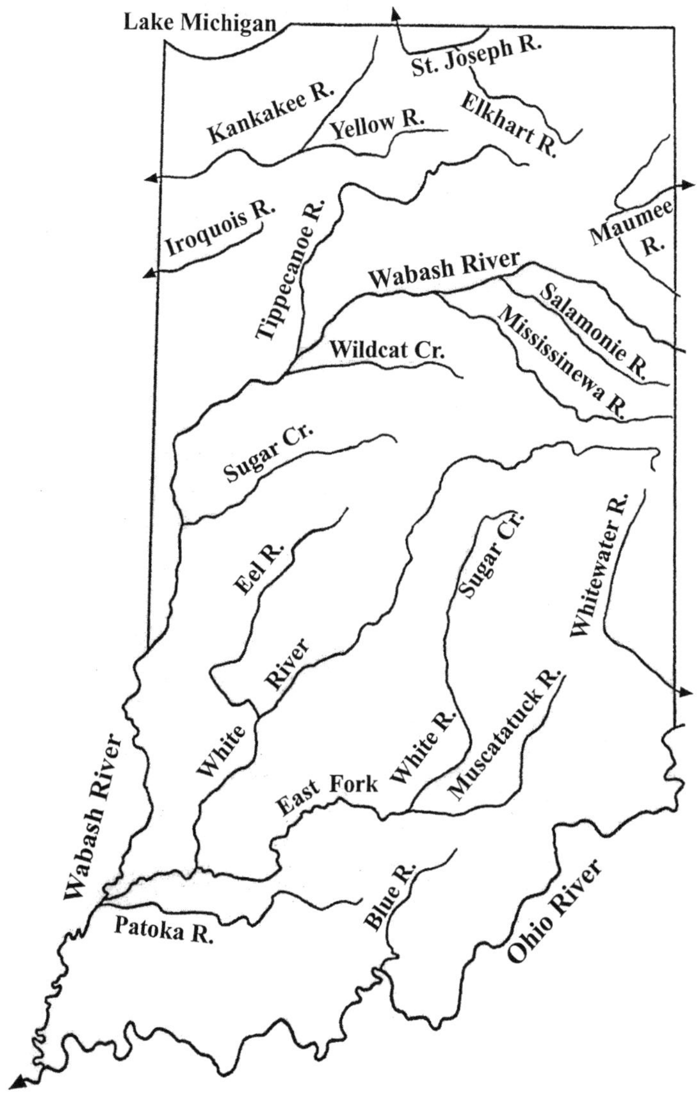

Map 1. Rivers of Indiana

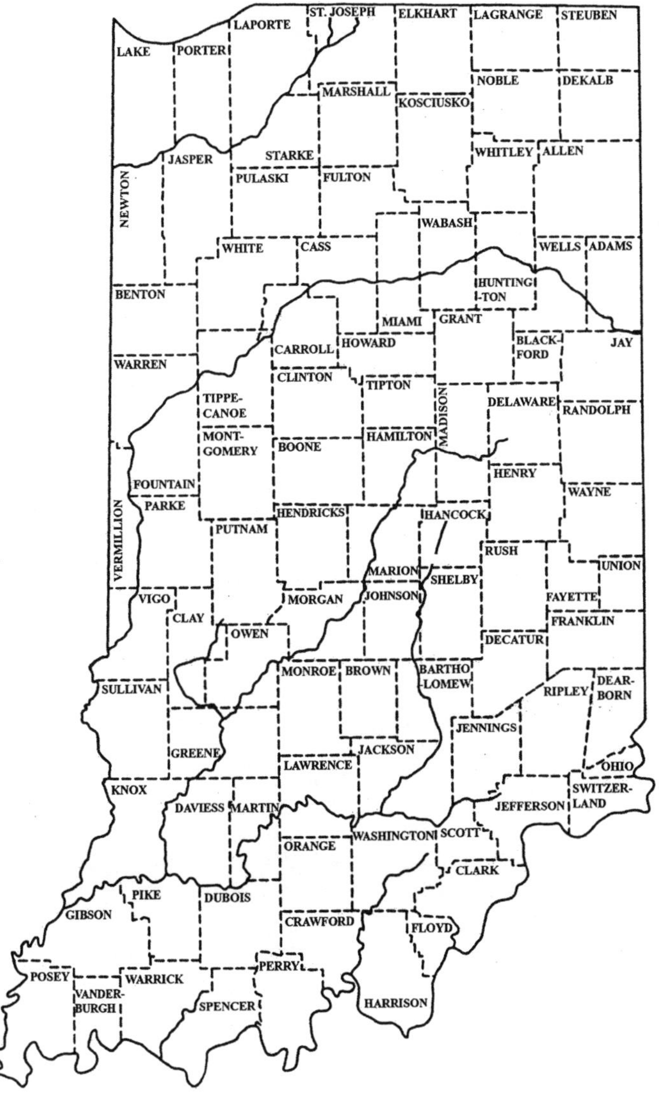

Map 2. Indiana Counties

1

The Great Water

The first physical phenomenon mentioned in the historic record that pertains directly to Indiana is Lake Michigan, the Great Lake that forms a part of the state's northern border. Although this extraordinary freshwater sea has played an important role in the lives of the original people of this continent since the end of the last ice age, the lake and an American Indian name for it did not enter European consciousness until the seventeenth century.

Samuel de Champlain's map from 1616 is the first document to indicate the existence of Lake Michigan. However, since neither this French explorer nor any other Frenchman had seen the lake by this time, its appearance on his map can only be attributed to information Champlain had gathered from native informants.[1] Later, during his second voyage to North America, Champlain would send Jean Nicollet, in 1634, on the first exploratory mission to the western Great Lakes. The latter's discoveries, embodied on Sanson's map from 1650, make it clear that Nicollet had only very limited knowledge of Lake Michigan, and no name for it.[2]

A map titled "Novvelle France" (New France), commonly referred to as the "Taunton map" and thought to be the work of Jean Bourdon from shortly after 1640, is the first document to evince a European name for Lake Michigan, at least for the northern section of the lake—*Lac des Eaux de Mer* (Lake of the Sea Waters).[3] However, it would be another half-century before Father Claude-Jean Allouez, an early French Jesuit missionary-explorer in the western Great Lakes, became the first European to mention an American Indian name for Lake Michigan.

After his arrival at Chaquamegon on the southern shore of Lake Superior in 1665 and through the year 1667, Father Allouez toured and charted the circumference of Lake Superior, all 1820 miles (2,910 kilometers) of it.[4] What is more, he embarked on the same journey three years later, having mapped in the meantime the extreme northern shores of Lake Michigan and the western shores of Green Bay. Then, in 1669, Father Allouez, along with Father Jacques Marquette, the former's mapmaker in the West starting in 1668, created an extraordinary map titled "Lac Tracy ou Supérieur avec les dépendences de la mission du Saint Esprit."[5] Four versions of this map, previously attributed incorrectly to Allouez and his Jesuit superior Claude Dablon, have survived. Although it is not the most accurate chart drawn in the West—Marquette's holograph sketch of his Mississippi excursion of 1673 is scientifically superior—this particular chart is unquestionably one of the few technical masterpieces of early midcontinental cartography.[6] What the Allouez-Marquette map demonstrates is that by 1669 French geographical understanding of not only Lake Superior but also Lake Michigan had grown exponentially as a result of Allouez's work. In a report from the same year, Allouez also wrote down the first recording of a Native American name for Lake Michigan, which was subsequently published in the form <Machihiganing>.[7]

Also in 1669 another important figure in the early geography of the Great Lakes played a decisive role in the formation of what in time would become the place-name "Michigan." In the course of his trip west in 1669–70, René-François Bréhant de Gallinée, a Sulpician missionary from Brittany, mapped for the first time in European experience the northern shores of Lake Erie and Lake Huron—all the way up to Sault Ste. Marie, at the entrance to Lake Superior—and with remarkable precision in light of the fiendish weather his expeditionary team encountered in the early spring of 1670.[8] Just as in the case of Allouez and Marquette, what Father de Gallinée drew is fascinating in its accuracy and what he did not see he intentionally left off his map. Like the Jesuits, he was impeccable in relating essentially only what he had observed firsthand.[9] In fact, after the time of Allouez, Marquette, and de Gallinée, France would enjoy neither integrity nor accuracy on its maps of the North American interior until the eighteenth century. In the interim, the works of explorers such as René de La Salle and Louis Hennepin would hold sway with their inexcusable inaccuracies, outlandish fantasies, or geographical propaganda.[10] On his own map and journal of the trip to Sault Ste. Marie, de Gallinée wrote the precursor of "Michigan" in the form <Michigané>.[11] However, the missionary-explorer did not apply this term to Lake Michigan, a body of water he was no doubt aware of, but instead to Lake Huron, which is a fact that may help in the analysis of modern "Michigan," for the etymology of this hydronym is not as transparent as some might think. Indeed, "Michigan" is probably as bedeviling as any of the most opaque American Indian place-names.

The commonly held belief is that "Michigan," a spelling whose direct ancestor is de Gallinée's <Michigané>, represents a reflex in an Algonquian language of Proto-Algonquian **meʔšikamyi*, "great-water," from the initial **meʔš-*, "great, big," the final **-(i)kamy*, "water," and the proximate singular inanimate noun suffix **-i.*[12] The fact that <Michigané>, de Gallinée's name for Lake Huron, was subsequently applied to Lake Michigan certainly appears to support this notion. In this connection, compare, for example, how the Iroquoian Huron–Wyandot cognate term "Ontario," from |õtar-iyo-|, "lake-be great," was the name used by speakers of that language for all the Great Lakes except Lake Superior.[13]

De Gallinée's <Michigané> is not, however, the same thing as Allouez's <Machihiganing>—unless the latter was grossly miscopied—and neither of these terms, *as written*, has anything to do with "great-water." Furthermore, the fact that both Allouez's and de Gallinée's place-names have an "n" instead of the "m" that occurs in the Algonquian "water" term is unusual and troubling.

Now, several variant spellings of Algonquian names for Lake Michigan made their appearance in the wake of the 1673 European voyage of discovery down the Mississippi River by Jacques Marquette and Louis Jolliet, a trip that sparked a new and vigorous round of mapmaking and hence of place-name attestations. In the late summer of 1675 the Québec cartographer Jean-Baptiste Louis Franquelin designed a map in honor of the governor general of New France, Louis de Buade, count of Frontenac, a chart known in French as "La Frontenacie." This was the second of the six maps drawn in Québec after the great Mississippi voyage, either with Jolliet's help or with information supplied by him.[14] Although at one time thought to be drawn by Jolliet himself, "La Frontenacie" does express what Jolliet *remembered* about the trip. The explorer had unfortunately lost one of the two original maps of the Mississippi created by his traveling companion and cartographer Jacques Marquette when his canoe upset in the St. Louis Rapids near Montreal in July 1674 while on his return to Québec from the West. It was not until the following summer that a copy of Marquette's journal and the other original Mississippi map that the missionary-explorer had made prior to Jolliet's departure for Québec in the spring of 1674 arrived in the hands of Claude Dablon, the Jesuit superior. In the meantime, Jolliet's memory of events of the Mississippi trip undertaken in the summer of 1673—at times accurate, at other times quite the opposite—and only his simplistic, amateurish geographical conception of the Mississippi Valley would proliferate both on maps and in print. Indeed, even when Marquette's scientifically superior second map, a copy of the one Jolliet had lost, finally arrived in Québec, it made little impression on European geographical thought since Jolliet's ideas, albeit skewed, had already firmly established in the minds of his compatriots a particular conception of the Mississippi Valley.

On the Jolliet-Franquelin map "La Frontenacie," the name for Lake Michigan, written <Missihiganin>, comes directly from Jolliet's memory, and Jolliet was not fluent in Ojibwa. Furthermore, Franquelin was a negligent monolingual copyist. For these two reasons, the spelling <Missihiganin> is not trustworthy. At the same time, <Missihiganin> is remarkably similar to Allouez's <Machihiganing>. That said, Jolliet's term, like the latter, contains no element that transparently means "great-water."

However, within ten years, a Native American name for Lake Michigan did appear spelled in a way that does mean "great-water." A widely disseminated map from 1681 by Melchisédech Thévenot, based on a copy of a map known today as "Manitoumie II" and drawing on the French place-name *Lac des Michiganis* from a map known as "la Manitoumie" designed previously by Father Dablon's Québec-based Jesuit assistant Thierry Beschefer in 1674, is the first chart to use the term <Michigami>. This spelling is an attempt to write Old Ojibwa–Ottawa **mehšigami,* "great-water."[15] Fourteen years later the same form would appear for the last time on a historical map, on a chart by Venetian friar Marco Vincenzo Coronelli, an associate of La Salle's influential friend Claude Bernou.[16] But neither Jolliet's <Missihiganin> nor Thévenot's <Michigami> persisted in the French geographical lexicon. What percolated out of this place-name stew composed of the ingredients <Machihiganing>, <Michigané>, <Missihiganin>, <Michiganis>, and <Michigami> was "Michigan."

Now, if "Michigan" does not represent "great-water," then its etymology is opaque and its meaning is unknown. If "Michigan" is in fact a garbled Algonquian term signifying "great-water," then this spelling seems to have developed in the following way. The original impetus for the establishment of an -n in this place-name would have come from de Gallinée's original <Michigané>. His incorrect spelling, or the miscopied spelling of his original recording, would no doubt have been picked up and used by Franquelin, our linguistically insensitive yet influential Québec-based French mapmaker. Franquelin never ventured west and thus probably never heard an Algonquian speaker pronounce a Native American name for Lake Michigan. However, since he was the king's official albeit neglected cartographer in New France, his own <Michiganay>, an obvious variant of de Gallinée's earlier <Michigané>—and surely a borrowing since both men lived in the small town of Québec at the same time—could have set the stage on both sides of the Atlantic for the adoption of the n-final spelling of "Michigan."[17] This would not be the first time the ingenuous Franquelin would influence the ultimate shape of American Indian place-name spellings. Finally, well-known intensive interaction between the French and the Potawatomi at the time this place-name was incubating in the French lexicon would have seen to it that "Michigan" would not have a final vowel. In other words, the Potawatomi language, in its diachronic development, lost the original final vowel of PA **-kamyi,* ultimately evincing |-gam|. A Frenchman would have no trouble, of course, hearing the Potawatomi *m.* However, in French, the letter -m at the end of written words is rare, whereas the letter -n is common. Final *-m* in the Old Potawatomi hydronym **mešigam* could have easily given way in the French spelling convention to a written final -n, or have been casually miscopied as an -n. The results of this development seem to be attested historically in the designation <Mécheygan>, the name recorded by the French trader and royal emissary Nicolas Perrot in the late 1600s, and in contemporaneous <Méchingan>, the term applied to a late-seventeenth-century fortified Potawatomi town in the Door Peninsula area.[18]

By 1750, the contours of Lake Michigan's name were effectively set in stone for Europeans. In that year the lake appeared in de Vaugondy's influential French atlas sporting the moniker *Michigan,* a spelling that had already been inscribed on the Delisle map in 1718.[19] This is of course the form of the place-name, both in English and French, that this Great Lake has borne ever since.

The name for Lake Michigan in the Algonquian languages spoken by peoples who know this lake combines a reflex of the Proto-Algonquian initial **keʔč-*, "big" and the final **-kamy,* "water," thus giving terms that mean "big-water": Menominee *keʔčekam,* Meskwaki *kehčikamiiwi,* Miami-Illinois *kihčikami(i)wi,* Ojibwa *gičikami,* Potawatomi *gčəgam,* and Shawnee *kčikami.* The Ojibwa hydronym *gičigami* was popularized by the poet Henry Wadsworth Longfellow in his "Song of Hiawatha," where it was spelled "Gitchee Gumee." Even though the bard was referring to Lake Superior, not Lake Michigan, his use of *gičigami* is an example not of poetic license but of Native American onomastic license.[20] As noted above, just as

Huron-Wyandot speakers used |õtar-iyo-|, "lake-be great" for four out of the five Great Lakes, Algonquians naturally referred to all the Great Lakes with their own very functional terms meaning "big-water." Certainly, for anyone who has ever stood on its shores, "Big-Water" is a name Lake Michigan naturally evokes—along with several exclamation points.

The natural wonders of Indiana include the extensive beaches and great sand dunes that lie along the state's Lake Michigan coastline. The Swiss linguist Albert Gastchet appears to have documented a Miami-Illinois name for these dunes in a term he learned from his Wea informant *wiikapimiša*. He wrote this name in the form <Nekáwi kamiûngi>, which represents phonemic *neekawikamionki*, "at the sand-water" or, in everyday English, "the sand-water place." This toponym is composed of the "sand" initial *neekaw-*, the "water" final *-(i)kam* and a locative suffix in the form *-ionki* signifying "at" or "on."[21]

One of Lake Michigan's principal sources is the St. Joseph River. This stream rises in southern Michigan and flows for over two hundred miles, mostly within the state of Michigan. However, for approximately forty-two miles the St. Joseph bends down into Indiana in northern Elkhart County, flows west into St. Joseph County, and then bends once again, this time northward (at the city of South Bend), to return to the state of Michigan before emptying into the Great Lake from the southeast.[22] The French apparently learned about the St. Joseph River long before they saw it. Champlain's map from 1616 is the first French chart that appears to indicate the river's existence, if indeed the squiggle visible at the southern end of Lake Michigan represents a bona fide watercourse and is not simply an artistic embellishment.[23] If the river depicted on this and other seventeenth-century maps is the St. Joseph, then its cartographic appearance at this early point in history, just as in the case of Lake Michigan discussed earlier, probably reflects information French traders and missionaries had managed to gather from native peoples. Even in the 1660s, the French king was not yet granting permission to any of his subjects to venture as far south as the St. Joseph River—and there is no record that any did. Therefore, it seems unlikely that Europeans saw the St. Joseph before 1669. Indeed, French traders first entered the southern peninsula of Michigan only with the 1668 licensing of soldiers in the Carignan-Salière regiment for trade. However, given the fact that these soldiers-turned-traders, numbering upward of three hundred or more, were like a tsunami sweeping over the western Great Lakes in 1669 in search of the potential riches to be made from the beaver fur trade, it is not impossible that a Frenchman could have stumbled upon the St. Joseph River around that time.[24] Yet despite this impressive and sudden advance of Europeans into the Great Lakes area, no visit to the St. Joseph River by a Frenchman is documented for several years after 1668, and maps appearing soon after 1669 do not provide an American Indian name, or even a French name, for the stream. However, the St. Joseph River is prominently featured on a Franquelin-Jolliet collaborative map from 1674, a chart known as "La Carte de la Colbertie ou des Griffons," and is also visible—and unnamed—on "La Frontenacie," the Franquelin-Jolliet map from 1675 mentioned above.[25]

The distinction for being the first European to see the St. Joseph River as well as the first European to set foot on the land known today as Indiana has been commonly accorded to the French explorer and entrepreneur René de La Salle. Nevertheless, neither of these firsts is true. It is true that La Salle's report, transcribed into the third person by his friend Bernou, a French abbot, states that the explorer found himself in the fall of 1679 at the southern end of Lake Michigan, "where the wind forced him to make landfall."[26] However, that event occurred *four years* after other Frenchmen had already traveled to the same place. In fact, the historical record clearly shows that the first Europeans to touch the land we today call Indiana were Jacques Largillier, known as Le Castor (The Beaver), Pierre Porteret, and the renowned Father Jacques Marquette.

Marquette's group arrived in Indiana in the last week of April 1675 during the attempt made by Largillier and Porteret to transport the mortally ill priest by canoe from the Kaskaskia village on the upper Illinois River to the Jesuit house at St. Ignace at the Straits of Mackinac. Arriving at Lake Michigan from the Illinois River by a previously unknown route, they paddled their canoe eastward along the Lake Michigan shoreline then northward up the eastern shoreline of the lake toward their intended destination, thereby becoming the first Europeans to enter what is now Indiana and the first to see the Indiana dunes.[27] The three would have had to stop every evening on Indiana's shoreline during their long journey, as there would not have been enough light for the travelers to paddle safely at night on those uncharted waters. In the last week of April 1675 the new moon was but the slimmest of crescents in the western sky and would have set early in the evening. In other words, beaching their canoe at night in what is today Indiana would have been obligatory. Father Marquette's rapidly failing health allowed him to venture no farther than the site of modern-day Ludington, Michigan, where he died on May 18, 1675.[28] In the meantime, he and his two companions not only stopped off in

Indiana but also, as April turned to May, canoed past the mouth of the St. Joseph River. Accordingly, these three can now take their rightful place in history as the first Europeans to enter Indiana as well as the first to see the St. Joseph. It would be four and a half years, on October 28, 1679, to be exact, before La Salle, following the same route along the southern coast of Lake Michigan as that taken by Marquette, Largillier, and Porteret, arrived in what is now Indiana. This was near the end of a forty-three-day-long paddle that carried him and his men from Washington Island near the entrance to Green Bay down the western side of Lake Michigan, around its southern rim, and up its southeastern side to the mouth of the St. Joseph River. On November 1, 1679, La Salle saw this stream for the first time.[29] Although he was not the first European to lay eyes on the St. Joseph River, La Salle would soon be, along with his French party, the first to paddle upon it. In fact, in the three years that followed his arrival in the area, La Salle saw the river at least seven different times, his last visit coming in early December 1682.[30]

Soon after his arrival at the St. Joseph, La Salle found a group of Atchatchakangouen and Wea, both of whom are Miami-speaking bands, along with some Mascouten, living near the headwaters of the Kankakee a little west of the St. Joseph, at what is now the western section of the city of South Bend. These folks had recently arrived from the Wisconsin area, where they had lived as refugees during the Iroquois wars of the second half of the seventeenth century.[31] The French hydronym *la rivière des Miamis* (the River of the Miami), a name created by La Salle himself on account of this very encounter in 1679 with this particular group of Indians near the St. Joseph, is in fact the first name on record for the St. Joseph River.[32] In fashioning the name *la rivière des Miamis* for the St. Joseph River, the monolingual La Salle simply played the French place-name card, designating in his own language a locale inhabited by Indians particularly important and memorable to him. Such French place-names are plentiful across the historical North American landscape: *la rivière des Outaouais, le pays des Illinois, la prairie des Mascoutens, la rivière des Moingouena, la rivière des Missourites,* and so on. Unfortunately, La Salle, who collected many Native American place-name data, failed to get a Miami-Illinois name for the St. Joseph River despite his numerous dealings with Miami and Wea who were living in its watershed during his several visits to the area in the early 1680s.

However, given the manner in which history unfolded, *la rivière des Miamis* turned out to be only a transitory place-name, for the Miami's sojourn on the St. Joseph was a highly unsettled affair. Although seasonal movements related to hunting and gathering activities in and around a particular area were representative of the Miami's centuries-old way of life, sudden, far-flung, conflict-induced displacements unrelated to food procurement were common for the tribe during the latter part of the seventeenth century. This unstable situation developed for a number of reasons: the local impact of French imperial and commercial policies, constant and brutal harassment by the Iroquois to the east, internecine warfare with the Illinois to the west, unpredictable devastating violence from Siouans to the northwest, and a suffocating conflict with the Ottawa and allied Potawatomi right in the Miami's own midst. In fact, for almost twenty years the Miami moved in, out, and around the St. Joseph Valley, pushed hither and yon by the unrelenting forces of intertribal warfare, European-introduced pestilence, French brandy, and international political intrigue. In fact, as early as 1695, less than twenty years after they began moving from southern Wisconsin into the St. Joseph River Valley, the Miami were motivated by the precarious nature of life on this stream to move out. Under continued pressure from the Potawatomi following the crisis at Detroit in 1702, and with the easing of tensions with the Iroquois to the east by the treaty of 1701, most of the Miami on the St. Joseph had shifted residency toward the southeast by 1715.[33]

Like the Miami, the Potawatomi, another Central Algonquian language-speaking people, were particularly intimate with the St. Joseph River in early historical times.[34] The Potawatomi had been forced by Iroquoians sometime about 1641–43 to flee from their late prehistoric estate,[35] situated in the northern part of the lower peninsula of Michigan, to islands and headlands near the Door Peninsula. The latter areas were then the Potawatomi's general location when they encountered the French for the first time. However, by 1679 the Potawatomi had begun inching their way down the western coast of Lake Michigan, and by 1695 some had reached the St. Joseph River.

Whereas early historical Native American settlement patterns on the St. Joseph indicate there were at least Miami and Potawatomi names for the river, early primary-source documents from the 1700s and early 1800s do not evince any Indian language names for it. In fact, La Salle was not the only European who failed to record a native name for the St. Joseph. Indeed, it was not until after the American Civil War that an Algonquian name for the St. Joseph River even appeared in the record—on Daniel Hough's map in the form <Sawkwawksilbuck>.[36] Hough neither translated this term nor ascribed a linguistic origin to it. It was not until the early twentieth century that the Indiana historian Jacob Dunn, working with speakers of Miami-Illinois and Potawatomi, brought the St. Joseph's native names into focus.

A highly respected Miami leader of the late nineteenth and early twentieth century, *waapanahkikapwa,* a fluent native speaker of Miami, gave Dunn the Miami name for the St. Joseph River, which the latter wrote <Sakiwäsipi>.[37] The Miami glossed this place-name "Coming-Out River," which is an adequate albeit ambiguous translation. This place-name ultimately derives from the PA II verb stem **sa·ki·-,* "it outlets," whose initial is **sa·k-,* "out, protruding." This verb stem was then the foundation for the PA noun **sa·ki·wi,* "outlet (of a river)," whose noun stem is **sa·ki·w-.* It was the latter term that served as the initial component for a derived Miami-Illinois verb in the form *saakiiweeki,* "it outlets," an expression attested in the early historic primary sources of the Miami-Illinois language.[38] With the dropping of the verbal suffix *-ki,* this derived stem was then combined with the Miami-Illinois hydronymic final *-(i)siip,* "river," and the proximate inanimate noun suffix *-i* to produce *saakiiweesiipi,* spelled <Sakiwäsipi> by Dunn, which signifies "outlet-river."

This same Miami man also provided Dunn with this Miami-Illinois place-name in the form of a locative noun, which the latter wrote <sakiwäyungi>. This spelling represents *saakiiweeyonki,* "at the outlet" or, in common English parlance, "the outlet place."[39] This term refers to the site where the St. Joseph River flows into Lake Michigan, at today's Benton Harbor, Michigan. The term "outlet" as applied to the St. Joseph River seems to refer to the notion that for the late prehistoric Miami this stream, within the territory familiar to them, was the principal water course that flowed out of the midcontinental landmass into the vastness of Lake Michigan. According to Miami tradition, the name indicates where the Miami emerged as a distinct people.

Dunn also noted the Potawatomi name for the river, which he wrote <Sagwah sebe>. Thomas Topash, the Potawatomi man who gave him this place-name, glossed the term "Mystery River."[40] Topash, who based on the evidence was not a fluent speaker of Potawatomi, accounted for the "mystery" by saying that the name commemorated an unexpected visit among the Potawatomi people living on the St. Joseph River by a taciturn stranger who during his stay with the tribe never disclosed his name.[41] Such a tale, however, is the very stuff that folk etymologies are made of. Topash's <Sagwah sebe> is in fact simply a Potawatomi place-name form cognate with the Miami-Illinois place-name noted above, perhaps Potawatomi **zagwzibə.* In addition, Hough's somewhat garbled recording <Sawkwawksilbuck> is ostensibly a related Potawatomi locative noun, possibly **zagwəg-zibəg,* which would translate to something like "at the place where there is an outlet river."

Iroquoian-speaking peoples have also had a connection dating to prehistoric times to the lands located between Lake Erie and Lake Michigan, including northeastern Indiana. Moreover, French and Indian Detroit, where the Jesuit missionary Pierre-Philippe Potier lived with an Iroquoian Huron-Wyandot–speaking population during the eighteenth century, was intimately connected commercially to the St. Joseph River. It is no surprise, therefore, that Potier's papers contain a Huron name for the St. Joseph River, which he wrote in the form <araonde>.[42] Because of its unusual, antique shape, <araonde> could be a recording that Potier lifted from an earlier work on Huron, perhaps from one composed by Pierre-Joseph-Marie Chaumonot. Potier, who was fluent in Huron-Wyandot, translated <araonde> to both *Riv. aux roches* (River with the Rocks) and *La riv: s jos:* (The St. Joseph River).[43] Although <araonde> is a very unusual transcription for Huron-Wyandot "rock," this spelling does in fact represent this term. The -o- is a miswritten or miscopied -e-. (A Huron-Wyandot term for "river" is missing from Potier's records for this particular place-name.)

In Northern Iroquoian, "rock" is phonemic **xahrẽ́ʔneh.* In the case of <araonde>, Potier failed to write the symbol "˛" under the first -a-. This symbol along with the sound *a* would represent the third-person neuter agent prefix, which is *ka-* in Proto-Northern Iroquoian and became *xa-* in Huron before evolving into *ya-* in Huron-Wyandot.[44] In <araonde> the segment spelled -raon- represents the Proto-Northern Iroquoian root for "rock," which is **-hrẽ́ʔn–*. The Northern Iroquoian morphophonemic form for the complete term signifying "rock" is |yo-hrẽ́ʔn-aʔ|, which in Huron is phonemic *ohrẽ́ʔnaʔ* and phonetic [ohrẽ́ʔndaʔ]. Note that, in Potier's <araonde>, the segment spelled -nd-, pronounced [nd], is the phonetic realization of *n* before an oral vowel. Later Huron-Wyandot evinced **u·rẽ́ʔnaʔ* for the term for "rock," where the root *-hrẽ́ʔn-* appears phonetically as [(·)-hrẽ́ʔnd-]. Finally, the twentieth-century Huron-Wyandot form would have been phonetic [u·rẽ́ndaʔ].[45] In the late 1600s, Father Allouez indicated that the St. Joseph River was full of rapids, a fact which supports a Huron-Wyandot name meaning "Rock River" for the St. Joseph.[46]

Two names have survived for one or more Potawatomi villages located on the St. Joseph River at the "South Bend" in the early 1800s. One of these, located at what was an important river crossing known as the "Grand Traverse of the St. Joseph," is written <Maskobeeninonk> in the published papers of John Tipton.[47] This spelling, however, represents either a mishearing of the original term or a miscopying of it. Tanner's atlas and

Dunn's unpublished notes spell this same place-name <Maskobinong>. The second n is unexpected, although it could represent a nasalization of the final vowel through assimilation to the first "n" (see additional notes on this phonological phenomenon in chapter 7). Indeed, what is represented here is Potawatomi *mskopənəg,* "at the red potato" or, in everyday English, the "red-potato place." The term *mskopənəg* is a locative noun composed of the initial *msko-,* "red," the "potato" final *-pən,* and the locative suffix in the form *-əg* meaning "at." This toponym referred historically to the marked local presence of pond lily (*Nuphar advena*), also known as cow lily and spadderdock, which will be discussed at length in chapter 4 in connection with the Kankakee River tributary known as Potato Creek. The other American Indian village name on record for a site in the South Bend area is written <Sanbawodonek>.[48] This spelling represents Potawatomi *zə́nbawodanəg,* "at ribbon town," from Potawatomi *zə́nba,* "ribbon," *-w-,* a noun + noun connector, and *odanəg,* "at the town," which itself can be parsed *odan,* "town" and *-əg,* a locative suffix. "Ribbon" in this toponym is perhaps a reference to the site's importance as a trading center, where items such as ribbons for decorating clothing could be had.

There are several streams within the state of Indiana in the neighborhood of Lake Michigan that bear historically documented Native American place-names. These include the Grand Calumet River, the Little Calumet River, the Elkhart River, the Pigeon River (formerly known in English as White Pigeon River), and Trail Creek.

The earliest English names for Trail Creek, which runs its entire course to Lake Michigan within La Porte County, are "Road River" from 1815 and "Chemin River" from 1818.[49] These names derive from an earlier French name for this stream: *la rivière du Chemin* (i.e., the Trail's River). This French hydronym is in turn a translation of the Potawatomi name for this stream, *myewes-zibiwe,* "trail-creek."[50] The term *myewes,* "trail" is the diminutive form of *myew,* "road," and *zibiwe* is "creek." (Compare Potawatomi *zibə,* "river.") Dunn attested this Potawatomi place-name in the spellings <Mēéhwaysēbēway> and <Miéwĕsibíwe>.[51] Both of these terms nicely exhibit the diminutive suffix in *zibiwe.* In fact, Dunn's recordings also demonstrate particular linguistic acumen on his part, since he obviously heard the postconsonantal *y,* represented here by the first -ē- of <Mēéhwaysēbēway> and by the first -i- of <Miéwĕsibíwe>. In the terms for "road" and "trail," this sound occurs in Potawatomi but not in her close sister language, Ojibwa-Ottawa. The referent for *myewes-zibiwe* is the old footpath and horse trail known historically in English as the "Potawatomi

Trail." This trace led from Chicago, skirted the southern edge of Lake Michigan, ran east along Trail Creek and passed by the western end of *le lac du Chemin* (the Trail's Lake), known today as Hudson Lake. It then proceeded to the French Fort St.-Joseph and to the nearby Jesuit mission located on the site of present-day Niles, Michigan. From there one of the trail's forks went to Detroit, while the other led to the Miami villages at the headwaters of the Maumee.[52] Even though Potawatomi *myewes-zibiwe* dates only to the turn of the eighteenth century, it may be a reformulation in Potawatomi of a much older original Miami-Illinois name for this creek, now lost. Naturally, the age of the basic place-name *concept* depends on how long the trail has been there as well as how far back in time local historic or prehistoric Indians associated the trail with the creek.

The Pigeon River is a major tributary of the St. Joseph River. Its waters begin their journey toward Lake Michigan in northeastern Steuben County, then flow generally west by northwest across Lagrange County into the state of Michigan. There they merge with those of the St. Joseph. The name Pigeon River does not refer to a bird but to a man who was so identified. The person in question was a historical Potawatomi leader known as *wabmimi*, "White Passenger Pigeon." His Potawatomi name is inscribed on the Treaty of Greene Ville from 1795, while a translation of his name is found in three letters written by William Henry Harrison in the autumn of 1812. *wabmimi* was a follower of the Shawnee leader *tkamhse*, commonly written "Tecumseh" in the early nineteenth century, and an enemy of Harrison, which explains why he figures in the latter's correspondence.[53]

For the Potawatomi name for Pigeon River, Hough has <Wabmenic>, which could be the Potawatomi locative noun *wabmimig*, "at White Passenger Pigeon" or in everyday English, "White Passenger Pigeon's place."[54] The constituents of *wabmimig* would be the initial *wab-*, "white," *mimi*, "passenger pigeon" (*Ectopistes migratorius*), and a locative suffix in the form *-ig*, "at." If <Wabmenic> does represent a genuine Potawatomi locative noun-based place-name, it is important ethnolinguistically speaking, since it would demonstrate that this particular place-name was a native eponymous place-name, not just a place-name originally conceived in English and then reformulated back into Potawatomi. However, in light of the known copy errors on Hough's map, discussed in the introduction, the spelling <Wabmenic> could just as well be an inaccurately reproduced "Wabmeme," for *wabmimi*, that is, simply a spelling of the man's name, where the right descender of an original second "m" was thought to be an

-i- and where an original final written -e- was mistaken for a -c-. If this analysis is correct, the name as such would not then be grammatical for a *place-name* in Potawatomi. For this reason, it is impossible at this point to determine whether the English language place-name "Pigeon River" is a translation of an actual American Indian place-name or simply an American creation. Historically attested Potawatomi eponymous place-names do exist, however, and *wabmimig* could well be a genuine Potawatomi name that was once applied by the Potawatomi to Pigeon River to designate a place where *wabmimi* lived at one time, perhaps his wintering place. However, additional evidence is needed to prove that this is the case.

The Elkhart River, which rises from multiple sources in central Noble, southwest Lagrange, northern Kosciusko, and southern Elkhart Counties, flows generally northwest to join the St. Joseph River in northeastern Elkhart County. Late-eighteenth-century and early-nineteenth-century English forms of this stream's name include "Elks-heart River," "Eltsheart River," and "Elkheart River." The French form of this hydronym, *le Coeur de Cerf* (the Elk Heart), was documented as a local place-name by at least 1749, when it was noted by the French that a Miami village was located on the river.[55] The elk in this case refers—at least indirectly—to the extinct eastern elk (*Cervus elaphus canadensis*).[56] Historically recorded Native American names for the Elkhart River are found for both Miami-Illinois and Potawatomi. The name for the Elkhart River is attested for Miami-Illinois in Gatschet's recording <miciwia-téhi sipiwi>.[57] This is *mihšiiwiateehi siipiiwi,* "elk-heart river."[58]

Dunn wrote the Potawatomi place-name in the forms <mēshĕ́wehou-dehík> and <micĕ́wĕhúdehĭ́k>, where the third "h" in both recordings indicates the sound *ʔ*, the glottal stop.[59] These spellings represent the Potawatomi locative noun *mžəweodeʔig,* "at (the) elk heart."[60] The constituents of this place-name are *mžəwe,* "elk," the dependent noun *-deʔ-*, "heart," and a locative suffix in the form *-ig,* signifying "at, in, on." Although Dunn said that the name of this river refers to the shape of the island at its mouth, this can only be a folk etymology. It appears that "Elk heart" is a prehistoric place-name and could in fact refer to the Kaskaskia, as this tribe was known to the Miami as *mihšiiwiateeha,* "elk-hearts."[61] A Kaskaskian association with the Elkhart River would not, of course, refer to where this Miami-Illinois–speaking tribe lived during the late 1600s and throughout the 1700s, but to their original late prehistoric location before the Algonquian diaspora of the 1600s.[62] Such antiquity for "Elk heart" as a place-name could explain why this name seems to have "always" been around and cannot be pegged down regarding its age.[63] As far as the modern English form of this river's name is concerned, it should be noted that English speakers in the 1800s "cleaned up" the old name by shifting graphic "Elk heart" to modern euphemistic "Elkhart." In addition, the modern English pronunciation [ɛ́l-kart]—pronounced like "go-cart"—instead of the original English pronunciation [ɛ́lk-hárt], further obscures the meaning of the original native place-name.

Mishawaka, the name of a modern city located on the Elkhart River, derives from an Algonquian language toponym that literally means "firewood-tree land," that is, "dead-tree land." Dunn mentioned the Potawatomi name for this area and wrote it <m'shḗhwakēk>, <m'shḗhwahkēēki>, and <m'cḗwakíki>. His translation for the name is "country of dead trees, a deadening."[64] Nevertheless, the latter two so-called Potawatomi terms are, with their final vowel, unusual for Potawatomi. Their strange form can perhaps be attributed to the fact that Dunn's Potawatomi informant, Thomas Topash, was not a fluent speaker of Potawatomi. In fact, one of Topash's grandfathers was Miami, which may explain why the inventory of "Potawatomi" place-names that Dunn gathered from Topash seems to be a jumble of Potawatomi, Miami, and Potawatomi-Miami hybrid terms. In the case of "Mishawaka," these so-called Potawatomi recordings by Dunn contain both Potawatomi and Miami elements.

In Miami-Illinois, the term in question is *mihswaahkwahkiki,* literally "it is firewood-tree land," attested in the form <miss8ac8aki8i> in the Illinois-French dictionary created by the Jesuits in the Illinois Country around the turn of the eighteenth century.[65] The word *mihswaahkwahkiki* is a conjunct II verb composed of the "firewood" initial *mihs-*, the noun + noun connector *-w-*, the "wood, tree" medial *-aahkw-*, the "land, country" final *-ahk(i),* and the appropriate verb ending *-ki.* Dunn also recorded this same Miami-Illinois verb in the conjunct order with his <mäswakwakiki>.[66] Evincing first-syllable ablaut, the latter term is phonemic *meehswaahkwahkiki.* Miami-Illinois *mihswaahkwa,* literally "firewood-tree," derives from PA **mehsiwa·xkw(i).*[67] The place-name in question was applied, at least, to an early-nineteenth-century Potawatomi village that Guernsey located at the confluence of the Elkhart and St. Joseph Rivers,[68] which was ostensibly named "the land of dead trees" because of its environmental situation. The Potawatomi name from which the modern toponym "Mishawaka" directly derives, which is represented by Dunn's <m'shḗhwakēk>, may have been **mšwakig,* "at (the) firewood-tree land."

The place-name <Mongoquinong> seems to have been applied in the early 1800s to a prairie and/or a village near the hamlet of Lima in Lagrange County. *The Historical Atlas of Lagrange County* mentions this place-name and gives it the incorrect translation "Big Squaw Village." Tanner's atlas also has this toponym and says that it refers to a Potawatomi village. Guernsey's map mentions this name, too, and says it means "Big Squaw Prairie." Finally, Hough's map, while not translating <Mongoquinong>, applies the name, curiously enough, to the east fork of the Elkhart River above its confluence with Turkey Creek.[69] <Mongoquinong> represents Miami-Illinois *maankwahkionka,* or more likely the contracted pronunciation [maankohkioŋga], signifying "In-the-Loon-Land." The term's constituents are the initial *maankw-*, "loon," the final *-ahk,* signifying "land, country," and the locative suffix *-ionk(i),* meaning "in." Note that the third -n- of <Mongoquinong> is a miscopied -o-.[70] This same miscopying of "n" for "o" can also be seen in the historical place-name <Passea*n*ong> discussed in chapter 7. As used in Indiana, *maankwahkionka* ~ [maankohkioŋga] was not a place-name but a name used by a Miami man who was a signatory to the treaty of 1840.[71] Because the major threat to their lives and cultures came from the south with the arrival of Virginians, Kentuckians, and Americans beginning in the latter part of the eighteenth century, ethnically and linguistically diverse American Indian groups, including some Miami who opposed the treaties, loss of land, and/or removal to lands across the Mississippi, came to reside in the far northern lake district of Indiana at that time.

Along with the Kankakee River, the Grand Calumet River and the Little Calumet River have undergone more catastrophic manmade changes since the nineteenth century than any other major streams in Indiana, so much so that the modern local hydrology would likely confuse a prehistoric or historic Indian. What we today refer to as the Little Calumet River rises in western La Porte County and flows west. Southeast of Ogden Dunes in northern Porter County some of its waters have been artificially diverted directly north to Lake Michigan while the rest continue on west all the way into Illinois. Then, south of Chicago at the bluffs of Blue Island, an important area archaeologically, the modern Little Calumet makes a spectacular hairpin turn, bending back to the east to meet the modern Grand Calumet, which, despite its name, is today just a short stream that flows west from its source about two miles east of the harbor at Gary. Together these combined modern Calumet rivers flow briefly northward in the state of Illinois before disappearing into Lake Michigan in South Chicago. The modern hydrological picture and the historical hydrological picture are like night and day.

First, the river known *historically* as the Grand Calumet essentially followed the long course of today's Little Calumet River. But after the big bend at Blue Island, it did not flow north to Lake Michigan, as the Little Calumet does today. Instead, it continued back eastward from that point, essentially following the bed of today's Grand Calumet River—but in the opposite direction. The *historic* Grand Calumet then entered Lake Michigan east of Gary's harbor.[72] In other words, the original Grand Calumet River basically followed the course of today's Little Calumet in the same direction and that of the Grand Calumet of today in the opposite direction. Second, what was known *historically* as the Little Calumet River was simply the short south-to-north section of today's combined Calumet rivers that flow into Lake Michigan in South Chicago. The historic Little Calumet River was just a brief, wet portage route connecting the historic Grand Calumet River and Lake Michigan. From these descriptions one can easily imagine how someone from the 1600s, 1700s, or early 1800s would find today's Calumet rivers baffling.

Father Jacques Marquette and his two companions, Jacques Largillier and Pierre Porteret, would have been the first Europeans to see the Grand Calumet, at its mouth, in the spring of 1675. However, the first historical attestation of an original, historical American Indian name for the Grand Calumet River did not appear until the early eighteenth century. *La Riviere de Kinouickomy,* a French name for this river, is first seen in a memoir composed by a local French commandant and authoritative source Pierre-Charles Delliette, a younger relative of Henri de Tonti, Cavelier de La Salle's famous lieutenant. In his memoir Delliette discusses his extensive and culturally in-depth experience with the Miami-Illinois peoples in the Illinois Country in the late 1600s.[73] Since of the local Indian languages he could speak only Miami-Illinois, and he lived only among the Miami-Illinois–speaking Illinois and Wea, Delliette's <Kinouickomy> can be none other than Miami-Illinois *kinwikami,* "long-water," which is composed of the initial *kinw-,* "long," the "water" final *-(i)kam,* and the singular proximate inanimate noun suffix *-i.*[74] The complete Miami-Illinois hydronym, based on comparative onomastic evidence within Miami-Illinois, may have been **kinwikamisiipi,* "long-water river," composed of the initial *kinw-,* "long," the "water" medial *-ikam-,* the hydronymic "river" final *-isiip* and the inanimate noun suffix *-i.* This analysis would in fact make the Miami-Illinois term a complete and direct translation of

Delliette's *La Riviere de Kinouickomy.*[75] Certainly the name "Long-Water River" aptly describes the original flat, sluggish old Grand Calumet, which traveled west for over sixty miles in a relatively straight line and in an essentially parallel fashion to Lake Michigan, without ever falling into it, and then did an abrupt about-face and traveled back toward the East for another thirty miles before entering the lake. There was certainly no other river in the entire region that was this long or took this form. Moreover, the fact that the *concept* "long water" as a place-name exists elsewhere in the Algonquian languages provides ethnolinguistic support for the foregoing analysis. Indeed, the same name was attested by La Salle in the 1680s as an Algonquian designation for the Cumberland River.[76]

Native American names for the Grand Calumet River and Little Calumet River are also represented in the French hydronyms written down in the forms *le grand quenomic* (the Great Quenomic) and *le petit quenomic* (the Little Quenomic), names that appear on an anonymous untitled French map created sometime around the middle of the eighteenth century.[77] Nonetheless, it is difficult to determine just what the spelling <quenomic> represents. Since these place-names come from the time when the Potawatomi controlled the area, <quenomic> could be a garbled or miscopied Old Potawatomi locative noun meaning "at the long water," which would, of course, make it cognate with the Miami-Illinois name discussed above. But at this point the meaning of <quenomic> remains a mystery, despite the fact that the American Jedediah Morse wrote an English-language rendition of <quenomic> in the form <Kannomic> on his map of 1792, and in the same decade a British cartographer wrote the name of the Grand Calumet River in the form <Kannome>.[78] In addition to these spellings, there is a set of related spellings that could represent locative noun forms of <quenomic>. These include <Kennomekin> from 1828, <Kannomokonk> from the mid-1800s, and <Kenomokonk>, of unknown provenience but said to be Potawatomi.[79] These terms—and others like them in the literature—seem to contain Algonquian locative suffixes, represented here by the spellings -in and -onk.

Finally, from the early nineteenth century also come several spellings for what is apparently a single American Indian place-name for the Grand Calumet River: <Callamank> and <Callimick> from 1812, <Calimic> from 1815, and <Callamink> from 1821.[80] However, this is a very unusual group since, phonologically speaking, these names cannot be Potawatomi even though they appear to be somehow related to <quenomic> and to the K-initial forms discussed directly above. Importantly, they are all nonsensical. That said, the fact that <Callamank>, <Callimick>, <Calimic>, and <Cal-

lamink> sound so much like "Calumet" suggests that perhaps an original French name for the Grand Calumet River in the form *Calumet* was borrowed by an Algonquian-speaking group and then transformed grammatically into their language by adding a locative suffix. In the end, the form and meaning of the original Miami-Illinois name for the Grand Calumet River is firm. However, there are obviously unresolved issues concerning this river's historical Potawatomi name.

<Kennomkia> is a moniker Dunn applied to the Grand Calumet River that he also obtained in an interview with Thomas Topash.[81] Even though this place-name resembles those discussed above, and has been lumped together with them in the literature, it is no doubt a different word. In fact, given its apparent meaning, <Kennomkia> could be a Native American term once applied to the Deep River, a major tributary of the Calumet that rises south of the Valparaiso moraine. The explorer René de La Salle was probably the first European to see this creek, which he had to ford on a makeshift raft.[82]

If the word represented by <Kennomkia> existed in Potawatomi at the turn of the twentieth century, it apparently has disappeared. Still, <Kennomkia> could represent an archaic Potawatomi cognate of the attested Miami-Illinois conjunct II verb *kiinoonki,* "it is deep" or even of the Miami adverb *kinoonke,* "where it is deep." In fact, the <Kennomkia> spelling could actually be an attempt to write the second of these Miami-Illinois terms. Although I have not seen any other instance in Miami-Illinois where an adverb served as a place-name, Miami-Illinois *ee* generally palatalizes after *k*. The result, in the case of this place-name—if it is in fact a place-name and not simply a descriptive phrase about the stream—would be phonetic [kinóoŋgye], which reasonably reflects Dunn's and Guernsey's <Kennomkia>, where the -e- of <Kennomkia> is an "alphabet E," and the final -e is an "alphabet A," historical vernacular English spelling practices discussed in chapters 5 and 7. Again, it could be that Topash gave Dunn a Miami-Illinois place-name and called it Potawatomi. Topash glossed <Kennomkia> as "deep and long." Though impressionistic, his translation does manage to hover closely over the semantic area visited above in the interpretation of this late historical recording. If <Kennomkia> represents a Potawatomi place-name, it could date to the eighteenth century; if it is Miami-Illinois, it would probably date at least as far back as the early 1700s.

2

‹8AB8SKIG8›, *Ouabachi,* and Beyond

In late June 1673 Jacques Marquette, Louis Jolliet, and their five French companions passed by the confluence of the Mississippi and the Ohio. This was the first known sighting by Europeans of the Ohio River, Indiana's magnificent southern boundary.[1] The name <8AB8SKIG8> on Marquette's holograph map of the Mississippi, a term whose application is specifically defined by Marquette in his narration of this famous voyage, designates precisely the water course we know today as the Ohio.[2] This place-name was recorded four years after Claude-Jean Allouez recorded a name for Lake Michigan and is, after another name for the Ohio examined in chapter 3, the third Native American place-name ever recorded that relates directly to Indiana.

The cryptic spelling of Marquette's <8AB8SKIG8> has allowed it over the centuries to elude analysis. The pronunciation and the meaning of this term were certainly not transparent to Claude Dablon, Marquette's superior and the person responsible for the minor editing of the missionary-explorer's narration of the Mississippi trip.[3] Moreover, the pronunciation of this place-name was not clear to Dablon's scribes, Thierry Beschefer and Antoine Dalmas.[4] All three Jesuits tacitly acknowledged their ignorance of the correct pronunciation of Marquette's original term by taking the judicious approach of leaving the spelling of the place-name essentially intact.

However, once Marquette's place-name got back to France, people with neither experience with North American languages nor any guidelines to comprehend the phonological intentions couched in Marquette's spelling ingenuously transliterated <8AB8SKIG8> to *Ouabouskigou.*[5] They got the first syllable right, since initial 8a- in French missionary shorthand always stood for the sequence oua- in standard French spelling, pronounced [wa(a)]. The French letter "8," a fashionable symbol in the seventeenth and eighteenth centuries, was routinely transcribed as "ou." However, someone transcribed Marquette's last syllable, -G8, incorrectly. Consequently, no one has been able to figure out what *Ouabouskigou* meant since this term, as written, is pure nonsense.

The warping of the original recording <8AB8SKIG8> to *Ouabouskigou* stemmed from the ephemeral nature of this place-name. No one but Marquette and Jolliet ever noted <8AB8SKIG8>. Jolliet was not proficient in the native languages, and Marquette died before he had a chance to tell who provided the term and to explain what it meant. However, scholars have completely ignored Marquette's and Jolliet's odd-looking and understandably formidable <8AB8SKIG8>, while they have gone on popularizing the transliteration *Ouabouskigou* as if it were the spelling that these two French explorers had actually written down.

To understand <8AB8SKIG8>, one must look at several items. To begin, it is important to know about the recorder of this name. Father Jacques Marquette had excellent academic credentials, distinguished success as an Algonquian scholar, and a deliberate nature as suggested by both his writing style and his handwriting. He also possessed technical expertise as demonstrated by both his Mississippi map and his earlier map of the upper Great Lakes noted in chapter 1. These personal characteristics thus lend credence to the notion that the hydronym <8AB8SKIG8> is inherently intelligible. Second, the Marquette map that contains this place-name, the only surviving document from the Mississippi voyage in Marquette's or Jolliet's hand, is one of two identical maps of the great river drawn by the missionary himself at his relative leisure in the St. François-Xavier Mission at Green Bay. In other words, this chart was not slapdash work. Third, the maps drawn in the town of Québec with Jolliet's assistance after the Mississippi voyage but before the arrival of Marquette's map in Québec in the summer of 1675, and based solely on Jolliet's *memory* of the trip, also contain this same name for the Ohio River.[6] The facts enumerated above therefore indicate that *somebody* called this big river by the name Marquette and Jolliet recorded in the form <8AB8SKIG8>.

For at least three years prior to their trip down and back up the Mississippi River, Marquette and Jolliet—especially Marquette—undertook a great deal of fact finding among Indians concerning the lands that they were intending to explore. The Frenchmen had at least one map of the land they expected to travel through drawn with native assistance. Importantly, Marquette had the opportunity to consult with Mississippi Valley Illinois Indian traders who visited the Jesuit mission at Chaquamegon on the southern shore of Lake Superior. At the same mission he also spent two and a half years learning the Miami-Illinois language with the help of an Illinois boy who had been a slave among the Ottawa.[7] Then, on the way to the Mississippi, Marquette would have been able to gather geographical information during the explorers' stopover at the large Mascouten-Miami town located near present-day Berlin, Wisconsin.[8] Given the fact that the French team was embarking into territory never before seen by Europeans, Marquette would probably have also consulted the two Miami guides from this town who led the Frenchmen to the portage between the Fox and Wisconsin Rivers. This is a reasonable assumption since these two Miami men were chosen for this task not only because they possessed expert geographical knowledge of the country but also because they and Marquette spoke a common language—Miami-Illinois.[9] Thereafter, down on the Mississippi River itself, we know Marquette talked about geography with the Miami-Illinois–speaking Peoria, who received him and his companion Jolliet in grand style at their village located near the Mississippi on the Des Moines River.[10] Later, Marquette could even have inquired about the geographical as well as the onomastic aspects of his trip with a Dhegiha Siouan speaker near the confluence of the Mississippi and Arkansas Rivers who was able to converse with Marquette in Miami-Illinois.[11] Finally, since the French explorers were on an important and official geographical fact-finding mission for King Louis XIV of France, Marquette may have gone over his notes with another Miami-Illinois–speaking tribe, the Kaskaskia, whom the French explorers encountered near present-day Ottawa, Illinois, on their return trip. In fact, the only people that the French party saw in the course of their entire Mississippi adventure—after leaving St. Ignace on the coast of the Upper Peninsula of Michigan and until returning to Green Bay—with whom Marquette could have communicated orally were speakers of Miami-Illinois. Therefore, the evidence concerning which Native American groups in the area could have provided the hydronym <8AB8SKIG8> to Marquette points suggestively, if not magnetically, to speakers of that language.

For whatever reason, the hydronym <8AB8SKIG8>, as noted above, seems to have disappeared from usage before the 1690s. Neither Jacques Gravier, a French Jesuit missionary in the Illinois Country from roughly 1688 to 1705, nor any of the other missionaries who followed him to the Illinois missions ever mentioned this hydronym. Indeed, by 1699, Father

Gravier had recorded various geographical and Native American place-name data for the lower Ohio Valley and was even in possession of a copy of Marquette's original Mississippi voyage narration, which, like the latter's map, also contains the name <8AB8SKIG8>. However, he never mentioned the name <8AB8SKIG8>.

In the Miami-Illinois language there exist two syntactic possibilities for <8AB8SKIG8>: it is either a verb or a noun. The first prospect, while grammatically possible for a place-name, is unlikely in this case. If *o* ~ *u*, which are the same phoneme in Miami-Illinois, is the sound represented by the final "8" of <8AB8SKIG8>, this sound occurs in word-final position exclusively in certain imperative verb forms. If *oo* ~ *uu*, which are the same phoneme in Miami-Illinois, is the sound represented by the final "8" in <8AB8SKIG8>, this sound occurs most of the time in certain first-person singular verbs. However, a command form of a verb or a first-person singular verb used as the name of a river is a preposterous idea. Hence, <8AB8SKIG8> appears to be a noun.

Ostensibly, <8AB8SKIG8> can be parsed into at least two elements. The first segment, <8AB->, represents the Miami-Illinois initial *waap-*, "white." In Marquette's work, as in that of other early French missionaries working with the Miami-Illinois language, *-p-* in the term *waap-* is characteristically written -b-. In fact, the Illinois-French dictionary always writes -b- for *-p-* in *waap-*. Among its copious examples are <8abicanate8i>, translated *os blanc decharné* (defleshed white bone), for *waapikanahteewi,* and <8abans8nsa>, glossed *petit lieuvre, espece de manit8 de jongleur* (little rabbit, a kind of shaman spirit) for *waapansoonsa.* The recently discovered French-Illinois dictionary penned by the Jesuit Pierre-François Pinet at Chicago starting in 1696, also writes *p* in this fashion, as in <8aban8a>, translated *le dieu des reveurs* (the god of the dreamers) for *waapanwa.*[12]

The -SK- of <8AB8SKIG8> represents Miami-Illinois *sk* ~ *hk.*[13] In fact, the -G- also stands for preaspirated *hk.* Although *hk* was rarely heard as [g] in the recordings of the Miami-Illinois language, it was known to happen, as in Gatschet's <sákgwa> for phonetic [hsáhkwa], "badger."[14] Marquette naturally did not mark preaspiration, represented here by *-h-*, when he wrote -G-, as the failure to hear and/or mark preaspiration was a routine mistake made by Europeans, especially those new to the Miami-Illinois language. This fact is evidenced by the three surviving dictionaries of that language compiled by the Jesuits in the late 1600s and early 1700s, as well as by later recordings such as those made by various researchers in the late 1800s and early 1900s.

Understanding the final -8 of <8AB8SKIG8> requires an examination of the French usage of this digraph. In word-initial position, "8" can represent *w,* sometimes *oow* before a vowel, and *oo* before a consonant. Between two vowels it stands for *w,* sometimes *o(o)w.* When it appears between two consonants, "8" represents *o(o).* Between consonants that are not followed by *w* and a following vowel, it stands for *o(o)w.* In word-final position, "8" typically represents *o(o).* This synopsis lays out the commonly recognized phonological possibilities of "8," and determining this symbol's intended pronunciation in any given word *within these contexts* is not problematic. However, early Mississippi Valley Jesuit missionaries also used "8" to signify *wa* and *waa,* and with these two additional phonological possibilities rose the specter of ambiguity—for 99 percent of the people back in Québec and France appear to have had no idea that these were possible values for the letter "8."

Just like the dictionaries of the Miami-Illinois language compiled by the French that contain numerous examples of the use of "8" for *wa* and *waa,* Marquette's map of the Mississippi casually evinces this phonological shapeshifter. <P8TE8TAMI>, for example, is his spelling of *pooteewaatamii,* the Ojibwa name for the Potawatomi. Here his first -8- predictably signifies *oo,* but his second -8- represents *waa.* Another example on the same map is his <8chage>, which was intended to represent Miami-Illinois *waašaaši,* "Osage."[15] Here again 8- stands for *waa.* A further example of the missionary's use of "8" is found in his holograph journal in the form <Chachag8essi8>, the name of the famous Illinois Indian trader who assisted the priest during the winter of 1675 near present-day Chicago.[16] In this man's name the first -8- stands predictably for *w,* but the final -8 was intended by Marquette to represent none other than *wa.* Although word-final -8 was certainly transliterated quite regularly and uncritically to ou, as in the "Chachagwessiou" spelling commonly seen in the literature, this is an incorrect rendering of the term, which is actually *šaahšaakweehsiwa,* "copperhead" *(Agkistrodon contortrix),* with final *wa.* Not only does the last syllable of "Chachagwessiou" not line up with the other recordings of this term, which are all in agreement, but also the word-final vowel sequence *-io,* represented here by the spelling -iou, does not even exist in Miami-Illinois.[17] A few from among the many examples of the use of "8" for phonemic *wa(a)* produced by Jesuits in the Illinois Country in the early 1700s are <p8ro>, glossed *fume* (Smoke!—the command form of this verb), for *(a)hpwaaro*; <irenans8>, translated *boeuf* (bison) for *irenaswa,* the Old Miami-Illinois term for "bison" (*Bison bison*); and <panghitam8>, glossed *perroquet,* for *pankihtamwa,* "Carolina parakeet" (*Conuropsis carolinensis*).[18] Moreover, the indiscriminate transposition of original "8" representing *wa(a)* to written ou is not uncommon in historical French documents.[19] Thus in the case of the final -8 of <8AB8SKIG8>, *wa* is what Marquette intended, not bizarre, inexplicable *o(o)* ~ *u(u)*, the sound represented by the meaningless final ou of the freak spelling *Ouabouskigou.* This analysis finds historical support in the Jesuit historian Camille de Rochemonteix's more informed rewriting of Marquette's <8AB8SKIG8>: *Ouaboukigoa.* Here de Rochemonteix's oa for the original final -8 is a correct French orthographic representation of the sound *wa.*[20] However, even though de Rochemonteix was apparently one of only a very few Frenchmen aware that "8" could represent *wa(a)*, his revision of Marquette's original <8AB8SKIG8> to *Ouaboukigoa* was also successful at eluding analysis—for his refashioning of the middle -8- of <8AB8SKIG8> to -ou-, just as in the earlier *Ouabouskigou,* resulted in yet another nonsense term.

Determining the phonological value of the middle -8- of Marquette's <8AB8SKIG8> requires a process of elimination. In terms of the sounds it could represent, *wa* and *waa* are out of the question since this analysis would yield a word that is simply babble. It is very unlikely to find *o* ~ *u* in the same context since this vowel rarely occurs *initially* in Miami-Illinois independent nouns or stems in general—and initial long *oo* ~ *uu* is extremely rare in the same position. Indeed, in the case of Marquette's term, none of the customary transcriptions of the letter "8" fits the context. The implication, therefore, is that this "8" is a mistake. But what is the nature of the mistake?

Europeans often heard what they thought was [ɔ] or [o] for actual native phonetic [ɑ(ɑ)]. Copious examples of this mishearing are found in the work of the Jesuit missionary Jean-Baptiste Antoine-Robert Le Boullenger. His <chig8oc8o>, translated *cedre,* "eastern red cedar" (*Juniperus virginiana*), is simply one good one. Here, medial -8o- clearly stands for [wɑɑ] and final -8o for [wɑ], since the name for this evergreen in Miami-Illinois is *šinkwaahkwa.*[21] Pierre-Charles Delliette wrote -komy for Miami-Illinois *-(i)kami,* "water."[22] Constantin-François Volney, a French traveler in the United States in the late 1700s, and Charles Trowbridge, an American ethnographer and linguist of the early 1800s, also provide important evidence that Europeans could hear [ɔ] or [o] for Miami-Illinois [ɑ] between consonants—and before preaspirated *hk*—a fact that is relevant to the analysis of <8AB8SKIG8>. In the interview Volney conducted with the Miami leader *mihšihkinaahkwa* in Philadelphia in 1797, he wrote, for example, <moxkoua> for phonetic [mɑhkwɑ́], "bear" (*Ursus americanus*). Trowbridge wrote the Miami-Illinois name for the site of Vincennes, *čiiphkahkionki* as <Tshipkohkeeōāngee>.[23] It appears then that Marquette, just like his fellow Frenchmen Volney and Le Boullenger, and just like Trowbridge, *thought* he heard the mid-back vowel ɔ or *o*, which he expressed obliquely as "8." But what his Native American informant actually said to him was the low back vowel [ɑ].

In the final analysis, <8AB8SKIG8> represents Miami-Illinois *waapahkihkwa*, which can mean either "white drum" or "white pots," composed of the initial *waap-*, "white," *ahkihkw-*, "drum, pot" and *-a*, the proximate singular animate noun marker or the plural inanimate noun marker.[24] Although Marquette spoke Ojibwa-Ottawa and was in contact with Ojibwa-Ottawa speakers before his Mississippi excursion, the presence of a final vowel in <8AB8SKIG8> would preclude the possibility that an Ojibwa-Ottawa cognate was the source of this place name. "White drum" would most likely refer to the resounding, brilliant white limestone Falls of the Ohio; "white pots" to the brilliant white, pot-shaped limestone holes carved by the surging, swirling waters of the falls.[25] Today, what remains of the falls, which were originally two and a half miles in length, can be seen at present-day New Albany. These falls are the only place in the *entire* course of the Ohio River where the stream cuts through bedrock composed of fossiliferous limestone from shore to shore—and these are the Ohio's one and only falls. Hence, they were the most outstanding landmark of the Ohio as well as a prime fishing spot and popular ford for untold millennia. In both a visual and auditory sense, the Falls of the Ohio are—and were more so in the past—the single most striking feature of this very long, flat, broad, meandering waterway. Owing to their unique nature, there is good reason to believe the Ohio River would have borne a name referring to these waterfalls, especially one created by people who knew them. Prehistoric and early historic Miami-Illinois speakers would have been familiar with this site and the river defined by <8AB8SKIG8>.

The formal similarity of the Gallicized American Indian terms *Ouabouskigou* and *Ouabache*, the latter being the most common French refashioning of the Miami-Illinois term that is the origin of modern English language hydronym "Wabash," has been the bane of historians ever since the birth of Ohio Valley history. Most have postulated that the *Ouabouskigou* is the origin of *Ouabache*. For example, historian Reuben Gold Thwaites wrote in the early 1900s, "Ouabouskiguo [*sic*] ... which the French corrupted to Ouabache." In the same vein, the Indiana historian Jacob Dunn thought that <8AB8SKIG8> was a dialect form of <Wahbahshikki>, his first attempt at spelling the Miami-Illinois name for the Wabash River. Toward the midpoint of the twentieth century, the New France and Mississippi Valley historian Jean Delanglez considered *Ouabouskigou* the "earliest form of 'Wabash.'" Recently, the historians Schwartz and Ehrenberg stated that *Ouabouskigou* was "a name that the French changed to 'Ouabache.'"[26] However, these statements and many like them fall wide of the mark. Moreover, no one has ever explained how such a change could have taken place.

In truth, the two terms are not the same, for it is impossible to derive *Ouabache* from *Ouabouskigou*, or even <8AB8SKIG8>, according to any known rules of phonology. The initial *waap-*, "white," which takes the form Ouab- in *Ouabouskigou*, has no doubt been the great temptation leading earlier scholars to conclude that the two terms are connected. However, *waap-* appears in *countless* expressions in Miami-Illinois; indeed, cognate terms occur in countless expressions throughout the Algonquian language family. Yet no one assumes, for example, that Miami-Illinois *waapikoona*, "snow (on the ground)" is the same word as *waapikinaahkwa*, "whooping crane" (*Grus americana*) simply because the two words share the initial *waap-*.[27] By analogy, no one believes that English "white dog" means the same thing as "white cat" simply because both expressions contain the term "white." Aside from the fact that the names *Ouabouskigou* and *Ouabache* share the term for "white," these terms are phonologically and semantically unrelated—and not only that. They referred, as we shall see, to essentially *two different rivers*.

Although he never saw the Wabash, the seventeenth-century French explorer René de La Salle was the first person in history to record a Native American name for this legendary river. Since La Salle is such an important figure in Indiana's place-name history, a brief look at this man is relevant and useful.

René de la Salle, whose original name was Robert Cavelier, was a very bright person with an insatiable desire and a very simple personal agenda—riches and fame—and he was thoroughly intent on achieving his goal. From the skeletal details of his youth it is difficult to gain an insight into the roots of his personality. It is known, however, that the major defeat for young Cavelier was his repeated failure to secure permission from his Jesuit superior in France to travel as a foreign missionary to China, after having spent eight years as a novice. Overcome with frustration and resentment, the young man dropped out of the order, changed his name for fear of reproach, and sailed for Québec, forever harboring profound and unmitigated hatred for his former religious order.

La Salle's Jesuit past and his thwarted desire to go to China continued to haunt him in Canada.[28] Moreover, in North America, the intrigues that he engendered contaminated and destroyed the lives of an untold number of Indians and Frenchmen, thus shaping the course of history. Indeed, by his rash designs and unenlightened duplicity in his relations with the Iroquois and their Algonquian enemies, La Salle almost singlehandedly precipitated the second wave of the seventeenth-century Iroquois conflagration, which was far more devastating to both the Native American populations and the French interests in North America than the first one had been. Lasting nearly twenty years, the latter conflict even directly endangered the very survival of the colony of New France. In sum, La Salle's actions consistently reveal an impatient, overbearing, arrogant, and what Campeau characterized as a "paranoical" personality.[29]

Then, on March 19, 1687, five years after his Mississippi expedition, La Salle's volatile emotions got him assassinated by his own men in Texas, an event that was but the end result of the desertions by those in his employ as well as the scheming by his French competitors and enemies that constantly beset his career in the New World. Even so, La Salle's tragic death is not in the least surprising. For in the course of his final misadventure, he led hundreds of French men, women, and children to their deaths at Matagorda Bay on the Texas coast in his obstinate, ill-conceived attempt to found a settlement in extremely inhospitable land and among equally inhospitable Indians. At the same time, La Salle was a religious man who protected those who were loyal to him and was in fact killed in the course of his attempt to save his suffering Texas colonists.

What then did La Salle discover for France that might in some small measure make up for his disastrous undertakings? Not much, really. Not Lake Erie or the Ohio River, as some even today continue to believe, and certainly not the Mississippi. Marquette and Jolliet had seen the Mississippi almost nine years before La Salle, all the way down to the Arkansas River, while the Spaniard Luis de Moscoso had already explored its distal end, including the Delta, over a century before La Salle's arrival on the scene.[30] In truth, La Salle's sole claim to discovery was the Kankakee marsh—not a bad catch, of course, as discoveries go, but nothing to equal the important European discoveries made by his French-speaking rivals Jacques Marquette and Louis Jolliet, a Jesuit and a friend of the Jesuits, whom La Salle despised and tried his best to discredit. Oddly enough, although he discovered only the Kankakee for the European community and clearly left grave humanitarian crises in his wake, La Salle managed to garner for himself some place-name fame. He was the first European to mention the Ohio River by its modern name as well as the first to provide American Indian names for the Maumee River, the Kankakee River, the Vermilion River of Illinois, and the White River–West Fork of Indiana, the latter three Miami-Illinois hydronyms picked up in the West between January 1680 and September 1683. So even though he failed as a monolingual soldier of fortune, La Salle, ever keen on the pragmatics of geographical understanding, left his mark on history and the future by coining for Europeans a few distinguished and enduring North American place-names. He was also the first European who tried to determine the location of the Wabash River, even though his initial attempt to do so roiled in confusion. But this comes as no surprise.

It was in 1682 that La Salle first spoke of a river, which he had only heard of and which, in his imagination, began near the western end of Lake Erie and ran the width of what is today northern Indiana all the way to the Illinois River south of Chicago. He called the stream *Ouabanchi*.[31] Even though La Salle's conception of the course of the Wabash, a river that Europeans would not see until the end of the first decade of the 1700s, found immediate cartographic expression in France in the work of his friend Claude Bernou, one can only describe the explorer's depiction of the river as unintentional high comedy—and this map is the brainchild of but one of La Salle's geographical delusions.[32]

Bernou was an abbot friend of La Salle living in France who strove to hype the public image of the explorer into a figure on the scale of Hernán Cortez, the conqueror of Mexico. Largely through the efforts of this cleric, who had connections within French royal society, La Salle's geographical conceptions came to hold sway over the European mapmakers of his time, including the French cartographer Jean-Baptiste Louis Franquelin at Québec. Still, while geographical information circulating among Bernou, Franquelin, King Louis XIV of France, and others managed to establish La Salle as a prime force in North American place nomenclature, Bernou's chart establishes the explorer's position among the ranks of the geographically befuddled. Outlandish geographic conceptions issued from La Salle's mind not only because he often did not see the places he described, but also because he lacked an important ingredient in understanding the lay of the land: knowledge of American Indian languages. In fact, in his nearly twenty years among the Indians, he never succeeded in learning a single native tongue.[33] Of course, the Jesuits would have yanked any hapless missionary with comparable linguistic incompetence right out of *les pays d'en*

Haut and likely sent the poor fellow packing back to the motherland. But the impatient La Salle regularly rushed in where Jesuits dared to tread only after they had equipped themselves with some native language skills. As a result, circumstances constantly forced La Salle to rely on interpreters possessed of varying degrees of ability, such as an Eastern Algonquian Indian from New England brought west to translate for him when the explorer landed among the Miami and Illinois Indians.[34]

As one might guess, problems inevitably arise with respect to some of the explorer's place-name data, and these difficulties often sport an occasional comic twist. For example, La Salle declared that the Iroquois called the upper Mississippi River <Gastacha>.[35] This spelling, however, is not the name of any river; it appears to represent the Old Seneca expression **o(ʔ)kastáhæʔ*, "it isn't there."[36] In this case, La Salle's Iroquoian consultant was apparently attempting to point out on a map that something was not where La Salle was looking for it, while the explorer was under the impression that the Seneca was giving him the name of the great river.

Most of La Salle's language problems stemmed from his abysmal relationship with the Jesuits. In fact, with the arrival of this powerful and clever yet rancorous and volatile personality in the West, the Jesuit mission simply dissolved into thin air. However, it was precisely the Jesuits who held the keys to the native languages, through their continuous direct contact with the Indians and in the grammars and dictionaries they compiled. However, the borrowing of Native American place-names and the coining of them into French place-names did not stop when the Jesuit mission in the Illinois Country temporarily shut down. People with far less linguistic ability, including especially La Salle, went right on coining, and the end results, utilitarian as they might have been, were often, linguistically speaking, far from perfect. However, it is not as if La Salle got everything wrong. Because of his devouring ambition, which, as mentioned above, included a desire to grasp local geography, La Salle was an inveterate, enthusiastic sleuth. Preternaturally driven to collecting geographical information that would further his ambitions, he gathered such data, including place-names, continuously from the day he arrived in New France at the age of twenty-four in November of 1667.[37]

Moreover, despite the fact that Delanglez took La Salle to task over the creation of the fanciful *Ouabanchi* river (or <Aramoni>, as the explorer also called it), this obviously incorrect conception, when critically examined, demonstrates that what La Salle recorded, although patently distorted, was *essentially factual*.[38] Whoever was serving as the explorer's interpreter at the time appears to have not understood his Miami-Illinois–speaking informant, and what was lost in the translation was the fact that *portages* would have been required in order to travel by canoe from Lake Erie to the Illinois River via the Wabash-Vermillion-Vermilion. The first of these portages, noted on maps as early as 1684, linked Lake Erie's Maumee River to the Wabash.[39] La Salle's intended waterway would then have led down the Wabash to the fork of the Vermillion River and then up the Vermillion to the second portage, one of less than seven miles, which linked this waterway to the separate and distinct Vermilion River of Illinois, a stream known historically as the <Aramoni>, La Salle's imagined alternate name for the Wabash. Indeed, there was a riverine passage from Lake Erie to the Illinois Indians residing on the upper Illinois River that traversed what is now Indiana and eastern Illinois. But La Salle got less than half the story right. He erred in thinking that it flowed directly east to west across northern Indiana and northeastern Illinois, that it was one continuous waterway, and that in traveling upon it one would always be going *downstream.*[40]

Irrespective of La Salle's linguistic incompetence, such a geographical blunder—if we ignore the hubris behind it—is essentially pardonable. In 1681, at the time he created his faulty conception of the Wabash, all of Indiana with the exception of the Kankakee Valley, the St. Joseph Valley, and the Lake Michigan shoreline was terra incognita for the French. However, La Salle's *Ouabanchi,* notwithstanding its skewed geographical placement, is the very first historical appearance of the name we today write "Wabash."

Although La Salle's relative success in recording place-names generally outdistanced his geographical understanding, Franquelin's map of 1684 managed to pull together additional data that La Salle had obtained since 1681. This chart, which Franquelin designed in Paris from La Salle's personal map and with the explorer's personal assistance, presents a new form for the name of the Wabash River: *Ouabache.* It was precisely this spelling that the French came to adopt in their language as the name of the river, and it is this spelling by La Salle that led directly to the form of the modern English language place-name "Wabash."[41]

Linguistically speaking, *Ouabache* can in one way be considered an improvement over the earlier *Ouabanchi,* since La Salle had gotten rid of the nonexistent *n* sound. However, the explorer, or else his mapmaker Franquelin, failed in typical seventeenth-century French fashion to put an acute accent over the final "e." La Salle's term, which was originally pronounced [wabašé] ~ [wabaší] by the French, with the last syllable being the strong one, should read *Ouabaché,* as the name sometimes appears historically. However, this *spelling error*—the failure to add an accent over the final "e"—was critical in that it led directly to a pronunciation error in French that was ultimately responsible for the form and pronunciation of French *Ouabache* and thence English "Wabash," *without a final vowel sound.*[42] This sort of mistake is expected, not only because La Salle and Franquelin were characteristically lackadaisical when it came to handling Native American language terms but also because French orthographic standards were much more lax in the seventeenth century than they are today regarding the use of accent marks. Geographically speaking, however, the course of the Wabash River is very well conceived on Franquelin's chart, the location of the stream instantly recognizable to anyone familiar with the contours of Indiana and Illinois.

Nineteen years after La Salle recorded his first *Ouabanchi* the Jesuit missionary Jacques Gravier also recorded this place-name as it was being used at that time in the French language. It was in the following way that Gravier described the river he called *Ouabachi,* a spelling that more accurately reflects the original Miami-Illinois pronunciation of the place-name: "[I]t is said to have three branches, one coming from the Northeast, which flows at the rear of the country of the *Oumiamis* … which the wild people properly call *Ouabachi* [i.e., the modern Wabash River]; the second comes from the Iroquois, and is what they call the Ohio; the third from the South-Southwest, on which are the *Chaouanoua* [Shawnee]. As all unite to fall into the Mississippi, the stream is commonly called Ouabachi."[43]

Notably, Gravier states that *Ouabachi* was originally the name of a waterway far greater in length than that currently designated today by the term "Wabash." Indeed, according to its original usage, *Ouabachi* bracketed the course of the modern Wabash River and *the lower Ohio River* below the confluence of today's Wabash and Ohio Rivers. In other words, it was the name for a water course that stretched from the source of today's Wabash River in western Ohio all the way down to the Mississippi. There is broad agreement on this point through the centuries. During the French era, Pierre-Charles Delliette, who lived among the Miami and Illinois in the late 1600s, said, "The Wabash River, of which I have just spoken, on which part of the Miami are settled, is a very beautiful river, and all the wild people call it such. I do not know where it has its source, but I know that it is not very far from the Iroquois country. It flows continuously southwest and empties into the Mississippi sixty leagues from the mouth of the Illinois River. It is wider than the Mississippi." Jacques-Charles de Sabrevois de Bleury, the French commandant at Detroit from 1714 to 1717, in describing the relationship between the Ohio and Wabash Rivers, noted that the Ohio "falls into the ouabach." William Darby, an American writing about Indiana a hundred years later, said that "the French of Canada ... considered the Wabash the main branch, and gave the united rivers its name." The historian Jacob Dunn, two centuries after Sabrevois, arrived at the same conclusion independently, as did Delanglez in 1939. The latter concurred that "the course of the river [i.e., the Ohio] from where it received the Wabash was generally called by the French 'Ouabache,' while the Ohio River was considered a tributary of the Wabash."[44]

Of course, it would be unwise for us to presume that the ways early historic American Indians conceived certain river courses should reflect our modern formulations. In the case of the Wabash, this was, first of all, an impressively broad, meandering stream, especially in its southern reaches. Though varying from report to report, the historic width of the Wabash as it approached its confluence with the Ohio was consistently enormous.[45] Second, and very important, at the mouth of the Wabash there is a big island that divides the Ohio into two currents, each of which joins the Wabash. This division of the Ohio makes the Wabash at the confluence of the Wabash and the Ohio appear to be the bigger river.[46] Third, every local Native American in the seventeenth and eighteenth centuries knew that by following the west bank of the Wabash one would arrive in seamless fashion at the Mississippi. Gravier's description of *Ouabachi* indicates that what we today know as the Ohio River, sidling in from the east to meet the Wabash at the southwestern tip of Indiana, was in the minds of Miami-Illinois–speaking groups a tributary of the Wabash.

The constituent morphemes of Gravier's *Ouabachi* are the Miami-Illinois initial *waap-*, "white" and the Miami-Illinois II final *-aahši(i),* "shine."[47] In Miami-Illinois, the same final can be seen in Le Boullenger's <misc8*achi*ki kipikat8i>, "red metal" (*metail rouge*), which is Old Miami–Illinois *miskwaahši(i)ki kiipihkatwi,* literally "the metal shines red." It also appears in <8ab*achi*8i atta8ane>, "transparent wood" (*bois transparent*) for *waapaahši(i)wi ahtawaani*; and in <8abanteï*achi*8i>, "luminous metal" (*metail lumineux*) for *waapaanteeyaahši(i)wi.* The term for "shine" is also attested as a medial in the form *-aahši-*, as in <8abachite8i>, for *waapaahšiteewi,* "metal whitened in the fire" (metail blanchi en feu).[48]

After the many recordings of the Miami-Illinois–based French placename *Ouabachi* in both French and English language documents of the 1700s, where the name essentially has the same form given initially by La Salle and Gravier, it was not until the mid-1800s, in the work of the Indiana book collector and Indian place-name researcher Daniel Hough, that we find a recording of the actual Miami-Illinois name for the Wabash River on which La Salle's and Gravier's terms derived. Hough wrote the name <Wahbahshikka>.[49] Then, a few decades later, when Jacob Dunn began his American Indian place-name work, he simply recycled Hough's term. However, he changed the latter's antique vernacular final -a, which represents phonetic [e] ~ [i], to orthographic -i, giving <Wahbahshikki>.[50] Later, after working extensively with native speakers of Miami-Illinois, Dunn revised this old form of the place-name, which had first been recorded ostensibly by an early English-speaking soldier or pioneer, if not Hough himself. Dunn's later renditions, which he glossed "it is bright white," include <wápachĭkĭ> and <wapáciki>, where his "ch" and "c," respectively, stand for š. In addition, the Swiss linguist Albert Gatschet recorded the Wea Miami name for the Wabash River three different times: <wapaxshíki>, <wapáhshíki> and <wapashíke sípiwi> for *waapaahši(i)ki siipiiwi*.[51] The term *waapaahši(i)ki* is a conjunct II verb meaning "it shines white" (*siipiiwi* signifies "river"). It is clear that these Miami-Illinois expressions, including Gravier's recording, refer to the transparent and/or reflective quality, indeed the luminescence, of concrete objects in general. And in the case of our place-name, there is no reason to doubt Dunn's claim that the referent, as explained to him by the Miami leader *waapanahkikapwa*, is the dolomitic limestone that forms the bed of the upper river between Huntington and Carroll Counties.[52]

Naming the Wabash after one of its most important geological features is consistent with indigenous place-naming practices. Indeed, research in the Ojibwa language, a close relative of Miami-Illinois, demonstrates that whereas half of the place-names in that language are noun-based, the rest are verb-based—and the verbal place-names are precisely of the type found in *waapaahši(i)ki*, II verbs composed of an initial + a final + the requisite verb ending. For Ojibwa, Hartley has pointed out that this kind of construction represents very descriptive place-names, and ones that usually refer to *aspects of topography*.[53] Such a notion clearly corroborates Dunn's explanation for the use of the Miami-Illinois hydronym *waapaahši(i)ki*.

In a speech presented at the Tippecanoe Battleground on June 16, 1907, the Miami leader *waapanahkikapwa* said that the Miami name for the Wabash meant "White Stone River." This is a beautiful, crystalline translation that brings us full circle to the original connotation of Miami-Illinois <8abachi8i>, which in the Illinois-French dictionary is translated *pierre transparante* [*sic*], *ou argent* (transparent stone, or silver).[54]

When Miami-Illinois–speaking peoples first created the place-name *waapaahši(i)ki siipiiwi* is not known. However, since one of the Miami-

Illinois names for the Ohio River, examined below, is prehistoric, *waapaahši(i)ki siipiiwi* could be a relatively ancient place-name whose usage stretches back into late prehistoric times and, perhaps, into the dreamtime, for the unique quality of the Miami-Illinois name for the Wabash and the unique geology of the river itself suggest that this stream may have an extraordinary spiritual undercurrent. Since the upper Wabash exhibits a monumental display of shining white stone, and since shining white stone is a principal attribute of the North American spirit known as the Underwater Cat or Underwater Panther, the Wabash may be one of its special abodes. Certainly, a river with such a conspicuously luminous bed would naturally lend itself to being constellated within the domain of the Underwater Cat.[55] In support of this notion is the fact that there are other place-names that refer to this spirit along the Wabash and in its watershed, as we shall see below, but, curiously, nowhere else in Indiana, Illinois, or the nearby areas of Wisconsin, Iowa, and Missouri, where the Miami-Illinois peoples lived in historical times.

In the early 1680s, during La Salle's heyday in the midcontinent, yet another name shows up in association with the Wabash River, in the guise of three historically attested variant spellings: <Agoussaké>, <Agouassaké>, and <Agouasaqué>. Before launching into an examination of this admittedly cryptic artifact, the reader should bear in mind that this term, provided by La Salle to his friend Bernou, to the mapmaker Franquelin, and to the royal French engineer Minet, could be a reflection of La Salle's confused picture of the Ohio Valley or his occasionally intoxicated linguistics—or both.[56] As noted above, La Salle never saw the Wabash River, and there is no evidence whatsoever that he ever laid eyes on the Ohio River at any location except during two fleeting moments in his canoe on the Mississippi as he passed the mouth of the Ohio on his famous excursion down to the Gulf of Mexico and back in 1682: in February southbound on the Mississippi and in June northbound on the great river.[57] Thus it is difficult to give absolute credence to the place-name <Agoussaké> and its variants as applied by the explorer and his associates. Archaeologist James B. Griffin was correct in stating that there is no reason to consider La Salle a reliable source of information on the Ohio Valley.[58] Indeed, the explorer's Ohio River watershed conception is impressionistic at best, full of baseless suppositions and hearsay. The confusing data that La Salle compiled for the midcontinent in general in the 1680s include nonexistent waterways—a situation that occurred in part because he placed disproportionate reliance on the writings of earlier Spanish explorers such as Garcilasco de la Vega and Ferdinand de Soto for the locations and names of rivers and tribes.[59] Still, La Salle occupies a significant place in the history of North America simply for having sent back to France important geographic, botanical, zoological, and onomastic information. It would therefore be irresponsible to toss <Agoussaké> ~ <Agouassaké> ~ <Agouasaqué> on the scrap heap of historical scholarship, since the explorer's use of this name seems to imply that *some* Native American group applied it, or *something like it,* to *some* watercourse. However, when entertaining the likes of place-names such as this one, it is important to remain circumspect lest the air fill with smoke and mirrors. But with this caveat in mind, let us proceed to an examination of at least the available information concerning this curiosity from La Salle's bag of place-name surprises.

<Agoussaké> was in fact the name La Salle gave the Wabash River in his letter of 1683.[60] That much is clear. The first appearance of the spelling <Agoussaké> *as a hydronym* is found in a letter from the explorer, later transcribed by Bernou, on the subject of the Mississippi drainage. Although La Salle composed the original missive most likely in early 1683 at Starved Rock on the upper Illinois River soon after the completion of his fort there, it is not known where he actually learned the name. However, Franquelin's map of 1684, which as noted above is based on both La Salle's personal, direct assistance and La Salle's own map of the area, calls the Wabash River *Rivière Ouabache,* while the name <Agouassaké> is distinctly applied only to that part of the Wabash *above* the "Forks of the Wabash," that is, the Wabash upstream from present-day Huntington, Indiana. Even so, it is important, again, to keep in mind that neither La Salle nor any other Frenchman in the 1600s ever saw the Wabash, and the foregoing information was thus not based on direct personal experience. It could be good information or it could be bad.[61]

Like the cartographer Franquelin, the royal naval engineer Minet, who, as noted above, was also a *direct* beneficiary of La Salle's geographic and onomastic conceptions, wrote <Agouasaqué> on his own map of 1685.[62] Minet's spelling is the same as Franquelin's save for a small Latin twist—Minet wrote the sound *k* as "qu" instead of "k." That said, on the Minet map the name is applied *to the Wabash* as we define it today, while *Ouhabach* is the moniker given to the Ohio. Since Franquelin's and Minet's charts were drawn at the same time, and both with La Salle's help, one has to wonder if La Salle was feeding people different stories, or if perhaps Minet did not trust La Salle's data and relied on other sources for his information.

The place-name <Agoussaké> ~ <Agouassaké> ~ <Agouasaqué> might be an imperfect French transcription of a reflex in some Algonquian language of

PA **wa·kwehšaki,* "foxes." This term commonly turns up in historical French documents in the form <Ouagoussak>, which does resemble <Agoussaké>. <Ouagoussak> was the name for the fox clan within the larger indigenous group known to the French in the 1600s and 1700s by the generic ethnonym <Outagami>, from Ojibwa *otakaamiik,* "people of the other shore."[63] These were the people known in French as *les Renards* (the Foxes), in English as the Fox, or Meskwaki. The initial A of <Agoussaké> could be miscopied 8, standing for *waa-*, or the scribe might have left off an original initial 8- of an original *8agoussaké. As an ethnonym, <Ouagoussak> first appeared in the mid-seventeenth century and probably went into French from Ojibwa-Ottawa, which has *waakušak,* "foxes," or even from Potawatomi.[64] If an Ojibwa-Ottawa-Potawatomi term for "foxes" is what La Salle intended by <Agoussaké>, and the place-name is genuine, then it probably refers to the Wabash as a way leading to and having its source in the late prehistoric estate of the Fox, ostensibly in northwestern Ohio.[65]

There is also a second and somewhat attractive avenue of interpretation for La Salle's elusive place-name, especially if Bernou miscopied La Salle's original spelling by incorrectly reading the second "a" as an "s." Even though they do not match perfectly, the spellings <Agouassaké> and <Agouasaqué> bring to mind the Miami-Illinois noun *aankwaahsakwa,* "driftwood," which is a term that is part of a Miami-Illinois place-name attested historically *for an Indiana tributary of the southern Wabash.* (For a discussion of this place-name see chapter 9.)

Despite the poverty of data relating to the place name <Agoussaké> ~ <Agouassaké> ~ <Agouasaqué>, it is known that La Salle heard about a river as well as an American Indian designation for it. However, because of his poor linguistic skills, he apparently at first confused this stream with the Wabash itself and then later realized, at least as suggested by the cartographic evidence, that it was a tributary or a source of the Wabash. In the end, however, the place-name <Agoussaké> ~ <Agouassaké> ~ <Agouasaqué>, like Marquette's <8AB8SKIG8>, soon vanished from French reports and maps. It does not show up on Franquelin's map of 1688 or, as far as this author has been able to determine, on any subsequent European chart or document. This would make perfect sense if indeed the term does refer to the Fox, since the Fox had abandoned the area near the western end of Lake Erie by the mid-seventeenth century. The eponymous place-name referring to these people would have then naturally disappeared since it would no longer have applied to reality—the Fox had fled to the land now known as Wisconsin.

A very unusual name for the Wabash River is the historian Hiram Beckwith's <Quiaaghtena>. Beckwith failed to provide a translation for this term, even though he declared it Iroquoian in origin.[66] Why he thought the place-name was Iroquoian is anyone's guess. Beckwith's spelling, however, does resemble another equally curious recording of a local putative Native American place-name also applied historically to the Wabash River: <Quaxtanana>. This name was one Lewis Evans collected, but likewise left untranslated, between 1749 and 1755 and placed on his map in 1766.[67] <Quiaaghtena> and <Quaxtanana> are not, however, Iroquoian, or that problematic, for that matter—the spellings were simply sufficient unto themselves and understandable to the general public in the 1700s. For these recordings are just improperly transcribed anglicized versions of Miami-Illinois *waayaahtanwa*, "Wea," the Miami-Illinois–speaking group discussed in chapter 8. Early British maps characteristically associate the Wea in particular with the Wabash, since their principal summer villages were located on the river just west of present-day Lafayette. In <Quiaaghtena> the -gh- is the silent English orthographic gh typically observed in such words as "thought" and "caught." The scribe wrote -aagh- to account for the long low back vowel [ɑɑ]. As for the "Quaxtanana" spelling, the -xt- can be none other than a valiant and rather successful attempt to write the preaspirated consonant *ht* of the original Miami-Illinois term. Indeed, the use of "x" to write Miami-Illinois preaspiration appears in other Miami-Illinois language-related documents, as for example in Volney's <moxkoua> noted above. Finally, in <Quiaaghtena> and <Quaxtanana>, the initial "Q" represents a copy error. Unfortunately, this same mistake has been reproduced even in modern times in spellings such as "Qabache" and "Quabache" for *Ouabache.* Examples of this blunder can be seen in the silly names for some Indiana parks, including "Quabache Park" near Attica, "Quabache State Park" near Blufton, and "Quabache Trails Park" near Vincennes.

3

‹Ohio›, *Ouabachi*, and Beyond

During the fall, winter, and spring of 1668–69 the explorer-to-be René de La Salle entertained a small group of Seneca at his fief in view of the St. Louis Rapids near Montreal.[1] In plying the Indians for information about what still lay hidden to Europeans between that French outpost and the Mississippi he learned the name of a great river that took its rise just south of the Seneca homeland in present-day western New York state and then ran in some undetermined way through the heart of the continent. The Seneca called the river *ohi·yoʔ*. Though the French had already heard about the Ohio, as evidenced by its appearance on Bourdon's map from around 1640,[2] it was La Salle who coined for the French this Iroquoian language name for the river and paved the way for its universal modern usage in the form "Ohio."

Iroquoian Seneca *ohi·yoʔ* was translated by the French to *la Belle Rivière*, "the Beautiful River." This Seneca term is parsed |o-h-iyo-ʔ|. The simple noun prefix |o-| carries no meaning, |-h-| is "river," |-iyo-| is the verb "be good, be nice," and |-ʔ| is the required simple noun suffix in the form of a glottal stop, which also has no meaning. The only thing that remains of **-iyh(õh)*, the Proto-Iroquoian root for "river" in Seneca *ohi·yoʔ*—and in the modern spelling "Ohio"—is the *h*. In Seneca, *y* before *h* is automatically deleted, and the *i* of **-iyh(õh)* is lost after a prefix beginning with a vowel.[3] Notably, the waterway that the historic Seneca called *ohi·yoʔ* was not simply the Ohio River as we know it today; it was also one of the Ohio's sources, the Allegheny River, as well as the southern section of the Mississippi below the Ohio-Mississippi confluence—*all the way down to the Gulf* *of Mexico.* This is a completely reasonable hydrological conception from the Northern Iroquoian perspective.[4]

The linguistic "anatomy" of "Ohio," however, also has a deeper level. The original meaning of the verb stem |iyo| in Proto-Iroquoian was probably "be big."[5] Therefore, according to its presumed ancient meaning, the hydronym "Ohio" would be cognate with various Algonquian names for the Mississippi that derive from PA **meʔšisi·pi·wi*, "big-river." The meaning of the Seneca name for the Ohio River, expressed in French as *la Belle Rivière,* evolved apparently because the Northern Iroquoians conflated the idea of bigness with the ideas of goodness and beauty. This conflation can be observed in Huron, where the cognate verb stem means both "be beautiful, be good," and "be big." Likewise, in Tuscarora, a non–Northern Iroquoian language, the same verb means "be great," "be big," and "be beautiful."Another way of looking at this situation is that the verb stem |iyo| encompasses more meanings than most simple English verbs. The earliest Iroquoians may have used this verb essentially for describing bigness, but because of a great positive value placed on large things, the verb's semantic field also included ideas of goodness and beauty.

Since La Salle was the first European to record "Ohio," it has often been assumed that he actually descended the river. This is not the case. However, it is true that when word got out in the early summer of 1669 that there was going to be a non-Jesuit expedition to the West, the anti-Jesuit La Salle, hungry to assume the role of explorer for the French colony, liquidated his holdings near Montreal and, posing as an Iroquois language interpreter, joined the exploration team that included the Sulpician priest Father Bréhant de Gallinée of "Michigan" fame (discussed in chapter 1). (For a related note, see chapter 2, note 33.) The members of this expedition, accompanied by the Seneca with whom La Salle had just spent the previous several months, embarked from Montreal on July 6, 1669, their destination Sault Ste. Marie, between Lake Huron and Lake Superior, the site of a Jesuit mission.[6] Although many Frenchmen had already ventured into the interior north of Lake Erie, even as far west as Lake Superior, this was the first group of Europeans ever to travel west along the northern shores of Lake Erie. Before 1669, Iroquoians had always steadfastly denied the French this experience.

Two months into the voyage, before the explorers had gone beyond the eastern end of Lake Erie, La Salle was caught in a lie about his stated ability to speak Seneca. This embarrassment, at least, led to his abandoning the party near the eastern end of Lake Erie, and from there La Salle headed off with his Seneca friends into the forests of the Iroquois country. The next summer he was seen on the Ottawa River. Finally, in the early 1670s, La Salle undertook an exploratory adventure to the lands south of Québec, journeying there with the blessings of the *intendant* Jean Talon and Governor Frontenac and with the knowledge of Louis XIV's minister Jean-Baptiste Colbert.[7]

Therefore, had La Salle discovered the Ohio, the private papers of all three men would be wildly *abuzz* with discussions of such a discovery. It is not impossible that during the summer of 1673 La Salle could have seen the Allegheny River. However, he never mentioned such an event. Indeed, there is not one reliable report that says La Salle saw the Ohio River or the Mississippi until he descended the Mississippi in the late winter of 1681–82. Not only the extreme paucity of data but also the poor quality of the data one sees concerning La Salle's so-called discovery of the Ohio is exemplified in an anonymous memoir in Margry that reads, "He [La Salle] followed it [the Ohio] all the way to a place where it falls from a great height into a vast marsh."[8] It is hard to figure out what planet that particular Ohio River was located on, but it certainly was not Earth. This sort of account differs immeasurably from those concerning Jolliet's and Marquette's exploration of the Mississippi, even when we figure in Jolliet's occasional hyperbole. La Salle would not see the Ohio River, except at its mouth—and that would be nine years after Marquette and Jolliet had seen it.

In the summer of 1673, Father Jacques Marquette, Louis Jolliet and their fellow explorers became the first Europeans to see the Ohio River, at its mouth, and to learn an Algonquian name for it. Yet within eight years of Marquette's recording of his <8AB8SKIG8>, discussed in chapter 2, Jean-Baptiste Louis Franquelin, the Québec-based royal mapmaker, working with geographic data supplied to him by La Salle, spearheaded the popularization of the Seneca name for the Ohio River that La Salle had recorded.[9] French versions of Seneca *ohi˙yoʔ* started to show up on French maps between 1681 and 1684, when La Salle was at the height of his career. Because of his connection direct or indirect to Franquelin, the royal naval engineer Minet, and the Italian Franciscan friar and influential mapmaker Coronelli, all of whom occupy the pantheon of the early historic cartographers of North America, La Salle naturally, and probably unintentionally, began swaying European geographical thought in the direction of the Seneca place-name. The maps of these men and those of their contemporaries serve to illustrate this Iroquoian slant. And in time the fate of this river's future and universal name would be sealed within the language of the Seneca.

However, it is necessary to bear in mind that the French experienced the Ohio River for the first time in 1673 and for nearly forty years thereafter *from the perspective of the Mississippi Valley.* It was the Mississippi that served as the essential French point of view upon the lands south of the western Great Lakes when France was the major European power operating in the area. In fact, until the mid-1700s, the Iroquois effectively barred the French from venturing down the Ohio from the direction of Québec or up the river east past the Ohio-Wabash confluence. At the same time, southern tribes hostile to the French, such as the Chickasaw and the Cherokee, also made the Ohio dangerous.[10]

As discussed in chapter 2, the waterway known today in English as the Wabash River ends where it meets the Ohio River and it is the Ohio that enters the Mississippi. However, as discussed in chapter 2, the historic French in North America consistently used the French hydronym *Ouabachi ~ Ouabaché ~ Ouabache,* derived from Miami-Illinois *waapaahši(i)-*, to refer to the waters coming out of northwestern Ohio, meandering through Indiana and flowing all the way down to the Mississippi. This hydrological conception, first explained by the Jesuit missionary Father Jacques Gravier in his report from the Illinois Country in 1700, maintained throughout the French regime. In 1726, Étienne Périer, the governor of Louisiana, wrote, "About 120 miles above the Arkansas there flows into the Mississippi the Ouabache river formed of four other rivers." In 1752, a mere decade before France lost North America to England, Antoine-Simon le Page du Pratz, a French military engineer, was still using this same time-honored Miami-Illinois hydrological definition when he called the waters below the Ohio-Wabash fork *Ouabache.*[11] The itineraries gathered by another Jesuit missionary, Pierre Potier, at Detroit from the mid-1700s, authoritative documents replete with an impressive array of descriptive place-names used by local French traders of the era, demonstrate that the latter were using the names *Ouabache* and *le petit Ouabache* to describe the river we today call the Wabash, while using the moniker *le grand Ouabache* to designate the combined waters of the Ohio and the Wabash that flowed down to the Mississippi.[12] It was then only natural that the French living in the West developed conceptions of these rivers and gave names to them in accordance with the practice of the local Miami-Illinois–speaking peoples friendly to the French.

Even so, concurrent with the use of *Ouabache* as described above, La Salle's Iroquoian name for the Ohio was fast becoming a fixture in the French geographical lexicon. Indeed, once La Salle had become a major player—and reporter—in the West starting in 1679, and once he had begun popularizing the Seneca name for the Ohio, the French were destined to have a binary naming system for the river, one Iroquoian and the other Algonquian. As one might expect, this approach did not come without a certain amount of confusion. In some cases, the French used "Ohio" basically according to its essential Iroquoian usage. On a map from 1697 drawn by Louis de la Porte de Louvigny, a French military leader stationed at Michilimackinac, the name *Ohio,* the standard modern spelling, is the name for the Ohio precisely as we use it today, while his *8bache* is our modern Wabash River.[13] Not surprisingly, Henri de Tonti, in 1700, also used his former master La Salle's hydronym and hydrological conception when he applied *Oyo* to the Ohio River as we know it today.[14]

However, since the French in the late 1600s and on into the 1700s used *Ouabache* and *le petit Ouabache* for today's Wabash, and *le grand Ouabache* for the lower Ohio below the Wabash-Ohio confluence, they sometimes reserved the name "Ohio" only for that section of the Ohio River *above this fork.* The very popular Delisle maps of the early eighteenth century, produced by a cutting-edge house of cartography that characteristically based its maps on reams of intensively researched data, are for the most part consistent in defining these waterways in this fashion.[15] Still, *Ouabache* not only predominated as the name for the lower Ohio, but also competed with "Ohio" in an unexpected way. Many a French traveler and/or mapmaker used the name *Ouabache* or one of its variants in a fashion that shows they were oblivious to the subtleties involved in using this hydronym correctly. Contemporaries and fellow residents in the West of de Louvigny and Tonti such as André Pénicault in 1700 and Pierre Le Moyne in 1702, both of whom saw the mouth of the Ohio in person, applied *Ouabache* to what we know today as the *entire* Ohio River, just as the French royal naval hydrographer Jean-Baptiste Minet, mentioned above, had done fifteen years earlier.[16] Likewise, Pierre-Charles Le Sueur's data from 1702 refer to the entire Ohio as *R. d'Ouabache.*[17] Nevertheless, prudence, experience, and awareness are evidenced on the French map designed after 1719 at Kaskaskia by the Jesuit missionary Jean-Baptiste Le Boullenger, wherein he deemed it best to offer the viewer a choice between the two names for the lower Ohio.[18]

In truth, what any particular Frenchman called the Ohio River seems to have depended on what crowd he was running with. A case in point is the map that has been attributed to the Jesuit missionary Gabriel Marest but which is actually in the handwriting of his colleague and fellow missionary among the Miami-Illinois peoples, Jean Mermet. On this chart the entire Ohio River is called <Acansea>. This term is a prehistoric Miami-Illinois name for the Ohio, one that we will examine below.[19] In the end the French ways for defining and naming the Ohio River and the Wabash River would not be leveled out, codified, and simplified to the way they are used today until the arrival of English speakers in the midcontinent after the turn of the nineteenth century.

Names for the Ohio River exist for other Native American languages. In the 1700s and early 1800s, Wyandot villages existed in present-day northwestern Ohio, even in west-central Indiana, and Wyandot names for the Ohio River have survived. One of these appears on Guernsey's map in the form <Ohezuh>.[20] His recording, attributed to the U.S. Indian agent John Johnston, represents phonemic *uhyì˙žuh,* "big-river" the Wyandot cognate of Seneca *ohi˙yoʔ.*[21] The components of this term are |yu-hy-ižu-˙|: |yu-| is the third-person singular neuter patientive marker, |-hy-| is "river," |-ižu-| is the verb "be great," and |˙|, the raised dot or vowel length marker, is the stative aspect marker. (PI *-*iyo-* went to *-ižu-* in Wyandot. Also, the final *h* of *uhyì˙žuh* is epenthetic, present in Wyandot after a word-final short vowel.)[22]

Now, since the Wyandot people were present historically in Indiana, it is important to comment briefly on the Wyandot language. Wyandot was an amalgam of Northern Iroquoian languages, mostly Tionontati along with Huron and Petun. Although, according to the Jesuits, the three tribes known as the Tionontati, the Huron and the Petun spoke the same language, this appraisal is superficial. In truth, they spoke three distinct languages that comprised a mutually intelligible linguistic continuum. There were significant differences among these languages, and between them and the later Wyandot language that evolved out of their mixing.

Of course, the term Wyandot not only applies to the language; it also refers to the sociopolitical entity composed of the tribes mentioned above, along with some Neutrals and Wenro, all of whom were not only linguistically but culturally related. After being forced to flee their contiguous homelands in southern Ontario in the face of the genocidal war waged against them by the Seneca and Mohawk in 1649, these people clustered into two bands. The refugee group that in time would become the more documented contingency settled at Lorette, Québec, where their descendants live today. The second group fled before 1660 all the way to the banks of the Mississippi. Eleven years later, they began making their way back east, passing by the Jesuit mission at Chaquamegon. From there, and for a brief time in the company of Jacques Marquette, they lived and traveled along the southern shore of Lake Superior. Then, after many years, they arrived near their ancestral homeland in the area at the western end of Lake Erie in the early 1700s.[23] The year 1718 found these folks living on the

Detroit River, where ten years later the Jesuits established a mission for them. In the meantime, they were joined there by the Lorette group, whom the Seneca had temporarily chased out of Québec. It was during this era that the combined bands became known as the Wyandot.

<Oheyandewa> is a garbled recording for another Wyandot name recorded for the Ohio River. This term was published in 1883 on Hough's map and later appeared in the *History of Perry County,* where it is attributed to the Wyandot.[24] While this ethnolinguistic attribution is correct, the spelling of this hydronym was corrupted, probably by Hough's engraver. However, this same place-name was first recorded by the U.S. government Indian agent John Johnston and published in the recognizable form <ohezuhyeandawa>.[25] The first segment of Johnston's <ohezuhyeandawa>, ohezuh-, is the same *uhyì·žuh* ("big-river") described above. The second segment, spelled -yeandewa, represents phonemic *yáhnawaʔ*, "current." The morphophonemic analysis of the latter term is |ya-hnaw-aʔ|, where |ya-| is the third-person singular neuter agentive marker, |-hnaw-| is "current" and |-aʔ| is again the noun suffix.[26] Potier wrote this term <ąnda8a> and glossed it *riviere flot courant d'eau* (tidal river current of water).[27] The " ̨ " mark of Potier's spelling represents the sound *y*. The "d" of -yeandewa is not a copy error; it represents a regular sound change in Wyandot whereby phonemic *n* became partially denasalized, giving [ⁿd] before an oral vowel such as *a*.[28] In other words, *n* went to [ⁿd] at the phonetic, or spoken, level in a phonological context such as we find in *yáhnawaʔ*.

Other non-Iroquoian names also exist for the Ohio River. Delaware Indian names for the great river have survived from the Munsee language and the Southern Unami language, both of which, as noted in the introduction, were spoken by a people living temporarily in what is now Indiana in the very late 1700s and early 1800s. The Munsee name for the Ohio was recorded in the latter half of the eighteenth century by the Moravian missionary John Heckewelder, who wrote it in the form <Gichthanne>. His spelling represents Munsee **kihtháne·w,* "big river," where *kiht-* is a prenoun meaning "big" and **-háne·w* is a noun final meaning "river."[29] The absolute age of this particular hydronym is unknown, but it would surely date at least to late prehistoric times. The Unami name for the Ohio River, as it appears in the "Voegelin Word List," is *me·xáne,* which Voegelin glossed "the big river, the Ohio." This is an unusual form that appears to be an inanimate noun but may in fact be a misheard verb in the form *me·xáne·*.[30]

In addition to his "Ohio," La Salle recorded an Algonquian name for the Ohio River in the form <Mosopeleacipi>. <Mosopelea> itself is an ethnonym, the name of an enigmatic Ohio Valley tribe that was dispersed by the Iroquois in the 1600s. The -cipi segment of La Salle's term represents an Algonquian term for "river."[31] Wheeler-Voegelin's explanation that <Mosopelea> stands for Shawnee *mhš-*, "big" plus *peleewa,* "turkey" is either whimsical or forced.[32] Such an analysis does not stand up to philological scrutiny. In fact, in her eagerness to designate the term Shawnee, the historian failed to realize that <Mosopelea> first came from the plume of Jacques Marquette in 1673 and appeared subsequently on the maps describing the Mississippi voyage that were based on the intelligence gathered by his companion Jolliet—but there is no evidence that either man ever met any Shawnee Indians. If so, they would not have been able to communicate with them in Shawnee, since the French could not speak Shawnee. Although related, the Shawnee language is profoundly different from and mutually unintelligible with the six native tongues that Marquette knew. Moreover, the Shawnee people in 1673 had not yet had the opportunity to learn any French.

Now, Marquette's early *relation* of 1669–70, written from Mission du St.-Esprit at Chaquamegon on the south shore of Lake Superior, does speak of a visit that the Illinois had received earlier *in their own country* from some Shawnee.[33] In fact, the Illinois boy from whom Marquette learned the Illinois language had witnessed that very visit. However, again, there is no hard evidence that Marquette met any Shawnee in his lifetime, and Jolliet himself would have obtained information about the Mosopelea from the Illinois, not from the Shawnee. Of course, these facts do not imply that the people known as the Mosopelea were not Shawnee speakers; they simply show that the historically recorded hydronym <Mosopeleacipi> did not come from the Shawnee language.

Given the earliest recording of <MONS8PELEA>, the prototypical spelling of this ethnonym on Marquette's map of the Mississippi; given the year the name was coined, 1673, a time well before any contact between Frenchmen and Shawnee had occurred; and above all, given the word's internal linguistic evidence, presented below, <Mosopeleacipi> appears to be a Miami-Illinois hydronym—provided that the -l- represents a mishearing by Marquette of *l* for *r*.[34] Aside from this one problem, the linguistic and historical evidence points very strongly to Miami-Illinois as the source language of the ethnonym originally recorded by Marquette.

Marquette's <MONS8PELEA> appears to consist of two elements. The first is Miami-Illinois *mooswa,* "deer" (*Odocoileus virginianus*), pronounced [moonswa]. This term is found not only in Marquette's <MONS8PELEA>

but also in La Salle's writings in the form <Monso>, the name of a man that translates to French *chevreuil* (deer).[35] Bearing the same translation, the term is also found in the French-Illinois dictionary of the Jesuit missionary Jean-Baptiste-Antoine-Robert Le Boullenger, who spelled it <mons8a>, in Father Pierre Pinet's earlier French/Miami-Illinois dictionary, as well as in the Illinois-French Jesuit dictionary, in spellings that support the present analysis: <M8ns8> and <mons8>, respectively.[36] These historical transcriptions of <MONS8PELEA> clearly exhibit the commonly occurring phenomenon of sibilant prenasalization, represented by orthographic -NS-, in the Miami-Illinois term for "deer." Among the Central Algonquian languages, this phonological phenomenon is for all intents and purposes unique to Miami-Illinois. Ojibwa is the only other Core Central Algonquian language that exhibits nasalization in a similar context, but its appearance in that language is rare and in fact nonsystemic.[37] In the Miami-Illinois language, this prenasalization, as well as the optional voicing in Old Miami-Illinois of *s* to [z], are noncontrastive features that ultimately derive from the preceding *m*. This voicing of *s* to [z] shows up historically in the French naval engineer Minet's La Salle–based spelling of this same ethnonym: <Mozopelea>.[38]

<MONS8PELEA> would be pronounced [moonzwapilia] and could evidence another use by Jacques Marquette of the letter "8" to indicate *wa(a)*, just as we see on his Mississippi map. A less likely but not impossible explanation is that the *-wa-* of **mooswapilia* contracted to *o* in the dialect or idiolect of the speaker from whom Marquette got this ethnonym, giving *[moonzopilia] with an initial in the form **mooso-*. As noted in chapter 6 in the discussion of Fall Creek as well as in note 2 in chapter 2, the sequence *-CwaC-*, where *C* stands for a consonant, has been shown to go to [-CoC-] in the speech of some Miami-Illinois speakers. However, given his proven propensity to use "8" for the sound *wa(a)*, Marquette's "8" in <MONS8PELEA> is probably *wa*, and later forms of this tribe name spelled with an "o" for his original "8" likely represent, as in the case of <8AB8SKIG8> in chapter 2, a misinterpretation by copyists of the sound he intended with "8."

There is good reason to believe that -PELEA, the second segment of <MONS8PELEA>, is an allomorph of *pileewa*, the Miami-Illinois term for "turkey" (*Meleagris gallopavo*). The *-w-* present in the independent noun *pileewa* does not occur in the composite term <Mosopeleacipi> because in Miami-Illinois, trisyllabic words with a short first vowel such as *pileewa* lose the *-w-* when they are prefixed.[39] The result of this phonological change is present, for example, in *araamipinšia*, a name for the Underwater Panther, literally "the under-bobcat," where we see the reduced *-pinšia,* "bobcat" in lieu of the simplex noun *pinšiwa,* and in *lenimahwia,* "coyote" (lit. "ordinary-wolf"), where *-mahwia* is a reduction of the simplex noun *mahweewa.* In fact, the very form spelled -PELEA meaning "turkey" in Marquette's <MON-S8PELEA> occurs in another "turkey"-related word in Miami-Illinois, the term for the domestic turkey. This expression also evinces a loss of *-w-* in *pileewa,* as seen in Gatschet's <wapipilía> and Dunn's <wapĭpilĭa>, recordings that stand for phonetic [waapipilia].[40]

Thus *araamipinšia, lenimahwia* and *waapipilia* reflect the same phonological reality as that found in Marquette's <MONS8PELEA>. In other words, the underlying *pileewa* of <MONS8PELEA> is no longer trisyllabic, and therefore does not evidence *w.* Further, in light of the fact that the French often heard [e] for *i,* as in Volney's <népé> for *nipi,* "water" and <mintchepé> for *miinčipi,* "corn," Miami-Illinois *-pilia* is likely the -PELEA of <MONS8PELEA>.[41]

In light of the facts noted above, the ethnonym <Mosopelea> could be analyzed as **mooswapilia,* "deer-turkey," with La Salle's hydronym <Mosopeleacipi> being **mooswapiliasiipi,* "deer-turkey river," where *-(i)siip* is the Miami-Illinois hydronymic noun final signifying "river,"and *-i* is the singular proximate inanimate noun marker. Finally, in my estimation, the ethnonym *mooswapilia* ~ **moosopilia* is not a "compound noun" but a complex statement involving related societal entities, one being known as the "Deer" and the other as the "Turkey."

As for the ethnic identity of the Mosopelea, the only thing that is known for certain is that they were originally a middle Ohio Valley population whose lives were shattered by the Iroquois in the mid-1600s and reduced to just a few individuals. That is obviously not much to go on. The Mosopelea could have been Shawnee speakers, as Wheeler-Voegelin suggested, in spite of the fact that her hypothesis rests partially on her mistaken belief that where they appear on Marquette's map, the Shawnee appear on the Franquelin-Jolliet map known as "La Frontenacie" and on Randin's chart.[42] On the Franquelin-Jolliet map, however, the Shawnee are in fact living up a southern tributary of the lower Ohio later identified cartographically as the "River of the Shawnee," while the Mosopelea are located below the Arkansas River opposite the Taensa. In contrast, on Marquette's chart, his firsthand experience with some members of this tribe is reflected in his <MON-S8PELEA>, which is written just below the mouth of the Ohio on the east bank of the Mississippi.[43] Now, historical accounts agree that the Mosopelea fled *south* out of the Ohio Valley when the Iroquois invaded the region in the mid-1600s. Therefore, since we know that the Shawnee had long established connections with southern tribes, the Taensa, for example, it is not impossible that the Mosopelea were Shawnee. Additional observations by Wheeler-Voegelin with respect to the Mosopelea are also noteworthy. Especially attractive is her suggestion that they were the Indians described on the Manitoumie maps as having guns, and noted by Marquette as being at war with the Quapaw. Furthermore, her statement that some Seneca had told La Salle in 1668–69 that the Mosopelea were Shawnee is also curious.[44] In fact, this is perhaps the strongest aspect of her theory, and at this point I could almost tentatively agree with Wheeler-Vogelin's hypothesis and further propose that Marquette's <MONS8PELEA> may refer to either the Deer and Turkey clans of the Shawnee or the Deer band/moietie of the Turkey clan of the Shawnee.[45] Still, this theory concerning the ethnic identity of the Mosopolea requires additional and convincing support.

Another Miami-Illinois language name for the Ohio River is *pileewa siipiiwi,* "turkey river," recorded by Gatschet in the form <pilãwa sipíwi>.[46] This is also the translation of the Shawnee name for the Ohio River, which is the cognate term *peleewa(a)θiipi.* The Shawnee name appears on Hough's map in the form <Palawatheepee>, ostensibly recorded by an English speaker, where it is correctly glossed "Turkey River" but incorrectly ascribed to the Delaware.[47] The terms *pileewa siipiiwi* and *peleewa(a)θiipi* could be ethnonymic in nature and could, in fact, be reductions of La Salle's <Mosopeleacipi>. If they are reductions of <Mosopeleacipi>, this fact would for all intents and purposes eliminate the possibility that the Mosopelea were Shawnee, since Algonquian place-naming practice prohibits the naming of a river after one's own people. Ethnonymic river names used by one people always indicate another people toward whom or from whom a particular river is flowing.

Curiously enough, a slightly garbled version of Miami-Illinois *pileewa siipiiwi,* "Turkey River" attained brief national prominence in the late 1700s, when Thomas Jefferson proposed that Congress assign the designation "Pelisipia" to one of the tramontane states that he had conceived for the new republic.[48] Had Jefferson's territorial divisions found acceptance among the lawmakers of his time, the state of "Pelisipia" would have included some land within present-day Indiana. The northern boundary of "Pelisipia" would have encompassed territory south of a line extending from near Oolitic in Lawrence County directly west along the northern Knox county line to the Wabash River, before proceeding on into Illinois. The eastern boundary would have gone from Oolitic directly south to the

Ohio River in eastern Perry County. The Ohio River would have been the southern boundary of "Pelisipia."[49]

This study has already discussed four Miami-Illinois names for all or parts of the Ohio River: *waapahkihkwa (siipiiwii)* for the Ohio River, *waapaahši(i)ki siipiiwi* for the Wabash and lower Ohio, as well as *moo-swapiliasiipi* and *pileewa siipiiwi* for the Ohio River. But there is one more Miami-Illinois name for the Ohio to be discussed, a name that was briefly noted above.

<Acanseasipi> is the Jesuit missionary Jacques Gravier's spelling of a Miami-Illinois language name for the Ohio River. His spelling represents phonemic *akaanse(e)asiipi.* Not only is this the most enduring of the five Miami-Illinois names for the Ohio River, but like <Mosopelacipi>, it is also prehistoric—much older than Gravier himself when he became the first person in history to record it about the year 1700.[50] Gravier was missioniz-ing among the Kaskaskia and Peoria at that time, for whom *waapaahši(i)ki,* adapted by the French Jesuits to *Ouabachi,* was, as explained above, the name for the Wabash River plus the Ohio River below the fork of the Ohio and the Wabash. However, it is obvious that a coeval hydrological con-ception among the Miami-Illinois speakers also existed under the name *akaanse(e)asiipi.* This name, like Marquette's <8AB8SKIG8>, denoted the Ohio in accordance with our modern conception of it. Although Gravier's description of <Acanseasipi> does not make it entirely clear whether this name referred to all of the Ohio or simply a part of it, Marest's and Mermet's map from the same year shows that it applied to the entire river.[51] Therefore, the implication is that the segment of the Ohio below the Ohio-Wabash confluence was covered by two names in Miami-Illinois: *akaanse(e)asiipi* and *waapaahši(i)ki siipiiwi.*

The hydronym *akaanse(e)asiiipi* is, first of all, a tenacious place-name. Documents from the turn of the eighteenth century evince it. It shows up, for example, in a letter written in 1700 by Henri de Tonti, La Salle's lieu-tenant and Gravier's acquaintance in the Illinois Country, and at the same time in French cartography on Delisle maps.[52] In addition, this place-name is also found a couple of years later on the famous Delisle map from 1703.[53] Then, even though *akaanse(e)asiiipi* eluded 99 percent of all cartographers' drawing boards from that point on, it still remained alive among the French Jesuits and, of course, the Indians. Indeed, Dunn found it thriving in the Miami-Illinois language two hundred years later.

Dunn's Miami consultant *waapanahkikapwa* glossed the hydronym "Pecan River," a translation that was popularized in an article by Dunn in 1912.[54] This was perhaps a believable etymology at that time since pecan trees (*Carya illinoiensis*) are indeed native and common to the lower Ohio River, having a natural range that extends just slightly north of the river into extreme southwestern Indiana.[55] Even so, "Pecan River" is an incorrect translation and a native folk etymology. Indeed, *waapanahkikapwa* translated the Ohio River's Miami-Illinois name to "Pecan River" since the Miami-Illinois term for "pecan" includes the term *akaansea* of our place-name, which is in fact a tribe name.[56]

Early historical *akaanse(e)asiipi,* which had evolved to *kaanseeseepiiwi* by the time *waapanahkikapwa* gave the name to Dunn, literally means "Quapaw River." The constituents of these Miami-Illinois language terms are *-(i)siipi ~ siipiiwi,* "river" and *(a)kaanse(e)a,* "Quapaw," composed of the initial *(a)kaanse(e)-* and the singular animate gender marker *-a.* The latter term was originally a Siouan tribe name, the Common Dhegiha reconstruction being **hkã·ze* and the modern Kaw form being **kkã·ze.*[57] This tribe name was naturalized into Old Miami-Illinois according to Miami-Illinois morphology, and in fact by the time of Jacques Marquette it had become nativized in two different ways, to refer to two different tribes: *akaanse(e)a* for "Quapaw," where, as noted, the animate gender suffix *-a* was added to a stem in the form *akaanse(e)-*; and then *akaansa* for "Kaw," or "Kansa," where the animate gender suffix *-a* was added to a stem analyzed by native speakers as *akaans-*. The spelling <accansa> for *akaansa* appears in the Illinois-French dictionary, which dates to the early 1700s.[58] The same basic ethnonym is also found on Marquette's map from 1673 to 1674 in the form <KANSA>.

The initial *a-* in *akaanse(e)a* and *akaansa* is an ethnonymic prefix. However, short initial *a-* could drop in Miami-Illinois, especially so as the language evolved through time. And this is the process that was responsible for the form with initial *k* seen here. Therefore, in the name for the Ohio River offered to Dunn by *waapanahkikapwa,* which is pronounced [kàanzeenzeepíiwi], Old Miami-Illinois *akaanse(e)a* had become *kaansee-,* a term that more closely approximates the original Siouan term. In addition, the *-ii-* of the original Old Miami-Illinois hydronym's *-siipi,* "river" had become *-ee-* through assimilation to the *-ee-* of the preceding final syllable of the first element of this place-name. On top of this, the *-s-* of the more modern Miami-Illinois *siipiiwi,* "river" had become prenasalized through assimilation to the preceding syllable's original prenasalized *-s-*. According to rules of Miami-Illinois phonology, it had, like the preceding sibilant, voiced to [z]. All of these sound changes noted above are reflected in Dunn's <kanzänzäpiwi> ~ <Kanzä̋nzäpíwi> spellings and in his locative noun recording <kánzänzäpíungĭ>, where the river's name includes the ethnonym *(a)kaanse(e)-*, "Quapaw." The latter term is pronounced [kàanzeenzeepióŋgi], for underlying *kaanseeseepionki*, "on the Quapaw River."[59] A Shawnee cognate of the Miami-Illinois term for the Ohio River also exists: *kaaθeewiθiipi*, "Kaw River."[60]

It is crucial to note that, ethnohistorically speaking, Miami-Illinois ethnonym *akaanse(e)a* in late prehistoric times was probably not limited in scope to designating only the Quapaw. This was likely an old cover-term in Miami-Illinois for *all* Dhegiha Siouan speakers. Thus the name originally represented the relatively common situation in which a name of a subtribe or even a village is used as a cover term for a whole tribe. We see this onomastic phenomenon, for example, in Miami-Illinois in the term for "Cherokee," where *katoohwa*, the name of one of the historic villages of one of the subtribes of the Cherokee, is used for all Cherokees.[61]

Importantly, the place-name *akaanse(e)asiipi* is assuredly a prehistoric item in the Miami-Illinois lexicon as it describes a reality that was long gone by the time the name was first recorded by the French.[62] Though it was not the first Native American place-name recorded for Indiana, *akaanse(e)asiipi* is undoubtedly one of the oldest. Indeed, it appears to be emblematic of the antiquity of Miami-Illinois place-names throughout Indiana. Miami-Illinois speakers in late prehistory, alive at the time the Dhegiha Sioux were living on the Ohio, not only had this name for the Ohio River but also would have had names for sites, important rivers, lakes, and marshes lying between their more northerly homeland in the southern Lake Michigan ~ western Lake Erie watersheds and the Ohio.

The archaeological identity of the Dhegiha Siouans in the lower Ohio Valley has not been determined. However, the late prehistoric nature of the Miami-Illinois place-name and the fact that this hydronym was applied to the lower Ohio River suggest the possibility that the Dhegiha were the late prehistoric Caborn-Welborn people, who lived near the confluence of the Ohio and Wabash Rivers, as well as their possible predecessors, the Angel Mounds people, whose town was located on the Ohio just east of present-day Evansville, Indiana.

4

The Kankakee and Its Affluents

The Indiana place-name of Native American origin that has successfully eluded interpretation over the years is "Kankakee." However, this is understandable, for just like the French garbling *Ouabouskigou* in chapter 2, the English language place-name "Kankakee," as written, is a nonsense term.

"Kankakee" refers to a grand wet prairie and marsh that existed in northwestern Indiana prior to the twentieth century as well as to a river that rises just west of the St. Joseph River at South Bend, Indiana. The French indicated the existence of the Kankakee River nearly a decade before they got around to learning a Native American name for it—or at least before they recorded one. Even though American Indians have known of the Kankakee time out of mind, the first Europeans to see this river—at least in terms of how it is conceived in modern times—were Jacques Marquette, Louis Jolliet, and the five other members of their expeditionary team returning from the first European voyage in the middle Mississippi Valley.[1] There is no known earlier sighting of the Kankakee by Europeans. One of some three hundred soldiers permitted by the French king in 1668 to enter land on the eastern shores of Lake Michigan for the first time might have made it far enough south to have stumbled upon the Kankakee before the Marquette-Jolliet team saw it. But if they did, their visit went unrecorded.

Marquette's and Jolliet's memory of their direct observation in the last week of September 1673 of what we today consider the mouth of the Kankakee, that is, at the confluence of the Kankakee and Des Plaines Rivers, took form on Marquette's holograph map from 1673 to 1674 and on the Jolliet-directed and Franquelin-designed map of 1675. On these charts the distal end of the Kankakee River is unmistakably in evidence.[2]

As far as anyone knows, the first European to paddle the Kankakee River, starting from its headwaters at the South Bend portage, was René de La Salle, in the final two weeks of December 1679. Furthermore, this French explorer and entrepreneur came to know the Kankakee River better than any European alive between December 1679 and December 1682.[3] So while Marquette and Jolliet were the first Europeans to glimpse the Kankakee, La Salle was the person responsible for bringing the knowledge of the river into focus for the European community. Moreover, his descriptions of the Kankakee, unlike his confounding geographical reports from his Mississippi voyage of 1683, are well conceived, fascinating observations created by someone who knew the river very well. La Salle also holds the distinction for being the first European to record an indigenous name for the Kankakee. He apparently wrote the name <Téakiki> for the first time on August 11, 1681, while discussing events that had taken place during the previous November.[4] La Salle spent months on the Kankakee in the company of Miami-Illinois speakers and used this same name numerous times in his correspondence. Thus there is good reason to believe that the spelling <Téakiki> is a relatively accurate rendering of an original Miami-Illinois language place-name.

Importantly, alongside La Salle's <Téakiki>, the French were also using a French name for the Kankakee: *la rivière des Illinois.* By calling the Kankakee the "River of the Illinois [Indians]," the French were not simply referring to a river on which the Illinois Indians were living; they were operating within a hydrological framework that differs from our modern one. They understood, correctly, that what we today know as the Kankakee River was simply part and parcel of what we today call the Illinois River. In other words, for both the late prehistoric and early historic native peoples of this area, as well as for the historic French, one and only one river began near the St. Joseph River at the western end of the portage at present-day South Bend and flowed *all the way to the Mississippi.* The local Indians knew that water course by the name La Salle recorded in the form <Téakiki>.

La Salle stated explicitly on many occasions that the Kankakee and Illinois Rivers were considered historically one and the same. He says, for example, "the Illinois' river, called Teatiki [*sic*] by the wild people" (*la rivière des Islinois, appelée par les Sauvages Teatiki*)[5] and "the Colbert River [i.e., the Mississippi], into which flows the river of the Illinois, called Téakiki" (*le fleuve Colbert … dans lequel la rivière des Islinois nommée Téakiki se descharge*).[6] In fact, in La Salle's reports we can follow the stream's course accompanied by its Native American name all the way from its source near the St. Joseph right on down to the Mississippi. The explorer explains that "this river of the Illinois … is born in a marsh one and a half leagues from that [i.e., the river] of the Miami [i.e., the St. Joseph River of Lake Michigan]" (*cette rivière des Islinois … naist dans un marais à une lieue et demy de celle des Miamis*)[7] and that "the river of the Islinois takes its rise … only one and a half leagues away from that [i.e., the river] of the Miami" (*la rivière des Islinois prend sa source … n'est esloignée que d'une lieue et demie de celle des Miamis*).[8] Downstream, La Salle tells of an important tributary of the <Téakiki>, the Des Plaines River, which had two French names at the time: "Teatiki [*sic*] … receives on the right that [i.e., the river] of Chicago" (*Teatiki … reçoit à droite celle de Chicagou*)[9] and the "Divine River falls into that of Téakiki, or of the Illinois" (*la rivière Divine tombe dans celle de Téakiki ou des Islinois*).[10] La Salle then describes the course of the river below the Des Plaines confluence: "By following the Teatiki River, from its confluence with the Chicago" (*En suivant la rivière de Teatiki, depuis le confluent de Chicagou*).[11] Finally, in speaking of the confluence of the Illinois and Mississippi Rivers, he calls the mouth of the Illinois "the mouth of Teatiki" (*l'emboucheure de Téatiki*)[12] and notes that the "Mississippi, as you are going down the river, appears to flow toward the south-southwest at the outlet of Teatiki" (*Mississipi, en descendant en bas, paroist, au sortir de Teatiki, aller au sud-sud-ouest*).[13] Pierre-Charles Delliette, a relative of La Salle's famous lieutenant Henri de Tonti, had the same understanding as La Salle, witnessed in Delliette's own excellent, authoritative, firsthand account concerning the Illinois Country.[14]

Naturally, representations of this hydrological view soon appeared in early maps of the area. For example, the Illinois River as conceived by the Miami-Illinois peoples and La Salle is in evidence on Claude Delisle charts from 1700 and 1703, as well as on La Hontan's map from the same year titled "Carte Generale du Canada." On these maps *R des Ilinois* distinctly indicates the conceptually unified Kankakee-Illinois waterway.[15] Moreover, this particular notion did not vanish with the turn of the eighteenth century. The Jesuit missionary Pierre-Philippe Potier, a one-man information highway for his times, who was stationed at Detroit throughout the mid-1700s and was young enough to be La Salle's great-grandson, indicated that the *Teatiki* [*sic*] flowed from the South Bend portage all the way to the Mississippi.[16]

As noted, La Salle used his original spelling of this place-name, or slightly variant spellings, numerous times in his reports.[17] Nevertheless, his meaningless misspelling *Teatiki,* if indeed it reflects a mistake committed by La Salle himself, made its way onto Bernou's map in 1682 and in so doing came to be the most popular spelling for this place-name among the French.[18] Because of the influence he wielded in France, Bernou had no trouble in establishing this faulty spelling as the accepted French form of this native place-name. Even though the more common, and better, spellings by La Salle can be seen much later, such as <Teakiki> on the Charlevoix-Bellin map of 1744 and <Theakiki> in de Vaugondy's famous atlas published in 1750, the use of the *Teatiki* with its deviant middle -t- was absolutely pervasive.[19] Indeed, by the 1700s *Teatiki* had become firmly entrenched in the French lexicon—not only in France and Quebec but also, amazingly, in the western Great Lakes.[20]

Not surprisingly, La Salle failed to provide a translation for his original <Téakiki>. Of the various incorrect interpretations of <Téakiki> offered over the years, it is the one by the Jesuit priest Pierre François-Xavier de Charlevoix in 1721 which stands out as being at least interesting. Although his analysis was incorrect, Charlevoix said that La Salle's place-name meant "wolf country."[21] As we shall see below, the -ak(i)- segment of <Téakiki> indeed represents a historical Algonquian language reflex of the Proto-Algonquian final **-axky* meaning "land, country." However, there is nothing in the rest of <Téakiki> that means "wolf." In fact, the support that modern writers have given Charlevoix's flawed etymology is dumbfounding, since Father Charlevoix himself admitted to not knowing the source language of this place-name.[22] In truth, how could he have known the meaning of <Téakiki> if he did not even know what language the name came from? Although the historian Jacob Dunn was among those who published Charlevoix's "wolf country" idea, he later, correctly, expressed doubts about its validity in his unpublished notes.[23]

Charlevoix's "wolf country" could have resulted from his having triangulated the following information: La Salle's <Téakiki> spelling, La Salle's gripping description of the jet-black wolves that inhabited the Kankakee, and the term <Huakiki>, analyzed below, which is another American Indian toponym applied to the Kankakee at the time of Charlevoix's visit that does in fact mean "wolf country."[24] However, <Téakiki> no more means "wolf country" than does "Indianapolis."

Arriving at the true form and meaning of <Téakiki> first requires an understanding of the prehistoric and early historic environment of the upper Kankakee River and its marsh. But, just as it is difficult to see "Kankakee" in La Salle's <Téakiki>, the Kankakee region itself would be unrecognizable today to any local prehistoric or historic American Indian, or to any early historic European who once knew it. Until the turn of the twentieth century, the Kankakee Valley was an uncommonly rich, biodiverse natural area where the Carolinian biotic province, known for its magnificent hardwood forests lying generally to the east and south of the Kankakee, met the Illinoian biotic province, known for its vast prairies that extended generally to the west. Here, at the interface of these two environmental zones, and in proximity to various local micro-environments such as forested moraines and dry prairie tracts, was an immense, perennially wet prairie, complete with a fine and notably swift river running through it.[25] What we today refer to as the Kankakee River, winding for three hundred miles within a valley *only eighty-five miles long,* was the principal artery of a permanent one-thousand-square-mile marsh, punctuated only here and there by sand-blown ridges that rose "above the marsh and sandy outwash plains."[26] Although La Salle notes that he found it difficult to find good places to camp along the river itself,[27] he did appreciate the Kankakee's beauty as evidenced by his description of it: "[O]ne finds nothing but beautiful country as far as the eye can see, interrupted from time to time by a few groves" (*on ne trouve plus que de belles campagnes à perte de vue interrompues d'espace en espace de quelques bouquets de bois*).[28] The Native American name that La Salle wrote in the form <Téakiki> accurately describes this land.

The final -ki of <Téakiki> represents the Miami-Illinois conjunct II verb suffix *-ki.* As noted above, the -aki- segment stands for the final *-ahki,* which means "land" or "country" in Miami-Illinois composite terms. The initial segment Téa- represents the Miami-Illinois *teeyaa-,* which exhibits a range of meanings including "uncovered," "in the wind," "in the open," and "exposed." La Salle's <Téakiki> is thus Miami-Illinois *teeyaahkiki,* which can be effectively translated by any of the following English phrases—and by *all of them together* in order to get a feel for the original native term: "(it is) open country," "(it is) exposed land," "(it is) land in the open," "(it is) land exposed to view."[29]

Today's place-name "Kankakee" has been in use with this particular spelling since 1816, when it appeared on a map designed by St. Louis resident René Paul.[30] Paul was an important mapmaker and surveyor for his time who had both the ability and the opportunity to tinker with names and their spellings. Furthermore, owing to his position, his spellings came to be disseminated far and wide. Moreover, Paul was bilingual in French and English and may in fact have been the very person who created the "Kankakee" spelling we know today, for "Kankakee" is a transliteration into the English spelling convention of an older homophonous French spelling *Kinkiki,* attested in the late eighteenth and early twentieth centuries. We see it, for example, in the papers of the bilingual French- and English-speaking Wabash Valley trader Hyacinthe Lasselle.[31] In addition, *Quinquiqui,* a homophonous French variant spelling of *Kinkiki,* appeared in the late eighteenth century in the writings of the well-known Detroit trader Guillaume La Mothe.[32] Thus the historical spellings "Kankakee," *Kinkiki,* and *Quinquiqui* all represent the same place-name, and, as noted at the beginning of this chapter, this term has no meaning. In fact, even in the next layer down, that is, in the next older historically attested form of this term, which in fact represents a pivotal turning point in the place-name's development, we still find jabberwocky.

Although Lasselle's *Kinkiki* and La Mothe's *Quinquiqui* appeared in the latter half of the 1700s, this place-name had essentially been around since the early days of that century—for *Kinkiki* ~ *Quinquiqui* is simply a distortion of an older spelling by Charlevoix from 1721 in the equally nonsensical form *Kiakiki.*[33] The nasalization of the first syllable of *Kiakiki* to *Kinkiki* is just a simplified, careless rendering of the term by a French soldier or trader, although written forms of *Kiakiki* probably also contributed to the garbling of *Kiakiki* to *Kinkiki,* and to the latter form's proliferation among French speakers in North America. In fact, research into the history of aboriginal place-names in North America shows that the *spelling* of autochthonous terms appearing in French reports, letters, maps, etc., influenced the way these terms were pronounced by French speakers who ventured into the wilderness.[34]

Kiakiki and *Kinkiki* are no doubt the same word. Lasselle in fact used *both spellings* as the name for the Kankakee River, and, tellingly, he once wrote both of them in the same document.[35] Therefore, "Kankakee," *Kinkiki, Quinquiqui,* and *Kiakiki* are all four of a piece. But where then did Charlevoix's *Kiakiki* come from? Charlevoix's *Kiakiki* spelling represents the same Miami-Illinois word as La Salle's original <Téakiki>. The discrepancy between the first vowels in <Téakiki> and *Kiakiki* is not important, since Frenchmen who did not know Miami-Illinois often confused its *e* and *i* sounds. La Salle correctly heard *e*; Charlevoix, who had very little experience with the Miami-Illinois language, incorrectly heard *i* (and he probably heard it from a fellow Frenchman). Indeed, Charlevoix heard *i* just as other Frenchmen thought they heard *i* when they created forms such as *Tiakiki* and *Tiatiki,* additional meaningless variants of the original Miami-Illinois place-name that La Salle had originally recorded in the form <Téakiki>.

Therefore, the only significant difference between <Téakiki> and *Kiakiki* is in the initial sounds of these terms, that is, La Salle's T- and Charlevoix's K-. However, Charlevoix's K- either resulted from his mishearing the stop consonant *k* for the stop consonant *t,* which is a historically attested phonological tendency in New World French itself, or is simply a garbling of the original term accomplished by making all three consonants *k.* Charlevoix himself says as much: "Theakiki, which by corruption our Canadians name Kiakiki."[36]

The French-twisted place-name for the Kankakee made its way into English with the help of Ninian Edwards, an English speaker and the first American governor of the Illinois Territory, the first top-ranking American official in Illinois. Edwards's 1812 map was no doubt instrumental in disseminating the distorted French place-name, which he in fact wrote in the French manner: *Quinquiqui.*[37] There is every reason to believe that the Indian agent and cartographer Thomas Forsyth soon transposed the *Quinquiqui* used by Edwards into the English spelling convention by writing the name "Kankukii" on his own map also from 1812, perhaps under the influence of the French-recorded *Kinkiki* form used, for example, by Lasselle. Forsyth's "Kankukii" certainly lay on a trajectory that led in 1816 to René Paul's "Kankakee," the modern spelling.[38]

What is particularly interesting about the French pronunciation of *Quinquiqui* ~ *Kinkiki,* which is [kẽkikí], is that it was remarkably preserved in the modern English pronunciation of this place name, which is [kẽkəkí]. Here we see that the initial syllable of both the English and the French pronunciations naturally has a simple nasalized vowel, rather than a vowel plus the sound *n.* In addition, in English, the strong syllable is the *last* one, exactly as it was in the French pronunciation of *Kinkiki* ~ *Quinquiqui*—and, in fact, in every word in French having two or more syllables. In other words, the pronunciation of "Kankakee" as an English language place-name should have naturally followed the same stress pattern that we observe in "Kentucky"—and it would have, had it not been borrowed into English from French.

During the 1700s, the French in the Illinois Country used many forms of this same place-name, including La Salle's original <Téakiki>, along with *Tiakiki,, Tiatiki, Kiakiki, Kinkiki,* and *Quinquiqui,* with coexistent first-syllable nasalized and nonnasalized K-initial versions.[39] Also, during the 1700s and 1800s, the flawed K-initial forms of this place-name multiplied exponentially throughout secondary and tertiary sources. While La Salle's

<Téakiki> is the basis for all the T-initial spellings of the Kankakee's Miami-Illinois name that appear in the late 1600s and the early 1700s, Charlevoix's *Kiakiki* represents the birth of the K-initial distortions of that same Miami-Illinois name that began to show up by the second decade of the eighteenth century—at least those that reflect an actual phonological distortion of the original American Indian place-name.

While the T-initial variants such as <Teakiki>, <Theakiki>, <Tiakiki> and the infamous *Tiatiki* were flying off the pens of cartographers in France in the mid-1700s, a completely different name for the Kankakee River had long since appeared: <Huakiki>. Briefly mentioned above, this is a name for the Kankakee that Gabriel Marest, a Jesuit missionary among the Illinois, wrote down in 1712.[40] Marest's <Huakiki> was subsequently picked up by the Delisle house of cartography in Paris and, because of the pervasive influence wielded by Delisle maps, this name is commonly seen on both French and English maps from the eighteenth century.[41] <Huakiki> is present, for example, on an anonymous English map of 1730, on D'Anville's map of 1755, and on Fielding's chart from 1785.[42] The spelling of this place-name displays such an uncanny consistency through time that every one of its appearances in maps and texts after that on the Delisle's maps can be none other than clones of Marest's original spelling. In other words, they represent no additional contact with local Indians, no additional recordings.

Simply because of -akiki, the place-name's final three syllables, scholars down through the years have thought that Marest's <Huakiki> and La Salle's <Téakiki> represented the same Native American word. However, <Huakiki> is unrelated to <Téakiki> and therefore to "Kankakee." Furthermore, on some of the Delisle maps the name <Huakiki> occurs in close proximity to the tribe name "Potawatomi." This, however, is an unfortunate coincidental juxtaposition, since the term <Huakiki> is not analyzable in Potawatomi.[43] <Huakiki> in fact represents a garbled Miami-Illinois *mahweehkiki,* a conjunct II verb meaning "it is wolf country."[44] In *mahweehkiki,* the *-hk(i)* is an allomorph of *-ahk(i),* "land, country," the last syllable *-ki* is the appropriate verb suffix, and the first segment of the term, *mahwee-,* is the "wolf" initial, the simplex noun form for "wolf" being *mahweewa.*[45] It is possible Marest did not write the initial syllable *ma-* in his <Huakiki> spelling since it was not in a strong position, that is, not "stressed" or "accented," and he did not hear it, even though it would have certainly been there in the term for "wolf." However, the sound sequence consisting of a word-initial *m* plus a short vowel was typically devoiced in Miami-Illinois, that is, whispered, just as in other Algonquian languages. In fact, in Miami-Illinois there are many words beginning with *m* followed by a short vowel that drop the first syllable altogether. For example, the word for "bowstring" in the older language was *mihtekwaapinti*, but by 1700 we also find *tékwaapinti*.[46] On the other hand, <Huakiki> could also be a miscopied item that was originally a truer representation of the actual Miami-Illinois term.

By naming the Kankakee marsh "wolf country," Miami-Illinois speakers were referring to the actual presence of wolves (*Canis lupus*). As pointed out by La Salle, the wolf was a very common carnivore in the deciduous borderlands of the Kankakee marsh, where it hunted deer and elk. In fact, wolves were known to inhabit the area even into the early twentieth century.[47] Furthermore, it is the particular superiority of these canines in maneuvering on ice, a skill observed by modern wildlife professionals, that would have made the frozen Kankakee marsh an ideal winter hunting ground for them as they pursued the local cervid populations.

At the same time, it is not inconceivable that the toponym *mahweehkiki* could have also encompassed in the late 1600s and early 1700s, at least in a folk-etymological way, the notion of Loups (Wolves), the name the French applied to several Eastern Algonquian–speaking groups from New England and present-day southeastern New York state.[48] Locally, the referent would be the people from the east whom La Salle hauled with him on his trip down and up the Mississippi in the winter and spring of 1682, folks who settled in what is now northwestern Indiana.[49]

The Iroquois River is a tributary of the Kankakee River that rises from multiple sources in eastern and southern Jasper County, as well as northwestern White County, and wends its way in a basically southwesterly direction while in Indiana. Then, after traversing Newton County, the Iroquois River enters Illinois and eventually joins the Kankakee in that state after traveling almost a hundred miles. The first thing that is important to know about the Iroquois River's place-name history is that the French name *la rivière des Iroquois,* meaning "the Iroquois' River," is not a translation of any Native American hydronym. *La rivière des Iroquois* is purely a French creation, a name that enters the annals of history also by virtue of René de La Salle.

La Salle first saw the Iroquois River, at its mouth, in the final days of 1679.[50] However, it was not until eleven months later in November 1680 that his name for the land at the confluence of the Iroquois and the Kankakee first appeared: *la Fourche des Iroquois* (the Fork of the Iroquois).[51] The readers should note that *la Fourche des Iroquois* does not mean "the fork of the Iroquois River" but "the Iroquois' Fork," that is, it is the name of a *site* associated with some Iroquois. The name indicates that *the land located at the confluence of the two streams* was significant because someone had at one time witnessed or interacted with some Iroquois at that very place. It is not clear what historical event actually triggered the creation of the French toponym *la Fourche des Iroquois,* but it is common knowledge that the Iroquois created hell on earth for many Great Lakes native communities starting in the early 1640s and continued doing so for the next three decades—conducting invasions that were no small feat for foot soldiers in enemy territory six hundred miles from their home in what is now upstate New York. Then, in 1679, the Iroquois resumed their attacks in the West, reignited by their fury toward La Salle for his having established close relations with their enemies, the Illinois. Indeed, the following year an Iroquois offensive seared into local memory the total destruction by fire of the Great Kaskaskia summer village on the upper Illinois River near Starved Rock. This new phase of the decades-long war continuously ravaged *le pays des Illinois* throughout the remainder of the seventeenth century.[52]

After striking their targets in the Kankakee and Illinois Valleys, the Iroquois would often try to escape immediate revenge at the hands of the Illinois or allied Algonquians by hastily returning home. To do so, they either ascended the Ohio River watershed or else raced across the top of what is now Indiana, through the watershed of the Kankakee River. This was surely related to the reason why the French also knew Trail Creek in La Porte County as *la rivière aux Iroquois* (the Iroquois' River).[53] Accordingly, any of the movements of Iroquoian warriors into and out of the Illinois Country could account for the toponym *la Fourche des Iroquois,* although the better-known skirmishes between Algonquians and Iroquoians in present-day northwestern Indiana actually postdate the appearance of the two French place-names under discussion.

Since the toponym *la Fourche des Iroquois* first appeared in 1680—concurrent with the Iroquois' first devastation of the Great Kaskaskia Village—it is likely that this place-name dates to that year and is connected in some way to that event. For his part, Charlevoix, who passed the Iroquois River in 1721, nearly half a century after La Salle coined the place-name, attributed the creation of its name to a surprise attack by the Illinois on a few Iroquois warriors in the neighborhood, noting that many of the latter had died in the encounter.[54] It is not surprising that the confluence of the Kankakee and Iroquois Rivers, *la Fourche des Iroquois,* would be a historically significant site since it had a natural elevation offering an excellent place to camp in what was typically an inhospitable riparian environment.[55]

As a result of information sent back to France and Québec by La Salle, the Iroquois River first appeared on Bernou's map in 1682, and then two years later on one of Franquelin's charts.[56] However, in both instances, it bore no name. In fact, it was not until 1683 that La Salle finally coined *la rivière des Iroquois*.[57] This name then reappeared on a second known Franquelin map from 1684 in the form *Rivière aux Iroquois*.[58] Thus the evidence indicates the Iroquois River actually got its name from the earlier name applied to the land situated at the confluence of what we today term the Kankakee and Iroquois Rivers, *la Fourche des Iroquois*.

No American Indian name for the Iroquois River figures in any French document of the New World. Indeed, no local native name for the Iroquois River surfaces in the historical record until the American-dominated 1800s, when a term appears in writings in a medley of related variants: <Pickamik>, <Pickemink>, <Pecamink>, <Pickamink>, <Pickemink>, <Pecamink>, <Pekamink>, <Pinkamink>, and <päkamĭk>.[59] All the spellings listed above, except for the first, which might be Potawatomi, appear to represent the name for this stream in Miami-Illinois. <Pickamik> and <päkamĭk> seem to stand for the unchanged and changed form of the conjunct II verb "it is muddy water," *piikami(i)ki* and *peekami(i)ki*, respectively. These are composed of the Old Miami-Illinois initial *piik-/peek-*, "muddy," the "water" final *-(i)kami*, and the conjunct verb suffix *-ki*. The remaining spellings above represent the Old Miami-Illinois locative noun *piikaminki~peekaminki*, "at the muddy water," composed of the initial *piik-/peek-*, "muddy," the final *-(i)kam*, "water," and *-inki*, the conservative locative suffix meaning, "at, on."[60] The verb and the locative noun constructions here are grammatical for place-names in Miami-Illinois, and the Native American names for the Iroquois River are appropriate monikers for this stream: The watercourse is muddy as well as narrow and generally unnavigable.

Another major tributary of the Kankakee is the Yellow River. This stream originates from various sources in southern St. Joseph County, crosses northwest Kosciusko County, flows northeast into Marshall County, which it also crosses—from northeast to southwest—and then heads west across Starke County to meet the Kankakee. La Salle and his entourage would have been the first Europeans to see this stream, at its mouth, in December 1679. A French itinerary for this region composed in the 1700s describes the Yellow River as a wide stream that was difficult to cross.[61]

There are two attested Miami-Illinois names for the Yellow River. The earliest one on record, a French recording from the itinerary mentioned above, is <ossa sip>.[62] This spelling represents Miami-Illinois *oonsaasiipi*, composed of *oonsaa-*, "yellow, brown," the hydronymic "river" final *-(i)siip*, and the singular inanimate noun marker *-i.*[63] The second Miami-Illinois name for this waterway was recorded by Dunn in the form <ó^{n}zalamónakamíki>, which is *oonsaalamoonakami(i)ki*, a conjunct II verb that literally means "it is yellow ocher water."[64] The morphological parsing of this term is *oonsaa-*, "yellow, brown," the medial *alamoon-*, "vermilion, red ocher, paint," the final *-ikam(i)*, "water," and the verb suffix *-ki*. Besides meaning literally "yellow ocher" [$FeO(OH)\cdot nH_2O$], *oonsaalamooni* is the Miami-Illinois name for the bloodroot plant (*Sanguinaria canadensis*). Whether the hydronym *oonsaalamoonakami(i)ki* was premised on the mineral compound known as yellow ocher or the yellowish stain of the bloodroot, this place-name as well as the older *oonsaasiipi* indicate that the waters of the historical river were muddy, with a yellowish-brown cast. (See more on yellow ocher in chapter 7's discussion of the Salamonie River.)

A historically attested Potawatomi name for the Yellow River was recorded by the early-nineteenth-century American leader John Tipton in the form <Wizahokuhmik>. This spelling represents the Potawatomi *wezawgəməg*, "at the yellow water."[65] *wezaw-* is "yellow, brown," *-gəm* is "water" and *-əg* is the locative suffix meaning "at" or "on." The idea "yellow water" also figures in Dunn's <Waythŏ́wkahmik> and <Wethaúkamík>.[66] However, these two forms are problematic. While almost everything about these spellings suggests that they represent the Potawatomi place-name discussed above, the Potawatomi language does not have the sound theta (*θ*), represented here by Dunn's -th-.

There is an outside chance that <Waythŏ́wkahmik> and <Wethaúkamík> could represent Old Kickapoo **weeθaawikameeheki*, "at the yellow water."[67] If these spellings are in fact distorted representations of a genuine local Kickapoo place-name, or even a related Mascouten place-name, then the name could date to the first half of the eighteenth century. However, the obvious differences between Dunn's forms and this Kickapoo term certainly cast grave doubt on this suggestion. It is my sense that Dunn probably just misheard *θ* for Potawatomi *z*, or else the Potawatomi speaker who gave him <Waythŏ́wkahmik> and <Wethaúkamík> had a lisp.

Wolf Creek flows northwest from southern Marshall County, generally west of Argos, to meet the Yellow River in the south-central part of this county. The word "wolf" in this hydronym does not refer to the wild canine; rather, it is an abridged translation of Potawatomi *mkədemʔwe*, "Black Wolf," the personal name of a Potawatomi leader who lived along this stream around 1830.[68] Owing to the fact that *mkədemʔwe* strongly opposed the forced removal of his people from their homes in Indiana, his name turns up repeatedly in Tipton's letters from the early 1800s.[69] A treaty from 1832 contains this Potawatomi chief's name in the form <Muckkatahmoway>. Dunn spelled his name <Makŏ́tam'wha>, which is a rather nice premodern linguistic recording in that the apostrophe indicates a glottal stop.[70]

A Native American name for Wolf Creek itself is visible on Guernsey's map in the form <Katamwahseetewah>.[71] Aside from the miscopied -t- for -b- in the incorrectly written -seetewah for Potawatomi *zibiwe,* "creek," <Katamwahseetewah> is a good representation by an English speaker of Potawatomi *mkədemʔwe-zibiwe,* "Black Wolf Creek." Here, the final orthographic -ah, an old vernacular spelling practice I term "alphabet A" and will discuss in chapter 5, represents the Potawatomi diminutive suffix *-e.* Furthermore, the common loss of the *m-* in the initial unstressed syllable of <Katamwahseeteewah> for an original *Mkatamwahseebewah is an excellent indication that this place-name is a genuine eponymous hydronym from the Potawatomi language, as it reveals a natural loss of initial — that occurred in the casual speech of the Potawatomi person who was the source of this recording.

Located for the most part in German Township, Marshall County, and at one time considered a tributary of the Yellow River but today thought of as just a segment of the Yellow River, is a north-to-south-flowing waterway approximately fifteen miles long. Historically, the stream and/or the area around it was known in Potawatomi as *bkanəg,* "at the nut," or in everyday English "the nut place," from *bkan,* "nut" and *-əg,* the locative suffix signifying "at." Guernsey spelled this place-name <Poconak>.[72] Although I have been unable to verify this place-name's authenticity independently of Guernsey's publication of it, "beechy," the unusual translation Guernsey gave for this term, is not one that he could have made up or found in a Potawatomi word list based on the term *bkan.* Moreover, the Potawatomi place-name has indisputable botanical underpinnings, since this watershed is known for the prevalence of the American beech (*Fagus grandiflora*), a source of edible nuts. We know this stream meandered historically through a beech-maple biome that was unique for this extreme north-central part of Indiana. This small beech-maple niche was bordered on the east, west, and south by oak-hickory forests, as well as by lakes and prairies, all of which were typical of the landscape north of the Wabash River.[73] Thus this particular piece of botanical evidence supports the authenticity of *bkanəg* as an American Indian place-name despite Guernsey's failure to reference where he got the name as well as the translation "beechy."

Cedar Lake, one of Indiana's largest natural bodies of water, is located in southwest-central Lake County. It is the source of the southerly flowing tributary of the Kankakee known as Cedar Creek. This lake's original English name was Red Cedar Lake, which is closer to the original Potawatomi place-name than is the modern English moniker "Cedar Lake."[74] In Potawatomi, Cedar Lake is known as *mskwawak-nbəs,* "eastern red cedar lake." *mskwawak,* which literally means "red-wood," is the Potawatomi term for the eastern red cedar (*Juniperus virginiana*); *nbəs* is the independent noun meaning "lake." Hough's spelling of this Potawatomi name for Cedar Lake took the form <Musquaockbis>; Dunn wrote the same hydronym <Meskwahwahkmbéss>.[75] As a Potawatomi place-name, this lake's name would date to the early eighteenth century, since there is no evidence the Potawatomi lived in the Cedar Creek area prior to that time.

In a discussion of the Kankakee it is important to mention the Native American place-name recorded by the French in the form <Atihipi-Catouy>. Noted by Pierre Le Moyne as one of the first known historical locations of the Miami in what is now Indiana after the chaos of the late seventeenth century,[76] this term appears to be a gnarled form of Miami-Illinois *kiteepihkwanonki,* "at the buffalo fish." However, in this case the name does not refer to the famous Tippecanoe River but to a lake known to the early French as *Lac tipiconeau* (buffalo fish lake).[77] This particular body of water was formerly located in the Kankakee River directly above its confluence with Potato Creek. What remains of it today is located in La Porte County, where it is now known as Fish Lake. The French hydronym *Lac tipiconeau* implies a Miami-Illinois name for this lake in the form **kiteepihkwanwa nipihsi/mahkiikwi,* "buffalo fish lake." Though unproven, it is not impossible that this modern and somewhat unusual English language hydronym "Fish Lake" represents a vestige of an unattested English translation "Buffalo Fish Lake."

Potato Creek rises from multiple sources in southwestern St. Joseph County, including Worster Lake. It then meanders about twelve miles in a southwesterly direction to the Kankakee River. An aboriginal name for this stream, embedded in the French place-name *R. de Macopin* (Macopin River), began appearing in the early years of the eighteenth century on various Delisle maps.[78] A French-speaking trader's itinerary from the mid-1700s, recorded by Jesuit missionary Pierre Potier in Detroit, identified Potato Creek's location and called the stream *Riv: aux macopines.* Here French *Riv: aux* means "Riv[er] with" or "Riv[er] of," while *macopines,* as he informs us, refers to a "a root you can eat" (*racine qu'on mange*).[79] The root in question, that is, the "potato" in "Potato Creek," is not of course the Idaho potato but *Nuphar advena*—known generally as pond lily, cow lily, and spadderdock. This is clearly the plant that Pierre-Charles Delliette described as the *macopine* in his memoir concerning his stay among the Miami and Illinois peoples.[80] While there are three native aquatic plants in the Indiana area that produce large edible roots, the description of *macopine* recorded by Delliette, who is an authoritative source, matches *Nuphar* the best.[81]

The Gallicized Algonquian term *macopine(s)* represents Miami-Illinois *mahkohpina,* "bear-potato," composed of the "bear" initial *mahko-* and the underlying final |-hpen| "potato." Delliette, the explorer La Salle, and the English painter George Winter all wrote similar descriptions of how local indigenous peoples prepared *macopine.*[82] La Salle wrote, "They gather these roots in the marshes. They are as big as an arm. They make a hole in the ground in which they make a bed of fire-reddened stones, then one of leaves, one of *macopin,* one of reddened stones and so forth up to the top which they cover with earth and their roots sweat inside there for two or three days after which they have them boiled and eat alone or with oil. It is a rather good food, provided they are well cooked, which one can know by the color, which must be red. On the contrary they are whitish if they are not cooked enough, and then they grab the mouth so cruelly, on the palate, in the throat that one cannot swallow any. They can be kept in a dry state for a long time."[83]

Interestingly, it appears that Miami-Illinois *mahkohpina* underwent a native folk-etymologizing. Most of the historical French attestations of this word, including the one made by the Jesuit missionary Jean-Baptiste Le Boullenger in his French-Illinois dictionary, consistently show an -a- in the first syllable, giving *mahkohpina.* However, the form of this word in the Illinois-French dictionary as well as in several contemporary sources shows the sound *i* in the same position, giving *mihkohpina,* which is an animate noun composed of the initial *mihko-,* "red" and the "potato" final noted above. Thus two variants existed historically in Miami-Illinois for the name of this plant: *mahkohpina,* meaning "bear-potato," and *mihkohpina,* meaning "red-potato." (The plural forms are, respectively, *mahkohpeniiki* and *mihkohpeniiki.*) Supporting this notion is a parallel linguistic reality that existed for this plant in the historic Potawatomi language.[84] The creation of the "red-potato" word could have resulted from direct observation of nature—the potato turning red when it was baked. Or else speakers of Miami-Illinois and Potawatomi could have created the "red-potato" idea by reshaping the "bear-potato" term, which can be reconstructed for Proto-Algonquian.[85]

5

Trails to ‹Kekionga›

From its source in the state of Ohio the 90-mile-long St. Mary's River flows northwest into northeastern Indiana, a region brimming with the effects of continental glaciation. From its own source in the state of Michigan over 90 miles due north of the source of the St. Mary's, the St. Joseph River—the second stream by this name shared by Indiana and Michigan—makes its way in a southwesterly fashion and flows into the St. Mary's at the site of present-day Fort Wayne. From this point on to Lake Erie 160 miles away to the northeast these waters travel under a new name—the Maumee.

Another way of looking at this same reality—this time through the historical lens of James Riley, a captain in the U.S. military at Fort Wayne in the early 1800s—is that at Fort Wayne the St. Mary's River "turns suddenly south and assumes the name of Miami of the Lakes [i.e., the Maumee] … then turning gradually round again, these congregated waters [i.e., the St. Mary's and the St. Joseph] flow off in a northeast direction" toward Lake Erie.[1]

Naturally, Lake Michigan on Indiana's northern border is important to Indiana history, since it was along this shoreline that Europeans first entered the land now known as Indiana. However, Lake Erie is equally important. Indeed, the early history of the Wabash is inseparable from that of Lake Erie and cannot be excluded from any study of Indiana's earliest history.

Samuel de Champlain, in the very early 1600s, was the first European to learn of the existence of Lake Erie. However, the information he heard about it failed to find explicit cartographic expression. Champlain's early maps seem to imply the existence of Lake Erie, as evidenced by his location of an Iroquoian tribe known to the French as the Neutrals who lived near it. However, his early depiction of this Great Lake is simply two large bulges in a river running from Lake Huron to Lake Ontario, which is a portrayal that obviously did not come from his direct observation of this inland sea. Indeed, even on Champlain's last map of New France from 1632, Niagara Falls is not yet in evidence.[2]

Étienne Brûlé, one of Champlain's explorers, had not yet seen Lake Erie by 1618. But as one of four Frenchmen who spent time with the Neutrals between 1620 and 1632 in the vicinity of Niagara, Brûlé was undoubtedly the first or one of the very first Europeans to set eyes on Lake Erie—from its extreme northeastern shores—sometime between 1629 and 1632. The news of this sighting flowed from Brûlé to the explorer Jean Nicollet to the Jesuits.[3] And even though the Hurons soon killed Brûlé for trying to bypass them in the fur trade, his direct experience of Lake Erie in the first half of the seventeenth century finds clear expression on the French map from sometime around 1641 titled "Novvelle France," as well as in the Jesuit reports from 1640–41. "Novvelle France" distinctly portrays Lake Erie as a large lake and calls the body of water *Lac des Gens du Chat* (Lake of the Raccoon's People).[4] Wright has demonstrated that the <Érié> spelling clearly points to Huron *eríʔxe,* "at the cherry (tree)," composed of *eríʔ,* "cherry (tree)" and *-xe,* the external locative suffix.[5] The notion that the place-name <Érié> signifies "at the cherry (tree)" finds bioregional botanical support in early French references to the remarkable precontact abundance of fruit trees in the area south of Lake Erie. This analysis can also be seen in Gabriel Gravier's comment from 1895: *Le Lac Érié ou «des Cerises»* (Lake Erie or "of the Cherries").[6]

The first, and unnamed, appearance of Indiana's and Lake Erie's Maumee River also seems to be on the map "Novvelle France." Yet because of continuous conflicts with the Iroquois, it would be nearly forty years after Brûlé before the French would record another sighting of Lake Erie. Adrien Jolliet, the elder brother of Louis Jolliet of Mississippi fame, returning from Sault Ste. Marie in the company of his French hired man named La Sotière and an Iroquois warrior whom the Ottawa had released from captivity, partly paddled and partly walked the northern shore of this Great Lake from west to east in September 1669.[7] The geographical information that Jolliet had picked up and then imparted to his brother Louis likely contributed to the appearance of the Maumee River on Franquelin's map of 1674, since the cartographer drew this map with Louis Jolliet's assistance.[8] The broad and deeply engraved river at the western end of Lake Erie on this chart is not simply an artistic embellishment but surely an actual albeit impressionistic representation of the Maumee. It is also possible that Adrien Jolliet is the ultimate source for the information on the Bernou map of 1676, commonly known as the "Jolliet Smaller Map," which marks a portage extending from an unnamed river at the western end of Lake Erie and leading to the Ohio River.[9]

The first European to apply a name to the Maumee was René de La Salle. In collecting geographical information about the West the explorer mentioned the relative location of this river shortly after 1681. La Salle also managed to come by a fairly good rendition of what he thought was the Huron name for it, which he wrote <Tiotontaracton>. This place-name is morphophonemic |te-yo-at-õtar-aktõ-ʔ| dualic–third person singular neuter patient–reciprocal–"lake"–"curve"–stative, meaning "curved lake, crooked lake." The phonemic form of this term would be **teyotõtaráktõh,* where, in the sequence |o + a|, the |a| drops.[10] However, this recording appears to be a mistake committed by La Salle in collecting geographic and onomastic information, as there is better evidence for a different name for the Maumee in Huron, examined below. Indeed, La Salle's <Tiotontaracton> seems to describe simply the western end of Lake Erie, or the location of the Maumee's outlet at the western curve of Lake Erie. Nevertheless, in terms of its age, <Tiotontaracton> could well be an ancient figure in the Northern Iroquoian place-name inventory, given the well-documented late prehistoric presence of Iroquoian-speaking tribes near the southwestern end of Lake Erie.[11]

Although La Salle had <Tiotontaracton> in hand, and was in his day squarely on the cutting edge of European geographical understanding of this particular area, he, like all Frenchman at that point in time, had not seen the land southwest of Lake Erie and south of the Kankakee, part of which is known today as Indiana. Such a lack of knowledge finds nearly universal expression in the diffidence expressed by La Salle's geographer contemporaries toward portraying the Maumee River on their maps.[12] For example, in 1684 in Paris, the cartographer Franquelin depicted the Wabash River quite well, which is remarkable since La Salle had never seen it. However, on the same chart, Franquelin, working in La Salle's very presence, failed to provide even the slightest hint of the existence of the Maumee—three years after La Salle had described its location and attempted to record a Native American name for it. Even Minet's map from 1685 and Coronelli's work from 1688, also based on La Salle's intelligence, fail to show the existence of the Maumee River.[13] It is difficult to explain such an omission. However, de

Louvigny, the French officer mentioned in chapter 3, who was stationed at Mackinac Island for four years, did not indicate on his map of the region in 1697 that he even had any idea there was a Maumee River.[14]

In truth, in the 1600s the French had only a feeble understanding of what lay at the western end of Lake Erie. Save for the initial hearsay-based geographical reference collected by La Salle and the impressionistic indications on less than a handful of early maps, the Maumee River could not in fact figure in the European geographical conception of North America during the seventeenth century. This lack of direct experience on the part of the French of the Maumee Valley and of the entire southern shore of Lake Erie for that matter can, again, be directly attributed to their implacable Iroquoian foes, the Seneca in particular. With absolute and unflagging resolve, the Iroquois created a powerfully psychological as well as concretely brutal barrier that effectively denied the French access to the land south of Lake Erie during the seventeenth century. Even La Salle, who stands out among all the early French explorers for having ingratiated himself with the Iroquois, never succeeded, as noted in chapter 3, in entering the Ohio Country or the Ohio Valley itself, despite the occasional misinformed statement to the contrary.[15] Furthermore, the Iroquois' restriction on French travel in the area that La Salle and his contemporaries were subject to does not seem to have relaxed even after the treaty of 1701 known as the "Grand Settlement." It is therefore no understatement that, owing to the unbending intransigence of the Iroquois, the land south of this Great Lake was still an unknown quantity to the French even midway through the eighteenth century, *over two hundred years after the French had arrived at Montreal.* The area south of Lake Erie on the map that Father Joseph-Pierre de Bonnécamps drew during the first French expedition down the Ohio River in 1749 states in no uncertain terms, "*Toutte celle partie du lac est inconnue*" (All that part [i.e., side] of the lake [Erie] is unknown).[16]

After La Salle's death in 1687 it would be eighteen years before a definitive depiction of the Maumee would appear on a map.[17] Moreover, it would not even be until after the first decade of the eighteenth century that a Frenchman would tread on the banks of this river. As far as we know, this was the French officer Jean-Baptiste Bissot de Vincennes. Bissot was a friend of the Miami and the father of François-Marie Bissot de Vincennes, for whom the well-known French town on the lower Wabash known in the French era as *Le Poste* and today as Vincennes would receive its modern name.

Even though Bissot had already been among the Miami on the St. Joseph River of Lake Michigan by 1696, it was not until 1711 that he visited the headwaters of the Maumee, where a part of that tribe had taken up residence slightly earlier. He made several trips to the Maumee River from 1711 to 1712, and in both 1712 and 1715 accompanied bands of Miami who were relocating there from the St. Joseph.[18] Though not all the Miami were living at the headwaters of the Maumee in the opening years of the eighteenth century, almost all appear to have arrived there or at the nearby headwaters of the Eel River by 1715.[19] Thus French geographical understanding of the Maumee did not take shape until the arrival of Bissot—and any knowledge the French had of this watercourse came to the French as they followed along in the footsteps of the Miami. On one of the Delisle maps, this one from 1718, is found a cartographic testament to what Bissot had recently witnessed.[20]

This new residential opportunity for the Miami, brought about in part by their conflict with the Ottawa in the Detroit area in 1706, had become available only with the relaxing of tensions after the important peace treaty mentioned above, signed by the French, their Indian allies, and the Iroquois in 1701.[21] Locating their villages east of Lake Michigan earlier than this would have been unthinkable to the Miami in light of the Iroquois-engendered bloodbath that swept through the Great Lakes region and the Ohio Valley during the second half of the 1600s.

As historians have noted, the Miami's move to the Maumee was the result of interrelated factors, one of which was the relatively abundant natural resources available in an area that had not witnessed human habitation for over half a century. Another important consideration was the protection provided by the surrounding swamps, which could be formidable barriers to approaching armies, especially of the European variety on horseback and with cannon. The swamps were also good places to hide those unable to fight in the event of an enemy attack.[22] Hearsay concerning these swamps was already ringing in the ears of the French in the last quarter of the seventeenth century, many years before they actually saw them firsthand.[23] With its abundant water—its rivers and streams, its extensive wetlands, and nearby Lake Erie—there is every reason to believe that the Miami felt right at home here at the headwaters of the Maumee. Their newfound abode was located in the same glaciated Great Lakes environment where they had dwelt for many generations prior to the arrival of the French among them in the 1670s.[24]

Another of the Miami's motivations for settling at the headwaters of the Maumee was the location's pivotal geographic position. Here natural conditions lent themselves to the designs of the tribe in two essential ways. Predictably, the site was destined to become a major hub for French trade southwest of Lake Erie in the 1700s. In fact, the choice of this locale for their villages was based in part on the immediate economic potential the site presented for playing the French off the Iroquois. With the opening of Lake Erie to French traders, this geographic "turnstile," a characterization fittingly reflected in the hairpin turns of the St. Mary's and St. Joseph Rivers, proved to be of considerable service to canoes coming from Montreal and Detroit. At the Maumee headwaters, French traders were able to make important connections via ancient portages to trading sites in virtually all directions, even to the Kankakee basin and *le pays des Illinois* by way of a portage route first indicated on Coronelli's map of 1688.[25] Indeed, the discovery and opening of the Maumee-Wabash route was a godsend to the French, for it provided them a way to avoid having to navigate around the vast lower peninsula of Michigan in order to reach the Mississippi. So while the upper and middle Ohio River Valley was never open to French commerce, the Miami's location at the headwaters of the Maumee gave the French a relatively easy route to the Indian villages along the Wabash, to the lower Ohio below the Wabash confluence (if they dared risking encounters with the Chickasaw), and ideally to the Mississippi Valley itself.[26] The Maumee River was a gateway opening onto myriad points within the heart of the continent only recently released from the control of the Iroquois.

Finally, establishing themselves near the Maumee headwaters also placed the Miami in proximity to British commercial interests advancing westward across the Appalachian Mountains. Hence, it offered the tribe the opportunity to purchase better quality European-manufactured goods from the Britons than they could obtain from the French, and at prices lower than the French could offer.[27]

After the death of Bissot at the headwaters of the Maumee in the winter of 1718–19, France sent Commandant Charles Regnault, Sieur de Dubuisson, in August 1721 to the confluence of the St. Mary's and St. Joseph Rivers, where he immediately began the construction of a fort.[28] With its completion in May 1722, Dubuisson officially dubbed the structure *Fort St-Philippe* des Miamis in honor of the patron saint of his commander, Philippe de Rigaud, marquis de Vaudreuil, governor general of Canada. However, the French soon turned this long place-name into Fort des Miamis for short,[29] into *Les Miamis* for shorter, and into *Les Mis* for shorter still. In addition, the French naturally referred to the Maumee River in French as *la rivière des Miamis* (the River of the Miami), a French hydronym that had simply accompanied the Miami on their journey from the St. Joseph River of Lake Michigan to the Maumee.[30]

An early American Indian place-name recorded for the site of present-day Fort Wayne appears in the form <Kiskakon>.[31] However, this name is a conundrum, for this is none other than the common Gallicized Algonquian name for the historically famous bear totem band of the Ottawa.[32] Why would the French have applied the name of an Ottawa group to the Miami's principal town?[33] As a place-name, <Kiskakon> cannot refer to protohistoric occupancy of the Maumee by the Ottawa; such a notion is void of archaeological and ethnographic underpinnings. Whereas the Ottawa eventually did move to the lower Maumee Valley near Lake Erie, their residency in that area began only in the very late 1740s, several decades after the Miami founded their town. In truth, there is no logical explanation for why the French would have called the Miami town <Kiskakon> *if the name referred to the Ottawa.*[34] My sense is that it did not. In fact, <Kiskakon> most likely represents the *Ottawa* name for this site, and specifically an Ottawa term that *sounded something like* <Kiskakon> to the French. History supports this notion since the appearance of <Kiskakon> in the historical record as a name for the principal Miami villages coincides with the arrival of the Ottawa in the lower Maumee Valley—and the Ottawa would certainly have had a name for the important Miami-occupied site located upstream from where they were living. Moreover, unlike the Miami, the Ottawa were dependable French allies from whom the French would have naturally heard the names for places.

It is not easy determining what the original Ottawa term could have been, but <Kiskakon> could represent something like *kiiškakkam-*, a conveniently shortened and garbled form of Ojibwa-Ottawa *kiiškakkamikaang,* the locative form of the verb *kiiškakkamikaa* meaning "cut land" (from *kiišk-*, "cut," *-kkamik-*, "land," and the stative aspect marker *-aa*). As noted elsewhere in this volume, the French were known to hear and write Algonquian *a* as *o,* and in fact in the very sequence *-kam-*.[35] Furthermore, the *-ikaa* could have been dropped off of the end of *kiiškakamikaa* by the French, just as final syllables in Miami-Illinois were commonly lopped off by the French to create their own ethnonyms, toponyms, and hydronyms based on Native American terms. Examples of this practice noted in this book include *Ouabachi* for Miami-Illinois *waapaahši(i)ki* and *Ouiatanon* for Miami-Illinois *waayaahtanwa.* Moreover, the *-ikaa* could have dropped out of this place-name, especially under the "gravitational pull" of the already firmly established <Kiskakon> ethnonym, which the French had been intimate with since the mid-1600s. Finally, the *-m-* now exposed at the end of *kiiškakkam-* could have gone through the same word-final *-m* to *-n* process that we observed above in the discussion of the possible evolution of the place-name "Michigan." In sum, then, the French may have used <Kiskakon>, an old, comfortable Ottawa standard in lieu of the actual somewhat homophonous Ottawa expression.

The original referent for this name for the site of the Miami villages, evoking its salient geophysical nature, would have been the *steep bluff* near the confluence of the St. Mary's and St. Joseph Rivers upon which the French had located their fort. Information contained in an 1819 letter from an American officer at Fort Wayne as well as in the writings of the English painter George Winter from the late 1830s corroborates the observation made by a French-speaking British soldier that will be noted below in connection to another name for this site. All of these people pointed out that Fort Wayne was located *on a bluff* just below the confluence of the St. Mary's and St. Joseph Rivers.[36]

There is an additional name for the site where the Miami lived at the headwaters of the Maumee. Over the years many authors have stated that the Miami of the 1700s called their town <Kekionga>, even though there is no historically documented basis for such an assertion. However, before embarking on the analysis of <Kekionga>, it would be wise to give some attention to what this term does not mean. Although the historian Wallace A. Brice said <Kekionga> meant "berry patch," there is no linguistic basis for this notion. Even so, Brice's translation has enjoyed a considerable dissemination.[37] Furthermore, <Kekionga> is not, as Dunn conjectured, a corruption of the Gallicized Ottawa <Kiskakon>.[38] There is no linguistic basis for proposing this idea, either. <Kekionga> is not Miami-Illinois *(ah)kihkonki,* pronounced [kihkoŋgi], a locative nominal form of *(ah)kihkwi,* "pot, kettle."[39] Linguistically speaking, <Kekionga> and *(ah)kihkonki* simply fail to square up—despite the curious fact that the Shawnee, as we shall see below, called the St. Mary's River by a name that means "little kettle" in their own language.[40]

As far as the origin of <Kekionga> is concerned, a particularly enticing analytical trail does lead to Miami-Illinois *(ah)kihkionki,* "on the earth," pronounced [kihkioŋgi], which is the locative noun of *(ah)kihkiwi,* "earth."[41] Phonetically speaking, <Kekionga> and [kihkioŋgi] line up rather well. In fact, this analysis is attractive in view of a firsthand description we have from 1778 of the Maumee River site: "The Miami town country for several miles on this side of the St. Joseph river is always overflown [*sic*] in the spring so that the Indians cabins are always drowned at this season of the year, the ground where the french [*sic*] town is build [*sic*] seems to be the most advantageous spot for a fort."[42] The author of this description, a French-speaking British lieutenant by the name of H. Duvernet, adds that along its course the Maumee in general ran scarcely below its banks, but at the headwaters of the Maumee, which is where the French fort was located, the banks were high above the river. Thus, given the site's geophysical setting, one is inclined to see in Miami-Illinois *(ah)kihkionki* the source of <Kekionga>, that is, as a term referring to the only suitable, dry living space amid the surrounding, expansive swamplands and flood-prone valleys—*on the earth* rather than submersed in water. This is a curious theory, but it is offered here only in so far as it demonstrates how carefully one must handle place-names of undetermined reference and provenience. For this interpretation is also wrong.

Illustrious, enigmatic <Kekionga> has proved to be a very worthy opponent for analysts, and properly so, for in the realm of philology this toponym, as written, is the equivalent of a fun-house mirror. The correct analysis of <Kekionga> will demonstrate that this historic spelling is in fact an unusual distortion of an unusual Native American place-name for this site, and yet, oddly enough, it is a name that is expected.

People have long assumed—and without fail almost any history book will state—that <Kekionga> was the Miami's name for their town during its early history. However, neither French nor British records mention the term. In fact, the *prototype* of this place-name does not even appear in the historical record until the German native and Moravian missionary David Zeisberger wrote it down in 1784, in the form <Gigeyunk>.[43] This place-name was also used by his American colleague John Heckewelder, who spelled it <Kegeyunk>. Then, in October of 1790, the American general Josiah Harmar, shortly before the destruction of his army by the Miami war chief *mihšihkinaahkwa* and his warriors, recorded his own version of the place-name in the form <Kegaiogue>.[44] Like Harmar's term, the <Kekionga> spelling is an American recording—and the Americans did not succeed in forcing their way to the headwaters of the Maumee until 1794, nearly a century after the Miami had founded their town at this location.

To get to the bottom of <Kekionga> it is necessary to understand that English speakers arriving in the Old Northwest in the late 1700s occasionally drove the transcription of American Indian names to the tottering brink of the fantastic, and, in cases such as <Kekionga>, right into etymological black holes. In general, the notorious problems of modern English spelling encountered by every first grader today were magnified incalculably in the latter half of the eighteenth century, when this place-name was recorded.

This was a time when the English language was only beginning to enjoy a modicum of orthographic standardization with the arrival of Samuel Johnson's landmark dictionary in London bookshops in 1747—and any impact of Johnson's work on contemporary English-speaking Virginian and Kentuckian villagers living west of the Appalachians is dubious at best. Indeed, the writings of English speakers in the New World from the seventeenth, eighteenth, and early nineteenth centuries exhibit a broad range of spelling usages. On the one hand, some folks, such as the locally traveled British officer and mapmaker Thomas Hutchins, evidence an extensive education characterized by exposure to Latin, French, continental sound-symbol correspondences in general. On the other, many English-speaking colonials and their offspring acquired writing skills in total ignorance of other European languages. In fact, for early historical North American English speakers with limited education and with limited exposure to the greater European linguistic and cultural world of that era, the rote-recited English alphabet served in large measure as the foundation for their orthography. It wielded a powerful influence over the way words, especially foreign words, were spelled, and it led to spelling acrobatics the likes of which few people in the twenty-first century have ever witnessed, and <Kekionga> is its "poster child." Moreover, English spelling conventions did not, in general, prepare Britons and Americans for the task of recording the phonologically exotic languages of the American Indians they encountered. This is not to say that English speakers did not make valiant attempts to record Native American languages. Indeed, in the case of <Kekionga>, the internal evidence of the spelling itself reveals commendable diligence on the part of the recorder to get this name down as accurately as possible. Therefore, despite the fact that, as we shall see, <Kekionga> swims in a confusing "alphabet soup," this spelling actually rivals recordings made by some of the early Jesuit master linguists. Phonetically speaking, the transcriptions of the consonants in <Kekionga> are in fact *perfect*; it is rather the unexpected yet at the same time *predictable* sound-symbol correspondences of the vowels here that is so bewildering. Clearly, the person who coined the spelling <Kekionga> did not know French or Latin, both of which have had immeasurable effects on the spelling of modern English, that is, the English of every historian and linguist who has ever tried to understand what this place-name meant.

As in reciting "A-B-C-D-*E*-F-G ... ," the -e- of <Kekionga> is pronounced just as it sounds when one recites the alphabet, that is, the sound of the first -e- of "concede" or "concrete," a sound that phoneticians write

[i]. This phenomenon, which appears elsewhere in this book, will be called "alphabet E." The -i- of <Kekionga> represents phonetic [a^{i}], which rhymes with "eye"—just as in reciting "... H-*I*-J-K ..." The -o- of <Kekionga> does not present any problem, as it just stands for plain [o]. The -a of <Kekionga>, however, which for purposes of elucidation in the case of this place-name and many times elsewhere in this volume will be called "alphabet A," is the vowel sound of "A" in "*A*-B-C ..." The "bare-bones" phonetic symbol for this sound, that is, minus the inherent English glide, is [e]. "Alphabet A" has a curious tale to tell.

The quality of the recordings of Algonquian *i(i)* produced by English speakers in the 1700s and early 1800s, like that of their French counterparts, is simply erratic. As noted earlier, the French often heard Miami-Illinois *i(i)* as [e] and therefore commonly spelled it é(e) in accordance with accepted French rules of orthography. Examples include <Ouabaché> for Miami-Illinois *waapaahši(i)-*, discussed in chapter 2, and <Sipioué> for Miami-Illinois *siipiiwi*, "river."[45] Among English speakers in North America in the eighteenth and nineteenth centuries, there was a common vernacular spelling practice that wrote Algonquian *i(i)* as "a."[46] The reason for this is that English speakers, just like their French counterparts, would often hear Algonquian final *i(i)* as phonetic [e]. Then, *in accordance with their understanding of the ABCs*, they would write this sound as "a" or "ay," since "A" in the "ABCs" represents the sound [e]. In fact, the spelling <Kekionggay>, found in Winter's work from the late 1830s, is a good example of this transcription practice, as is the final -a of Hough's mid-nineteenth-century recording <Wahbahshikka> for actual Miami-Illinois *waapaahši(i)ki*.[47]

By taking into account the preceding description of the sound-symbol correspondences present in <Kekionga>, it is now possible to see that this historical place-name is Miami after all. <Kekionga> represents Miami-Illinois *kiihkayonki*, pronounced [kiihkayoŋgi], a term which literally means "at Kikaya" or, in common English parlance, "Kikaya's Place."Gatschet was successful in recording a good Miami-Illinois pronunciation of this place-name in the forms <kikayúngi> and <Kikayüngi>.[48] Here "Kikaya" is a personal name, a local American Indian moniker for Gen. Anthony Wayne, the American military officer responsible for the rout of a coalition of Indians at the Battle of Fallen Timbers in northwestern Ohio on August 20, 1794.[49] Just as Wayne's advanced age made such an impression on his own soldiers that they nicknamed him the "Old Man," this wizened soldier made a similar impression on the local Delaware Indians, from whose languages the term "Kikaya" originated.[50] With the construction of Wayne's fort at the headwaters of the Maumee, begun on September 22, 1794, and finished on October 22, 1794,[51] native peoples in the area came to call the land at the headwaters of the Maumee after the name of this American general, its new "owner."[52] Miami living in the early 1800s would have known that *kiihkayonki* referred to the fort named for General Wayne. However, a hundred years later, long after the general's passing, native speakers of Miami, such as one of Dunn's Miami language consultants, no longer knew the pronunciation, referent or meaning of this place-name. There were two reasons for this. First, the Miami commonly referred to Wayne as *alaamhsenwa*, "it is windy, there is wind."[53] Second, although *kiihkayonki* is ostensibly a Miami language place-name, *kiihkay-* was not originally a term from the Miami-Illinois language; it was a borrowing from Unami Delaware *khík˙ay*, "old person"and/or Munsee Delaware *kíhkay*, "elder."[54] The Miami-Illinois language has no cognate for these Delaware terms. Therefore, even though *kiihkayonki* is a Miami place-name, it did not come originally from the Miami-Illinois language. The Miami-Illinois place-name consists of a borrowed Delaware name for General Wayne—as well as some unusual Miami morphology.

With a term like *kiihkaya*, one would expect in Miami-Illinois a locative noun in the form **kiihkayenki*, **kiihkayinki*, or even **kiihkeenki*. However, in creating *kiihkayonki*, it is clear that the Miami borrowed not only the basic noun stem from the Delaware, which they retooled into the form *kiihkay-*, but they also used an unexpected Miami-Illinois locative suffix form, *-onki*. The reason they did this is that *-onki* was the closest locative suffix in Miami that sounded like the corresponding Delaware locative suffixes. Indeed, this unusual Miami name for the U.S. military fort near the confluence of the St. Mary's and St. Joseph Rivers was influenced by both the Delaware morphology and the Delaware phonology of the Delaware language names for the site.

With the uncommon ethnolinguistic heritage of <Kekionga> comes an equally curious ethnohistorical background: The Delaware names for this site were in use *before General Wayne arrived*. In other words, *the "old one(s)" or the "elder(s)" that the Delaware name referred to did not originally refer to Wayne*. "Old Man" Wayne simply filled the shoes of a Delaware "old person(s)/elder(s)"–related place-name for the Miami's principal town that had already been in use at least a full ten years before Wayne became *kiihkaya*. That said, it is not clear what the earlier Delaware name referred to. Perhaps it indicated that the principal chiefs, the elders of the Miami in the 1700s, as opposed to the leaders of other Miami bands such as the Wea and the Piankashaw, had their villages at the headwaters of the Maumee. Or perhaps the Delaware name was a sign of respect for the Miami. In any event, there seems to be no documentation for what Miami-Illinois speakers themselves called the site of the Miami villages at the headwaters of the Maumee during the French and British eras. However, there is indirect evidence suggesting it was known as *čečaahkonki,* "at the sand-hill crane,"[55] since *čečaahkwaki,* "sand-hill cranes" is the Miami self-designation. This idea is supported by the Huron name for the Miami town, which was recorded by Father Pierre Potier at Detroit in the forms <tochingoke> and <tochingooke>, glossed *aux mis* (at the Miami). These spellings represent *thohšinkóhke(h),* "at the sand-hill crane" (Fr. *grue* [*Grus Americana*]),[56] which is an exact translation of Miami-Illinois ethnonymic toponym *čečaahkonki.* Since it is a known that the Wea's village near modern Lafayette was known as *waayaahtanonki,* "at the Wea," either *čečaahkonki,* "at the sand-hill crane" or the generic *myaamionki,* "at the Miami" would naturally be expected, both grammatically and ethnologically speaking, to designate Miami villages in the Miami-Illinois language. Miami-Illinois speakers in the 1700s would certainly have recognized *čečaahkonki* and *myaamionki* as names for their villages.

The locative nouns *čečaahkonki* and *myaamionki* do not show up, however, in the literature as place-names for the simple reason that the French in the first half of the eighteenth century, as noted above, had firmly established a bevy of French names for the important location of the Miami's new home at the headwaters of the Maumee, and they were constantly recycling these names in conversation, in correspondence, on maps, and so forth. Since the French were the only ones writing down anything in those days, the names they recorded were often the only ones that survived.

The name of the river that flowed from the Miami's town to Lake Erie has posed its own particular set of problems to past analysts. Contrary to the commonly observed notion promulgated by Dunn, the name "Maumee" is in no way a corruption of the Miami's name for their own tribe.[57] Rather, this transcription, created by an English speaker—and perhaps coined by the American officer John Tipton—represents *(o)maamii* (sg.), which is the Ottawa language term for "Miami."[58] Not only is "Maumee" not a good match for Miami-Illinois *myaamia,* "Miami," the Miami would not have bucked the deeply engrained Native American place-naming tradition that prohibits naming a river one lives on after oneself. According to Ojibweyan specialist David Pentland, the unwritten proscriptive grammar of Ojibwa-Ottawa would suggest a possible form for this hydronym was **(o)maamiiwiziibi,* "Miami river." Another Ojibweyan specialist, John Nichols, has pointed out that the variant **(o)maamii-ziibi,* with the same meaning, was also possible. The latter is in fact suggested by the English spelling "Maumee."[59]

The historical Miami, on the other hand, referred to the Maumee River as the *taawaawa (siipiiwi),* "Ottawa (River)" since, as noted above, the Ottawa took up residence downstream on the Maumee near Lake Erie toward the midpoint of the eighteenth century. The expression *taawaawa* (*siipiiwi*) as a Miami name for the Maumee had already arrived on the tongues of non-French Europeans by at least 1781, when Zeisberger spelled it <Tawa>. The same spelling also occurs multiple times in a journal, composed in the summer of 1794 by an unknown ranking officer in General Anthony Wayne's army. Furthermore, this Miami name can be seen on maps by 1795.[60] Note, however, that neither Ottawa *(o)maamii(wi-)* nor Miami *taawaawa* was a component of an ancient hydronym. The hydronym *taawaawa* (*siipiiwi*) dates only to 1748, the year the Ottawa arrived along the lower Maumee from the Detroit area.[61]

Another commonly observed name for the Maumee can be seen on Antoine-François Tardieu's map from 1789 in the form <Omie>.[62] Instead of being a crude representation of Ottawa *(o)maamii,* this recording simply represents a segment of the colloquial French hydronym *la rivière aux-Mis,* "the River of the Miami." Here, *aux-Mis,* pronounced [omí], means "of the Miami." As mentioned above, *Mis,* a plural noun, was the historical French clipping of *Miamis.*[63] Tardieu's <Omie>, therefore, simply means "of the Miami" or "with the Miami."

Yet another historic Native American name for the Maumee River exists on record, this one from the Wyandot language. It first appeared in the form <Cagharendute> in a list composed by John Johnston, an Irish fur trader and United States Indian agent at Fort Wayne in the early 1800s, of various native place-names in the Ohio area, which was finally published in 1848. Beckwith spelled the same place-name <Cagharenduteie> and glossed it "River-of-the-Standing-Rock." He also properly attributed its origin to the Wyandot.[64] <Cagharendute> represents Huron-Wyandot *kahrɛ̃ʔnú·teʔ,* "standing rock." Its structural components are |t-ka-hrẽʔn-ot-eʔ| cislocative–third person singular neuter agent–"rock"–"stand"–stative (epenthetic -e). The Huron-Wyandot pronunciation of this place-name would be [ka·rɛ̃ʔndúteʔ].[65] Although *orthographic g* is present in the spelling <Cagharendute>, the *sound g* is not a part of the native word. The -g- of Johnston's recording together with the following -h- simply form the common silent English digraph gh, as in "bought." Here, as in the case of the anglicized Miami-Illinois name <Quiaaghtena> discussed in chapter 2, -gh- was used by the recorder in an attempt to render as closely as possible the perceived quality of the long vowel of the first syllable of the Wyandot term.

The source of the place-name *kahrε̃ʔnú·teʔ* was a large rock standing in the Maumee Rapids.[66] Although Americans have, for the purposes of navigation, eliminated the greater part of the rapids in which this rock is located, the rock from which this river got its Wyandot name is still standing and is located near Waterton, Ohio.[67] The Wyandot place-name that the rock inspired dates *at least* to the arrival of the Wyandot people in the Detroit area in the early 1700s. However, again in light of the occupancy of the western end of Lake Erie by Iroquoian-speaking peoples, this could very well be a much older Iroquoian language place-name, one that reaches back into late prehistoric times.

Curiously, the French translation of *kahrε̃ʔnú·teʔ* underwent folk etymologizing in the 1700s from *la Roche Debout,* which signifies "the standing rock," to *la Roche de Bout,* which means "the end rock." However, this folk etymology is logical since the famous rock that gave the Maumee its Huron name was located near the *end* of miles of rapids, as well as near the *end* of the Maumee River itself.[68]

The geological formation itself known as Standing Rock also has a Miami-Illinois name, which Gatschet got in the form <nepáweki sāne>. His spelling represents *neepaweeki (a)hseni,* "the stone is standing." The constituents of this toponym are *neepaweeki,* "it is standing" from the changed initial *neepawee-,* "stand" and *-ki,* the conjunct II verb suffix, along with *(a)hseni,* the inanimate "stone" noun.[69]

As noted above, there was also an old Huron name for the Maumee River, one much older than its eighteenth-century Wyandot name recorded by Johnston. In the Jesuit missionary Pierre Potier's papers composed in Detroit in the mid-1700s we find the entry <θotontaraton>, translated to French *R. des mis.* Potier also wrote the same term <Totontaraton>.[70] Here, the French translation *R. des mis* means "R(iver) of the Miami," indicating the Maumee as the river on which the Miami were living *at that point in time.* In other words, the French gloss is not a translation of the Huron term. <θotontaraton> could be a clipped version of the Huron name for the Mascouten, *totõtaratõhró·nõʔ,* "people surrounded by the lake." The term can be parsed |t-o-t-õtar-atõ-hro·nõʔ| dualic–third person neuter singular patient–semireflexive–"lake"–"encircle"–populative. The verb in question is | te- … -to~- |, which means to "enclose, put something around." The name could refer to an island or peninsular area near the mouth of the Maumee River and to the late prehistoric location of this tribe prior to the Iroquois wars of the 1600s.[71]

The St. Mary's River rises in western Ohio and, like the Mississinewa, Salamonie and Wabash Rivers, it skirts the southern edge of an extensive terminal moraine on its journey into northeastern Indiana. *La rivière de Ste-Marie,* like the name of its tributary, *la rivière de St-Joseph,* was a term coined by the French in the 1700s. The Miami, however, call the St. Mary's *mameewa siipiiwi,* "sturgeon river." The Miami term is composed of *mameewa,* "sturgeon" and *siipiiwi,* "river." Dunn wrote this place-name <maymáyiwahsepeway>,[72] which is an interesting spelling since the segment written ay indicates that he heard the long *ee* of the Miami term, realized it was a unique sound, and tried his best to express it. Dunn's later <Mameĭ́wasipíwi> for this same place-name is more modern, more continental in appearance, and reflects his growth as an amateur linguist.[73]

The name "sturgeon river" alludes to the fact that the St. Mary's once abounded in the giant, long-lived fish known as the lake sturgeon (*Acipenser fulvescens* Rafinesque), a cousin of the shark. This ancient denizen of the Great Lakes, whose numbers have been depleted by pollution and overfishing, would have used the St. Mary's for spawning.[74]

In this connection, it is important to note that the modern division of the St. Mary's and the Maumee into two different rivers is an arbitrary one. Hydrologically speaking, they are the same river, as Captain Riley, who was mentioned above, pointed out in the early 1800s, and as the French understood earlier. Father Pierre Potier mentioned a portage between his *R. des mis* (the Miamis' River) and a stream that flows into the Ohio (i.e., Loramie Creek and the Great Miami River), and Potier's *R. des mis* can refer to none other than the St. Mary's River. In this light, since the name *taawaawa (siipiiwi)* is a Miami creation dating only to the late 1740s, *mameewa siipiiwi* is probably the original Miami-Illinois name *for the entire St.-Mary's–Maumee waterway.* Moreover, the British trader George Croghan referred to the St. Mary's River as the "Miame river," thus connecting it onomastically to the Maumee.[75] As a place-name, Miami *mameewa siipiiwi,* whatever its ultimate application, may be quite ancient. Indeed, this hydronym could date to late prehistoric times, given our current understanding of the location of the Miami-Illinois peoples in late prehistory.

The spelling <Cakothekesepe>, glossed "Kettle River," is the name John Johnston recorded as the Shawnee name for the St. Mary's River. Both

Dunn and Beckwith repeated this information, but misspelled Johnston's original recording <Cokotheke sepe> and <Cokothekesepoie>, respectively.[76] The segment that Johnston spelled Cakotheke- seems to be the Shawnee diminutive locative noun **hkohkooθeki,* "at the little kettle." The -sepe ending of Johnston's term represents Shawnee *-θiipi,* "river." Therefore **hkohkooθekiiθiipi* would be "the river at the little kettle." That said, it appears that most of the far-flung dialects of Shawnee had undergone the shift of *s* to *θ* by the time Johnston recorded this place-name, and that shift would have taken earlier *siipi* to *θiipi.* In other words, Johnston's -sepe should have been spelled *-thepe. Presumably, Johnston's spelling represents a mishearing on his part.

Although **hkohkooθekiiθiipi* is one of the very few place-names in Indiana that survive from the Shawnee language, the name is difficult to date, as the Shawnee are associated with the St. Mary's watershed on various occasions historically and likely prehistorically. At the very latest, the name could date to the arrival of some Scioto Valley Shawnee in the Kekionga area after the American Revolution. A number of people from this tribe were certainly in residence on the upper Maumee from 1786 to 1790. On the other hand, this place-name could go back to the arrival in the Fort Wayne area of a Shawnee group who had been briefly on the St. Joseph River (of Lake Michigan) near the turn of the eighteenth century and were soon followed by about a thousand Shawnee from the Cumberland River. Finally, **hkohkooθekiiθiipi* could even reach back into prehistoric times as the Shawnee are commonly thought to have lived in the middle Ohio Valley in late prehistoric times, and would have been aware of the St. Mary's River.[77]

The referent for **hkohkooθekiiθiipi* is unknown. However, this place-name may refer to a smaller version of the geological phenomenon discussed in chapter 2 in the analysis of Jacques Marquette's <8AB8SKIG8> and also embodied in the name for the Chaudière River in Québec.

The St. Joseph River, the second hagionym created by the French in Indiana that was based on the name of this Christian saint, evinces a putative American Indian name which appears on Hough's map as <Kemmemsowah>.[78] Unfortunately, this term was completely twisted by some nineteenth-century English-speaking copyist, perhaps by the engraver of Hough's map. Hence, it is not analyzable in the languages spoken in Indiana in historical times. It would have to be Algonquian, however, as the sound *m,* if it was properly written down here, does not occur in Iroquoian. Moreover, the -wah ending suggests an Algonquian noun + noun connector in the form

**-wi-* that would have preceded a "river" noun. If that is true, it eliminates the possibility that <Kemmemsowah> was a Miami-Illinois place-name, since Miami-Illinois does not have such a connector. At the very least <Kemmemsowah> does not appear to be even an extremely disfigured spelling of the Miami name for this river, which is *kóčiihsasiipi,* "bean river," from *kóčiihsa,* "bean," the hydronymic "river" final *-(i)siip* and the singular inanimate noun marker *-i.* Jacob Dunn, citing *kiilhsohkwa,* the granddaughter of *mihšihkinaahkwa,* attested this Miami name for the St. Joseph River in the form <Kōchísahsēpē>, which he later respelled <Kōtchĭsahsípi>.[79] The first historical use of "Bean Creek," the English translation of the Miami place-name, seems to be in the journal mentioned above compiled by an officer in General Anthony Wayne's army in 1794.[80]

The referent for Miami *kóčiihsasiipi* was not indicated historically. Indeed, on the surface, this Miami name for the St. Joseph does not even appear to be amenable to analysis based on any known ethnobotanical or historical fact. However, there is one possible referent: the beanlike seeds of the honey locust tree (*Gleditsia triacanthos*).[81] It is known that the French referred to the seeds of the honey locust tree as *fèves,* meaning "beans." The local Miami may have also used the Miami term *kóčiihsa,* "bean" in designating the seed of the honey locust tree, and may have applied the term to this stream because its banks supported an abundance of honey locust trees.

The forty-mile-long major tributary of the St. Joseph River known as Cedar Creek originates in two principal sources in northern Dekalb County and then flows southwest into north-central Allen County before shifting directions and flowing southeast to the St. Joseph.

Documentation for a Native American name for this stream exists only in Potawatomi, and is represented by Dunn's earlier <Mĕskwáhwahsḗpē> and his later <Mĕskwáwasípi>.[82] The garbling of these spellings by Dunn indicates that he did not get them from a native speaker of Potawatomi. However, his forms do stand for Potawatomi *mskwawak-zibə,* "red cedar river." The first segment of this place-name is *mskwawak,* "eastern red cedar" (*Juniperus virginiana*), literally "red-wood"; the second part is *zibə,* "river."[83] It is interesting that the literal translation of this Potawatomi hydronym into English survived for a while as a place-name among English-speaking Americans. In other words, in 1836, the name for the creek appeared cartographically as "Redwood Creek." [84]

There is no telling where Dunn got his place-name, but he seems to have taken it from a related toponym recorded in 1823 in the form <Muskwa-

wasepeotan>, which is *mskwawak-zibə odan,* "cedar river town," literally "red-wood-river town."[85] This was the name of a Potawatomi village located on the banks of Cedar Creek. Beckwith says that this site was located nine miles above Fort Wayne and was home to the Potawatomi leader Metea.[86] Beckwith's statement would place the village near the confluence of Cedar Creek and the St. Joseph River. The Potawatomi may have coined this name for Cedar Creek or they may have borrowed the idea for it from a preexisting yet now lost Miami place-name, since the eighteenth-century Miami no doubt had a name for this stream, so near it was to their principal villages at the headwaters of the Maumee River. In fact, it is a mystery why the Miami name for this stream did not survive. Then again, maybe it did. Perhaps it is couched within the meaning of the Potawatomi name itself. It is hard to say. Clio, the muse of history, is unwilling to reveal all of her secrets.

6

The White River and the People from the Dawn

In Indiana's Randolph County, within thirty miles of the Ohio state line, the waterway known as the West Fork of the White River rises from humble beginnings. However, in flowing in a westerly direction through central Indiana and then bending southwest to its distant encounter with the southern Wabash, it transforms by virtue of its enormous drainage system and its long history of glaciation into one of Indiana's premier streams. Because of its impressive breadth and length, the White River–West Fork naturally figured in the very earliest European accounts of the land that lay south of the Kankakee. In those days it bore the French designation *la rivière Blanche,* "the White River." Again, as in the case of the Kankakee, the Wabash, and the Iroquois Rivers, it was the French explorer René de La Salle who coined this French name and introduced the White River–West Fork to Europeans. That said, he never saw the stream in person. In fact, there appears to be no record of when the first Frenchman came upon it. But the first European sighting of it would not have occurred until the arrival of the French at the headwaters of the Maumee in the second decade of the eighteenth century.

<Oiapikaming> is the first name on record for the White River–West Fork. It was collected by La Salle in the Illinois Country and then given to the cartographer Jean-Baptiste Franquelin when they collaborated in Paris in 1684 on one of Franquelin's maps of North America from that year.[1] However, this term harbors a misspelling, attributable in all likelihood to Franquelin's unreliability as a scribe. The initial Oiap- of <Oiapikaming> should be Ouap-. Hobbled by the same spelling mistake, this same name for the river

is also on Franquelin's map of 1688 in the form <Oiapigaming>. This second incorrect spelling is disconcerting, however, since Franquelin had managed to get the name right on an earlier map when he wrote <Ouapigaming>.[2]

All of Franquelin's spellings are based on La Salle's data and, whether distorted or not, represent the Miami-Illinois locative noun *waapikaminki,* "on the white water, at the white water," the constituents of which are the initial *waap-,* "white," the final *-(i)kam,* "water," and underlying |-enki|, phonemic *-inki,* pronounced [-iŋgi], a conservative locative suffix meaning "on" or "at." The complete name is pronounced [wàapikamíŋgi]. The -ing of the La Salle–Franquelin spellings is expected, since *k* in Miami-Illinois naturally voiced to [g] following a nasal consonant, in this case *n.*

Miami-Illinois *waapkaminki* as a name for the West Fork of the White River probably dates to late prehistoric times; it is impossible to give a precise age for it. Even so, it has certainly enjoyed a long life since European contact. Trowbridge recorded the name in 1824 in the form <Waupeekomēē̆kee>, and two hundred years after La Salle recorded this hydronym the Miami were still using it, as Dunn heard the same name among his early-twentieth-century Miami speakers. He first penned the place-name in the traditional English phonetic spelling <Wápikahmēki> and then later modernized it to <Wápĭkamiki>. His translation "white waters"[3] is incorrect, since, grammatically speaking, the plural form of *waapikami* could not be ***waapikami(i)ki.* Dunn's spellings actually represent *waapikami(i)ki,* a singular conjunct II verb meaning "it is white water," composed of the initial *waap-,* "white," the final *-kam(i),* "water," and the requisite verb suffix *-ki.* Gatschet's recording <Wapikamikingi> is the same place-name as Dunn's and evinces a locative suffix in the form of *-inki* attached to an II verb. This same grammatical form can be seen, for example, in Miami *peehkonteekinki,* "last night."[4]

There are three major rivers in Indiana whose Native American names include the word "white": the White River–West Fork, the Wabash River, and the Whitewater River. As far as the West Fork of the White River is concerned, the Miami-Illinois term for "white water" must refer to some quality of the river that produced a white visual appearance. But since, unlike the Wabash, the White River–West Fork does not have any limestone bed to speak of, limestone would not be the source of the river's name. Apparently the only possible source of the "white" is the stream's "broad ripple." This expression, which is now the name of an Indianapolis neighborhood, refers to the shallow water and extensive rapids of the White River located upstream from downtown Indianapolis.[5]

In addition to being very familiar to Miami-Illinois–speaking populations in the eighteenth century, the White River was one of the homes of the Delaware Indians. As noted above, "Delaware" is an English language term applied with a broad brush by early East Coast British folks to culturally and linguistically related Eastern Algonquian Indians whose original homeland included the New York City area and New Jersey. The local Miami called the Delaware *waapanahkiaki,* "people of the dawn-land." However, the peoples known as the Delaware did not speak the same languages.[6] In Indiana there were Delaware Indians who spoke Munsee and others who spoke two different dialects of a closely related language known as Unami. The ethnonym "Munsee" comes from this tribe's self-designation *mən'si·w* (sg.), a term that originally indicated a person from Minisink, an ancient island habitation site in the Delaware River. *lənáˑpe* (sg.), "ordinary person, real person, original person," commonly written "Lenape," is the Unami self-designation. This term consists of the initial *lən-*, "ordinary, real, original" and the final *-aˑpe,* "person." The tribe name "Unami" derives from the Munsee language term *wə̆náˑmiˑw,* "downstream person."[7]

Delaware Indians began filtering into present-day Indiana from the east around 1770, and nearly all the Munsee and the Unami were living on the upper West Fork of the White River by the late 1790s.[8] Despite their relatively short stay in what is now Indiana, which lasted only until around the years 1818 to 1820, these peoples applied place-names to an area that had never before borne Delaware language names.[9] In this connection, it is important to note that, even though some Miami-Illinois toponyms and hydronyms in Indiana may exhibit a time-depth of several hundred years or more, local place-names created by the historic Delaware, as well as those that come from the Potawatomi, are relatively recent creations. In some cases, the toponyms and hydronyms fashioned by the latter groups may represent an overlay of earlier, mostly Miami-Illinois names that are now lost.

The historical recording <Opeecomecah> is the first appearance of a Delaware name for White River–West Fork. This place-name was recorded at a meeting between Delaware leaders and the U.S. government in Princeton, New Jersey, on May 10, 1779.[10] In 1801, Abraham Luckenbach, a native German and a Moravian missionary who lived with the Delaware on the upper White River between May 1801 and September 1806, also wrote down a Delaware toponym that included the name for the river. His <woapicamikunk> designated specifically a Delaware town that derived its name from its being located on the river. This was the home of the Delaware leader *pahkančíhəlaˑs,* whose name is commonly written Buckongehelas in the literature. Curiously, Luckenbach translated <woapicamikunk> "White Grave."[11]

The English spelling <Opeecomecah> appears to stand for Southern Unami _*ɔ·p·i·k·amí·k·a,_ "that which is a white house," the participle of the verb _*ɔ·p·i·k·amí·k·at,_ "it is a white house." Luckenbach's recording <woapicamikunk> is the cognate Northern Unami locative noun form of this term and signifies "at the white house." In Southern Unami this would be _*ɔ·p·i·k·amí·k·unk._[12] Just why the river was so named is not clear. However, the "White Grave" translation of this place-name provided by Luckenbach, an authoritative source, suggests that _*ɔ·p·i·k·amí·k·a_ is a Klammerform. In other words, based on Luckenbach's gloss, the segment _-ík·ami·k·a,_ "that which is a house" seems to have been intended to represent _mahčí·k·ami·k·a,_ "that which is a grave," which is literally "that which is a bad-house." The _-ík·ami·k·a_ segment of this place-name was apparently used to signify "grave" based on an inferred _mahčí·k·ami·k·a._[13] That the French were already referring to the White River as the _Maison blanche_ (White House) by 1748, long before the Delaware arrived in the midcontinent, adds an unusual twist to this place-name's history, and seems to imply that the French were aware of the Delaware name for the White River before the Delaware moved there.[14]

Another possible avenue of analysis suggests that, since the Delaware settled on the White River with the permission of the Piankashaw, they might have borrowed directly into Unami the name that eighteenth-century Piankashaw and other Miami-Illinois–speaking peoples applied to the White River: _waapikami(i)ki._ This term would have been easy for the Unami to pronounce since it sounded very much like their participle for "white house," _*ɔ·p·i·k·amí·k·a._ But instead of _translating the place-name_ into their language, the Unami could have, according to this scenario, created their own place-name by simply _mimicking the sound_ of the Miami-Illinois original. This phenomenon, known as paronomasia, would have produced a name that is a near-homophone of the original Miami-Illinois term, but which means something entirely different. An attractive theory, this notion implies that in time the Unami forgot that they had borrowed Miami-Illinois _waapikami(i)ki._

Before this discussion of the local Indian names for the White River–West Fork comes to an end, it is important to mention the term "Wapihani," sometimes spelled "Wapehane."[15] This expression, commonly attributed to the local historic Delaware, has enjoyed _widespread_ recognition in Indiana as _the_ Delaware name for the White River. However, this is not a Delaware word. It is simply a nonsense vocable composed of two Northern Unami terms fused together in an ungrammatical fashion.[16] Therefore, "Wapihani" could not have been an original Delaware name for the river. The observation about this term made by the native Southern Unami speaker Lucy Blalock agrees with that offered by the Delaware expert Ives Goddard when he states that it is ungrammatical. Blalock said that it sounded like a "made-up word."[17]

Hough refers to the historic Munsee town on the upper White River located on the site of modern Muncie, Indiana, as <Outaunink>. This is the same place-name that Dunn spelled <útĕnĭnk> and glossed "place of the town," which is a loose yet acceptable translation. However, Dunn also came up with the curious alternative translation "the place where the town was," which is incorrect. <Outaunink> simply represents the Southern Unami locative noun *o·t·é·nink*. The Munsee cognate would be *o·té·ne·nk*. Both expressions mean "at the town," a toponym that is about as generic as place-names get.[18] The Delaware name for the village that was under the leadership of a Delaware chief known as Anderson, an area now known as Anderson, Indiana, appears in local Moravian correspondence in the forms <Woapiminschi> and <Woapiminschijeck>. In his own spelling convention Dunn wrote a related <Wápĭmĭ́nskĭnk> [*sic*], a term of unknown provenience.[19] All of these forms above have to do with the American chestnut tree (*Castanea dentata*). The spelling <Woapiminschi> itself represents the term for the chestnut tree in either Munsee, which has *wa·pi·mí·nšəy*, or Unami, which has *wa·p·i·mə́·nši.*[20] In general, since the historical spellings of Delaware language terms characteristically lack phonetic precision, one cannot tell in many cases whether a lone Delaware language word is Munsee or Unami. Etyma from these two closely related languages can sometimes appear indistinguishable amid the mishmash of historical English or German spellings. Dunn's <Wápĭmĭ́nskĭnk>, the first "k" of which should be an "h," probably represents Munsee *wa·pi·mí·nšink* rather than Northern Unami **wa·p·i·mə́·nšink*. In Munsee and Northern Unami, respectively, the morphological parsing of this term is *wa·p-* and **wa·p·-*, "white," connective *-i-*, the "tree" final *-mí·nšəy/*-mə́·nši,* along with *-ink,* the locative suffix meaning "at."

Regardless of the source language for Dunn's term, both Munsee *wa·pi·mí·nšink* and Northern Unami **wa·p·i·mə́·nšink* are inherently ambiguous as both terms can refer to a site endowed with either a single chestnut tree or a grove of chestnut trees. However, in the case of this particular locale, we are fortunate to have the relevant historical Moravian recording <Woapiminshijeck> and the translation "where the chestnut trees grow."[21] This spelling seems to represent Northern Unami **wa·p·i·mə́·nši(y)í·ke·*, "there are a lot of chestnut trees," "(the place) has a lot of chestnut trees." That having been said, <Woapiminshijeck> may have lost parts of itself in the recording process, and, in fact, could have originally been something like **énta wa·p·i·mə́·nši(y)í·ke·k*, "where there are a lot of chestnut trees."[22] In any event, we at least know from this recording that the name for the site of Anderson's village referred to a place that was endowed with an impressive stand of chestnut trees.

Entering the White River some twenty miles downstream from Anderson is a stream known today as Pipe Creek. This White River tributary rises in northwestern Delaware County, runs most of its length across western Madison County, then pokes into Hamilton County for about a mile before joining the White River. "Pipe" appears to be a translation of the personal name of a local late-eighteenth-century Unami leader commonly known in the literature as Captain Pipe. Guernsey's map calls the stream <Hopoakan>, which represents Unami *hupɔ́·k·an,* "pipe."[23] However, since the term *hupɔ́·k·an* itself is not, grammatically speaking, a place-name, it is difficult to determine the authenticity of Guernsey's offering. In fact, the spelling <Hopoakan> insinuates that Guernsey, aware of the history of upper White River Valley, and aware that the English place-name "Pipe Creek" refers to Captain Pipe, simply created a "Delaware" place-name by looking up the Unami word for "pipe" in the Moravian missionary Daniel Zeisberger's eighteenth-century dictionary, which has exactly the same spelling <Hopoakan>.[24] While the Unami leader *hupɔ́·k·an,* based on the very English language place-name Pipe Creek, was connected to this waterway in some way, there is no evidence that the Delaware knew the stream by a name that included the name *hupɔ́·k·an* as an element. In fact, it is not known what the Delaware called Pipe Creek.

Even so, *hupɔ́·k·an* was an important figure in the late 1700s in what would later become Indiana, and much has been written about his exploits. In the Pennsylvania-Ohio area in the year 1773 he attained the position of Wolf chief, a title he inherited from his uncle Pakanke, also known historically as Custaloga.[25] Indeed, *hupɔ́·k·an* was an active pro-British Delaware leader and a principal player in the Indiana area and in the Old Northwest in general during the last quarter of the eighteenth century. He died in August 1794.[26]

One of Indiana's three Duck creeks originates in northwest Madison County and flows southeast into northeastern Hamilton County, where it meets the White River at the ancient American Indian site known historically as Strawtown. Hough's map has <Wenavaktanoo> as a Native American name for this stream, a term which he glossed "Duck Creek."[27] However, <Wenavaktanoo> does not mean "duck creek" in any known Indian language. In fact, the "Duck" in this case can be none other than a miswritten "Buck," and in this case "Buck" would not be the term for a male deer but instead the English nickname for the historical Delaware leader known in English as Killbuck.[28] Importantly, however, Hough's <Wenavaktanoo> does not mean "Killbuck." <Wenavaktanoo> is in fact a garbled spelling of an *Iroquoian name* that Killbuck used, evidenced by his signature on a letter to William Henry Harrison from September 9, 1808, where it is spelled <Wenavakhenon>.[29] The use of Iroquoian names by Delaware Indians developed out of the complex relationship that had evolved between the Iroquois and Delaware by the mid-1700s. <Wenavakhenon> seems to be from a Northern Iroquoian language, but it is not Wyandot, Seneca, or Tuscarora. Morphophonemically speaking, these spellings represent |w-a-hnaw-akta-nyon| third person singular neuter agent–linking vowel–"rapid"–"be next to"–distributive, which translates to English "several places near the rapid."[30] Why Killbuck chose this particular name is not clear.

Finally, it is not impossible that the Iroquoian word represented by the spellings <Wenavakhenon> and <Wenavaktanoo>, just as in the similar case of Pipe Creek above, could have been used in some form as part of a hydronym by local Indians for Duck [*sic*] Creek when Killbuck resided there. However, there appears to be no available evidence that supports this notion.

Fall Creek, which rises in northwestern Henry County, doglegs in a generally southwesterly direction across the bottom of Madison County and the southeastern corner of Hamilton County before entering the White River in central Marion County. This stream bears attractive and topographically descriptive names in both Delaware and Miami-Illinois. Its modern name is a translation of one of the Native American place-names discussed below. Dunn's writings evince this waterway's name in Unami and spell it <Soosoocpahaloc>, a term that he lifted from Chamberlain's mid-nineteenth-century gazetteer. Although it is misspelled, Hough's map also bears this term. <Soosoocpahaloc> stands for Southern Unami **susu·kpéhəla·k*, a participle meaning "(water) spills down continuously."[31] Dunn glossed the term "continuous waterfalls," which properly reflects the semantics inherent in the reduplication of the initial syllable of **susu·kpéhəla·k*. The first -a- of Chamberlain's <Soosoocpahaloc> is an example of the "alphabet A" phenomenon discussed in chapters 5 and 7. Moreover, it should be noted that the term *énta*, "where," may have also been a part of this place-name just as in the case of the Northern Unami name for the site of Anderson discussed above. Therefore, <Soosoocpahaloc>, though a genuine and readily analyzable term, may have been only one component of the original complete Delaware name for Fall Creek.

According to the Miami leader *waapanahkikapwa*, the Miami referred to Fall Creek as <Chắnktūnóongi> (also written <Tcắnktunúngĭ>). He translated this name to English "Makes a Noise Place."[32] Both of these spellings represent a Miami-Illinois toponym based on the II verb *čiinkwihtan-*, meaning literally "noise-flow, thunder-flow" but signifying "waterfall," accompanied by the locative suffix in the form *-onki*. <Chắnktūnóongi> and <Tcắnktunúngĭ>, recorded by Dunn, represent specifically *čeenkwihtanonki*, which exhibits first-syllable ablaut. This is a toponym signifying "at the noise-flow, at the thunder-flow," that is, "at the waterfall," or in everyday English, "the waterfall place." The independent II form of this verb, which can function grammatically as a noun, can be seen in the Illinois-French dictionary composed by Jesuit missionaries near the turn of the eighteenth century in the entry <tching8itan8i>, which represents phonemic *čiinkwihtanwi*. The dictionary's gloss is *sault, rapide, eau qui fait du bruit en tombant* (waterfall, rapid, water that makes noise in falling).[33] The local Miami place-name *čeenkwihtanonki* refers to the site that embodies the most outstanding feature of Fall Creek—the cascade near Pendleton, which was originally nine feet high.

The Miami name for Fall Creek itself would have been *čeenkwihtanki siipiiwi*, "it is a noise-flowing river, it is a waterfall river." This notion is fully supported by Gatschet's recording of this Miami-Illinois language hydronym for Fall Creek in Oklahoma in the form <Tchänk8tangi sipíwi>. Interestingly, Gatschet also recorded a related II verb–based name for another stream in Oklahoma, which he wrote <Tchínk8sanwi>.[34] The first of these Gatschetian recordings, also evincing first-syllable ablaut, is our phonemic *čeenkwihtanki siipiiwi* noted directly above; the second is phonemic *čiinkwihsinwi*, which signifies "it noise-lies, it thunder-lies." Notably, however, since Gatschet used the symbol 8 for short *o* and never for *wi*, both of his spellings indicate that there was a contraction of phonemic

-kw- + *-ihtan/-ihsin* to phonetic [-kohtan]/[-kohsin] in either the dialect or the idiolect of the person he got the name from. These forms would have thus been pronounced, respectively, [čeeŋgohtaŋgi siipíiwi] and [čiiŋgohsinwi].

Eagle Creek, another White River tributary, begins its course in extreme northwestern Hamilton County and continues down the extreme southeast portion of Boone County into northwestern Marion County before entering the White River about five miles south of the Fall Creek and White River confluence. As far as we know, the Delaware did not know this stream by a phrase in their language that translates to "Eagle Creek." In fact, the origin of this English hydronym is enigmatic. However, "Eagle Creek" does appear on very early local American maps, at a time when newly arriving Americans were still carrying on the time-honored practice, begun by the French, of adopting aboriginal place-names into their languages.[35] Chamberlain somehow acquired what he believed to be the original Delaware name for Eagle Creek, which he published in the form <Lauashingapaimhonnock> and glossed "Middle of the Valley Stream." His is a curious translation in light of what can be said about the etymology of this term.[36] Dunn attempted to analyze <Lauashingapaimhonnock> on the premise that it came from a Delaware language. He believed the lawi- segment meant "middle," and indeed this spelling appears to represent Northern Unami **la·wi-*, "middle." He also thought the -schingeu- part signified "level,"[37] and in fact this spelling would represent an allomorph of Unami *-šínk·e-*, a term referring to level wooded lowlands. The final element -paimhonnock, which he did not analyze, actually represents **pe·mháne·k*, a participle meaning "stream."

There is a problem, however, in reconstructing the original form of this place-name. Goddard notes that it is not known what shape *-šínk·e-* would have taken when forming composite terms with a participle as a second member. It could have been *-šínke·í·i-*, or even a prenoun in the form *-šínke-*.[38] In the spelling <Lauashingapaimhonnock>, if it is trustworthy, the "a" of -shinga- is no doubt an "alphabet A." (See the discussion of this spelling phenomenon in chapters 5 and 7.) But even knowing this does not help solve the problem that Goddard elucidates, since "alphabet A" could represent *e, e·*, or even *e·í·i.*

Furthermore, as in the case of the Delaware name for Anderson discussed above, the word *énta,* "where" could have been a part of the Unami name for Eagle Creek. But Chamberlain's term does not include this item.

Thanks to Chamberlain, however, the general "contour" of the putative Unami name for Eagle Creek, which he gives us in the form <Lauashingapaimhonnock>, is relatively clear. However, it is simply impossible, for the reasons presented above, to offer a grammatically and morphologically reliable reconstruction for it.

Rising in southern Boone County and descending the length of east-central Hendricks County to meet the White River in central Morgan County is White Lick Creek. A presumed Native American name for this waterway appears on Guernsey's map as <Wapimahonink>, which ostensibly signifies "at the white salt lick."[39] However, Guernsey did not reveal where he got the word, and thus its authenticity cannot be established. While it is not impossible that this place-name is genuine, Guernsey could have simply taken the Northern Unami initial for "white," which he wrote Wapi-, and added the Brinton and Anthony dictionary spelling of the Unami locative noun form for "salt lick."[40] Therefore, Guernsey's <Wapimahonink> lacks the necessary supporting evidence that would verify its authenticity. In this connection, it should be mentioned that the word for "salt lick" has disappeared from modern Unami. In the early 1800s, the Moravian missionaries Zeisberger and Heckewelder certainly heard it and wrote it <mahóny> and <mahony>, respectively.[41] James Rementer, a modern Southern Unami language specialist, worked with a Lenape man born in 1867 who remembered the word and translated it "a place where animals gather."[42] Although speculative, the locative form for this term could have been phonemic *_ma·ho·nink_.

Further down the White River, down below the confluence of White Lick Creek and the White River, is the mouth of a White River tributary known in English as Beanblossom Creek. This stream originates in northern Brown County and snakes through the uplands of south-central Indiana in a westerly fashion to meet the White River just south of Gosport in Owen County. Beanblossom Creek bears a possible Delaware language name as well as a possible Miami-Illinois language name. Yet whereas both terms appear to be related to the modern hydronym, each has its problems.

On Guernsey's map a putative Delaware name for Beanblossom Creek, recorded in what seems to be German spelling, takes the form <Hakiachhanne>.[43] Where Guernsey got this spelling is unknown, but this is such an unusual term that he could not have made it up. First, -hanne would represent an allomorph of the Unami verb final _-háne·_, "river, stream, creek."[44] Second, although the generic or common term for "bean" in modern

Southern Unami is *ma˙láxkwsi˙t,* where the root *ma˙l-* means "striped" and *-áxkwsi˙t* is the "bean" final, Zeisberger's dictionary also has an ancient "bean" term from Unami which he recorded in the obviative case in the form <Hackiachksitall> and glossed "beans, wild earth beans."[45] This term, the proximate form of which is *hakiya˙láxkwsi˙t* (sg.), "earth bean," is in truth the "bean" term related to Guernsey's word.

The twentieth-century native Unami speaker Nora Thompson Dean was aware of the word *hakiya˙láxkwsi˙t,* although she did not know what plant the historic Unami applied it to.[46] That said, at the turn of the nineteenth century and before that time, *hakiya˙láxkwsi˙t* must have been an expression for some wild "bean"-producing plant, perhaps a name for groundnuts (*Apios americana*), given that the most edible portion of this plant is under*ground.* Even though Guernsey's Hagiach- and *hakiya˙láxkwsi˙t* are obviously not mirror images of each other, *hakiya˙láxkwsi˙t* seems to be related to our place-name since the segment <Hagi-> of <Hagiachhanne> represents the initial signifying "earth."[47] In this light, whatever its historical referent might be, the spelling <Hagiachhanne> could be

1. a confused or imperfectly copied recording in which *hakiya˙láxkwsi˙t* was a component, as Hagiach- could represent the *hakiya˙láx-* segment of *hakiya˙láxkwsi˙t;*
2. an Unami place-name originally composed of the term *hakiya˙láxkwsi˙t* that was reduced to a trade jargon place-name; or
3. a Klammerform in the shape of a verb **hakiáhəne˙,* where *haki-* alone stood for "bean."

However, in the light of the problems noted above, it seems unwise to draw any conclusions at this point about what exactly the Delaware name for Beanblossom Creek was.

Not to be bested by the possible Delaware name for Beanblossom Creek with its problems are the presumed Miami-Illinois names for this stream. First, <Kochisahsepe>, a term applied to this stream on Guernsey's map, seems to have been just Guernsey's idea. No early documents contain such a name for Beanblossom Creek.[48] It appears Guernsey simply assumed that, since the Miami name for the St. Joseph River (of the Maumee) is *kóčiihsasiipi,* "bean river," Beanblossom Creek must have had the same name in Miami. But again, Guernsey's annoying lack of documentation for his work does not help in any way to settle this question. Second, Beanblossom Creek is identified on Hough's map as <Coshespaweset>.[49] Contrary to what McPherson suggests, this word is not Huron.[50] His opinion is based on having incorrectly taken the abbreviation "H." on Guernsey's map to mean "Huron," whereas it actually stands for "Hough." More important, the Huron language does not have the sound *p*, or any bilabial consonants for that matter. Yet it is difficult to tell what <Coshespaweset> really is. No doubt recorded by an English-speaking American, the term is quite twisted. It is not impossible that it represents a genuine Miami-Illinois language expression, where <Coshes-> stands for **kóčiihs-*, the Miami-Illinois "bean" initial—provided the -sh- of <Coshespaweset> is a miscopied original ch. In fact, good evidence for the name's being Miami-Illinois is the final segment, spelled -set, which could well be a miscopy of -sep for Miami-Illinois *-(i)siipi*, "river." This same copy error, committed by other English speakers, can be seen in chapters 4 and 11. Unfortunately, however, the middle -pawe- segment of <Coshespaweset> is not readily analyzable.

In sum, then, the presumed -set copy error as well as sh for apparent ch suggest not only that this particular hydronym does refer to "beans" but also that it passed through the hands of at least two scribes before coming to rest in its jumbled <Coshespaweset> form. Yet while <Coshespaweset> could represent the historical Miami-Illinois name for Beanblossom Creek, its complete etymology is opaque.[51]

The Eel River of southwest central Indiana takes its rise in two principal sources, one of which originates in south-central Boone County under the alias Big Walnut Creek. Skirting the northwest corner of Hendricks County, Big Walnut crosses Putnam County diagonally from northeast to southwest and then meets Mill Creek, which is the Eel River's other major source, in the southwestern part of that county. The name Eel River Township in Hendricks County, just west of Indianapolis, indicates that American pioneers originally knew Big Walnut Creek as the Eel River. For its part, Mill Creek begins in west-central Hendricks County and forms the border between Morgan and Putnam Counties. It then flows southwest into northwestern Owen County before turning northwest and joining Big Walnut Creek in southwestern Putnam County. United and now called the Eel River, these waters enter eastern Clay County, wind through most of that county, edge along southwestern Owen County, and eventually enter the White River in north-central Greene County. This long-winded description of the Eel River should tell us at least one thing: At around 120 miles in length it is one of Indiana's longest waterways.

Although it is possible, in fact likely, that the English hydronym "Eel River" derives from an earlier American Indian name, no historical recording of a Native American name for the Eel River seems to exist. The spelling <Shoamaque>, which, in my estimation, represents *šɔ˙x˙ame˙k˙w-í˙i-*, the initial element meaning "eel" of an incompletely transcribed Unami hydronym **šɔ˙x˙ame˙k˙w í˙i-sí˙p˙u*, signifying "eel-river," is found in the work of George Winter, an early-nineteenth-century English-born painter and chronicler of Indiana's historic Indians.[52] However, Winter's <Shoamaque> refers to the Eel River in *northeastern* Indiana. Even though he was quite familiar with the northern Eel, the painter never visited southern Indiana's Eel River.

In the spring of 1929, the State Conservation Commission gave the newly formed state park near Jasonville the name "Shakamak," which is an English spelling of the Southern Unami simplex noun *šɔ́˙x˙ame˙k˙w*, "eel." How the commission came up with this name as well as this spelling is unknown. But it is clear from the proceedings of the meeting in 1929 that the members of the commission, in their desire to have an American Indian name for the park, chose "Shakamak" thinking that this was what the local historic Kickapoo called the nearby Eel River. That was certainly not the case.[53] Indeed, there is no evidence for what the local Kickapoo called this stream—but they did not call it "Shakamak." The Kickapoo term for "eel" is *keneepikwa,* not "Shakamak."

7

The Northern Wabash Valley

Numerous rivers, creeks, and lakes help to create the Wabash River in its journey of nearly five hundred miles through Indiana. Many of these bodies of water either currently bear American Indian names or at least have historically documented ones. Surviving aboriginal place-names occur for the most part up the Wabash from Terre Haute, since Miami-Illinois speakers continued to live in the northern part of the state after the Americans took control of the Indiana area in the early 1800s. In contrast, the Miami-Illinois–speaking Piankashaw and Wea, living at or below the Vermillion River in the late 1700s and early 1800s, were among the first local indigenous groups forced out of Indiana to lands across the Mississippi. Consequently, very few Miami-Illinois language names for the southern Wabash tributaries made their way into the historical record. Down the river from Terre Haute, the oldest place-names tend to be French, vestiges of an array of French place-names that once lined the Wabash Valley.

After entering Indiana from its source in Mercer County in western Ohio, the Wabash soon receives the combined waters of the Little Wabash River and the Aboite River. Both of these streams were once important segments of the famous portage route that connected France, Québec, Montreal, and Detroit to the Indian villages and French posts on the Wabash and the Mississippi Rivers. The French did not see the Wabash River for the first time until the second decade of the eighteenth century, and they first came upon it by way of the Little Wabash and Aboite Rivers. (See chapter 5 for more on the early history of the headwaters of the Maumee.)

There are two excellent firsthand sources from the 1700s describing the portage that began at the second of two French forts, finished in 1752 and formerly located along the St. Joseph River in the vicinity of Lawson Park in present-day Fort Wayne, Indiana. One of these sources is a trader itinerary collected by the eighteenth-century Jesuit missionary Pierre Potier at Detroit and the other is the journal composed by Henry Hamilton, a British commandant at Vincennes during the American Revolution.[1] By studying the information in these two accounts, one can see that the portage from the second French fort began on the far side of the St. Joseph opposite the fort and then headed southwest overland until it met the Little Wabash River. The portage route then utilized the Little Wabash down to its confluence with the Aboite River, before continuing on down to the Wabash.[2] However, the reader should note that in the 1700s the Little Wabash was considered a tributary of the Aboite, rather than the other way around. Finally, thanks to Hamilton's journal we know that the portage bracketing the Little Wabash and the Aboite Rivers involved the arduous task of dragging and toting boats, canoes, trade goods, and gear for *miles,* at times down a rivulet under low-lying branches where snakes dangled, then through slow-moving waters dense with water lilies.[3] Nevertheless, the Little Wabash River, despite its name, could also be as broad as the upper Wabash itself or even the St. Joseph River at South Bend when the weather was wet.[4]

The earliest name applied by the Americans to the Little Wabash was "the Little River." This hydronym, which appeared cartographically as early as 1795, is a surviving direct translation of the original French name for the Little Wabash River, *la petite rivière.*[5] The Little Wabash River's Miami-Illinois language name was recorded by Dunn in the forms <Pawwḗkŏm-sēpe> and <Pawwíkamsípi> and translated to "standing still river" and "no current river."[6] His recordings represent Miami *pwaawikamisiipi,* "weak-water river," composed of the initial *pwaaw-,* "weak," the "water" medial *-ikam-,* the Miami-Illinois hydronymic "river" final *-isiip,* and the proximate inanimate noun marker *-i.*[7]

The Aboite River runs generally north to south in west-central Allen County, about nine miles west of the Miami's principal villages in the eighteenth century in what is now downtown Fort Wayne.[8] In historical times the Aboite traversed a marsh known to the French as *le Marais de fiatro* (Fiatro's Marsh, i.e., Filliatrault's ~ Filiatrault's Marsh).[9] It is not known why the marsh bore this French family name. Evidently a person named Filliatrault was identified with it in the 1700s for some reason.[10]

The Aboite River's modern name comes from the early French name for the stream, *la rivière à boîte,* "the river with mud." *Boîte,* commonly pronounced [bwɛt] in traditional North American French, and often written *bouette,* means "mud" (literally "little mud").[11] The French name seems to be related to the Miami-Illinois name for the creek, for in Miami-Illinois the Aboite River is known as both *neekawikami,* "sandwater," composed of the initial *neekaw-,* "sand," the "water" final *-(i)kam,* and the singular proximate inanimate gender marker *-i.* The stream is also known as *neekawisiipi,* "sand river," the components of which are the "sand" initial *neekaw-,* the hydronymic "river" final *-isiip,* and the inanimate gender marker *-i.* Both of these terms were recorded by Dunn: <Nakaúwíkamĭ> and <Năkŏwwēsḗpe> ~ <Năkŏwwēsḗpe>.[12] The "sand" of these names refers to the large beds of glacial drift sand present in the Aboite River watershed.

The combined waters of *pwaawikamisiipi* and *neekawikami* enter the Wabash near modern Huntington at a spot the eighteenth-century French called *la fourche de la Ouabaché* (the fork of the Wabash). English speakers know this site as the "Forks of the Wabash." The French place-name naturally arose from that moment in history when the French, portaging from the St. Mary's River, encountered the Wabash for the first time. For their part, the Miami know the Forks of the Wabash not for a hydrological reason but for a geological one. Their name for this place is *wiipičahkionki,* "in the flint land" or, in everyday English, "the flint place." This toponym means just what it says. The land at the Forks is both underlain and heavily strewn with Liston Creek chert, a locally important prehistoric lithic resource. This type of flint outcrops from the Forks on down the Wabash River to the vicinity of Peru.[13]

The lexical form of this Miami place-name is attested in the earliest records of the Miami-Illinois language. The Illinois-French dictionary from around the turn of the eighteenth century has it in the spelling <8ipitchaki8i>, translated *endroit ou il y a des pierres a fleches* (place where there are arrow stones).[14] <8ipitchaki8i> represents Miami-Illinois *wiipičahkiwi,* which is, formally speaking, an independent II verb signifying "it is flint land" and, functionally speaking, a deverbal noun signifying "flint-land."

Dunn wrote the Miami-Illinois name for the Forks of the Wabash in various ways: the antique spellings <Wepecháhkioong> ~ <Wḗpēcháhkioong> ~ <Wēpēcháhkióong(i)>, and his modernized <Wípitchákiúngi>. He translated the name to "place of flints."[15] This Miami-Illinois name for the Forks of the Wabash is composed of the "flint" initial *wiipič-,* the final *-ahk,* which signifies "land" and "country" in composite terms, followed by *-ionki,* a locative suffix meaning "at" or "in." Again, as with certain other Miami-Illinois toponyms, both Dunn's older spellings with -ioong(i) and his modernized spelling with -iúngi are typical English representations of Miami-Illinois *-ionki.* On the one hand, the lack of a final -i in three of his spellings is not surprising, since short vowels in final position in historic Miami-Illinois apparently were apt to devoice, they often escaped the notice of Europeans. On the other hand, the -g- of -(i)oong(i) and -(i)úngi in Dunn's and in transcriptions made by other people of Miami-Illinois *-(i)onki* is an example of good linguistic fieldwork. Orthographic "g" in these cases represents the systemic voicing of *k* to [g] in Miami-Illinois when *k* follows a nasalized syllable. Thus phonemic *-(i)onki* was pronounced [(i)úŋgi] ~ [(i)óŋgi].

The first major watercourse entering the Wabash downstream from *wiipičahkionki* is the Salamonie River. This stream rises from numerous sources in Jay County and flows in a northwesterly direction through Black, Wells, and Huntington Counties before entering the Wabash in east-central Wabash County. Today's spelling "Salamonie," reflecting its French heritage, represents a reduction of the actual Miami-Illinois place-name, which is *oonsaalamooni.* The word *oonsaalamooni* literally means "yellow ocher." Also known in English as limonite, yellow ocher, with chemical signature $FeO(OH)\cdot nH_2O$, is a mixture of hydrated iron oxide minerals. It is found near oxidized iron deposits or other ore deposits, as well as in sedimentary beds. Historically, yellow ocher was ground into a powder and used as a source of yellow paint. *oonsaalamooni* is composed of the initial *oonsaa-,* "yellow, brown," and *alamoon-,* which is the Miami-Illinois term for the mineral hematite (Fe_2O_3), otherwise known as red ocher and commonly glossed *vermillon* in historical French sources, followed by *-i,* the singular proximate inanimate noun suffix.

Notably, the historical record does not show "yellow ocher" as an English translation for recordings of the Miami-Illinois term *oonsaalamooni.* In fact, this Miami-Illinois word, aside from its appearance in translation as a French place-name that was not glossed, was not even recorded until around the turn of the twentieth century, at which time it was being used in Miami-Illinois only as the term for the bloodroot plant (*Sanguinaria canadensis*), the rhizomes of which are an important botanical source of a reddish juice producing a yellowish stain, also used by local historic Indians as paint. However, Goddard's discussion of yellow ocher suggests that Miami-Illinois *oonsaalamooni* as the name for the bloodroot plant is a secondary attribution based on this plant's virtue to produce a yellowish stain resembling yellow ocher's.[16]

As far as I can determine, the earliest surviving mention of the Salamonie River by name is found in a Wabash Valley itinerary from the mid-1700s by either Charles Chevalier or Charles Chaboillez. In fact, the French trader's <Salamani> is clearly a direct orthographic ancestor of the modern English language spelling of this river's name.[17] In the early 1900s, Dunn transcribed the Miami-Illinois name for the Salamonie River in the forms <ō^{n}sahlắmōnee> and <Onzalắmoni>.[18] These recordings represent *oonsaalamooni.* Although there is no recording of the Salamonie's Miami-Illinois name that includes a term for "river," it is safe to assume, by analogy, that the stream's full name was **oonsaalamooni siipiiwi,* "yellow ocher river" or "bloodroot river." In modern American English, Salamonie is pronounced [sǽləmòni].

Early English recordings of this hydronym, which reflect its French spelling origins, made their way from <Salamonie>, a form from the treaty with the Miami in 1818, to <Salimaniae> in 1826, <Salamonie> in 1827, <Saalimanie> in 1835, and <Salamania> in 1838. The 1835 form is particularly interesting from a linguistic point of view since the double -aa- spelling seems to reflect the actual long *aa* of the original Miami-Illinois term. A later attestation of this hydronym spelled <Salimony>, probably an adaptation of the recording that appears on the 1834 treaty between the Miami and the U.S. government, could well have become the established modern form of the river's name had it not been for the copious correspondence of Fort Wayne Indian agent John Tipton concerning local Indians. In his capacity as the most important local government official of his time, Tipton unintentionally saw to it that the French-based spelling that he used would prevail.[19]

A popular belief has grown up around the name for the Salamonie River—that it derives from the cognate Miami name of a famous Miami chief whom the French called le Gros (the Big One).[20] This notion is untenable, however, since the river's name is documented before Le Gros' time. *oonsaalamooni* appears to mean just what it says—that the banks of the Salamonie held either an important deposit of yellow ocher or a stunning abundance of bloodroot plants. Both items were important to the prehistoric and historic native peoples, and each certainly had the requisite cultural clout to inspire a place-name.[21]

Butternut Creek is the modern name for the Salamonie River's principal tributary. This stream begins in south-central Jay County and zigzags north to meet the Salamonie southwest of Portland. The fact that this relatively insignificant waterway has a Miami-Illinois name simply shows how almost every stream, large or small, used to have a Native American name. Nevertheless, *kiinošiši,* "butternut" (*Juglans cinerea*) is not the term used in Miami-Illinois when referring to this creek. "Butternut Creek" appears to be an American settler's invention.

The surviving American Indian name for this stream is first mentioned in the treaty between the Miami and the U.S. government in 1818, where it is spelled <Atchepongqwawe>. This same place-name appears a year later as <atcheponggawawee seepe> in the memoir of the local English-speaking pioneer Joseph S. Allen. In creating his own work on Indiana's native place-names, Dunn copied the antique English spelling <Atchepongqwawe> from the 1818 treaty. Later, however, during a conversation with *waapanahkikapwa,* he wrote the hydronym <ätchípangkwáwa>.[22] Dunn translated both of his spellings "snapping turtles eggs." However, only his second spelling can mean that. Indeed, Dunn's <ätchípangkwáwa> form, which is the exception among the spellings noted above, seems to be a *reformulation* by *waapanahkikapwa* of the original place-name. Finally, Guernsey's map has the 1818 treaty form <Atchepongquawe>, which he translated to simply "snapping turtle." In his bedeviling characteristic fashion of handling his material, Guernsey did not indicate where he got his translation.

The 1818 treaty form <Atchepongqwawe> and Allen's <atcheponggawawee seepe> must be considered authoritative spellings for this place-name. The final -e and -ee of <Atchepongquawe> and <atcheponggawawee>, respectively, clearly represent "alphabet E," the sound of "e" in the recited English alphabet, that is, phonetic [i]. Hence, these old historical forms represent *eečipaankwaawisiipi,* "snapping turtle egg river," composed of the "snapping turtle" initial *eečipaankw-,* the inanimate noun stem *waaw-,* "egg," the hydronymic "river" final *-isiip,* and the singular inanimate noun marker *-i.*[23] However, there is also a chance that <atcheponggawawee> of <atcheponggawawee seepe> could represent simply an initial allomorph of the "snapping turtle" initial, and that this term was folk etymologized by native speakers of Miami to "snapping turtle egg" because it resembled the latter expression. In any event, in light of the facts presented above, this Miami-Illinois place-name probably referred to the notion that in early historic times Butternut Creek was a prime snapping turtle nursery. Snapping turtles (*Chelydra serpentina*) prefer to live in slow-moving, or nonflowing, water.

The river town of Wabash was once the site of a well-known spring known as Treaty Springs or Paradise Springs to English speakers in the 1800s. The

Miami call this place *tahkinkamionki,* "at (the) cold water, at the spring," that is, a toponym composed of the initial *tahkin-,* "cold," the final *-(i)kam,* "water," and *-ionki,* a locative suffix meaning "at."[24] As a local place name, Dunn recorded *tahkinkamionki* in the forms <Tahkinggáhmēóongi>, which he glossed "cold water place" and "running water place." He later "modernized" his original spelling of this place-name to <Tákĭnggámĭungĭ>, which he translated to "cold (running) water place."[25]

After leaving *tahkinkamionki,* the next major stream that one encounters when going down the Wabash is the Mississinewa River. Like the Salamonie, this one-hundred-mile-long waterway forms in the country southeast of the Wabash, with its principal headwaters in Darke County in western Ohio. In Indiana, the Mississinewa flows west across the entire breadth of Randolph County, then eventually bends northwestward through Delaware and parts of Grant, Wabash, and Miami Counties before entering the Wabash River.

The early-nineteenth-century painter George Winter was one of the first English speakers in this area to record the Miami name for the Mississinewa, which in 1839 he wrote <Nanmatchessinawa>.[26] A few years after Winter recorded this name, Hough recorded the same hydronym in an equally antique English spelling: <Nemahchesinway>. Hough's -ay-, like Winter's -a, are examples of "alphabet A," an old English vernacular spelling that stands for phonetic [e], although in these particular cases -ay and -a actually represent mishearings by English speakers of Miami-Illinois *i.*[27] Dunn offers two slightly different forms for the Miami name of the Mississinewa River. The first, <nimatchissĭnewĭ sipiwĭ>, is a term given to him by the nineteenth-century Miami leader *šipaahkana.* The second is <Nämátcĭsĭnwĭ> ~ <Nämáhchissínwi>, which probably came from his Miami consultant *waapanahkikapwa.*[28] The term from *šipaahkana* represents Miami-Illinois *nimačihsinwi siipiiwi,* while the other two recordings by Dunn stand for the *neemačihsinwi,* that is, exhibiting unusual first-syllable ablaut. The words *nimačihsinwi* ~ *neemačihsinwi* are variant forms of the independent II verb meaning "it-downward-lies," that is, "it lies on an incline." Dunn's translation is "it lies on a slant."[29] This verb is composed of the initial *nimač-,* whose fundamental meaning is verticality,[30] the final *-ihsin,* meaning "lie," and *-wi,* the appropriate verbal suffix. This place-name refers to the Mississinewa's underlying geology, or as *waapanahkikapwa* put it, there is "much fall in the river," that is, the stream has a steep gradient.[31] Indeed, the Mississinewa falls on average 3.3 feet per mile, making it one of the swiftest rivers in Indiana.[32]

The place-name *nimačihsinwi* is one the French garbled almost from the very beginning, and that garbling was the very basis for what is now the modern English form of this name. Although I am confident this Miami-Illinois hydronym was recorded earlier by the French, the first time I have found it in the record is for 1748, in the French recording <Massissinoüi>.[33] It then crops up in 1762 as <Massissinoué>, a French language form of this place-name written down by Thomas Hutchins, a British lieutenant who could speak French and who collected the name firsthand along the Wabash River.[34] Clearly, the essential spelling of this place-name has scarcely changed since it was first recorded over two and a half centuries ago. Furthermore, the French pronunciation represented by <Massissinoüi> and <Massissinoué> survived relatively intact even into the twentieth century—*in English*—for Dunn stated that local Americans in his day, in the late 1800s and early 1900s, pronounced the river's name "Mássissínēway," which is phonetic [mæsIsÍniwe]. Importantly, this pronunciation has phonetic [a] in the first syllable and phonetic [e] in the last, both of which represent the corresponding sounds in Hutchins' French term.[35] In the twentieth century, the pronunciation, influenced by twentieth-century sound-symbol correspondences, came to be [mIsəsÍnəwɑ] ~ [mIsəsÍnəwə].

With the flood of English speakers into the Wabash Valley in the early 1800s, the Mississinewa River naturally figures prominently in early-nineteenth-century Miami history. Thus there are many recordings of this Miami-Illinois name from that time, including <Massasinewa> in a letter from Wabash Valley residents John Gibson and Francis Vigo to William Henry Harrison in 1805, <Mississiniway> by Harrison himself in 1805, <Mississinway> by Harrison's assistant Peter Jones in 1809, and <Mississineway> again by Harrison in 1810.[36] The year 1810 also saw the U.S. Indian agent and fur trader John Johnston write the term at least four different ways, *three in the same letter:* <Mississinaway>, and then <Massasinnway>, <Massissineway>, <Massasinneway>. The spelling <Mississinawa> is also present on the French-speaking American René Paul's maps of 1815 and 1816. In 1822, the geographer Jedidiah Morse wrote the name <Missasinua>.[37] In these recordings, we can see the persistence, especially in Johnston's work, of the *-ma-* of the original Miami-Illinois *nimačihsinwi*. However, we can also see the beginning of the Mi- spelling, apparently instigated by William Henry Harrison, and very likely premised on the spelling of well-known "Mississippi." Perhaps the most intriguing of the early historical recordings of this place-name comes from the quill of a *fluent speaker of Miami-Illinois,* William Wells, adopted son of the Eel River band Miami leader *mihšihkinaahkwa.* In his letter to Harrison on 20 August 1807, Wells wrote the river's name <Massacenwa>.[38] His spelling is curious evidence for at least what this particular speaker of Miami was calling the river in the early 1800s when he was using English.

Finally, a folk etymology, perhaps of Native American origin, grew out of the somewhat unusual place-name *nimačihsinwi.* Beckwith's writings reveal that "Mississinewa" had come to be analyzed as "missi ... great" and "assin ... stone."[39] Despite its lack of grammaticality, this folk etymology was probably convincing enough to many, given that the Mississenewa River *is* known for its huge and visually impressive rocks—argillaceous dolomitic siltstone and silty dolomite, calcareous in some places. These rock formations, long sacred to the Miami, are located between the city of Marion and the southwestern corner of Wabash County, and some are now under the waters of the Mississinewa reservoir.[40]

Canoeists floating down the Wabash through Miami County will suddenly come upon a two-mile-long stretch of water that is extraordinarily straight, flanked today by the town of Peru. This beeline stretch of the Wabash River is known in Miami-Illinois as *iihkipihsinonki,* which literally means "at straight-lie" or, in common English parlance, "the straight place." Dunn wrote this term <ikkēpissínnong> and <íkkĭpĭssĭ́nnung>.[41] Gatschet has <ikipissínungi> and <ikipisshinŭ́ngi>.[42] Both men glossed their terms "straight place." Underlying this place-name *iihkipihsinonki* is Miami-Illinois *iihkipihsin-,* "lie straight," an II verb comprised of the initial *iihkip-,* "straight," and the II final *-ihsin,* "lie."[43] Like *čeenkwihtanonki,* the Miami-Illinois name for Fall Creek discussed in chapter 6, *iihkipihsinonki* is intriguing from a grammatical point of view as it combines an II verb stem and a locative suffix in the form *-onki.*

The mouth of one of Indiana's three Pipe Creeks is located downstream on the Wabash from *iihkipihsinonki.* This particular Pipe Creek begins in western Grant County, meanders into the northwestern part of that county, and then heads northwest across Miami County to meet the Wabash in eastern Cass County. Dunn says Pipe Creek was known to the Miami as <Pwakána>,[44] a spelling which represents Miami-Illinois *(ah)pwaakana,* "pipe." However, there is no evidence available indicating how the term "river" or "creek" was expressed in the original native hydronym that Dunn recorded. Still, Gatschet was able to get the complete Miami-Illinois name for Pipe Creek which he recorded in the form <Pokanni kamí>. This spelling stands for *(ah)pwaakanikami,* "pipe-water," composed of the initial *(ah)pwaakan-*, "pipe," the "water" final *-(i)kam*, and the singular inanimate noun marker *-i*.[45]

Chevalier's or Chaboillez's Wabash River itinerary is the first document I am aware of that mentions Pipe Creek by name: *Riviere au Calumet*, which can literally mean "Pipes River," "River of the Pipe," or "River with the Pipe."[46] The *au* of this French place-name indicates that there is a logical connection between the river and the pipe, although it does not elucidate the specific nature of that connection. One thing is clear, however. Since this itinerary dates to the early to mid-1700s, this French place-name cannot refer to the Unami known in English as Captain Pipe (*hupɔ́·k·an*), who is discussed in chapter 6 in connection with the West Fork of the White River, also known as Pipe Creek. *Riviere au Calumet* was recorded in advance of Captain Pipe's arrival in the area. *Riviere au Calumet* could point to a place where, in the mists of early history, some local native people presented the French with a peace pipe.[47] However, Hutchins' map, based on his 1762 trek through Indiana, evinces the French hydronym *Riviere a Calumet* (Pipe's River),[48] where the colloquial possessive *a* (for *à*) and the lack of a definite article implies that the "pipe" in question is in fact a personal name. If this analysis is correct, the time period in which this name appears suggests that *Calumet* is the French translation of the Miami-Illinois name of a particular Miami-Illinois–speaking person of that era. This notion finds support in a number of ways. First, in Algonquian, "pipe" can be a personal name. Second, as we shall see in chapter 8, there are other French-recorded hydronyms, eponymous place-names, with a similar form, *including the use of the definite article*, that distinctly contain the names of Indian individuals. In other words, definite articles were definitely used by the French when translating native given names, as we see in La Demoiselle, La Tortue, and Le Baril, French names for three well-known Miami leaders of the mid-1700s. And third, the occurrence of the possessive noun form in the earliest English version of this place-name from 1796, "Pipes R."[49] If the "Calumet" of *Riviere a Calumet* does refer to a person, his association with this stream probably involved a winter village, as it would have been unlikely for a Native American family in the eighteenth century to live alone during the warm months of the year.

Historically, Pipe Creek also bore another American Indian hydronym, recorded by Hough in the form <Powlonsepewa>.[50] This spelling is a fascinating linguistic hybrid. The -sepewa segment of <Powlonsepewa> is the Miami-Illinois inanimate noun *siipiiwi*, "river." Since Europeans rarely recorded Miami-Illinois long vowels, the only significant difference between the historically recorded form of this "river" term and the phonemic one is the final vowel. Hough's final -a clearly represents ultimately phonemic *i*, just as in the case of the final a of Winter's <Nanmatchessinaw*a*> discussed above and in many other historic recordings appearing in this volume. The other part of <Powlonsepewa> is not Algonquian but French. In the historical English language sources, <Powlonswa>, for *palanswá*, represents the Miami pronunciation of the French name *François*, pronounced [frãswá] in French. In the case of this particular place-name, this personal name refers to François Godfroy, a famous Miami leader, born in March 1788, who in later life took up residence on Pipe Creek. Godfroy's name in Miami was written <Powlonswa> for a couple of reasons. First, the Miami-Illinois language does not have the sound *f*. Therefore, in pronouncing French words with *f*, historic Miami-Illinois speakers chose the closest sound in their language to replace it with, which was *p*.[51] Second, in the Miami-Illinois language spoken at least after 1790, the sound *r* was no longer in use. By that time this sound had shifted to *l*.[52]

Furthermore, the first vowel of <Powlonswa> is a linguistic curiosity. This -o- (actually phonemic *a*) represents a natural Miami-Illinois epenthesis, that is, the insertion of a vowel by Miami-Illinois speakers between the *p* and the *l* in order to facilitate the pronunciation of the consonant cluster [pl], which is not a possible sound combination in the Miami-Illinois language. And finally, <Powlonsepewa>, as written by Hough's engraver, is unusually and unexpectedly contracted. The reason for this is unclear. Hough could have misheard or miswritten an original **palanswá siipiiwi*, his engraver could have miscopied the place-name, or the Miami themselves could have reshaped the name in their language when they created this hydronym by creating an initial in the form **palans-*.

Dunn said the historic Miami called the southern tributary of Pipe Creek <Ahpắssyah> and <apḗssĭa>. Gatschet also recorded a toponym for this creek in the Wea subdialect of Miami-Illinois in the form of a locative noun: <Päđiukamíngi>.[53] While Dunn's spelling simply stands for Miami-Illinois *apeehsia*, "fawn" and is not, technically speaking, a place-name, Gatschet's recording is a bona fide place-name representing Miami-Illinois *apeehsiokaminki*, "at the fawn water." This term is composed of Old Miami-Illinois *apeehsiwa*, "fawn" (modern *apeehsia*), whence we get the *-o-* in this place-name, *-(i)kam*, the "water" final, and phonemic *-inki*, the conservative locative suffix meaning "at, on," realized as phonetic [-iŋgi]. This stream, which runs its entire course within Cass County, is not known in English as "Fawn Creek" but as Little Deer Creek. Consequently, the "Little Deer" of the English version of this hydronym could be a translation of Miami *apeehsia*, "fawn," or else the "Deer" by itself could be an oblique translation of Miami *apeehsia* at the same time that the qualifier "Little" could simply be an American artifice tacked on to the front of the place-name in order to distinguish this stream from its larger, neighboring stream, Deer Creek.

The Miami-Illinois language name for Little Deer Creek can only be an eponym. Virginia deer (*Odicoileus virginianus*) inhabited all the resource zones in historic Indiana and would therefore have been an inconceivable referent for a local native place-name. Simplex noun terms for mammals *common to all of the resource zones* do not appear in Miami-Illinois as names for rivers or streams unless the hydronyms are eponymous or ethnonymous in nature, that is, unless they refer to people whose personal names are mammal terms, or to tribe names that are mammal terms. In the case of Little Deer Creek, *apeehsia* could well refer to the same person whose name graces nearby Deer Creek, examined below.

The physical reality of the Eel River of northern Indiana begins its impressive journey of some 110 miles in a handful of sources in northwest Allen County, southern Noble County, and in Blue Creek, a stream formerly known in English as Blue Grass Creek. The Eel River then courses in a generally southwesterly direction to enter the Wabash downstream from Pipe Creek.[54] Blue Creek is historically important, as the celebrated Miami war chief *mihšihkinaahkwa* (Little Turtle), a child of the third generation of Miami born in this area after the Iroquois wars, was born near its headwaters in 1752. Several important historic Miami villages were located on the banks of the Eel River in the eighteenth century. The historical reality of the Eel River comes into view on Franquelin's map of 1684 and on Minet's from the following year.[55] In fact, Franquelin's chart from 1687 indicates a portage from the Eel River's headwaters to those of the Elkhart River. As noted previously, Franquelin and Minet used the French explorer René de La Salle's geographical information to draw their maps, and in both cases the Eel River remains nameless. This fact is not at all surprising since La Salle never saw the Wabash. Chaboillez's or Chevalier's Wabash itinerary from the early to mid-1700s seems to be the oldest extant document that mentions the name of this stream: *La R. à l'anguille*.[56] This French hydronym can be translated "the River with the Eel(s)" or "the Eel's River."

The Miami-Illinois name for the Eel River, which is the basis for its French name, is premised on the term *kineepikwameekwa*, "American eel" (*Anguilla rostrata*). This term consists of the "snake" initial *kineepikw-*, the "fish" final *-ameekw*, and *-a*, the singular proximate animate gender marker.[57] When combined, these terms form the Miami-Illinois word for "eel," *kineepikwameekwa*, which literally means "snakefish." The Miami-Illinois name for the Eel River refers to the stream's former abundance of American eels during their so-called yellow phase. Dunn wrote <Kēnăpēkwōmä́kwa> and <Kinapíkwomäkwa> as the Miami name for the Eel River, and <kinäpíkwamä́kwa> as the name for the animal itself. Gatschet made a linguistically excellent recording of the river's complete name with his <Kineepikomeekwa siipiiwi>, representing phonemic *kineepikomeekwa siipiiwi*. The front end of this stream's Miami-Illinois name also appeared as early as 1819 in the slightly garbled form <Kenpecomaqua>, which for the times is not a bad rendition of this place-name by an English-speaking recorder.[58] It should be noted that *kineepikwameekwaki*, "Eels," an ethnonym of unknown antiquity, is a name for a historic band of Miami that lived on this river as well as at Thorntown.

Beckwith says the Eel River was also known in Miami-Illinois as <Kinapeekuoh Sepe>.[59] This spelling stands for *kineepikwasiipi*, "snake-river." Since the Illinois historian obtained this place-name from the longtime Wabash Valley resident Mary Ann Baptiste, there is reason to believe that Beckwith's designation could represent an authentic Klammerform place-name, a kind of hypocoristic version of the original name—something on the order of a nickname—where the term *kineepikwa*, "snake" was used and understood to represent *kineepikwameekwa*, "eel" (i.e., "snake-fish"). Either that was the case, or the Eel River's name in Miami may have simply confused some speakers of Miami-Illinois, since the native hydronym possesses an inherent potential for being confused. Yet another explanation for *kineepikwasiipi* would be that some people, like Mary Ann (Dagenais) Baptiste, who lived on the Wabash between 1817 and 1848 with her first husband, the Wea leader and native Miami-Illinois speaker Noël Dagenais, simply knew the Eel River as *kineepikwasiipi*.

A Delaware language name for the Eel River is also attested historically. The English painter George Winter, traveling through Indiana in the late 1830s, wrote down a name for this stream in the form <Shoamaque>. Winter's *spelling* is noteworthy for two reasons. First, he got the initial vowel of this term correct. Second, his form demonstrates the difficulty that historic English speakers experienced in attempting to write the Delaware fricative *x*. In fact, in his case, Winter did not even try. (Zeisberger's Germanic <Scháchamēk> accomplishes this function with its second -ch-.)[60] Chronologically speaking, Winter's recording is an unusual one in that most of the Delaware Indians had left Indiana by 1818 to 1820. However, the place-name somehow managed to survive. In my estimation, the final -e of <Shoamaque> is an "alphabet E." Thus <Shoamaque> represents the initial component meaning "eel" in the form *šɔ·x·ame·k·w í·i- of a Southern Unami hydronym in the form *šɔ·x·ame·k·w í·i-sí·p·u, "eel river," literally "slippery-fish river."[61] For additional information on this place-name, see chapter 9's discussion of the Eel River in southern Indiana.

The historic Miami and Wea used the term *saakiiweeki* to designate the place where the Eel River empties into the Wabash, now the site of the city of Logansport. Gatschet recorded this place-name from *wiikapimiša* in the form <Sakiwéki>, and specifically in the Wea subdialect form <đākiwäki>, glossing the latter "A town called Eel River." Dunn later recorded the same place-name as <sákiwäk> and <sákĭwäkĭ>. As a purely lexical item, this term is also found in the dictionary composed by the early-eighteenth-century Jesuit missionary Jean-Baptiste Le Boullenger, who spelled it <saki8eki>. Gatschet also recorded the word in the forms <sākiwäki> and <sakiwéki>.[62] All of these spellings stand for Miami-Illinois *saakiiweeki.* Although "fork (of a river)" is the traditional translation of this term, this is a somewhat free translation. The term *saakiiweeki* is in truth a conjunct II verb meaning "it is the outlet (of the river)." Le Boullenger also recorded a related locative noun in the form <saki8ei8nghi>, representing *saakiiweeyonki*, "at the outlet," which is phonetic [saakiiweeyúŋgi]. The Jesuit missionary also got a related etymon <saki8a8iki>, for *saakiiwaawiki*, to which he added the gloss *l'endroit ou elle se partage la fourche* (the place where the fork divides).[63] Additional details on these terms' morphologies can be found in chapter 1's discussion of a related Miami-Illinois name for the St. Joseph River. What is curious about the Miami name for the forks of the Eel River is its generic character—the expression *saakiiweeki* can apply to the outlet of *any stream*. Therefore, the use of this term to designate *in particular* the mouth of the Eel River appears to underscore the significance of the outlet of the Eel River for the historic Miami-speaking peoples.

The English-American painter George Winter identified a little creek west of Logansport by the name <Kchemanitousepewah>. He was referring to a tiny, unnamed stream that empties into the Wabash opposite the little islands just north of Clinton township, the little creek that briefly parallels Cass County road 350 West. Winter translated his recording "Big Snake Creek." His spelling represents Potawatomi **gčə-mnədowzibiwe* ~ **gčə-mnədo-zibiwe*, "big spirit creek, big snake creek." The first phonemic form is composed of the initial *gčə-*, "big," *mnədo*, "spirit, snake," the noun + noun connector *-w-* and *zibiwe*, "creek"; the second is composed of the initial *gčə-*, "big," *mnədo*, "spirit, snake," and the inanimate noun *zibiwe*, "creek."[64] Even though I could not find a name for this little stream, it obviously made a great impression on local historic Potawatomi, judging from its Potawatomi name. Also, **gčə-mnədowzibiwe* ~ **gčə-mnədo-zibiwe* may be connected to the Algonquian spirit known as the Underwater Panther, since the Great Serpent is one of the figures constellated within the archetype of the Underwater Panther. The reader is referred to the discussion of Wildcat Creek below as well as to that of the Wabash River in chapter 2 for more on the Underwater Panther's connection with the Wabash.

The many headwaters of Rock Creek, another Wabash tributary, are located in southeast Carroll County. In collecting these sources the stream meanders basically west to meet the Wabash in northern Carroll County. Gatschet seems to have been the only person who recorded a native name for Rock Creek, which he wrote <ashipá:k8-sa:núngi>.[65] This spelling contains the Miami-Illinois animate noun *aašipehkw-*, "rock face, cliff," a term that refers in particular to rock faces that have or could have water falling down them. Notably, the base of these geological formations is a common abode of the Underwater Panther.

Gatschet's <ashipá:k8-sa:núngi> is phonemic *aašipehkwihsinonki*,[66] literally "at the rock-cliff-lie," or in common English parlance, "where the rock cliff lies," or simply "where the rock cliff is." It is composed of the "cliff" initial *aašipehkw-*, the II final *-ihsin*, "lie," and *-onki*, the locative suffix. According to Gatschet's recording, as in the case of <Tchínk8sanwi> discussed in chapter 6, <ashipá:k8-sa:núngi> evinces a contraction of phonemic *aašipehkwihsinonki* to phonetic [aašipehkohsinoŋgi] in the dialect or idiolect of the person from whom he got the name.[67]

Today the name Deer Creek is applied to seven Indiana waterways, at least. Although the names of all of these streams could be of American Indian origin, only two of them have certified native credentials. One of these is Little Deer Creek, discussed above; the other is a Wabash tributary that rises in both northeastern Howard County and southwestern Miami County. The latter stream flows almost directly west across the bottom of Cass County and then through the heart of Carroll County to join the Wabash below the Eel River–Wabash confluence a little south of the town of Delphi. Indiana historian Jacob Dunn said the historic Miami called Deer Creek <Passeanong>.[68] Although the meaning of this recording is transparent, <Passeanong> is not an actual recording made by Dunn. The idiosyncratic nature of this spelling reveals that Dunn had to have lifted it from an earlier source. Indeed, he explicitly states he found the term in "various treaties." Gatschet also attested the same place-name with his <pässiungi> spelling,[69] even though his is a recording of a place-name created by Miami-Illinois speakers after their exile west of the Mississippi and refers to a creek in Oklahoma. In any event, both <Passeanong> and <pässiungi> represent Miami-Illinois *apeehsionki,* "at the fawn" or, in everyday English, "the fawn's place," which is composed of the "fawn" initial and *-ionki,* the locative suffix.[70] In Gatschet's and Dunn's spellings the initial unstressed *a-* of *apeehsionki* naturally deletes, giving phonetic [pѐehsiúŋgi].

In Dunn's version of this toponym, orthographic -ea-, intended to represent the vowel sound in the English verb "eat," stands for the *i* of the original Miami word. Although he was not a linguist, Dunn never transcribed Algonquian *i* in such a prosaic, traditional, and obtuse manner as -ea-. Hence, the spelling <Passeanong>, obviously created by an English speaker, belies its own relative antiquity, dating it to the early to mid-nineteenth century. Furthermore, Gatschet's recording demonstrates that the first "n" of Dunn's <Passeanong> is a miscopied "o" of what would have been originally *Passeaoong. Dunn himself may have realized this "n" was an anomaly for he added a grammatical clarification to his brief discussion of this place-name—and such observations are practically nonexistent in his published works.[71]

Although this Miami-Illinois place-name is clearly eponymous, it is not known who it refers to. Indeed, the knowledge of the existence of some local eighteenth-century Indian leaders survives only in the occasional place-name, and Deer Creek is a case in point. The Indiana place-name *apeehsionki* could derive from the personal name of a Miami man known in history as <Obassea>, that is, *apeehsia,* "Fawn," whom Hopkins mentioned in his 1804 "Mission to the Indians at Fort Wayne."[72] Hopkins' English-based spelling <Obassea> represents essentially the same term for "fawn" that is present in Dunn's <*Passea*nong>. In <Obassea>, the initial O- is a vernacular spelling of initial unstressed Miami [ɑ]. As noted in discussing Little Deer Creek above, this vowel dropped in late historic

Miami-Illinois, thus producing the p-initial recordings seen here. But by no means is this erroneous O- unexpected. A similar mistake took form in <Ongwasakwa>, Dunn's spelling of the initial element of the Miami-Illinois name for the East Fork of the White River, which is in truth *aankwaahsakwa*, "driftwood." In this case, Dunn wrote O- for initial long [ɑɑ]. Finally, the -b- of <Obassea> seems to be a mishearing by an English-speaking recorder of [b] for actual Miami-Illinois unaspirated *p*.

Hough's map has a different name for Deer Creek—<Kewawasipi>.[73] As written, this place-name is nonsense. Although it is impossible to discern with complete confidence what the original transcriber intended by this garbled spelling, <Kewawasipi> seems to represent a Miami-Illinois eponymous place-name in the form *(ah)kiwanasiipi*, "his-Beak-river/his-Nose-river." This hydronym would be composed of *a*-, the third person possessive prefix, *-hkiwan*, the "beak/nose" dependent noun, *-isiip*, the hydronymic "river" final, and *-a*, the proximate animate noun marker indicating this *ahkiwan*- is a personal name. Here the -e- of <Kewawa> would be an "alphabet E" representing the sound *i*. The second handwritten -w- would be a miscopied "n", which is a very common copy error.

If the foregoing analysis is correct, *(ah)kiwanasiipi* would be an eponymous hydronym that likely refers to the historical Potawatomi figure whose name in Miami-Illinois is typically spelled Kewanna, from whom a Fulton County town took its own name. Working in favor of this hypothesis is the fact that Kewanna, who was a supporter of the Shawnee leader Tecumseh, was known to have resided in the central Wabash drainage in the early 1800s. In fact, it is known that some late historic Potawatomi were living as far south as the Indianapolis area.[74] Thus, if this reconstruction of the garbled <Kewawasipi> is correct, and if this is indeed a Miami-Illinois language place-name deriving from Kewanna's name, it would date to sometime after the turn of the nineteenth century.

The next native-named watercourse whose mouth is located downstream on the Wabash below Deer Creek is the Tippecanoe River.[75] One of the primary sources of this important Indiana waterway is Tippecanoe Lake located in eastern Kosciusko County, far north of the Wabash in the glacial lake country of northern Indiana. Although Hough noted a putative native name for Tippecanoe Lake, which he wrote <Misquabuck>, it is not known if the historic Indians themselves used this term in referring to this body of water.[76] <Misquabuck>, a recording done by an English speaker, represents Potawatomi "copper," literally "red metal," composed of the initial *mskw*-, "red" and the "metal" final *-abək*. In the case of this historical recording, the name does not refer to metallic copper but rather to a nineteenth-century Potawatomi leader, whose name can be found in the 1832 treaty between the Potawatomi and the United States. Tipton also mentioned this man later, noting at the time that he was living near present-day Oswego in Kosciusko County during the early 1800s and that he died in Indiana around 1837. In fact, the English painter George Winter, mentioned above, met *mskwabək* and painted a picture of him, which has survived.[77]

After forming at Tippecanoe Lake, and long before its lengthy and historically significant waters come into view along the north bank of the Wabash, the Tippecanoe River receives streams that bear native names, one of which is Chippewanuk Creek. This waterway has its ultimate source in Rock Lake, which forms the border between Kosciusko and Fulton Counties. Chippewanuk Creek then flows for some fifteen miles in a northwesterly direction through a small portion of southwest Kosciusko County before crossing the northeast side of Fulton County and meeting the Tippecanoe River a few miles north of Lake Manitou.

A Native American name for Chippewanuk Creek is present in Dunn's work in the forms <Chipwahnŭ́k> and <Tcĭ́pwanuk>.[78] Even though this place-name often appears with the translation "Chippewa Creek," it has nothing to do with the Chippewa, or Ojibwa. "Chippewanuk" stands for Potawatomi *ǰibəywanəg*, "at the ghost hole, at the corpse hole, at the grave." The term can be parsed *ǰibəy*, "ghost, corpse," *wan*, "hole" and *-əg*, the locative suffix meaning "in, at." What the referent of this place-name might be has not been determined, aside from the possibility that there is an old Potawatomi cemetery located somewhere along this creek.

Another source of the Tippecanoe River is Lake Manitou. This English hydronym appears so early in the 1800s that its antiquity implies that it derives from an original, unattested Native American hydronym, presumably Potawatomi, in the form **mnədownbəs* ~ **mnədo-nbəs*, "spirit lake, snake lake."[79] The first term would be composed of *mnədo*, "spirit, snake," the noun + noun connector *-w-*, and *nbəs*, "lake"; the second would be *mnədo*, "spirit, snake," plus *nbəs*, "lake." (See the discussion of the Ojibwa name for the Maumee River in chapter 5 and the accompanying note 59 for ideas concerning the use of the noun + noun connector in Potawatomi.) Dunn was of the opinion that "Manitou" in this lake's name referred to the deity known as the Underwater Panther that lives in its depths. In Potawatomi, this divinity is known as *mšəbži*, "great cat."[80]

Another important tributary of the Tippecanoe River, which has been known variously as Big Monon Creek and Metamonong Creek, begins its journey in extreme southwestern Starke County and flows south through Pulaski County to meet the Tippecanoe River in north-central White County. The first historical occurrence of an American Indian name for this stream that I have found, in the form <Mtomonong>, appears in a letter by John Tipton to Superintendent of Indian Affairs Lewis Cass dated October 19, 1827. The place-name is also common in Tipton's subsequent correspondence in the form <Metomonoung>, as in his letter of December 2, 1827, to Edward McCartney, a local trader. The same place-name crops up again in a Tipton abstract from September 1, 1828, detailing local trading licenses, where this time it is spelled <Mettomonong>. Cass himself, in mentioning the establishment of a trading post at the fork of the Tippecanoe River and Big Monon Creek in his letter to Tipton dated January 15, 1828, wrote this place-name <Motomonong>.[81] The historically famous fork of the Tippecanoe and Big Monon Creek, known to the early French as *la fourche de Tipiconneau*,[82] was the location of a short-lived early American trading post in the early 1800s.

A curious and long-running tradition has grown up around the sequence of the letters M-o-n-o-n. At least by the 1880s, Americans were informally calling the Chicago, New Albany, and Louisville Rail Road Company the "Monon." The explanation for why they did so is elusive, but the story goes that since the word "monon" meant "carry" in Potawatomi, and these trains carried passengers and cargo up and down what was once Potawatomi territory, then "Monon" was the "perfect" name for the railroad. However, two mistakes occurred somewhere down this line of thinking. First, "monon" is not a Potawatomi word. Second, it does not signify "carry" either in Potawatomi or in any local Native American language. When I discovered that Big Monon Creek's earliest recorded English language name was "Old Woman's River," the Kickapoo term *metemooha*, "old woman" came to mind as a possible origin of "Metamonong," as there are obvious similarities between the Kickapoo term and this historical spelling as well as the historical spellings noted above.[83] In addition, women leaders were not alien to the historic Kickapoo or, in fact, to other historic native cultures in what is now Indiana or Illinois.[84] Therefore, a place-name created for an important woman's village would not be out of the question. Importantly, the Kickapoo lived in various locations in west-central Indiana in the 1700s in the vicinity of Big Monon Creek.[85] That having been said, the Kickapoo term "old woman" in the form of the locative noun *metemooheki*, meaning literally "at the old woman" (i.e., "the old woman' s place"), which would be the expected grammatical form in Kickapoo for such a place-name, does not match the historical recordings of the native name for Big Monon Creek noted above in a convincing enough manner to allow one to feel secure that *metemooheki* is the source of "Monon"—at least its direct source.

The timing of the recording of the historical native name for Monon Creek actually indicates that it is probably from the Potawatomi. This notion is also supported by the -o(u)ng endings for the Potawatomi locative noun suffix *-əg* following stems ending in *n* found in recordings of Potawatomi place-names just as we find in these recordings for Big Monon Creek. (For example, see the Potawatomi name for the Tippecanoe River below.) Whether this apparent nasalization was because of a mishearing by English-speaking recorders or of an assimilation of the nasal consonant of an *n* in the preceding stem to the locative suffix in the Potawatomi dialect that was recorded has not been determined. In any event, the historical spellings of Big Monon Creek's name seem to point to Old Potawatomi **mdamənəg*, "at the corn," modern Potawatomi *mdamnəg*. However, unless *mdamnəg* as a place-name could be justified by being a location where the historic Potawatomi gathered to trade their corn with the Americans in the early nineteenth century, "at the corn" has the feel of a folk etymology. In fact, it is my opinion that the historical spellings penned by Tipton and others could represent a hybrid term. In other words, "Monon" does in fact appear to derive from Kickapoo *metemooheki*, "at the old woman," but in an *indirect* way. When the Potawatomi moved into the area, they could have borrowed an already existing Kickapoo place-name and reformulated it into Potawatomi by way of paronomasia. In other words, it seems that the Potawatomi borrowed the *sound* of the original Kickapoo place-name meaning "at the old woman," added their own Potawatomi locative suffix, and ended up with a new place-name that meant, incongruously, "at the corn." As the reader can see elsewhere in this volume, the Potawatomi are known to have borrowed local place-names from other native groups previously established in the areas that the Potawatomi moved into.

The Tippecanoe River is a grand watercourse with many far-flung sources, not only in Tippecanoe Lake and Rock Lake, but also in numerous streams in southeastern Starke County, southeastern Marshall County, northwestern Miami County and especially Fulton County. All of these waters eventually gather in Fulton County before flowing in a northwesterly direction into northeastern Pulaski County. The Tippecanoe River then descends the length of that county, as well as that of White and most of Carroll Counties, before finally joining the Wabash in northeastern Tippecanoe County after a journey of nearly 170 miles. The British lieutenant Thomas Hutchins noted on the map he created from data compiled during his local travels in 1762 that the river was 100 yards wide at its mouth.[86] The Tippecanoe seems to have made its historical debut on Franquelin's map in 1684.[87] Although the French had not yet seen this river by even 1712, Franquelin's depiction of it does imply they had at least gotten wind of its existence. And well they should have, since the Tippecanoe was an important north-south thoroughfare in north-central Indiana, a "highway," as it were, that was very popular with historical Miami-Illinois speakers, and later with French traders. The Tippecanoe River was in fact a connective link between the St. Joseph River and the Kankakee River in the north and the Wabash River to the south.

The English language place-name "Tippecanoe" is a shortened form of an Algonquian name for a species of carp known in English as the buffalo fish. As noted in the introduction, *Ictiobus cyprinellus* is the scientific name of the big-mouth buffalo fish and *Ictiobus bubalus* that of the small-mouth buffalo fish. The attested variants phonemic *kiteepihkwana* ~ *kiteepihkwanwa* ~ *kiteepihkonwa*, a term that is not a literal translation of English "buffalo fish," represent the Miami-Illinois name for these carp.[88] The Miami-Illinois etymon is apparently neither reducible nor analyzable.

In Indiana, the earliest albeit most twisted recording of a Miami-Illinois place-name meaning "buffalo fish" comes from the French in the form <Atihipi-Catouy>.[89] This place-name marks one of the first known historical locations of the Miami in Indiana after they ventured southeastward out of the *refugia* where they had spent over half of the seventeenth century during the Iroquois wars. In this case, however, <Atihipi-Catouy> does not refer to the Tippecanoe River or even today's Tippecanoe Lake, but to a body of water whose Miami-Illinois name was translated by the early French as *Lac tipiconeau* (buffalo fish lake).[90] The reader can turn to chapter 4 for a discussion of this lake and its native name.

The Wabash Valley French traders Chaboillez's or Chevalier's recording <Tipiconnoa> from sometime after 1732 is the first recording of a Native American name for the Tippecanoe River that I am aware of.[91] This early spelling already demonstrates the elusive nature of the actual initial *ki-* of this river's Miami-Illinois language name insofar as the ears of Europeans were concerned, which is a fact that would eventually determine the modern spelling "Tippecanoe." Nevertheless, the form <Quitepiconnae>, recorded by the French-speaking U.S. emissary Antoine Gamelin in 1790, as well as <Quetepiconnuais>, written in the same year by the American Arthur St. Clair, then governor of the Northwest Territory, are also eighteenth-century recordings of this same hydronym that did succeed in catching its initial consonant and short vowel.[92] Even so, William Henry Harrison, like Chevalier/Chaboillez, did not get the initial *ki-* when he wrote <Tepaconoe> in his letter to the secretary of war on June 14, 1810.[93] In fact, the general's spelling of this place-name, just as in the case of the Mississinewa River discussed above, seems to indicate that he was insensitive to the sounds of the languages of the native peoples he was dealing with. But just as with "Mississinewa," his spelling for the Tippecanoe River's Miami-Illinois name appears to have set the stage for the establishment of this place-name's modern English form. Harrison's <Tepaconoe> no doubt led to the <Tippicanoe> spelling by his junior officer and important successor John Tipton seen on the latter's map from 1824.[94] Indeed, Tipton's spelling is, for all intents and purposes, the modern spelling.

Even so, <Ktepicanoe> is the form of this river's name penned by the surveyor and mapmaker René Paul in 1815.[95] His recording is mentioned here because it exhibits syncope in the initial syllable, a fact that supports the notion that the initial vowel of the Miami-Illinois term was short. In Miami-Illinois, short unstressed vowels in odd-numbered syllables are naturally deleted, a process known in linguistics as vowel syncope.

Further support for the reconstructed vowel lengths of *kiteepihkwana* is found in <Ketắpkwon>, Jacob Dunn's Miami version of this place-name.[96] His spelling does not show *i* between the *p* and *k*, making it an example of a historical recording of naturally occurring syncope in a Miami-Illinois term. In other words, this spelling provides support for the vowel length—short *i* instead of long *ii*—since long vowels do not undergo syncope.

Understandably, since the Tippecanoe River was very important to the historical Potawatomi, the name for this stream is also attested in their language. Dunn, citing early-nineteenth-century Baptist minister Isaac McCoy, wrote the Potawatomi name for the Tippecanoe River as <Kĕtắpekwŏn>, a spelling Dunn later modernized to <Kitắpĭkŏn>.[97] Unfortunately, the term for "buffalo fish" is no longer attested for Potawatomi, and no cognates appear to have survived in other Algonquian languages. Thus, the exact phonological shape for this fish name in Old Potawatomi is uncertain. But, if McCoy's Potawatomi transcription is *generally* reliable, the word may have been early on **kətepik(w)ən.*

The Tippecanoe River no doubt received its name from the remarkable abundance of carp in its slow-moving, relatively shallow waters. Indeed, Chevalier or Chaboillez noted explicitly that this species of fish was the origin of this river's name. Dunn's unpublished notes also reveal that early-nineteenth-century American settlers marveled at the quantities of buffalo fish that would clog the millraces of the Tippecanoe River.[98]

It is a well-known historical fact that the land where the Tippecanoe and Wabash Rivers meet figured prominently in the history of this area. This site first came into the historical limelight in the very early eighteenth century with the arrival, noted above, of Miami-Illinois speakers from lands located northwest of present-day Indiana where they had lived as war refugees during the Algonquian diaspora that dragged on throughout the second half of the seventeenth century. The Tippecanoe-Wabash confluence area again attained preeminence in the early 1800s, when it became the home of the Shawnee Prophet *teenhskwaatawe*, the brother of *tkamhse*, whose names are commonly spelled Tenskwatawa and Tecumseh. John Tipton identified the remnants of the Indian settlement known in English as Prophetstown during his survey of the islands of the Wabash River in March of 1828. He located the site three miles below the Wabash-Tippecanoe confluence.[99] Dunn wrote <Kitäpīkŏnnong> and <Kētắpēkŏnnūng> for the Potawatomi name of the area in and around the confluence of the Tippecanoe and Wabash Rivers.[100] These forms are, again, unusual, with the nasalized locative suffix in the form -ong and -ūng for modern Potawatomi. In fact, Dunn may have reconstructed <Kitäpīkŏnnong> and <Kētắpēkŏnnūng> simply on the basis of Isaac McCoy's spelling of the Old Potawatomi name for the buffalo fish.

Now, a curious historical spelling of this place-name in the form <Kithtippecanunk> is commonly seen in history books. This spelling is related to an earlier variant, <Kathipacanunk>, which appeared on Abraham Bradley's map in 1804.[101] Both <Kithtippecanunk> and <Kathipacanunk> are unusual spellings in that they fail to line up well, phonologically speaking, with *any* of the expected forms of this term in the several Algonquian languages spoken by the compatriots of *teenhskwaatawe* and *tkamhse*. However, through the process of elimination, <Kithtippecanunk> seems to be simply a poorly written representation of the Miami-Illinois language name for this site. Although unattested, the Miami-Illinois term would be **kiteepihkwanonki* ~ **kiteepih-*

kononki, "at the buffalo fish (river)" or, in everyday English, "the buffalo fish place," composed of *kiteepihkwan-/kiteepihkon-*, the "buffalo fish" initial, and the locative suffix meaning "at" in the form *-onki*.

Wildcat Creek enters the Wabash River above Lafayette after following an impressively serpentine course from its origin more than seventy-five miles to the east. This stream originates from multiple sources in Tipton, Howard, and western Grant Counties, traverses the breadth of Howard and Carroll Counties, and enters the Wabash River in Tipton County. The mouth of the Wildcat is located approximately halfway between the mouth of the Tippecanoe River and the Wea village known in French as *les Ouiatanons*, discussed in chapter 8. A fate similar to that of the Elkhart River befell Wildcat Creek. American settlers soon "cleaned up" the accurate early English place-name "Wildcat Paunch Creek," a translation of the original Miami-Illinois hydronym, transforming it to the less graphic and in fact ambiguous "Wildcat Creek."[102] The Miami-Illinois name for Wildcat Creek derives from Miami-Illinois *pinšiwa-amootayi*. The term *pinšiwa* signifies "bobcat" (*Lynx rufus*) and *amootayi* means "its stomach, its pouch," from *a-*, "his/her/its," *mootay-* the "stomach, pouch" dependent noun, and *-i* the inanimate noun suffix. Dunn gives three spellings for this place-name: <pizháywahmoti>, <Pinjā́wahmṓtai>, and <P̆injíwamótai>. Gatschet wrote it <Pižiwa mutáyi>, while Hough offers the slightly garbled <Peshewamotia>.[103]

Contrary to what many have asserted, Wildcat Creek was not named for the famous Miami leader Jean-Baptiste Richardville, born in 1761 and reared near the headwaters of the Maumee. It is true that after living on the Salamonie River, Richardville, whose Miami-Illinois name was *pinšiwa*, did settle on the banks of Wildcat Creek, at the age of thirty-five.[104] But while many have speculated that local Miami-Illinois speakers created this place-name to mark Richardville's arrival in the Wildcat Creek area, the place-name actually predates him. The Jesuit missionary Pierre Potier at Detroit, who, as noted, preserved Chaboillez's/Chevalier's Wabash River itinerary for posterity and who was one of the few folks to record this hydronym, in French, in the eighteenth century, died in 1781. But Richardville, who was born in 1761, did not move to Wildcat Creek until 1795. Since the French version of this place-name, *la panse au Pichou* (the belly of the Bobcat),[105] was already established by the early to mid-1700s, the "bobcat" in question could therefore not refer to Richardville.

However, we now have the precise referent for *pinšiwa-amootayi*, which is indicated explicitly in Chevalier's or Chaboillez's itinerary. The French trader says that *Panse au pichou* was originally the name of the *cove* located at the mouth of Wildcat Creek, not the name for Wildcat Creek itself. In fact, he only mentions the creek as an afterthought.[106] Of course, *pinšiwa-amootayi* does not mean that this cove on the Wabash River was known for bobcats. The *pinšiwa* of this hydronym refers to the Algonquian deity known in English as the Underwater Cat or the Underwater Panther. In Miami-Illinois, it has several names: *mihšipinšiwa,* "great bobcat," *araamipinšia,* "the under-bobcat," *ariimipinšia,* "the within-bobcat," *akimarenia,* "chief-man," *waapipinšia,* "white cat," and *wiihkweepinšia,* whose meaning is unknown but which could be a Klammerform for **wiihkweekamiwipišia,* "cove cat."[107] Because of its association with the Underwater Panther, this Wabash Valley landmark known as *pinšiwa-amootayi* must have been a well-known location to the historical native peoples.

8

The Southern Wabash Valley

Throughout the 1700s, several Native American groups lived in western Indiana, including, importantly, Kickapoo and Mascouten. However, the Miami-speaking Wea and Piankashaw were by far the predominant human presence in this area during the eighteenth century.

The ethnonym Piankashaw is an English language spelling of Miami-Illinois *peeyankihšia,* "torn-ears person," from *peeyank-,* "tear," *-ehši,* the dependent noun meaning "ear," and *-a* the proximate animate singular noun gender marker. The Piankashaw, more numerous in 1700 than the Crane band Miami (*čečaahkwaki*) or the Wea, were according to the French a subgroup of the Wea.[1] By the second decade of the eighteenth century, the Piankashaw were living in the middle and lower Wabash Valley, with their principal summer village located near the confluence of the Wabash and the Vermillion Rivers. Their historic residency on the banks of the Vermillion followed their many years far west of Lake Michigan as well as on the Mississippi during the Iroquois wars of the seventeenth century. The wanderings of the Piankashaw during their cautious return east in the aftermath of these wars included brief sojourns at Starved Rock in northern Illinois and on the Kankakee River. In this chapter, we will look more at the Piankashaw as we descend the Wabash. But first, just a few miles below Wildcat Creek on the Wabash was the location of the major summer villages of the Wea during the early and mid-eighteenth century.

The English language ethnonym "Wea" is an adaptation from French *les Ouyas.* This spelling, sporting the French plural marker -s and pronounced [lewiá] in French, is itself a handy reduction of the French language ethnonym *les Ouiatanons*. The latter is a French corruption of this Miami subtribe's Algonquian name, analyzed below, which comes from the name of the unknown original prehistoric ethnonymous site associated with this people. In referring to the Wea, the French used both of the foregoing terms on an everyday basis: *les Ouiatanons*, pronounced [lewiatanõ], with the stress on the last syllable, and *les Ouyas*, often written *les 8ias* for short, which also has the stress on the last syllable. The reader should note that where the term *Ouiatanons* ends belies the French speaker's unconscious predisposition to anticipate that the strong, or "stressed," syllable of any foreign word represents its final syllable. In other words, in the original Miami-Illinois place-name *waawiaahtanonki* from which French *Ouiatanons* derives, the penultimate syllable *-on-* is the naturally strong one. At the same time, the final vowel of the Miami-Illinois place-name underwent a natural devoicing on the tongue of Miami-Illinois speakers, while the *k*, pronounced [g], was not aspirated. Thus, besides lopping off the first syllable *waa-* of the original Miami-Illinois term, the unknown, untutored (i.e., non-Jesuit) French soldier or trader who coined the *Ouiatanons* spelling obviously did not catch this devoiced, unstressed final vowel as well as the preceding consonant or just dropped them off when he spelled the term because it was too big a mouthful. Following his French ear, the Miami-Illinois word appeared to end with *-on-*, and it was this mishearing that led to the creation of the French place-name in the form *les Ouiatanons*. As a French place-name, *les Ouiatanons*, also spelled conveniently *8iatanon*, was transposed into English as "Ouiatenon," which is today pronounced [wiάʔnɑn] locally. Where and when the Wea acquired this tribe name is not known, but it was already being applied to them by at least 1672, when they were refugees west of Lake Michigan during the Algonquian diaspora of the seventeenth century. The French first recorded the Wea's name in the form <Ouaouiatanoukak>, a spelling that represents an Ojibweyan plural form of this tribe name.[2]

Just as the French crown sent the junior military officer Jean-Baptiste Bissot to follow the Miami to the headwaters of the Maumee near the turn of the eighteenth century, it first assigned an ensign by the name of François Picoté de Bellestre and a handful of soldiers under his command to live among the Wea. Picoté arrived in 1717 among the Wea at a site about three miles down the Wabash River west of present-day Lafayette. The following year responsibility for this site fell to Captain Charles Regnault, Sieur de Dubuisson. The first French traders to visit the Wea at this location were Pierre Cosmes, Claude L'Espine, and two unknowns, all of whom possessed a single *congé,* or official trade permit, and Joseph Larche, Jacques Monboeuf, and Estienne Roy, who together held another *congé.* These traders all went to the Wea in the same year as Regnault.[3]

In the course of the Wea's move into what is now Indiana following the Iroquois wars of the second half of the seventeenth century, some members of this Miami-Illinois–speaking group arrived on the Wabash as early as 1691. However, during the last decade of the seventeenth century, most of the Wea lived in the Chicago area and continued to reside there until at least 1702. Then, while a few Wea apparently lingered in the north, others moved down to the banks of the Wabash. It appears that by 1717, the year Picoté arrived, all of the Wea had finally made their way to *les Ouiatanons.*[4]

The Miami-Illinois–derived French name *les Ouiatanons,* when first recorded for Indiana, identified the Wea's summer villages located, as noted above, west of present-day Lafayette. However, since eponymous place-names referring to seminomadic peoples naturally travel with them, the same name, this time recorded by English speakers, would also later refer to Wea villages in the Terre Haute area. The Miami-Illinois name for Wea villages appears in two forms. The older form, spelled <Wahweahtunong> by O'Hair as well as <Wahweahtenon> and <Wahweottanon> by Hough,[5] represents *waawiaahtanonki,* "at the whirlpool (person)," or, rephrased in everyday English, "the whirlpool (person's) place," that is, "the Wea's place." The constituents of this term are *waawiaahtanwa,* "whirlpool person," and the locative suffix *-onki. waawiaahtanwa,* "whirlpool person, Wea" is itself composed of the initial *waaw-* meaning "egg, circle, round," the II final *-ihtan* meaning "flow," the third-person independent verb suffix *-w-*, and the singular animate gender marker *-a,* which in this case indicates a person. The other form of this eponymous place-name appears in Michelson's recording <waiyátā́nuñgi> and in Dunn's <waiátanung>, both of which represent *waayaahtanonki,* "at the whirlpool person, at the Wea."[6] Note that here, *waaya-* for "egg, circle, round" exhibits a normal sound change of *wi* to *y.* Hence the components of this form of this more modern Miami language place-name are the same as those of the older form mentioned above.

There is a notable cluster of modern place-names south and southwest of *les Ouiatanons* that derive from the names of local historical Indian groups. These include Wea Creek, Little Wea Creek, Kickapoo Creek, Shawnee Prairie, and Big Shawnee Creek. All of these place-names memorialize folks who once called the *les Ouiatanons* area home.[7] Moreover, given the timing of these peoples' residencies near *les Ouiatanons*, the foregoing English language place-names Wea Creek, Kickapoo Creek, Shawnee Prairie, and Big Shawnee Creek are assuredly translations of original French place-names that apparently have not survived in documents. That said, it should be noted that, since the Miami-Illinois–speaking Wea and Piankashaw were the first people to move into this area after the peace treaty was signed with the Iroquois in 1701, these streams would have originally borne Wea-Piankashaw names, which are now lost.

In addition to the waterways located in the neighborhood of *les Ouiatanons*, there are some Wabash tributaries downstream from there that deserve mention before the historically important Vermillion River comes into view. One of these, known today as Flint Creek, rises in southwestern central Tippecanoe County and meanders for over ten miles in a northwesterly direction before entering the Wabash opposite the riverside landmark known as Black Rock. Because the English place-name Flint Creek is mentioned in the early history of this area, this name may derive from an underlying yet unrecorded Native American language term.[8] The name Flint Creek refers to the presence of Attica chert, also known as Indiana green chert, which was an important prehistoric lithic resource.[9] Indeed, Attica chert was used as far back as Paleo-Indian times, that is, locally some eleven thousand years ago.

An important prehistoric trail, noted on Guernsey's map, connects this flint resource to the Strawtown mounds on the West Fork or the White River as well as to the Whitewater River and Ohio River. This appears to be a good link for the Fort Ancient and Oneota connections observed by archaeologists for late prehistoric Ohio and central Indiana.[10] It may also relate to the Siouan Tutelo in the Ohio Valley, from whom the Miami-Illinois language borrowed the word for "eight," *paraani*.

A French name for Big Pine Creek can be seen on McMurray's map from 1784 in the colloquial French form *R. à la Tortue* (the Turtle's R[iver], the R[iver] with the Turtle).[11] This place-name does not refer to a reptile but to an eighteenth-century Miami-Illinois–speaking Wabash Valley Miami leader known to the French of that era as La Tortue (the Turtle). He was a son of the famous Miami chief *meemeehšikia* (known in French as La Demoiselle, or "The Dragonfly") and, like his father, was an important friend of the Britons in the mid-1700s. It is commonly thought that La Tortue and his father were Piankashaw. However, there appears to be no solid evidence to support this notion. Although the historic British sources do refer to *meemeehšikia* as the "Piankashaw King," the French sources do not speak of him at all as being Piankashaw and in fact locate his original home at the headwaters of the Maumee, home of the Miami.

Like his father, La Tortue was involved in the Pickawillany affair, in which a British-leaning contingency of local native peoples led by Maumee River Miami settled at the headwaters of Loramie Creek in west-central Ohio. (See chapter 5, note 27.) Although La Demoiselle lost his life when the French and their Ottawa allies destroyed Pickawillany, his son managed to escape with his. In fact, the association of La Tortue with Big Pine Creek dates to the time when he and his people, having fled to the White River of Indiana in 1752 in the aftermath of Pickawillany's destruction, went on to make their home near *les Ouiatanons* area in 1754.[12] The hydronym *R. à la Tortue* thus dates to around the mid-1750s and to the final years of the French regime in North America.

Wabash Valley historian Hiram W. Beckwith found an English language recording of the Miami-Illinois name for the Miami leader La Tortue in the form <Mushequanockque>. This recording demonstrates that this man bore the same personal name as the later and more famous Miami leader Little Turtle. The word *mihšihkinaahkwa,* the proper form for the name of both of these Miami-Illinois–speaking warriors, is etymologically "big-turtle" (*mihši-,* "big" + *-hkinaahkw,* "turtle" + *-a,* the singular proximate animate noun gender marker) and is the Miami word for the painted terrapin (*Chrysemys picta marginata*).[13]

The Miami leader *mihšihkinaahkwa,* son of *meemeehšikia,* lived in several places in the Wabash Valley following his days at Pickawillany, as evidenced by the appearance of his name in other area hydronyms. In 1762, Hutchins was also alluding to the same person when he recorded the French place-name *Riviere a la Tortue* (the Turtle's River) for today's Big Creek, a western tributary of the Wabash located below the Vermillion River.[14] Another reference to *mihšihkinaahkwa* is found in the English language place-name Turtle Creek, an eastern tributary of the Wabash whose source is located in western Sullivan County.

Apparently, only one Native American name has survived for Big Pine Creek. Beckwith, in some way, came by the spelling <Puckgwunnashgamucksepe>, which he translated to "White Pine of the Bark Peeling Variety."[15] Beckwith's spelling has an unmistakable Potawatomi appearance, with the letter "u" being the typical historic spelling by English speakers of Potawatomi *ə.* The segment of <Puckgwunnashgamucksepe> spelled -gamuck appears to represent Potawatomi *-gəməg,* "at the water." The segment spelled

Puckgwunn- seems to represent Potawtomi *bəkwan,* "bark roof mat," while Puckgwunnash would be *bəkwanəš,* a pejorative expression meaning "inferior bark roof mat."[16] Thus *Puckgwunnashgamuck- may signify "at the inferior bark mat water," and <Puckgwunnashgamucksepe> "the river at the inferior bark mat water." Although it is not clear what the referent is, Beckwith's translation suggests that it referred to a local tree. In his opinion, it was the white pine (*Pinus strobus*). However, another species of evergreen, the eastern red cedar (*Juniperus virginiana*), which has a known history of native use for bark mats, could have been the intended referent.

The early to mid-eighteenth-century French hydronym *Rivière de Boisrouge,* literally "redwood river," could be a place-name of Native American origin. This is a noteworthy place-name simply for having had through the years almost as much mobility as running water itself. In other words, three different creeks along this section of the Wabash River have borne or are thought to have borne this name at one time or another: Little Wea Creek in southwestern Tippecanoe County, Indian Creek, which rises in northwestern central Tippecanoe County and flows southwest to the Wabash, and Redwood Creek in Warren County.[17] The eastern red cedar obviously created quite a stir in the place nomenclature of this area. However, in the end, the Warren County waterway located west of West Lebanon in Warren County prevailed in holding on to this tree for its name. Today this local stream is known as Redwood Creek, just as it was on a map of Indiana in 1858.[18]

Beckwith called Redwood Creek <Musquametigsepe>, explaining that <Musqu-> means "red" and <-metig> "tree" or "wood."[19] However, he failed to tell us what language this hydronym came from, if in fact he ever knew. <Musquametigsepe> is clearly not a Wea~Piankashaw place-name, that is, a term from the Miami-Illinois language. Although Miami-Illinois has a reflex of the Proto-Algonquian derived initial **meçkw-,* "red," which can occur either in Miami-Illinois in the form *miskw-* or the changed *meeskw-*, the name of the eastern red cedar in Miami-Illinois is *šinkwaahkwa,* a term that refers to the tree's resinous character, not to the color of its wood. <Musqumetigsepe> is not from Kickapoo or related Mascouten, either. The orthographic "u" would be a very unusual English transcription of the sound *e,* which is the vowel in the Kickapoo form of this particular initial. However, the first "u" of Beckwith's recording is a letter, as noted above, that was very commonly used by early English-speaking recorders attempting to write the Potawatomi vowel *ə*. Thus the form of the initial segment,

Musqu-, strongly suggests Old Potawatomi **məskw-*, "red," which in modern Potawatomi is *mskw-*. At the same time, the segment spelled -mitig ostensibly derives from PA **meʔtekw-*, "wood, tree." Indeed, -mitig would be an expected historical English spelling for the Old Potawatomi reflex of this term. Therefore, Musqu- + -metig would theoretically signify "red-tree" in Potawatomi, and thus denote the eastern red cedar.

However, the problem with this analysis is that the standard Potawatomi term for the eastern red cedar is *mskwawak*. At the same time, I am confident that Beckwith did not invent <Musquametigsepe>. His Musqu-metig- could therefore be a local Potawatomi dialect variant for the eastern red cedar, an idiolectal variant, a pidginized Potawatomi name, or even a Potawatomi trade jargon name for the tree. There is certainly good reason to believe that the Potawatomi would have had a name for Redwood Creek, since documented early-nineteenth-century Potawatomi villages were located nearby at the mouths of both Big Pine Creek and Kickapoo Creek on the Wabash. Furthermore, in the same time period, there were Potawatomi reserves along the Wabash River below the Tippecanoe confluence, especially at the mouths of Big Pine Creek and Flint Creek.[20]

As the Wabash begins its descent along the western edge of Indiana it receives from the northwest one of its major tributaries, the Vermillion River. It was on the Vermillion near its confluence with the Wabash River that the Miami-Illinois–speaking Piankashaw, mentioned above, had their principal summer village throughout the greater part of the 1700s.

The Vermillion River originates in east-central Illinois and enters Indiana as well as the Wabash River after traversing Vermillion County, Indiana. The modern place-name, including its spelling, derives directly from the eighteenth-century French name for the Vermillion River, which was *le grand vermillon jaune,* "the Great Yellow Vermilion." But the French hydronym itself is of American Indian origin.

There are only two documented native names for the Vermillion River. One is an Algonquian term found and preserved by Hough in the form <Osanamon>, the other a Huron-Wyandot moniker, to be examined below.[21] Perhaps unexpectedly, given the Miami-Illinois–speaking Piankashaw's extended presence on the Vermillion, Hough's <Osanamon> does not represent a Miami-Illinois term as some have thought. The presence of the first "n" in his spelling dismisses the possibility of a Miami-Illinois origin since this language does not have *n* in the third syllable of the term in question; it has *l* instead, giving *oonsaalamooni,* which means literally "yellow ocher."

<Osanamon> is assuredly a representation of **osanəmən,* the Old Potawatomi term for yellow ocher, or limonite. This is the mineral compound $FeO(OH)\cdot(nH_2O)$, a source of yellow paint, discussed above in chapter 7 in reference to the Salamonie River. The well-documented residency of the Potawatomi along the Wabash upstream from the Vermillion during the second half of the eighteenth century and into the early nineteenth century adequately supports a Potawatomi origin for the spelling <Osanamon>. Moreover, the use of the Potawatomi term for yellow ocher indicates the Vermillion River was once an important source of this substance. George Croghan, an early American government emissary and captive among the Indians, saw this river in person and thought its name came from "red earth," as he put it.[22] Croghan's "red earth," by which he was referring to hematite, does in fact occur historically in regional place nomenclature—in Louis Jolliet's hydronym *Pierres Sanguines* (bloody stones). The latter term is a French translation by Jolliet's companion Jacques Marquette of the Miami-Illinois place-name obtained from the Kaskaskia in 1673 for the Vermilion River of *the Illinois River Valley.* Jolliet was the first European to use such a designation for this Illinois River tributary, and he did so because it relates to the stream's name in the Old Miami-Illinois language, *aramooni (siipiiwi),* "hematite, vermilion, paint" (river).[23] René de La Salle, following in Jolliet's tracks, was the first European to record this hydronym in its native form, in the very early days of 1680s. His <Aramoni> entered the French lexicon via the Bernou-Peronel map from 1682, Coronelli's chart from 1688, and Guillaume Delisle's work from 1703.[24] Later French cartographers, foregoing the use of any native name for the Illinois River tributary, fell into the habit of using only the French translation *Vermillon,* a term which English-speaking Illinoisans later borrowed and respelled "Vermilion" in accordance with English orthographic standards.

However, as far as the Vermillion River, tributary of the Wabash, is concerned, Croghan's idea that the name referred to hematite can only be incorrect. Granted, hematite (red ocher [Fe_2O_3]) like limonite, can occur in the Pennsylvanian age rocks over which the Vermillion River flows. However, the very forms of the Vermillion River's name in Potawatomi and French soundly refute Croghan's notion that the former was its origin. As noted above, the complete French name for the river was not simply **le vermillon,* but *le (grand) vermillon jaune.*[25] The term *vermillon jaune* means "yellow vermillion," that is, yellow ocher (limonite), and is a direct word-for-word reflection of Old Potawatomi **osanəmən.* So while the tributary of the Illinois River known as the Vermilion and the tributary of the Wabash known as the Vermillion bear the same name in the twenty-first century, they had morphologically as well as semantically different Algonquian and French names historically.

The development of the Vermillion River's modern name through time and across languages probably occurred in the following manner. The French place-name _le grand vermillon jaune_ was surely a translation of the original Wea-Piankashaw (i.e., Miami-Illinois) name for the river, in use long before the Potawatomi arrived and began using their own translation of the name. It was the Piankashaw in particular who had the earliest, strongest, and indeed unique historical ties to the Vermillion River, having arrived on the Wabash at and below Ouiatanon by 1705, many years before the French and the Potawatomi came to the area.[26] Given the early occurrence of this French place-name, it stands to reason that the Old Potawatomi cognate *_osanəmən_ as a name for the Vermillion River entered the language of the late-arriving Potawatomi _as a borrowing from earlier Piankashaw_ *_oonsaalamooni._ The Miami-Illinoisan Piankashaw form failed to get recorded because the French were in the habit of using place-names from their own language. Indeed, in the case of this stream, the French early on adopted the Miami-Illinois name for it, translating it to French _le (grand) vermillon jaune._ However, it was the Potawatomi form of this place-name that managed to make its way into the historical record at some point in the late 1700s or early 1800s. Finally, the <Osanamon> spelling indicates it was written down by an English-speaking person who was in contact with the local Potawatomi people.[27]

In addition to Algonquian names for the Vermillion River, there is a Huron-Wyandot name for it that appears in the papers of the Detroit-based Jesuit missionary Pierre Potier. Potier recorded the place-name in two ways: <ąnnod8> and <ekąnnod8>.[28] The first thing that is clear about Potier's recordings is that his <ekąnnod8> is simply the locative form of <ąnnod8>. In other words, <ekąnnod8> signifies "at ąnnod8," or, in common English, "the ąnnod8 place." Here, the Huron-Wyandot cislocative _et-_, in combination with _y(a),_ the initial segment of the following morpheme spelled ą by Potier, becomes phonetic [eky(a-)].

That said, it is not clear what <ąnnod8> itself signifies. Potier did not translate the term, and there appear to be no cognates for it in other Iroquoian languages. Thus a phonemic transcription and a translation for this place-name are necessarily speculative. The Iroquoianist Blair Rudes has suggested that the unextended form might be *_xanṍnoʔ,_ with the extended form with the instrumental suffix _-hkw-_ being *_xanõnóhkwaʔ_[29] This is an attractive thesis, since Potier actually recorded the latter term in the form <ąnnodok8a>, and translated it to *rouille* (rust).[30] Moreover, the similarity between <ąnnodok8a> and our Huron-Wyandot names for the Vermillion River suggests that <ąnnod8> came from the verb from which <ąnnodok8a> derived. In light of the Algonquian names for the Vermillion River, Huron-Wyandot <ąnnod8> might mean "yellow ocher." On the other hand, if it should be a term signifying "red ocher," then the Huron-Wyandot name for the Vermillion would represent a misinterpretation of the river's Algonquian name or its French name.

Sugar Creek—the west-central Indiana Sugar Creek—rises from multiple headwaters in southern Clinton County and northwestern Boone County. It then flows southwest for approximately a hundred miles, flanked by an ancient prairie in its upper reaches and by spectacular glacial moraines near its destination with the Wabash River. Sugar Creek's many sources include Little Potato Creek, whose English language name, given its antiquity, is probably of Native American origin. Moreover, an early-nineteenth-century Indian healer appears to have lived on the banks of this stream at the same time that the English place-name appeared in history.[31] Even though a historically documented Native American language form for Little Potato Creek does not exist, this hydronym, as in the case of Potato Creek in northern Indiana discussed in chapter 4, refers to the cow lily or pond lily, otherwise known as spatterdock (*Nuphar*).

Sugar Creek itself has two Miami-Illinois names. The more common one is *ahsenaamiši siipiiwi*, "sugar maple tree river." Around the turn of the twentieth century, Dunn got this hydronym in the form <Sänahmĭ́ndjĭsipíwi> from one of his three Miami or Wea consultants mentioned in the introduction. The natural phonologically predictable dropping of the short initial unstressed vowel *a-* of *ahsenaamiši* is readily apparent in Dunn's recording.[32] The term *ahsenaamiši siipiiwi* is pronounced [(a)hsènaamĭ́ži siipíiwi]. The *š* in the final syllable of *ahsenaamiši* is voiced to [ž], for according to the rules of Miami-Illinois phonology, a sibilant becomes voiced when it follows a syllable with an initial nasal consonant. In other words, in the actual pronunciation of *ahsenaamiši,* a linguistic phenomenon known as noncontrastive nasalization occurs, whereby the *š* is voiced to [ž] in the same environment in which this sound is prenasalized. The word *ahsenaamiši* is one of two documented in Miami-Illinois for "sugar maple tree."[33] It literally means "stone-tree," and cognate expressions of *ahsenaamiši* are common across the Algonquian languages.[34]

The second Miami-Illinois name for Sugar Creek is found in Hiram Beckwith's papers in the form <Pungosecone>.[35] At first glance, the curious thing about this recording is that it could not have been a *local* American Indian name for Sugar Creek. In other words, the Miami and Wea term for "maple sugar" is *pankoosaakani.* But in <Pungosecone> the first "e" is an "alphabet E" that clearly stands for the sound *i.*[36] Thus the spelling in question actually represents *pankoosikani,* which is the cognate term for "maple sugar" in Peoria, a nonlocal subdialect of the Miami-Illinois language. The authenticity of <Pungosecone> as a name for Sugar Creek is supported by two factors. One, the historic Peoria did not live very far to the west of Sugar Creek and would have naturally had a name for the stream. And two, the woman who gave Beckwith this name lived with Miami-Illinois speakers near Sugar Creek *for decades.*

Sometime prior to 1878, in the course of compiling data for his Indiana county histories, Beckwith, the first president of the Illinois Historical Society, began exchanging letters with a woman in Kansas named Mary Ann Baptiste. Baptiste was born Mary Ann Isaacs in April 1800 in Oneida County, New York, her mother of Iroquoian and Mohegan ancestry and her father a European American. A member of the Brotherton Indians in her youth, she came to Indiana in 1817 and in 1820 married Noël Dagenais at Isaac McCoy's Baptist mission on Big Raccoon Creek near present-day Armiesburg, just south of Sugar Creek. Dagenais, an important leader of the Wea and native speaker of Miami-Illinois, was the son of a French trader named Ambrose Dagenais and a Wea woman named <Mechinquamesha> (for *mihšiinko(o)miša,* "Burr Oak"), who was the sister of another important Wea chief <Tackkekekah>, better known by his French name, Jacco Godfroy. Mary Ann Isaacs was not a native speaker of Miami-Illinois, but her marriage to Noël Dagenais and her long association, from 1817 to 1846, with the Wabash Valley and its aboriginal population no doubt familiarized her with the region's Miami-Illinois language place nomenclature. She certainly would have known what her Wea relatives called Sugar Creek, which is Big Raccoon Creek's closest neighboring large stream, located just a few miles to the north.

The Dagenais continued to live on Big Raccoon Creek until 1846, when the couple moved to Kansas, where Noël died two years later, at Coldwater Grove. In time, the widow Dagenais remarried, her new husband being "Batticy" Baptiste the Peoria, an important chief of the Peoria tribe. Baptiste, who was also a native speaker of Miami-Illinois, was born at the confluence of the Des Plaines and Kankakee Rivers in 1793. According to Beckwith's notes, he was not only a leader of his tribe, serving as its representative at the treaty of Edwardsville on September 25, 1818, but was also an interpreter for the U.S. government for thirty years. It was no doubt because of this man, and through his wife Mary Ann Baptiste, that Beckwith acquired the Peoria term <Pungosecone> as a name for Sugar Creek when he visited Mrs. Baptiste in Kansas soon after Batticy's death. However, in light of the fact that Mary Ann Baptiste lived for three decades with the Wea right in the very shadow of Sugar Creek, this Peoria place-name could also have had a Wea cognate, in the form **pankoosaakani (siipiiwi),* "maple sugar (river)."[37]

As a Miami-Illinois name for Sugar Creek, *pankoosikani* (*siipiiwi*) ~ **pankoosaakani* (*siipiiwi*) could have been in use at least by the early 1700s, and it would have highlighted the stream's importance as a resource area for the production of maple sugar. As indicated by the place-name *ahsenaamiši siipiiwi* mentioned above, the Sugar Creek watershed in the past housed an extraordinary abundance of sugar maple trees (*Acer saccharum*) as part of its unique and important beech-maple forest. Brelsford's account of the area's early history mentions stories about local American Indian sugaring, particularly the *kineepikwameekwaki* (Eel River Miami) living at Thorntown, who would descend the Sugar Creek Valley to make sugar.[38] This local preponderance of maple trees was apparent not only to the native peoples but also to American settlers, as evidenced on an early map of Montgomery County.[39] Indeed, the lower Sugar Creek basin, which formed the heart of early pioneer sugaring, is still known for its maple sugar industry. However, as far as the antiquity of Peoria *pankoosikani (siipiiwi)* is concerned, it is important to note that the native manufacture of maple sugar depended upon the arrival of the French and their metal cooking pot, known as *la chaudière.* It is for this reason that the Peoria subdialect place-name *pankoosikani (siipiiwi)* can date only to the early 1700s. It could not be a prehistoric name for Sugar Creek.[40]

Finally, the Miami-Illinois name for Sugar Creek, *ahsenaamiši siipiiwi,* naturally had a French incarnation before the English version was established. The old French name appears in 1805 in a letter from lower Wabash Valley residents Gibson and Vigo to Harrison concerning the Eel River band of Miami residing at that time on Sugar Creek at Thorntown. In this missive, Sugar Creek bears the name *Le Rabellaire,* which is a distorted rendering of French *l'érablière,* "maple tree woods."[41] In the 1700s the Wabash Valley French would have called Sugar Creek *la rivière à l'érablière,* which *in principle* is a decent translation of the Miami-Illinois name(s) for this stream in that it perfectly describes the local dendrography.[42]

A historic Indian town was located on Sugar Creek about twenty-five miles southeast of *les Ouiatanons.* Situated on the south bank of Sugar at its confluence with Prairie Creek, this site was originally the location of an eighteenth-century Miami-Illinois–speaking village and French trading post, home to nearly four hundred people. According to Dunn's Wea consultant *wiikapimiša,* the Wea knew this place as *(a)kaawinšaahkionki,* which Dunn wrote <Kawinjakiŭngī>. She translated the term to "Thorn Tree Place." The referent is the honey locust tree (*Gleditsia triacanthos*),[43] whose seed pods contain a sweet and edible pulp. If the English translation offered by *wiikapimiša* is accurate, the Miami-Illinois place-name *(a)kaawinšaahkionki* is the locative noun form of *(a)kaawinšaahkwi,* "honey locust tree." But the precision of the translation "Thorn Tree Place" is important for establishing this fact, since it would imply that a rounding dissimilation occurred that transformed underlying **(a)kaawinšaahkwionki* to *(a)kaawinšaahkionki.* Rounding dissimilation is known to occur occasionally elsewhere in the Miami-Illinois language.

In the early nineteenth century, Thorntown was also the location of a small reservation with a much smaller population—around two hundred and twenty-five people according to Tipton—comprised mostly of the Miami-speaking Eel River band, mentioned above, known in Miami as *kineepikwameekwaki,* "eels."[44] At that time, this site was known as *(a)kaawiahkionki,* "in the thorn land," or loosely, "the thorn land place." This term is composed of *(a)kaawi-,* which is a "thorn" initial, the "land" final *-ahk,* and the locative suffix *-ionki,* meaning "at."[45] While the Wea toponym noted above, *(a)kaawinšaahkionki,* is probably the older name for Thorntown since the principal Wea summer villages throughout most of the 1700s were located only a day's walk to the west, the Miami-speaking Eel River band's toponym, *(a)kaawiahkionki,* could be a later name for the site since the latter were latecomers to this area.[46] It was at *(a)kaawiahkionki* in the 1820s that *nkótikapwa,* "1-Flower," known in English as both Billy Flowers and Captain Flowers, was head of the Eel River Miami. Also in residence at *(a)kaawiahkionki* was the Miami man *(a)nikoonsa,* "Little Squirrel," a contemporary of *nkótikapwa.* He was the person after whom Indiana's Squirrel Creek in Howard County near Russiaville (i.e., "Richardville") and Squirrel Creek, the Eel River tributary in northeastern Miami County and northwestern Wabash County, were named.[47] The *kineepikwameekwaki* lost their land at Thorntown in the spring of 1828, three years after the American government commissioner Lewis Cass granted it official status as a trading post. However, various members of the tribe remained there until as late as 1835.

Also, with respect to Thorntown, Hough's map bears a strange-looking toponym: <Kowasikka>.[48] Here again, in characteristic early historical American English fashion, the final -a is an "alphabet A" standing for *e,* which itself was a mishearing by Americans of Miami-Illinois *i.* Furthermore, Hough's poorly engraved -s(i)k- represents a preaspirated *-hk-* misheard as [sk]. As a result, <Kowasikka>, although a distorted recording, simply represents Miami-Illinois *(a)kaawiahki,* "thorn-land," composed of the "thorn" initial *(a)kaawi-,* the "land" final *-ahk,* and the singular proximate inanimate noun marker *-i.* This term is grammatical and is, in fact, grammatically akin, for example, to documented forms of the Miami-Illinois name for Vincennes. While it is often twisted nearly beyond recognition, the original native name for Thorntown has a strong spirit. As the name for Thorntown High School's sports teams it persisted well into the second half of the twentieth century in the form "Keewasakees."[49]

Paralleling Sugar Creek to the south is a stream over eighty miles long known today as Big Raccoon Creek. This waterway rises in southwestern Boone County some ten miles south of Thorntown and moves in a southwesterly fashion across southeastern Montgomery County, northwestern Putnam County and then into southern Parke County. At that point Big Raccoon bends impressively to the northwest, directed by glacial moraines toward its eventual meeting with the Wabash River. As far as the modern name Big Raccoon Creek is concerned, the "Big" is an item added by American pioneers to the English translation of the original Native American name for this watercourse. Like the French when they created *le grand vermillon jaune* and *le petit vermillon jaune,* "Big" was added to this stream's original English language name "Raccoon Creek" in order to distinguish it from one of its neighboring streams, which the Americans had dubbed Little Raccoon Creek. Thus the "Big" of Big Raccoon Creek is neither a commentary on the size of any particular raccoon nor a part of the waterway's aboriginal name.

Although Big Raccoon Creek's name is copiously attested in the literature in both French and English language translations, it was not until around the turn of the twentieth century that the Miami-Illinois name for it was finally written down. The late-nineteenth- and early-twentieth-century Miami leader *waapanahkikapwa* gave this name to Dunn, who transcribed it in the form <äsepánasipíwi>. Dunn's spelling represents *eehsipana siipiiwi,* "raccoon river," from *eehsipana,* "raccoon," and *siipiiwi,* "river."[50] It is important to note that *eehsipana siipiiwi* does not refer to the raccoon (*Procyon lotor*), since this masked nocturnal omnivore is an animal that inhabits all of Indiana's resource zones. In other words, naming a local stream after the ubiquitous raccoon was not part of local native place-naming practice. *eehsipana siipiiwi,* pronounced [eehsípana siipíiwi], is an eponym. As in the case of the mid-eighteenth-century Miami leader *mihšihkinaahkwa* discussed above, *eehsipana* was the name of a prominent Wabash Valley Indian leader in the mid- to late 1700s. In fact, he was a nephew of *meemeehšikia* of Pickawillany fame and a cousin of *mihšihkinaahkwa* discussed above. As the year of his death seems to have been 1752,[51] the application of this name to this waterway probably dates to sometime shortly before 1752.

A similar yet slightly different Wea name for Big Raccoon Creek also exists: *eehsipanikami,* "raccoon-water," pronounced [eehsípanikámi]. This hydronym is implied by the name of the Wea village and reservation located along Raccoon Creek during the early 1800s, which was *eehsipanikamionki,* "on the raccoon-water," or in everyday English, "the raccoon-water place." The Wea speaker *wiikapimiša* gave this toponym to Albert Gatschet, who wrote it <essipaníkamiû'ngi>. The name is composed of the "raccoon" initial *eehsipan-,* the "water" final *-(i)kam* and the locative suffix *-ionki.*[52]

In the 1700s, Big Raccoon Creek was also associated with another Wabash Valley man whose name occurs historically in the English language form <Pishewaw>.[53] The exact shape and referent for a place-name involving the term <Pishewaw> are unknown. However, <Pishewaw>, which represents Miami-Illinois *pinšiwa,* "bobcat," might be the name of some Wabash Valley Wea or Piankashaw in the latter part of the eighteenth or in the early nineteenth century who would have lived on this stream. While the spelling <Pishewaw> stands for a Miami-Illinois term, its human referent could be a local historical Kickapoo leader whose name is spelled <Passheweha> in the literature. It is well known that the Kickapoo lived along the Wabash in this area. The name <Passheweha>, where the second -h- is a miscopied -w-, is Old Kickapoo **pešiwiwa,* "he is a bobcat."[54]

The historic French name for Big Raccoon Creek, recorded in Chaboillez's or Chevalier's Wabash Valley itinerary, was *la Rivière du Chat,* literally "the Cat's River."[55] This same French name was recorded, independently, by Hutchins in 1762 and placed on his map from 1778.[56] It is important to mention, however, that no Algonquian term for "bobcat" (*Lynx rufus*), or any other kind of feline, underlies this hydronym. New World French speakers of the Mississippi Valley called the bobcat *pichou,* which is a borrowing from Ojibwa *pišiw,* "bobcat, lynx." However, they used French *chat,* meaning "cat," and French *chat sauvage,* meaning literally "wild cat" to denote the *raccoon.* (The reader can read more about this French usage in chapter 5 in the discussion of Lake Erie.) French *chat* was correctly translated into English to create the name for a waterway located in eastern Vermillion County that enters the Wabash at Hillsdale—Little Raccoon Creek.[57] Therefore, regarding Big Raccoon Creek, Chaboillez's or Chevalier's *Rivière du Chat* properly translates to English "the Raccoon's river." This was, of course, a translation of the Miami-Illinois name for this stream, and again refers to the Miami leader *eehsipana* mentioned above.

The first historical reference to the land now occupied by the city of Terre Haute, Indiana, seems to come from the early to mid-1700s in Chevalier's or Chaboillez's *L'ile à la Terre haute* (The island at the high Land). This was a reference to a long, broad island in the Wabash, partially visible on the map of the Indiana geological survey for 1869.[58] Beckwith noted "the high land" referred to the fact that this was "the only high ground approaching the river for a distance of several miles."[59] Gatschet, quoting *waapanahkikapwa,* said that the Miami's name for Terre Haute was <kawizhakiû'ngi>. This recording represents Miami-Illinois *(a)kaawinšaahkionki,* "at the honey locust tree(s)," which is the same botanically descriptive toponym that the Wea applied to Thorntown on Sugar Creek.[60] Again, as in the case of Thorntown, the referent would be the honey locust tree.

In the years following the abandonment of *les Ouiatanons* near Lafayette,[61] the Wea established two villages in the Terre Haute area, which were known in English as Upper Wea Town and Lower Wea Town. In Miami-Illinois these towns would have been known collectively as *waayaahtanonki,* "at the whirlpool (person)," that is, "at the Wea." One of these Wea villages could be the archaeological site known as "Vigo 18" discussed in Helman's early survey of Vigo County.[62]

The famous French soldier François-Marie Bissot de Vincennes managed to induce some Piankashaw to follow him in 1731 from their principal summer village on the Vermillion River to the Vincennes area. However, most Piankashaw subsequently abandoned the lower Wabash site and moved back to the Vermillion River after this French leader was burned to death by the Chickasaw near Fulton, Lee County, Mississippi on Palm Sunday, March 25, 1736, while on a punitive expedition against that tribe.[63] The Piankashaw's general aversion to settling at Vincennes, despite French coercion, highlights the attitude that prevailed among Miami-Illinois–speaking tribes with respect to *inhabiting* the lower Wabash. Indeed, the perils of living in that area took a brutal form in the intensive campaign waged by the Chickasaw against the French-allied Piankashaw along the lower Wabash in the early 1700s, precisely the situation that led to the death of Bissot de Vincennes fils. Whereas the roots of this conflict between Muskogeans and Algonquians were probably far older than the documented attack by British-allied Chickasaw on the Illinois in 1703, the former's historically famous onslaught began in earnest around 1732.[64] Under these circumstances, the execution of their friend and ally Bissot de Vincennes fils by the Chickasaw was for the Piankashaw, residentially speaking, the proverbial straw that broke the camel's back, that is, it was the catalyst that hastened their return up the Wabash to the Vermillion, where they continued to live into the last decade of the eighteenth century.[65]

Miami leader *waapanahkikapwa* attended elementary school for a week in Vincennes and later in life told Dunn that the Miami called Vincennes <chípkahkyóongay>. This recording represents the same term as Dunn's later reformulated spelling of the place-name <Tcĭpkákĭúngi>, which he glossed "Place of Roots." Trowbridge had much earlier recorded the same place-name in the form <Tshipkohkeeŏ́āngee>.[66] All three of these spellings represent Miami-Illinois *(a)čiipihkahkionki,* "at the root land," that is, "the root-land place."[67] This, the earliest name for Vincennes, is comprised of the Miami-Illinois "root" initial *(a)čiipihk-,* the final *-ahk,* "land," and the locative suffix in the form *-ionki.*

Dunn's comment that this site's name referred to the local abundance of edible roots is correct.[68] Even today the Vincennes area is known for its wild sweet potatoes (*Ipomoea pandurata*). Although the Old Miami-Illinois language appears to have had only *ačiipihki,* an inanimate noun meaning "root," late Miami-Wea also had *(a)čiip(i)hka,* an animate noun also signifying "root." According to Dunn, it was the latter term which was applied to edible roots. *(a)čiip(i)hka* would then be the referent for the place-name in question. Dunn also stated that the Vincennes area was known as <Chippekoke>, which is the same name represented by the <Cippecaughke> spelling penned by the early tourist David Thomas a century earlier. Dunn seems to have lifted his <Chippekoke> spelling from Hough's map, which has <Chippecoke>. Hough also wrote <Chippekawkay>, as well as the extremely garbled <Chihkahwekay>.[69] All of the above are simply variant spellings of the same word and represent *(a)čiipihkahki,* "root-land." These forms are interesting, linguistically speaking, because they occur in the historical record prior to the time when syncope raked through the Miami-Illinois language, transforming the older pronunciation [ačìipihkáhki] to modern [čìiphkáhki].

Finally, according to R. P. Dehart, an Indiana historian, <Chepekakah> was a name applied to the Piankashaw.[70] The reliability of his report, however, is questionable. In <Chepekakah>, if the final -ah represents [a] or [ɑ], the resultant form ***čiiphkahka* would simply be ungrammatical in Miami-Illinois as a term for a person, that is, as a name meaning "root-land person." The actual Miami-Illinois term for someone from a place known for its roots would be *(a)čiip(i)hkahkia,* which would have had an expected historical spelling in the form **Chepekakiah—which we do not have. Therefore, the final -ah of Dehart's spelling must be an "alphabet A" representing the English *e* sound, for original Miami-Illinois *i.* In the end Dehart's <Chepekakah> seems to stand simply for *čiipihkahki,* "root-land" and is not, as written, an ethnonym. If Dehart's term should one day prove to be a genuine albeit garbled indigenous ethnonym, it is clear that it would have referred only to those members of the Piankashaw tribe who moved to the Vincennes area, not to the main body of the tribe that remained on the Vermillion River throughout the greater part of the eighteenth century. In addition, it is important to understand that **(a)čiip(i)hkahkia,* if it ever existed as a name for the Piankashaw, would not have been an ethnonym of long standing since it would have simply referred to the Piankashaw's brief association in the 1700s with the Vincennes area, the "root land." The lower Wabash River was of interest to the Piankashaw solely as hunting ground or as a place to pass through. There was never a consensus among the Piankashaw as far as their settling at Vincennes was concerned, despite the fact that the French had built a fort there.[71]

The name of the Patoka River, the one-hundred-mile-long waterway that meanders from its beginnings in southern Orange County across all of Dubois, Pike, and Gibson Counties westward to the Wabash, represents one of the most difficult recovery challenges involving Indiana's American Indian place-names. Curiously, even when this stream appeared on French maps during the time of the French in the Wabash Valley, it never enjoyed a name. In fact, I have been unable to locate any mention of the Patoka River in French colonial records. The only known itinerary that could have offered a name for it does not contain any information. In other words, the document consists of only a title. The itinerary was never written down.[72]

Now, a personal name with exactly the same spelling as modern "Patoka" does appear on a list included within the voluminous material recorded by the Jesuit missionary Pierre Potier at Detroit in the 1700s. The registry in which this name is found notes the names of the community's Native

American and French inhabitants, and there in bold capital letters is the name <PATOKA>.[73] However, one problem with Potier's attestation is that it represents neither a French given name nor surname. More important, no evidence exists indicating that this person, whoever he or she was, was ever associated directly with the Patoka River. Still and all, given the fact that this personal name was recorded in Detroit—and French Detroit was intimately connected commercially and militarily to the lower Wabash Valley—it is not impossible that the name once belonged to an eighteenth-century Indian individual who became identified in some way with the Patoka River. That said, a second avenue of analysis for the name of the Patoka River was offered by the place-name scholar George R. Stewart. In his opinion, the stream was named after a Kickapoo chief of the 1800s.[74] This is not an unattractive hypothesis since the Kickapoo, as noted, lived along the southern Wabash. However, I have been unable to locate any reliable data that would substantiate Stewart's notion.

Whoever it referred to, the *term* "Patoka," seen today as place-names and historically as a personal name in Illinois, Indiana, and Kentucky, probably ultimately derives, as Dunn surmised, from the Miami-Illinois ethnonym *paatoohka,* "Comanche."[75] This is certainly not to imply that the Patoka River was named after the Comanche tribe. Naming a major stream in southern Indiana the "Comanche River" would be almost tantamount to calling the Kankakee the "Eskimo River." However, the historical Miami-Illinois peoples did on occasion acquire Comanche slaves through far-flung trade networks, which is probably how this term entered the Illinois-Indiana-Kentucky region in the first place.

The earliest recorded spellings of "Patoka" as the name for the tributary of the southern Wabash come from the works of English speakers in the late 1700s. Indeed, the first person to use this place-name, and spell it in this manner, was apparently the American general Josiah Harmar, in the autumn of 1787. In that same century, the hydronym appeared as <Potoka>, and then in the early nineteenth century as <Petoka>. In the late 1800s the name was being spelled <Pataka>.[76]

Alongside Stewart's Kickapoo theory, the analysis of "Patoka" should probably include the possibility that the place-name is from a Delaware Indian language. This proposition is plausible, attractive, and in fact expected, since there were well-known and historically documented Munsee villages only a few miles north of the Patoka River at the forks of the White Rivers, and other Delaware villages elsewhere in the general vicinity.[77] In looking at this etymological problem through a Delaware language lens,

"Patoka" could represent Munsee *pehtáhkəw,* an II verb meaning "it thunders."[78] The first -a- of the old American English spelling "Patoka" could be an "alphabet A" indicating phonemic *e.* The written -o- could easily stand for phonemic *a,* which would be realized in Munsee very much like phonetic [ɑ] and thus easily confused by English speakers with *o.* Finally, the final orthographic -a of "Patoka" could easily represent Munsee *ə* since that is the same sound it represents in English. However, it should be noted that if "Patoka" does derive from *pehtáhkəw,* the Munsee expression was probably not a place-name at all, but simply a descriptive statement made by a Munsee individual about the river. If *pehtáhkəw* is the origin of "Patoka," the term would refer to the singular, important and *noisy* narrows and falls of the Patoka River at Jasper, site of the historically important Endlow Mill established in 1815.[79] Such a description would have thus served to distinguish this stream from the others in the immediate area since this is the only one that has an impressive waterfall in such proximity to the Wabash. Furthermore, the expression "it thunders" fits locally into the known historic Indian metaphorical world. In other words, a distinct semantic correlation exists between this Delaware term and *čeenkwihtanonki,* the Miami-Illinois language name for the site of the waterfalls on Fall Creek, the White River–West Fork tributary, where *čeenkwihtanwi,* "waterfall" literally means "it thunder-flows." Finally, although it is easy to see how *pehtáhkəw* could have been confused by English speakers with Miami-Illinois *paatoohka,* one can only conclude, as far as determining what or who "Patoka" derives from and refers to, that the jury is still out.

9

The Driftwood and Its Branches

If not disorienting, it is certainly peculiar that Indiana has two important waterways known as the White River. This situation is similar to that of a family's having two children with the same first name.[1] Even if these two rivers do eventually merge, as rivers are wont to do, calling both by the same name is still quite an unusual practice. Certainly, calling them by the same name would have been unthinkable to prehistoric or historic native peoples, for it would have only led to instant geographical confusion. Therefore, as we saw in chapter 6, the Miami-Illinois language name that translates to English "White River" refers to only what is today known as the West Fork of the White River. No one these days seems to be concerned about this situation. But Indiana author and educator Ross Lockridge Jr. proposed in the mid-1900s that the two streams be given separate names, the appropriate moniker "White River" for the White River–West Fork and the handsome label "Driftwood River" for the White River–East Fork.[2] Lockridge, however, did not pull the latter name out of a hat; his suggestion has old roots. Indeed, the first English language name on record for the White River–East Fork is "Driftwood Fork of the White River," a hydronym mentioned in 1805 in the Grouseland treaty executed by William Henry Harrison.[3] "Driftwood River" is certainly an appropriate designation for this long, relatively narrow, and extremely torturous waterway, often subject to flooding, that moves through what was once one of the planet's greatest mesophytic forests. Understandably, the East Fork's numberless meanders would have been a great environment for the accumulation of driftwood. In fact, an unintentional reference to this place-name is present in one of the first historical descriptions of the East Fork. On his visit to the river in February 1819, John Vawter "found ... both sides of Driftwood ... well timbered."[4] Why Harrison, Vawter, and others in their day called the river the "Driftwood" stemmed from the fact that this is a translation of original Algonquian names for it.

None of Dunn's Miami or Wea informants were aware of a Miami-Illinois language name for this stream, even though the name "Driftwood" originally came from Miami-Illinois. Indeed, no certifiable Miami-Illinois name exists in the record for any tributary of the White River–East Fork watershed. This unfamiliarity with the East Fork was a result of the treaties of the early 1800s that placed these people in relative isolation in various parts of northern Indiana, or else pushed them far to the west of the Mississippi—in either case far beyond the banks of the East Fork of the White River. Thus by the early 1900s, when Dunn got around to asking Miami-Illinois speakers in both Indiana and Oklahoma for this stream's name, they had long since lost their connection to it and hence the memory of what their forebears had called it. Fortunately, however, the Miami-Illinois name for the East Fork of the White River did survive in the record and is found in a history of Johnson County in the slightly distorted but transparently recognizable <Inquahsahquah>.[5] Dunn probably came across this particular spelling, or else a similar attestation of this Miami-Illinois place-name unknown to me, and then asked his Miami-Illinois–speaking informants for its proper pronunciation, which he wrote in the forms <Óngwahsahkah> and <Óngwasákwa>.[6] However, the Old Miami-Illinois sources indicate that *aa* not *oo* is the initial sound of the word for "driftwood." Costa has shown convincingly that in Miami-Illinois the first vowel of the word for "driftwood," phonemic *aankwaahsakwa,* is long *aa.*[7] Indeed, Dunn's Ó- is a vernacular spelling of long back [ɑɑ], phonemic *aa,* before [ŋg].

Since one of the Miami-Illinois names for the Ohio River, as we saw in chapter 3, is datable to late prehistoric times, the Miami-Illinois name *aankwaahsakwa (siipiiwi)* for the East Fork of the White River could also be of the same general age. Even historically speaking, this hydronym was a member of the Miami-Illinois place-name repertoire decades before the Delaware Indians borrowed it into their languages.

As noted in chapter 6, Delaware Indians, driven by British colonists from their homelands near the eastern seaboard into what is now western Pennsylvania and eastern Ohio, eventually established villages, with the consent of the Piankashaw, in the watersheds of Indiana's White River–West Fork and White River–East Fork during the last quarter of the eighteenth century.[8] Even though the Delaware did not found their well-known towns and villages on the upper White River–West Fork until after the Treaty of Greene Ville in 1795, some were already living on the Great Miami River of southwestern Ohio by 1754 and then in the land between the Ohio River and the West Fork shortly after 1770. History marks the appearance of Unami-speaking villages in the White River–East Fork watershed at least by 1790, and inference suggests the initial arrival of the first occasional Unami groups twenty years earlier.[9] It is for this reason that the watershed of the White River–East Fork has Delaware place-names.

The American military officer Colonel John Ketcham, in his reminiscences of the year 1812–13, called the East Fork of the White River <Hangonahakqua Sepoo>.[10] Although it contains a misspelling, -nahak-, for an originally written *-hanak (for phonemic *-həna·k*), where the "n" and the "h" have been switched, Ketcham's recording represents Unami **ankɔhəna·kwí·i-sí·p·u*, "driftwood river."[11] The final -a of Ketcham's <Hangonahakqua> is an example of an "alphabet A," an old English vernacular sound-symbol correspondence discussed in chapters 5 and 7, whereby English orthographic "a" can represent the sounds *e(·)* and *i(·)* and even, as we see here, the sequence *-í·i-*.

The English hydronym "Driftwood River," like its American Indian inspiration, originally delineated the entire White River–East Fork, all the way from the mouth of Sugar Creek in southwestern Shelby County down to the meeting of the White River–East Fork and the White River–West Fork south of Washington.[12] An intimation of the original usage of this place-name is found, for example, in the name of Driftwood Township in Jackson county, located at the confluence of the Muscatatuck River and the White River–East Fork. However, by 1836, "Driftwood River" had come to apply only to the waters *below* the Flatrock River on down to the mouth of the Muscatatuck, which is a usage that prevailed at least until 1860.[13] Since that time, prosaic, utilitarian "East Fork of the White River" has continued to apply to more and more sections of this waterway while the original, euphonious "Driftwood River" has come to denote smaller and smaller segments of it. Indeed, this has become true to such an extent that at the beginning of the twenty-first century the name Driftwood River now refers only to a mere sixteen miles of water lying above the mouth of the Flatrock. But the original native "Driftwood River" meandered for well over *two hundred miles*.[14] Certainly, Lockridge would have agreed that each shrinking of the use of beautiful "Driftwood River" represents a cultural loss for all.

All of the eight streams in Indiana known as Sugar Creek attest to the former and in some cases current glory of important beech-maple forests in the respective watersheds of these various streams. Although the name of each Sugar Creek could be of Native American origin, only two of these streams are known to have documented indigenous names. One of these, an approximately 120-mile-long tributary of the White River–East Fork, begins in extreme northwestern Henry County northeast of Indianapolis. After entering Madison County a couple of times for negligible distances, this particular Sugar Creek runs the full length of Hancock County, passes into Shelby County, and then flows down the eastern boundary of Johnson County. There, the stream joins the waters of the Big Blue River to become the Driftwood River, as the latter term is used today.

A spelling that no doubt has the appearance of being an American Indian name for Sugar Creek is found on Guernsey's map in the form <Achsinnaminschi>, which ostensibly represents a German language spelling of a Delaware language term meaning "sugar maple tree."[15] Of course, the authenticity of this term as an actual component of a Delaware place-name for Sugar Creek depends on our being able to determine its source, which Guernsey does not provide and which still today remains elusive. Therefore, we are left with two assumptions: (1) <Achsinnaminschi> could be a genuine recording by a German Moravian missionary that Guernsey turned up somewhere but failed to document, or (2) <Achsinnaminschi> is simply Guernsey's personal interpolation. In other words, since he knew that the English place-name "Sugar Creek" referred to sugar maple trees, and since he knew the Delaware had lived in the area, it is not impossible that he took this information and just made up this place-name by looking up the word for "sugar maple tree" in Zeisberger's dictionary—for Guernsey's and Zeisberger's terms have exactly the same, distinctively German spelling for the name of this tree.[16] This is not to say that the Delaware did not have a name for Sugar Creek, or that they could not have used words for "sugar maple tree" in their languages to name this creek, or even that <Achsinnaminschi> itself is not a good representation or indeed a genuine attestation of the initial component of such a place-name. The problem is that the spelling <Achsinnaminschi> as well as the precise form of the *complete* Unami or Munsee hydronym are, as far as I know, *undocumented* and therefore unknown.

The only genuine recording for a Native American name for Sugar Creek is Hough's <Thenamesay>. This spelling stands for Shawnee *(hah)θenaamiisi*, "sugar maple tree." Unfortunately, Hough's term represents just the front end of the place-name—it lacks the term for "river" or "creek."[17] Although it is not possible to state this with any certainty, the full place-name could have been **(hah)θenaamiisiiθiipi.*

While the attestation of a Shawnee place-name in this area may come as a surprise, its appearance seems to point to a distinctive Shawnee settlement pattern in the Indiana area during the late 1700s and very early 1800s. The Indiana historian William Anderson suggested that during the second half of the eighteenth century, many Shawnee were living in what is now central Indiana, between the Miami, Wea, and Piankashaw to the north and west and the Delaware to the south and east.[18] His early-twentieth-century theory finds support in various later works, including Helen Tanner's atlas, which indicates a Shawnee village on the lower White River in 1788–89, and Ferguson's dissertation, which notes that in 1800 Shawnee were living along the west fork of the White River.[19] In addition, intriguing native place-name evidence in this particular part of what is today known as Indiana points to historic Shawnee residency. When looking at American Indian place-names throughout the state, one notices the stunning dearth of Shawnee names—only a handful exist. But all of Indiana's Shawnee place-names are found in precisely where Anderson said the Shawnee had lived. In addition to two names for the Ohio River, there is one each for the St. Mary's River southwest of Fort Wayne, a waterway well known for Shawnee villages, Sugar Creek in Hancock and Johnson Counties, Six-Mile Creek in Jennings County, and Salt Creek in Brown, Monroe, and Lawrence Counties. In the same area, we also find the English-language place-name Shawnee Creek for a stream located in Rush and Fayette Counties.[20]

The local Shawnee were generally at odds with the Americans. So while the former would have had names for sites and streams in Indiana, they were not necessarily in a position to share them with the latter. At the same time, one must also bear in mind that there were only two requirements for a local place-name of Shawnee origin: a single historical Shawnee speaker who said the name aloud and a literate American sitting nearby with quill and ink. Hough's <Thenamesay> is such a Shawnee place-name.

The modern name of an important northern source of the White River–East Fork is variously spelled Shankatunk, Shankatank, or Shankitunk. Dunn tried to tie this stream's name to <Tāchanigeu->, a recording done by the Moravian missionary Zeisberger, which the latter glossed "where many old logs lie."[21] However, the shapes of the two terms do not even begin to match. Although the following analysis is speculative, when the linguistic evidence is dovetailed with the geophysical character of this stream, Shankatunk ~ Shankatank~ Shankitunk seems, in my opinion, to represent unattested Munsee **ša·xkíhtank,* "it flows-straight," which would be a dependent verb composed of the initial *ša·xk-,* "straight," the final *-ihtan,* "flow," and *-k,* the requisite verbal suffix.[22]

There are two reasons that make this an attractive hypothesis. First, Shankatunk Creek is *impressively* straight when compared to any of the area's creeks, all of which are *unforgettably* tortuous. For example, while the Little Blue River, located directly west of Shankatunk, meanders for all intents and purposes in circles upon itself, Shankatunk Creek drops like a heavy rope from the bottom of central Henry County straight down into Rush County. The conspicuous straightness of Shankatunk Creek could have had a direct visual impact on the Delaware and stirred them to name this creek in the same way that the straight stretch of the Wabash River at Peru, discussed in chapter 7, inspired Miami-Illinois speakers to create the toponym *iihkipihsinonki.* Second, even though the term <Shankatunk> and **ša·xkíhtank* are not mirror images of each other, it is only the first syllable of the historical spelling that presents any problem. However, the discrepancy between Shank- and *ša·xk-* is easily explainable in light of the great difficulty English-speaking Americans had in comprehending and recording the Munsee fricative *x.* In the case of Shank-, the -k- would naturally correspond to the sound *k* of *ša·xk-.* The -n- of Shank- would then represent either a replacive sound for the sound *x* of *ša·xk-,* mimicking and assimilating to the sound of the *-n-* of -atank ~ -itunk, or else the "n" could be an original miscopied "h," one of the oldest copy errors in the business. Finally, the second -a- of <Shankatunk>, especially in light of the specific Shankitunk spelling, is surely an "alphabet A," the English vernacular spelling practice mentioned above, which can ultimately represent, among other things, Delaware *i.*

The waters of the Shankatunk enter the Flatrock River in northwest-central Rush County. The Flatrock, whose name derives from the fact that its bed is composed of New Albany shale, begins in Henry County and flows southwest in a narrow channel through a constricted flood plain across southern Shelby County, skirting several bluffs and escarpments before falling into the Driftwood in central Bartholomew County. The English language placename "Flatrock River" was used as early as 1812. For that reason it could be a translation of an indigenous name for this river. However, Guernsey's <Puchkachsin>, by which is intended a Delaware expression meaning "flatrock" (i.e., Puchk-achsin), would only represent the initial component of a place-name.[23] Moreover, in general, roots in the Algonquian languages, which include the Unami initial *pàk-*, "flat," are idiosyncratic, and there is no attestation on record of a grammatical term meaning "flat-rock" that includes *pàk-* as the initial component and *ahsən,* "stone" as the second. That said, the -u- in Puchk- is an excellent rendering of Unami short *a,* which was pronounced [^], somewhat like the vowel in English "up." This fact alone lends an air of authenticity to Guernsey's term. At this point it is not impossible to say that the modern English place-name "Flatrock River" came from a Delaware hydronym meaning "flat-rock," but no grammatical historical spelling has yet been found that would corroborate this notion.

Ben Davis Creek, whose name derives from the American name for a local Delaware leader in the early 1800s, enters the Flatrock River some ten miles below the mouth of Shankatunk Creek. An early history of Rush county writes <Mahoning> as a Native American name for this stream.[24] This spelling indeed represents the Unami expression "at the salt lick." <Mahoning>, if it is a genuine recording, would indicate that Ben Davis Creek was known to the Delaware for one or more salt resources located along its banks. (See chapter 5 for additional information about the Unami term for "salt lick.")

Clifty Creek begins in southern Rush County, traverses the northwest quadrant of Decatur County and flows from the northeast into the Driftwood River south of the Flatrock. The English hydronym "Clifty Creek" likely refers to the same geological reality as that described by Guernsey's <Esseniahanhokqui>,[25] which stands for Southern Unami *ahsə́n(a) aha·nhúkwi.* The late Lucy Blalock, a native speaker of Southern Unami, supplied the present study with a gloss for Guernsey's <Esseniahanhokqui>, which according to her translates to English "rocks over and over again."[26] This term is composed of *ahsə́n(a),* "rock(s)" and *aha·nhúkwi,* "over and over again." At the same time, it is not clear if *ahsə́n(a) aha·nhúkwi* was an actual place-name; it may simply represent a descriptive statement about this stream. Or it is also possible that in some way <Esseniahanhokqui> is a reconstructed form, since the -ahanhokqui spelling in Guernsey's term is the very same spelling for "over and over again" that appears in the Brinton and Anthony dictionary, which Guernsey had access to.[27] Even so, the Esseni- segment of Guernsey's spelling is certainly peculiar, as it is not the way the word for "stone" is usually written in historical recordings of this Unami word. Moreover, there is no way that Guernsey could have translated the English hydronym "Clifty Creek" and come up with the Unami spelling <Esseniahanhoqui>. Therefore, we are left with at least the possibility that Guernsey's word is genuine, and that this Unami expression was, *in some form,* the original Unami name for this creek—or at least a descriptive phrase applied to it by an Unami speaker.

Sand Creek, another of the many tributaries of the White River–East Fork rises from multiple sources in central Decatur County. The principal one starts in the countryside northeast of Greensburg. Sand Creek then flows in a southwesterly manner through central Decatur County, cuts across northwestern Jennings County, and then runs for about four miles along the Jackson-Bartholomew county line before flowing into the East Fork. The historically attested American Indian name for this stream is first seen in 1812 in translated form in Gen. John Tipton's "Sandy Creek."[28] The only trustworthy recording of the aboriginal hydronym appears to be Hough's <Laqueouenock>.[29] In fact, although the final "o" of his spelling is a miscopied or misengraved "e," Hough's form is an admirable attempt from the early nineteenth century to write the Southern Unami participle *lé·k·aɔ́həne·k,* "that which is a sand river."[30] In this light, Tipton's "Sandy Creek" with its adjectival character reflects the grammar and meaning of this Delaware hydronym rather well.[31]

As in the case of other participle-based Unami place-names discussed in this book, *lé·k·aɔ́həne·k* may have only been a component of the entire place-name. The complete place-name may have originally been **énta lé·k·aɔ́həne·k,* "where there is a sand river."

The referent for this place-name is quite clear. *lé·k·aɔ́həne·k* speaks of the terraces composed of aeolian dune sediments along Sand Creek.[32] In fact, this is the second of two known "sand creeks" in the Native American place-name repertoire of Indiana, the other being a Miami-Illinois hydronym discussed in chapter 7.

Wyaloosing Creek starts in southwest Decatur County and meets Sand Creek in northwest Jennings County. Although Dunn correctly said this place-name derived from a Delaware language, it was his opinion that it did not originate with the Delaware Indians living in Indiana. He believed "Wyaloosing" was first applied to this creek by local American settlers who brought the name from the East with them, naming the Indiana stream after a tributary of the Susquehanna River in Pennsylvania known as "Wyalusing."[33] Unfortunately, Dunn provided no evidence to support his claim. In fact, it appears that no evidence exists as to whether this is an

American-imported place-name or a term created by local historic Indians and then borrowed locally by American settlers. Nevertheless, the *word* written "Wyaloosing" ~ "Wyalusing" does represent a genuine Munsee term, one that Zeisberger spelled <Machiwihilusing>.[34] Dunn wrote it <M'chwihillusink> and cited Zeisberger's Moravian missionary contemporary John Heckewelder as the source for his spelling as well as for the translation "at the dwelling place of the hoary veteran." This translation, however, is hyperbolic. What <Machiwihilusing> ~ <M'chwihillusink> actually stands for is the locative noun meaning "at the big old man," which in conventional English can be rephrased as "the big old man's place." The original form of this term is Munsee *(m)xmihló·ssənk,* comprised of the archaic prenoun **məx-,* "big," *mihlo·səs,* "old man," and the locative suffix *-ənk,* meaning "at." The term was pronounced [(m)xwihló·ssəŋg].[35]

After gathering to itself the waters of Sugar Creek, Shankatunk Creek, Flatrock River, Clifty Creek, Wyaloosing Creek, Sand Creek, as well as several smaller streams, the White River–East Fork flows in a southeasterly direction across Jackson County to meet the waters of its major tributary, the Muscatatuck River, on the Jackson-Washington county line. The Muscatatuck has many sources, but its principal one is located in southeastern Decatur County east of Greensburg. The name "Muscatatuck," which as recently as the early 1900s took the form "Muscackituck," is a philologist's field of dreams—or nightmares.

To begin, Muscatatuck, the modern form of the name, is pure nonsense. Furthermore, the "clear river" translation of this place-name given by Dunn, based on the spellings "Muschachetuck," "Mŏsch⊠chhittūk" ~ "Mŏschắchhíttūk", does not seem to work.[36] First, although Dunn did not identify these terms as such, they are actually his own reconstructions, no doubt premised on his belief that the first segment of this place-name was Zeisberger's <Moschachgeu->. Dunn, without noting it, surely went to Brinton's and Anthony's Lenape dictionary for the meaning of his term, since his gloss matches *verbatim* their unique translation, "clear, not turbid."[37] Second, Dunn's reconstruction, morphologically speaking, is not a possible formation with its two weak syllables in a row.[38] Therefore, if we are to sort out the meaning of this river's name, we must put Dunn's work aside and return to the known early historical spellings of the hydronym. However, the analysis will not be that simple, for the historical spellings themselves present confusing evidence.

The direct ancestor of modern spelling "Muscatatuk" is no doubt Tipton's <muscakituck>, which he penned in 1812.[39] His <muscakituck> may represent a Munsee term, composed of *máske˙kw,* "swamp" and *-ihtəkw,* "river."[40] This analysis is at least supported by the hydrology of the Muscatatuk River. Even so, it is difficult to offer complete support for this "swamp"-based analysis of "Muscatatuck." First, we have no historical attestation of a term meaning "swamp river" in Munsee. Second, there are early historical variants of our place-name that suggest its first syllable had the sound *š* and not *s.* Indeed, Hough's mid-nineteenth-century spelling <Meshcaquetuck>, which he says applied as well to the Graham Fork of the Muscatatuck River, harkens back to Dunn's "clear river" theory.[41] Chamberlain's <Meschcaquetuck>, which is the likely source of Hough's term, seems to reflect Dunn's interpretation of the place-name, except for the fact that Chamberlain translates the term "pond river"—and that gloss actually supports the "swamp river" analysis! Interestingly enough, the historical forms that support the "swamp river" theory occur in American documents starting *at least* six years before the Delaware began leaving Indiana.[42]

Also of interest is the development of the modern spelling "Muscatutuck." First, Tipton's original <muscakituck> displayed outstanding tenacity down through the years. Even in 1826, when the *spelling* of this place-name had shifted to <Muskakituck>, it still represented the *identical pronunciation* in English as that of Tipton's original recording—and this spelling persisted in English throughout the first half of the nineteenth century.[43] It was not until 1856 that the contorted and semantically opaque <Muscatatuck>, the form that we use today, sprang into being.[44] Notably, the linguistic phenomenon known as consonant assimilation, which gravitates like iron filings to the sort of phonologically charged environment exemplified by Tipton's term, was the factor responsible for the spelling change from his <musca*k*i*t*uck> to modern Musca*t*a*t*uck. In other words, the first [k] sound in Tipton's form shifted to a [t] sound under the influence of the second [t], which is an original native sound in this place-name. In the end, however, we can conclude with certainty only one thing about "Muscatatuck": In its original form, this was a hydronym conceived by local historical Delaware language speakers.

Dunn, citing an early atlas of Jennings County, stated that Six-Mile Creek, a tributary of the Muscatatuck River located in Jennings County, bore the native name <Chokoka>.[45] This spelling appears to represent Shawnee *šaakohka*, "flint." This surmise is supported by the fact that significant chert outcrops are found along Six-Mile Creek in the area where it falls rapidly. In addition, nearby Coffee Creek is also well endowed with chert.[46] However, it should be said that, if the spelling <Chokoka> does represent the Shawnee term for "flint," the exact original form of the *complete* Shawnee hydronym that it was part of is unknown.

Otter Creek is the name of a tributary of the Muscatatuck River whose sources lie in Ripley County. The former flows in a southwesterly direction into Jennings County where it meets the latter. The word for "otter" in Munsee is *kwə̀nə́moxkw* and in Southern Unami *kwənúmuxkw*.[47] Even though it is not clear which language it represents, <Connumock> on Hough's map certainly attests one of these words.[48] Furthermore, it is clear from this recording that the original European interlocutor did not hear Delaware *kw*, both at the beginning and at the end of either *kwənúmuxkw* or *kwə̀nə́moxkw*. In the case of <Connumock>, the original native *xkw* was mistaken for *k*, which both the initial C- and the final -ck in this spelling represent.

At the same time, it is important to mention that Hough's term *as written* is not a grammatical place-name; it is simply a Delaware language term meaning "otter." So despite the fact that Hough's recording may have been in some way a constituent of a Delaware language name for Otter Creek, important elements of the original hydronym are missing. For that reason it is impossible to state with any certainty what the original form of this place-name was. Still, if <Connumock> is in fact a component of a genuine Delaware place-name, the name could have referred to one of two things. It could have been a hydronym describing an area preternaturally endowed with otters (*Lutra canadensis*) or it could have been an eponym embodying the personal name of a Delaware individual named *kwənúmuxkw* or Munsee *kwə̀nə́moxkw* ("Otter") who would have lived on its banks near the turn of the nineteenth century. There are two other streams known in English as Otter Creek in southwestern Indiana, one at Terre Haute and another near Evansville. Since it is known that there were Delaware bands on the lower Wabash in the eighteenth century, particularly in the Vincennes area, the Wabash tributary known as Otter Creek could also refer to a person whose name was "Otter."[49] Because of the presence historically of Delaware Indians in extreme southwestern Indiana, the third Otter Creek, located in Warrick County, could also refer to a Delaware individual. In fact, all of these place-names could allude to the same person, if all three are eponymous. A historically notable Delaware leader known in English as "Otter," who was born around 1770 and died in 1815, was involved in Ohio Valley raiding in the late 1780s.[50]

Downstream from the Muscatatuck–White River confluence is a stream with an unusual name: Fishing Creek. A northwesterly flowing tributary of the White River–East Fork, this waterway originates in extreme northeastern Orange County and moves in a slightly northwesterly direction through Lawrence County toward its meeting with the East Fork. For a Native American name for Fishing Creek, Guernsey wrote <Nameshanne>. Names-, the first part of this term, is indeed Southern Unami *namé·s*, "fish," while -hanne would represent an Unami verb with various allomorphs that signifies "river."[51] However, Guernsey's spelling is problematic. As stated in the introduction and elsewhere in this book, no one knows where he got a great deal of his "Indian place-names"—including <Nameshanne>. Some he seems to have invented; others he clearly found in sources I have been unable to locate.

As written, <Nameshanne> could be a verb in the form **namè·sháne·*, "fish river." It could also represent a mishearing of the participle **namè·sháne·k*, "that which is a fish river." In fact, the complete hydronym could even have been **énta namè·sháne·k*, "where there is a fish river."[52] There is at least one thing working in favor of the authenticity of Guernsey's term: <Nameshanne> does not translate to "Fishing Creek."

Clear Creek, a tributary of Salt Creek, which itself is a major tributary of the East Fork of the White River, runs its entire course within Monroe County. Clear Creek then joins Salt Creek immediately before the latter descends into Lawrence County. On his map, alongside the term <Waseleuhanne>, the putative American Indian name that he offered for Clear Creek, Guernsey simply wrote "Clear Creek."[53] However, the actual meaning of the expression represented by <Waseleuhanne> is far more evocative than prosaic "Clear Creek."[54] Just like *waapaahši(i)ki (siipiiwi)*, the Miami-Illinois name for the Wabash River, <Waseleuhanne> is, seemingly, the Northern Unami verb ending in long *-e·* meaning "a shining river." In Southern Unami, the term for "it shines"· is *ɔ·s·əle·w*. The Northern Unami cognate appears in Zeisberger's dictionary in the form <Wasaléu>.[55]

Certainly, <Wasaleuhanne> would be a hydronym that holds a special place in the inventory of Indiana's Native American place-names, since a visitor to this stream today can still see why the Lenape would have given it such a name. Like no other waterway in the area, Clear Creek is but one seemingly endless series of rocky riffles reflecting the celestial luminaries.

The Muddy Fork is the modern name for another tributary of Salt Creek. This stream originates in northeastern Jackson County and then swings northwestward into southwest Brown County where it meets the south fork of Salt Creek. The name <Niskassieku> given for this stream on Guernsey's map could be his invention. <Niskassieku> is at the very least a careless miscopy of Zeisberger's dictionary entry <niskassisku>, which represents Unami *ni·skahsí·sku*, "dirty-mud." The Munsee cognate is *ni·skasískəw*.[56] In Algonquian the word for "mud" is constellated within the semantic domain of "slippery." Therefore, the term *ni·skahsí·sku* refers not only to something that is slippery, that is, *ahsí·sku*, but to something unclean, *ni·sk-*. Certainly, the Muddy Fork is sluggish and somewhat rank in character and has steep, often slippery, muddy banks.

In sum, it is an attractive hypothesis that Guernsey's miscopied <Niskassieku> in some way represents a segment of the original Unami name for the Muddy Fork of Salt Creek. Still, there seems to be at present no evidence that supports the notion that the Unami knew this stream by the name Guernsey applied to it.

Salt Creek itself rises from multiple sources within the highlands of Brown County and flows in a serpentine fashion toward the southwest to meet up with the White River–East Fork in Lawrence County west of Bedford. The name of this waterway derives from the presence of salt licks along it. An archaeological survey of Brown County conducted in 1990 by the Glenn Black Laboratory of Archaeology at Indiana University located four salt licks on Salt Creek. In addition, Jack Weddle, a Brown County archaeologist, has located not only numerous seeps along this stream but also a major salt lick along the north fork of Salt Creek.[57] In fact, the latter site was a very important local source of salt for settlers in the 1820s and 1830s, as mentioned by Bailey in her history of Brown County.[58]

<Wapepemay>, the American Indian name that Hough recorded for Salt Creek, bears a classic miscopy.[59] Here an original handwritten capital N- was thought to be a capital W-. Either Hough or Hough's engraver probably committed this error, and not only because of the similar "peak and valley" contours of capital N and W, but also because either man, and Hough in particular, might have been aware of Algonquian words beginning with wap- or wab, which are common spellings for historical language

reflexes of the Proto-Algonquian initial **wa·p-,* "white." Consequently, before either of those individuals got his hands on it, <Wapepemay> would have originally been written *Napepemay. In <Wapepemay>, that is, *Napepemay, the first a- is an "alphabet A," the antique English vernacular spelling representing *e.* The final -ay also represents a vernacular spelling that stands for the sound *i.* *Napepemay thus represents Shawnee *nepipemi,* "salt," literally "water-grease." The original Shawnee name for Salt Creek was then likely **nepipemiiθiipi,* "salt river."[60] This is probably the case since, although *θiipi,* the Shawnee term meaning "river," is missing from Hough's attestation, a complete Shawnee hydronym with the same meaning is recorded for a stream in Kentucky. In the early nineteenth century, the U.S. Indian agent and fur trader John Johnston wrote <Nepepimmesepe> for that state's Licking River, which is named for its famous salt licks.[61] Although the length of the antepenultimate vowel of Shawnee **nepipemiiθiipi* is not certain, Johnston's double mm preceding "e" supports the long *ii* hypothesis, for the doubling of a consonant in historical recordings done by Europeans commonly indicates that a long vowel is in the immediate vicinity. In Johnston's case, this would imply that he noticed vowel length in the speech of his Shawnee source but neither understood it nor properly recorded it.

Rising in southern Lawrence County and flowing west and southwest into Martin County to meet the White River–East Fork, southern Indiana's Beaver Creek may bear a name today that is a translation of an American Indian language name for the stream. Guernsey offers the spelling <Tamaquehanne> as a native name for this stream. Tamaque- appears to stand for Unami *təma·kwe,* "beaver," a noun evincing word-final *e.* The segment spelled -hanne, as we saw earlier, represents an allomorph of a verb meaning "river, creek," possibly a verb form ending in long *-e·*. Guernsey's <Tamaquehanne> could also be a either mishearing or a miscopy of either **təma·kwe·háne·k* or the changed **te·ma·kwe·háne·k,* a participle meaning "that which is a beaver river."[62] Moreover, as with other participle-based Unami place-names noted above, this one could also have been preceded by the term *énta,* "where," which was obviously not recorded.

Now, one thing certainly working in favor of Guernsey's term's being a genuine Unami place-name is the fact that the simplex noun for "beaver" in Unami was commonly written by English speakers with "o" in the first syllable—as a representation of Unami [^]. But <Tamaquehanne> has -a- in the first syllable, which happens to be an excellent candidate for an "alphabet A" representing the sound *e˙*, precisely the first vowel of the **te˙ma˙kwe˙háne˙k,* noted above, an example of first-syllable ablaut.

As in the case of other streams mentioned in this chapter, if <Tamaquehanne> were a spelling of a genuine Unami place-name, this name would probably be an eponym. And it would likely refer to the local late-eighteenth- and early-nineteenth-century Unami leader *təma˙kwe,* "Beaver," an associate of the more famous Killbuck discussed in chapter 6. The place-name would thus indicate where this individual and his people were living at one time. This Indian leader's name appears on various treaties signed by the Delaware and the United States in the opening years of 1800s. It is spelled <Tommaqua> in a letter addressed to William Henry Harrison, <Tomaguee> on the treaty of 1804, and <Tomague> on the famous accord executed in 1805 between the Delaware and the United States at Grouseland near Vincennes, not far from Beaver Creek. *təma˙kwe* also signed a letter to Harrison on September 9, 1808, and was a signatory to the general treaty of 1815.[63]

Lick Creek, whose name is related to the name of the modern town known as French Lick, originates south of Paoli in Orange County and flows northwest to join the White River–East Fork in extreme southern Martin County. This area was a favorite stopover for bison traveling across southern Indiana from the Wabash at Vincennes to the Ohio at New Albany, back and forth from the prairies of Illinois to the salt licks of Kentucky. Guernsey says the Delaware name for the stream was <Manonhanne>, which ostensibly is a hydronym having to do with "salt lick": Manon- [*sic*] for original *Mahon-, and -hanne for "river."[64] If authentic, this is either an Unami verb ending in long *-e˙* or a misheard participle with final *-k.*[65]

After its journey of nearly 250 miles, the waterway known today as the East Fork of the White River finally meets the West Fork of the White River where Daviess, Knox, and Pike Counties come together. An ill-fated Munsee village was located in this area shortly before 1789.[66] Guernsey's map calls the land at the confluence of these two streams <Lechauwitank>.[67] The complex syntactic nature of his spelling indicates that it represents a genuine native place-name. Moreover, in this case, Guernsey did not copy his term from Zeisberger, and given the grammatical structure of <Lechauwitank>, Guernsey certainly could never have made it up. But as usual, he did not indicate where he got it, which is unfortunate.

<Lechauwitank> is a descriptive moniker. If the Northern Unami form of this expression was like the Southern Unami form, this German spelling would represent Northern Unami **le·x·awí·tank,* a conjunct II verb meaning "it fork-flows." In Unami, the initial **le·x·aw-*, exhibiting first-syllable ablaut, means "fork," *-i·tan* is the verb "flow," and *-k* is the verb suffix.[68] This place-name, of course, refers to the confluence of the White River–West Fork and the White River–East Fork.

10

The Heart of the North Country

Numerous glacial lakes grace northern Indiana. Historically, these waters naturally bore Miami-Illinois place-names. However, beginning in the eighteenth century, this area became the hunting ground of the southerly advancing Potawatomi and in time the home for most of this tribe. Therefore, both Potawatomi and Miami-Illinois place-names are found in this part of the state.

Lake Maxinkuckee, the lacustrine jewel set in Marshall County, enters history set in the itinerary created by French traders Charles Chevalier or Charles Chaboillez for the overland trail between the St. Joseph River of Lake Michigan and the Indian villages and French fort just west of present-day Lafayette known to the French as *les Ouiatanons.*[1] In this, the earliest known guide to what is now north-central Indiana, we see that Lake Maxinkuckee was known to the French as *le grand lac* (the big lake). This is, of course, an appropriate label, since this lake is, strictly speaking, Indiana's largest *naturally formed* body of water.[2] Lake Maxinkuckee was important in the early history of this area for the simple reason that it was a very prominent landmark on this Indian trail/French trade route. On its way to the Tippecanoe River, this trace passed along the western side of Lake Maxinkuckee then proceeded south across a wet prairie, typical of regional topography, which was located at the south end of the lake.[3]

A variety of early forms of today's spelling "Maxinkuckee" exist in historical accounts. The year 1835 saw the appearance of the spelling <Meksinkakeek> in the survey report of the Michigan Road. In the same decade of the nineteenth century, English painter George Winter, during his travels in the area, recorded this place-name in four different ways: <Muxinkuckee>, <Muxinkuckkey>, <Muxenkuckee>, and <Maxeenickuckee>.[4] Winter's spellings are the direct forerunners of the modern spelling. In the next century Dunn wrote the lake's name <Mŏgsi̋nkiki> and <Mŏgsínkεεki> for Potawatomi and <Mängsā́nkiki> for Miami-Illinois,[5] and it was the Miami leader *waapanahkikapwa* who supplied Dunn with the Miami-Illinois place-name along with the translation "big stone country." Evincing expected unstressed short-vowel syncope, Dunn's <Mängsā́nkiki> spelling represents the Miami-Illinois conjunct II verb *meenkahsenahkiki,* "it is big stone country." This term, which can also serve as a deverbal noun meaning "big stone country," is composed of *meenk-,* the ablauted form of the initial *mank-,* "big," along with the "stone" medial *-ahsen-,* the "land" final *-ahk(i)* and the inanimate intransitive verb suffix *-ki.* Owing to a naturally occurring voicing as well as a vowel deletion process at work in the Miami-Illinois language of the early 1900s, phonemic *meenkahsenahkiki* in the time of *waapanahkikapwa* had come to be pronounced [meeŋghsenhkiki], for which Dunn's recording <Mängsā́nkiki > is a reasonably accurate representation. The Old Miami-Illinois cognate for this expression is attested in the early Jesuit missionary records in the independent order with the spelling <mangasinacaki8i> and glossed *lieu ou il y a de grosses pierres* (place where there are big stones).[6] The Miami-Illinois name for Lake Maxinkuckee alludes to glacier-transported boulders in the vicinity of the lake.

The age of the local Miami-Illinois language place-name *meenkahsenahkiki* cannot be precisely determined. However, it could very well date to late prehistoric times given our current understanding of the population distribution pattern of the late prehistoric Miami-Illinois–speaking peoples. On the other hand, Dunn's putative Potawatomi forms <Mŏgsi̋nkiki> and <Mŏgsínkeeki>, as well as Winter's spellings above, are problematic for Potawatomi. It appears that the Potawatomi simply borrowed the preexisting Miami-Illinois toponym wholesale, altering the pronunciation slightly—or else these spellings represent something in Old Potawatomi no longer attested, perhaps a miscopied/misheard Potawatomi cognate of the Miami-Illinois place-name.

The Potawatomi name ascribed by Guernsey to the body of water in Marshall County known today as Lake of the Woods is spelled <Copenuckconbes> on his map. This spelling represents Potawatomi *mkopənikkewnbəs,* "Bear-Potatoes-Gathering Lake."[7] It consists of the initial *mko-,* "bear," written Co-, the independent plural noun *pənik,* "potatoes," written -penuc-, the animate intransitive derivational suffix *-ke,* "gathering," miswritten -kc-, where -c- is an original miscopied "e," a connective *-w-*, written -o-, for making a composite expression, and the Potawatomi independent noun *nbəs,* signifying "lake." The potato in this place-name is the cow lily, or spatterdock (*Nuphar*), the same edible root represented historically by the French spelling *macopine* for Miami-Illinois *mahkohpina ~ mihkohpina,* a plant described on several occasions in this volume. Indeed, the *Nuphar* figures in more Native American place-names in Indiana than any other term. That the hydronym <Copenuckconbes> had to do with some kind of edible root was a fact not lost on local Americans at the turn of the twentieth century. Although he could not be more specific, the Marshall County judge and amateur historian Daniel McDonald said the historical native place-name referred to "a vegetable that grew spontaneously in that region."[8]

According to Guernsey, a historical American Indian name for another Marshall County body of water known today in English as Pretty Lake was <Quauckeubus>.[9] This spelling represents the Potawatomi expression *mtəgwagkiwnbəs,* "woods lake."[10] The form <Quauckeubus> clearly reflects an instance where an English-speaking recorder caught only the last part of the composite term, *-gwagkiwnbəs,* and failed to hear the front end of the place-name, *mtə-*, which was not recorded. Still, <Quauckeubus> is an excellent rendition in nineteenth-century English orthography of the final segment of the Potawatomi term in question. This place-name is based on *mtəgwagkik,* a locative noun meaning "in the woods." It also contains the noun + noun connector *-w-*, and *nbəs* the inanimate noun meaning "lake."

The shoddy nature of the recording of this place-name is not the only cruel fate that has befallen it. Strangely enough, someone may have misplaced this hydronym, for "Woods Lake" or "Lake of the Woods," which in Potawatomi is *mtəgwagkiwnbəs,* is the English translation of the name for another lake, discussed above. Thus the implication could be that *mtəgwagkiwnbəs* was the original name for Lake of the Woods, while *mkopənikkewnbəs* was the original Potawatomi name for what is known today as Pretty Lake. However, I have been unable to find documentation that could resolve this issue.

<Sagayiganuhniyug> is a name applied to a body of water once located in an area in Newton County now known as the Willow Slough State Fish and Game Reservation. Beckwith seems to have been the first person to run across this native place-name, which he translated to "Lake of the Bea-

vers."[11] Beckwith's statement that the <-ahnickyug> segment of this place-name means "of the beavers" can only be a bad guess. <Sagayiganuhniyug> cannot mean "Lake of the Beavers" since such a construction would violate Potawatomi grammar. Nevertheless, Beckwith's incorrect translation for <Sagayiganuhniyug> was successful in popularizing itself, finding its way, for example, onto Guernsey's map and into Hiestand's early archaeological report on Newton County.[12] Despite the fact that the area around this lake is well endowed with modern place-names referring to the beaver, such as Beaver Creek, Beaver City, and Beaver Township, the origin of these names is not necessarily Native American. In fact, the first cartographic occurrence of English "Beaver Lake" that I could find dates only to 1858.[13] Even though Beckwith's notion is unfounded, what <Sagayiganuhniyug> actually represents is not clear.

<Sagayiganuhniyug> could represent Old Potawatomi *_zagagən(ə)nəniyəg_, "ricing-pole-men," a plural noun composed of Old Potawatomi *_zagagən_, "ricing pole, nail," a pole used to mark off rice sheaths until the time that they can be harvested, and *_(ə)nəniyəg_, "men." According to the Potawatomi scholar Laura Buszard-Welcher, the modern pronunciation of the name would be _zgagənniyəg_, showing loss of the extra _n_ as well as vowel deletion.[14] Although it would be a mystery as to who these "ricing-pole-men" could have been, wild rice (_Zizania aquatic_) is a very common plant in this part of Indiana and was an important food source for local historic Native Americans.

At the same time, the -yi- segment of <Sagayiganuhniyug> could be an attempt to represent orthographically a glottal stop, thus suggesting a Potawatomi analysis in the form *_zag(ə)ʔəgən(ə)nəniyəg_, "lake men," a modern spelling with the old vowels reinserted in parentheses. This term is composed *_zag(ə)ʔəgən_, "lake" and *_(ə)nəniyəg_, "men." However, the problem with this interpretation as well as with the analysis offered above would indicate that Beckwith's <Sagayiganuhniyug> is not a Potawatomi place-name but simply a descriptive statement about or an informal moniker for the people who were living at this lake at one time. However, if we look at the final -ug of <Sagayiganuhniyug> as a locative noun suffix, which would be expected for a grammatical Potawatomi place-name, Beckwith's term might mean "at the little lake man" or, in everyday English, "the little lake man's place," *_zag(ə)ʔəgən(ə)nənəweyəg_, which evinces the diminutive suffix _-ey_ and the locative suffix _-əg_ meaning "at." Yet in the end, even that term does not match Beckwith's all that well. Thus the final analysis of <Sagayiganuhniyug> remains problematic.[15]

Shipshewana, the name of a town in southwestern La Grange County, was originally applied to the lake located just northwest of this town. This modern place-name represents the personal name of a Potawatomi man who lived in this area in the early 1800s. His name appears on the treaties signed by the U.S. government and the Potawatomi in 1832 and 1834.[16] Dunn wrote the name of this man, who was a contemporary of better known Potawatomi leaders such as Wisaw and Mota, in the forms <Shupshewáhno> and <cū́pciwáno>, where "c" stands for *š*. Dunn said the term meant "Vision of the Lion."[17] Not surprisingly, this translation, given to him by Thomas Topash, again reveals Topash's lack of fluency in Potawatomi. Indeed, the translation "Vision of the Lion," which has been repeated numerous times in the literature as the gloss for <Shipshewana>, is nothing but bizarre. In truth, <Shipshewana> is simply *mšəbžiwanəg,* "at the great cat den."[18] This Potawatomi toponym is comprised of the initial *mšə-,* "big, great," *bži,* "cat," *wan,* "hole in the ground, den," and *-əg,* a locative suffix meaning "in, at." The initial *m* of Potawatomi *mšəbži,* "great cat" would have dropped in casual speech, a fact that accounts for the historical spellings with initial Sh- rather than initial M—and which also accounts for the native language authenticity of these forms. However, the reader should note that the place-name <Shipshewana> was used by local English-speaking American military personnel and government officials as a means of designating where this Potawatomi man lived. So, while the term *mšəbži* is the name in Potawatomi for the spirit known as the Underwater Panther, <Shipshewana> was not a place-name used by the Potawatomi to describe a place sacred to this deity.

Lake Wawasee, the large body of water located in Kosciusko County that is one of the sources of the Elkhart River, is not the name that the early English-speaking settlers of the region used for this lake, which was a smaller body of water in its original form. They knew today's Lake Wawasee as "Nine-Mile Lake." The English language moniker "Wawasee" was originally the name of the small lake straddling the Van Buren and Turkey Creek township line in northeastern Kosciusko County known today as Dewart Lake.[19] Even so, the place-name "Wawasee" is noteworthy from an ethnolinguistic point of view. Although one might expect, as Dunn did, that the name is Potawatomi place-name, it is in fact a distorted Miami-Illinois language personal name. "Wawasee" is an abbreviated form of the name of a local Miami man who lived in the late eighteenth and the early nineteenth century. A contemporary of the famous Miami leaders Jean-Baptiste Richardville, François Godfroy, Francis Lafontaine, and Le Gros,

Wawasee signed various treaties between the Miami and the United States including the one drawn up in 1826, wherein his name appears as <Wau-weassee> and <Wauwaausesee>.[20] In the 1820s, Wawasee moved his band north of the Wabash and was living in what is now Kosciusko County. By 1831, he had moved further to the northeast, to the Elkhart River.[21] His name is in fact seen numerous times in Tipton's papers in a bevy of spellings: <Wawweessee>, <Waweeesse>, <Wawweahsee>, <Wauweeisee>, and <Wauwaausee>, to mention just a few.[22]

Although <Wauweassee> and <Wawweahsee> are, linguistically speaking, the best historical recordings of this individual's name that I am aware of, all of the spellings mentioned here are incomplete forms of the Miami-Illinois participle *waawiyasita,* "one who is round." Tipton, or whoever first recorded this name, barring an outright intentional clipping of the name, evidently did not catch the final syllable *-ta.* The reason for such an error would be that *-si-*, the next to the last syllable, is the strong one, while *-t-* was likely unaspirated and the following vowel *-a* was likely devoiced. This situation could have caused an English speaker lacking a deep enough understanding of the Miami-Illinois language to simply miss the last syllable of this term altogether. Still, the pronunciation of the English place-name "Wawasee" nicely preserves the strong-syllable pattern of the native pronunciation, that is, the English hydronym is pronounced "wawaSEE," not "waWAsee," as one would naturally expect for English.

It is not clear what the roundness of this man's name referred to. It could have been his body, his face, his personality or his spirit; it could even have referred to something that he was named for, such as the full moon or the sun, or to something unimaginable. But one thing is certain—he was not named after the lake. Neither Nine-Mile Lake nor Dewart Lake was round by any stretch of the imagination. Furthermore, it is important to mention that, even though the linguistic reality of this Miami man's name is transparent, no evidence exists indicating that "Wawasee" was ever used as a place-name by the Miami themselves. In all likelihood, as in the case of Shipshewana above, "Wawasee" was simply a designation applied by Americans to the site where they found *waawiyasita* living in the early part of the nineteenth century. Finally, though, one must give credit, it seems, to Col. Eli Lilly, the grandfather of Indiana archaeology, who spent many a warm month at Lake Wawasee in the early 1900s. As the story goes, Lilly relished the sound of the name "Wawasee" and, aware of the early history of this area, instigated the adoption of this term as the name for this beautiful lake.[23]

11

Indiana's Ohio River Tributaries

Although rivers and lakes bearing names of American Indian origin are common in north, central, and southern Indiana, the majority of the modern names for the state's Ohio River tributaries come from English, the foreign language that figured most significantly in this area's recent history. The primary reason for this situation is that the Ohio Valley watershed in Indiana was an important segment of the volatile front along which trespassing Virginians and Kentuckians challenged local, legitimately established Native American populations in a desperate struggle for control of the land.[1] Just like the Anglo-Saxon tribes during the conquest of Celtic England in the fourth and fifth centuries, English-speaking American villagers living west of the Appalachian mountains in the late eighteenth and early nineteenth centuries appear to have had, generally speaking, little incentive to use their enemies' place-names. For local indigenous peoples and newly arriving Americans, mutual massacre and village burning ruled the day, and many indigenous toponyms and hydronyms were lost in the flames. Furthermore, because of this dangerous situation, the extreme southern part of what is today the state of Indiana was not home to that many Indians around the turn of the nineteenth century. In this light, the entire Ohio Valley in Indiana—all 357 miles of it—is for the most part without documented American Indian place-names. However, because of their sheer age, one must allow for the possibility that the English language monikers for some Ohio River tributaries in Indiana, such as Blue River, Deer Creek, and Pigeon Creek, could be American Indian–related hydronyms. Shawnee and Delaware villages were certainly located along the Ohio in southwestern Indiana, and, in fact, Deer Creek and Pigeon Creek, the latter identified by name by 1765, are likely eponymous in nature and native in reference.[2]

Though located principally within the state of Ohio, the Great Miami River manages to swing into extreme southeastern Indiana for a little over a mile before returning to Ohio and falling into the Ohio River. This is one reason Indiana can claim this stream as one of its own. A more important reason is that the history of the Great Miami River is intimately entwined with that of Indiana.

As we saw in earlier chapters, the French referred at various times to two streams in present-day Indiana as *la rivière des Miamis* (the Miami's River)—the St. Joseph of Lake Michigan and the Maumee. However, in the case of the Great Miami River, its name did not come from the French; this is an English creation, and it dates to only 1749. "The Great Miami River" also appears to be a unique place-name in the local inventory since it was the only European place-name borrowed by a native language. The historic Shawnee took this English form and translated it **mhšimyaamiiθiipi*, "Great Miami River," from *mhš-*, "big, great," a connective vowel *-i-*, *myaamii-*, "Miami," from middle historic Shawnee *myaamiwa*, which is a loan word from Miami-Illinois, plus *θiipi*, "river."[3] The "Great" of the original British hydronym "the Great Miami River" simply served, and still serves today, to distinguish this river from its neighbor, the Little Miami River, whose name is also a British hydronym that dates to the same time period as "the Great Miami River." The "Miami" in both of these place-names refers to Miami-Illinois–speaking folks, chiefly Maumee River Miami along with some Wea and Piankashaw, who settled briefly at the midpoint of the eighteenth century in the area now known as western and southwestern Ohio in order to benefit from trade with the Britons. Since England and France at that time were locked in a struggle for control of the Indian trade west of the Appalachians, "the Great Miami River" certainly does not reflect reality as ideally envisioned by the French. Indeed, France never accepted the presence of Miami-Illinois speakers on the Great Miami River, and with the help of Algonquian allies she saw to their destruction and rout in 1752. The French in fact called the Great Miami River *la rivière à la Roche* (the River with the Rock), a place-name that can be seen on three anonymous French maps, one from 1749, as well as in the French military officer Pierre-Joseph Céleron's account on the first French trip down the Ohio that took place that same year.[4] *Roche* (rock) refers to how Father Joseph-Pierre Bonnécamps aptly characterized this river during Céleron's expedition: "[I]ts bottom is but one continuous rock."[5]

At a deeper level, however, the French hydronym *la riviere à la Roche* was not originally a French creation; it is the translation of the stream's Miami-Illinois name. This native place-name appears on Lewis Evans' map from 1758, where it is written in the garbled form <Assereniet>.[6] This twisted English spelling, intended to represent Miami-Illinois *ahsenisiipi*, "stone-river," contains *three* classic copy errors. The -r- of <Assereniet> is in truth an "n," as the first segment of this name was originally written *Assene- for Miami-Illinois *ahsen-*, "stone." The -n- of <Assereniet> was originally an "s." This mistake occurs when a handwritten "s" is tilted slightly clockwise and thus misread as an n. Each of the e's of <Assereniet> is an "alphabet E" (discussed in chapter 5) and represents the sound *i*. The -t of <Assereniet> was originally a handwritten "p"—a routine copy error, noted in chapters 4 and 6. By correcting these last two problems, one arrives at an original -isiep, which is both a praiseworthy and a predictable attempt to write in English the Miami-Illinois hydronymic "river" final *-isiip*.[7] The word *ahsenisiipi* is composed of the "stone" initial *ahsen-*, the inanimate noun "river" final *-isiip*, and the singular proximate inanimate noun marker *-i*.

The Miami-Illinois place-name *ahsenisiipi*, "stone-river" could date to late prehistoric times, since, as discussed elsewhere in this volume, it is believed that late prehistoric Miami-Illinois peoples lived in the southern Lake Michigan–western Lake Erie basin prior to the mid-1600s, and would therefore have known about this important riverine link to the Ohio. In addition, there is a stream in extreme south-central Wisconsin and northwestern Illinois that also bore historically the Miami-Illinois name *ahsenisiipi*. Furthermore, the Wisconsin place-name went through the same evolution as the Miami-Illinois hydronym in southwestern Ohio—from its original Miami-Illinois form through a French translation and then to an English translation. Even though the Wisconsin stream's modern English designation is "Rock River," this particular English place-name, like its historic southwestern Ohio counterpart, comes from the earlier French version, *la rivière à la Roche*, which in turn derives from Miami-Illinois *ahsenisiipi*, witnessed for example in the spelling <Assenisipi> on Jacques-Nicolas Bellin's map from 1744.[8] Moreover, as in the case of <Assereniet>, the double -ss- of Bellin's spelling is a transparent and astute attempt at writing the preaspirated *hs* of Miami-Illinois *ahsen-*.

The premier waterway of southeastern Indiana is the Whitewater River. Its multiple origins are located in Wayne, Henry and Fayette counties and even as far north as Randolph County in east-central Indiana. The waters from most of the Whitewater's sources meet on the south edge of Brookville, flow in an impressive narrowly defined valley toward the southeast, into Dearborn County, and then briefly enter the southwestern corner of the state of Ohio before joining the Great Miami River. The southern section of this river falls at approximately six feet per mile, making the Whitewater Indiana's swiftest stream. In 1826, this river was one hundred yards wide at its confluence with the Great Miami River.[9]

A putative native name for the Whitewater River appears on Hough's map in the historical English language garbling <Wahhenepay>,[10] which Hough probably originally wrote *Wahpenepay. In other words, the second -h- of this spelling is an incorrectly copied "p." In fact, this particular error represents one of *three* mistaken readings of "h" for "p" by the engraver of Hough's map.[11] Also, in <Wahhenepay> [*sic*], English orthographic -ay indicates a final native *i* that was misheard as *e* by the original recorder, whether by Hough himself or someone before Hough. It is impossible to ascribe a precise ethnic origin to <Wahhenepay>, since speakers of both Miami-Illinois and Shawnee resided and/or hunted in historical times in the Whitewater valley, and the term as spelled could come from either Miami or Shawnee. Superficially, the recording suggests **waapi-nipi* for Miami-Illinois and **waapi-nepi* for Shawnee, both *theoretically* meaning "white-water," as *waap(i)-* is a term meaning "white" and *nipi/nepi*, the independent noun meaning "water." However, although *waap-* can precede both noun and verb medials and finals in Algonquian, neither Miami-Illinois **waapi-nipi* nor Shawnee **waapi-nepi* is attested, and therefore each could well be ungrammatical.

A more convincing analysis of the place-name <Wahhenepay>, that is, *Wahpenepay, suggests that this spelling is the work of a slightly incompetent English-speaking recorder who failed to hear the *hk* and the following devoiced final *-i* in Miami-Illinois *waapihki-nipi*, "white water." This is in fact a grammatical expression in Miami-Illinois. The term *waapihki* is an attested prenoun meaning "white," and *nipi* is the independent inanimate noun meaning "water." Furthermore, both grammatically and onomastically speaking, the analysis *waapihki-nipi* finds support elsewhere in Algonquian, in the Menominee cognate expression *wa·peskiw nepe·w*, an authentic native hydronym in Wisconsin.[12]

An American Indian language term underlies the English hydronym Silver Creek, the modern name for a stream whose headwaters are located in both northern Clark County and extreme southern Scott County. Silver Creek flows in a southerly fashion and enters the Ohio River at the western end of the Falls of the Ohio near present-day New Albany, Indiana.

<Wahpachsinnink> is the name for this watercourse on Guernsey's map. Although, again, he did not cite the source of his term, the -ch- in Guernsey's spelling suggests that the spelling has a German origin, which would lend support to its historical authenticity, since German Moravian missionaries worked among Delaware speakers in Indiana near the turn of the nineteenth century. Moreover, the "i" of -ink in Guernsey's term is the expected vowel for the Unami locative suffix of the place-name in question.[13]

<Wahpachsinnink> would be Northern Unami *wa·p·ahsə́nink, "at the white stone" or, in conventional English, "the white stone place." The modern Southern Unami cognate is *ɔpahsə́nink*.[14] Here *wa·p·- and ɔ·p·-, the latter shortened to *ɔp-* before *ah*, signify "white"; *ahsən* means "stone"; and *-ink* is a locative suffix meaning "at."[15] The creation of this Delaware language place-name would date at the earliest to around 1770, to the time when Delaware Indians, coming from the East and down through the Ohio River watershed, first entered the Indiana area.

The translation of the Unami term for "white stone" to the "Silver" of Silver Creek is an American fantasy. There was no silver. What the Unami were referring to by "white stone" was the prominent light-colored argillaceous dolomitic limestone that outcrops along Silver Creek.[16]

An important historic feature in what is now southern Indiana was the Great Buffalo Trace. Hewn by bison since their appearance in Indiana in the 1400s, this road stretched from the Big Bone Lick in northern Kentucky all the way across southern Indiana into the Illinois prairies. In traversing southern Indiana, this magnificent road connected the crossing of the Ohio River at the Falls of the Ohio near present-day New Albany to the Wabash River crossing at Vincennes. A section of the trace can still be seen along the Springs Valley Trail System in Orange County south of French Lick. In truth, what is conveniently termed in the singular "the Great Buffalo Trace" became several trails as the bison negotiated the Norman Uplands of southern Indiana. All of these routes ultimately converged north of Jasper at great wallowing holes. Then, leaving their bovine mud baths behind, the bison, in this case traveling westward, had the choice of two crossing sites on the White River, one just northwest of Petersburg, the other near Portersville.[17] From these points they took direct paths to the crossing of the Wabash at Vincennes. In addition, I would like to point out that the site of Vincennes was no doubt strategically located by the French for their post on the lower Wabash because it lay precisely at the intersection of two great "highways"—the Wabash River and the Great Buffalo Trace.[18]

In his report on this buffalo trail Wilson stated that the Miami called it <Lananzoki Miwi>.[19] It is true that "Lananzoki" is a representation of the Miami-Illinois animate plural noun *(a)lenasooki*, "bison" (pl.). Wilson's spelling reflects the pronunciation of the term for "bison" common at least by 1790, which was phonetic [lenanzóoki]. Moreover, "Miwi" is Miami-Illinois *miiwi*, "trail, road." However, ***(a)lenasooki miiwi* is not a grammatical construction in Miami-Illinois. In fact, the outlandish syntax of <Lananzoki Miwi> indicates this is a place-name that either an English speaker or a partial speaker of Miami-Illinois invented, going from English into Miami-Illinois. This expression could not have been the creation of fluent speakers of the Miami-Illinois language, and therefore could not have been the original native odonym in question. In Miami-Illinois, to form the expression "bison trail" in a grammatical fashion, it is necessary to use the inanimate noun final *-ihkanaw*, "trail, path, road." The Illinois-French dictionary in fact offers two forms for the expression "buffalo trail": <irenans8icana8i>, glossed *chemin de boeuf* (buffalo road), which is phonemic Old Miami-Illinois *irenaswihkanawi*, and <irenans8cana8i>, which represents a contracted dialectal or ideolectal form *irenasohkanawi*.[20] The late Miami dialect form per se for the name of the Great Buffalo Trace was *lenaswihkanawe*. This is composed of the "bison" initial *lenasw-*, the "trail" final *-ihkanaw*, and the proximate singular inanimate noun marker in the form *-e*. Local late historic Miami-Illinois speakers would have pronounced this place-name [lenànzwihkanáwe].

Notes

Abbreviations

AGS	American Geographical Society
AMAE	Archives du Ministère des Affaires Etrangères
ANQ	Archives Nationales du Québec
ASJCF	Archives de la Société de Jésus Canada Français
BHM	Bibliothèque Historique de la Marine
BNF	Bibliothèque Nationale de France
IHS	Indiana Historical Society
ILS	Illinois State Historical Library
IUGL	Indiana University Geography Library
NL	Newberry Library
PAC	Public Archives of Canada
SHB	Bibliothèque Service Hydrographique
TCHS	Tippecanoe County Historical Society

Technical Considerations

1. David Costa, personal communication, February 14, 2006.

2. Wisconsin Native American Language Project, Records, 1973–1976, University of Wisconsin–Madison Manuscript Collection 20, Madison.

3. Costa, "Historical Phonology of Miami-Illinois Consonants," 365–93.

4. Voorhis, *Introduction to the Kickapoo Grammar.*

5. Voegelin, *Shawnee Stems.*

6. Goddard, "Delaware," 236.

7. Voegelin, "Delaware, an Eastern Algonquian Language," 130–57.

8. Goddard, *Delaware Verbal Morphology.* Also Goddard, "Historical Phonology of Munsee," 16–68.

9. Lounsbury, "Iroquoian Linguistics," 15:334–43; Chafe, *Seneca Morphology and Dictionary.*

10. Rudes, "Iroquoian Vowels," 16–69.

Introduction

1. For Gabriel Godfroy and *kiilhsohkwa,* see Rafert, *Miami Indians of Indiana,* 136–98, and 186, 191, and 200, respectively; also see Costa, *Miami-Illinois Language,* 23–24. For Sarah Wadsworth, see Costa, *Miami-Illinois Language,* 20, 22; and Dunn, *Indiana and the Indianans* 1:69. For Dunn, see Boomhower, *Jacob Piatt Dunn.* For Dunn's use of his consultant Gabriel Godfroy for native place-names, see Dunn, *True Indian Stories,* 9. The name *wiikapimiša* is the Miami-Illinois language term for the basswood tree (*Tilia americana*); *kiilhsohkwa* means "sun woman."

2. Dunn, *True Indian Stories*; Dunn, *Indiana and the Indianans.*

3. Hough, son of William and Keziah Hough, was born on June 11, 1827, near Fountain City, Indiana. He died on June 15. 1880, at Fountain City, where he is buried.

4. Beckwith, "Indian Names of Water Courses"; Hough, "Indian Names of Lakes, Rivers, Towns."

5. Beckwith, *Illinois and Indiana Indians.*

6. File SC 98 2/3, Beckwith Papers.

7. For Dunn's comments on Hough's work, see Dunn, *True Indian Stories,* 13.

8. Wabash County historian Mary O'Hair compiled a list of native place-names. Aside from a couple of novel entries, hers is essentially a copy of Dunn's work. See O'Hair, Index Glossary of Indiana Indian Names.

9. Guernsey, "Indiana," 1932.

10. Kari and Fall, *Shem Pete's Alaska,* 30.

11. Schwartz and Ehrenberg, *Mapping of America,* 132. For Native American map making, see Warbus, *Another America;* De Vorsey, *Keys to the Encounter;* also Wood, *Atlas of Early Maps.*

12. Lounsbury, *Iroquois Place-Names in the Champlain Valley,* 23–66; Day, "Place-names as Ethnographic Data," 26–31.

13. Eighty different cultural manifestations producing approximately as many typologically distinctive kinds of projectile points knew the Indiana area as home during its at least eleven-thousand-year-old human prehistory. See Justice, *Stone Age Spear and Arrow Points.*

14. Archaeological evidence indicates the presence of Iroquoian populations in northeastern Indiana in the Springwell phase, ca. 1200–1300. See Stothers, "Late Woodland Models," 201–5; also see McCullough, "Overview of the Oliver Phase," 52–55.

15. Mason, *Rock Island,* 213, 215; Brown and O'Brien, *At the Edge of Prehistory,* 152–54, 155–60; Esarey and Conrad, "Bold Counselor Phase," 55; Brown and Sasso, "Prelude to History on the Eastern Prairies," 213, 215.

16. Cree *we˙mistiko˙siw,* Meskwaki *weemehtekoošiha,* Kickapoo *eemehtekoo-siiha,* Menominee *wɛ˙mɛhteko˙sew,* Miami-Illinois *meehtikoošia,* Montagnais *məstuku˙šu,* Ojibwe *wemitigoož̌i,* and Potawatomi *wemtəgoži.* The Shawnee cognate *(m)tekohsiya* has the generic meaning of "white man" rather than the specific meaning of "Frenchman." Its origin is the Proto-Algonquian initial **mehθweθ-* (wood watercraft). See Goddard, "Heckewelder's 1792 Vocabulary," 173. For an in-depth, definitive examination of Algonquian linguistic terms such as "stem," "initial," "medial," and so on, consult Goddard, "Primary and Secondary Stem Derivation," 449–83. The history of the use of this ethnonym suggests to me that it originally referred to French-made watercraft, not to Indian dugout canoes as some have thought.

17. I gave some of the place-name analyses in this book to William Bright for his *Native American Placenames of the United States* (Norman: University of Oklahoma Press, 2004). My analyses of "Wabash" and "Kankakee" first appeared, respectively, in McCafferty, "Wabash, Its Meaning and History," 225–28; and Michael McCafferty, "Kankakee: An Old Etymological Puzzle," *Names* 52, no. 4 (December 2004): 287–304. Since the article on "Kankakee" was garbled by a computer at the press where it was printed, I have been told it will be republished either in hard copy or on the American Name Society web site. However, all of the information in that article is presented in this book.

Chapter 1: The Great Water

1. Samuel de Champlain, ["La Nouvelle France faict par le Sr de Champlain"], 1616, reproduced in Armstrong, *Samuel de Champlain,* 232. This map shows Lake Huron and Lake Ontario, but only a river where Lake Erie should be. The Northern Iroquoian place-name variously spelled <Karégnondi>, <Tekari endiondi>, and <Karegnon> on Nicolas Sanson's 1656 map, Pierre du Val's 1664 map, and Guillaume Sanson's 1669 map, respectively, is apparently the first native name on record applied to Lake Huron. See d'Abbéville, "Le Canada, ou Nouvelle France, &c.," 1656, reproduced in Karpinski, *Bibliography of the Printed Maps of Michigan,* 9; Du Val, "Le Canada faict par le Sr de Champlain," 1664 (original at McGill University). This chart is based on Champlain's map of 1632. For a subsequent printing of this map, see Karpinski, *Bibliography of Printed Maps of Michigan,* 13. The same Du Val map, reproduced in Paris in 1677, is reproduced in Verner and Stuart-Stubbs, *Northpart of America,* 33. Guillaume Sanson, "Amérique Septentrionale," 1669, reproduced in Karpinski, *Bibliography of the Printed Maps of Michigan,* 12. Though Champlain may have heard of the place-name <Tekari endiondi> early in the seventeenth century, the term is not on his map from 1612, "Carte Geographique

De La Nouuelle Franse," reproduced in Armstrong, *Samuel de Champlain*, 174–75; nor is this place-name on his map from 1632. Armstrong, *Samuel de Champlain*, 308–9. The original recorder of this name is unknown. It may be Champlain or his assistant Nicollet. These recordings are not Huron but represent either Mohawk or Old Onondaga *kahrɛ̃ʔnyṍ·nih*, "rock extends there." The place-name's constituent morphemes are |t-ka-hrɛ̃́ʔn-yõ·ni-h| cislocative–third person singular neuter agent–"rock"–"extend"–habitual. I am indebted to Blair Rudes for this linguistic analysis. The extensive writings of Pierre-Philippe Potier, the Jesuit missionary from Belgium who lived in the Detroit area from 1744 until his death in 1781, offer a Huron-Wyandot term related to *kahrɛ̃ʔnyṍ·nih*, which he wrote <ekarendiñiondi>. Robert Toupin, personal communication, December 13, 1999. Judging from Potier's gloss *là où il y a une pointe de rocher q(ui) avance* (there where there is a rock point extending), it is clear that, rather than being an Iroquoian name for Lake Michigan—as it was misused on French maps—the term referred to a rocky prominence jutting out into Lake Huron. Du Val's map of 1669 also contains an Iroquoian place-name that appears to denote therein the upper peninsula of Michigan: <Tarontorai>. See Du Val, "Le Canada faict par le Sr de Champlain," 1669, reproduced in Verner and Stuart-Stubbs, *Northpart of America*, 33. (Karpinski noted that this map has a twin in the William L. Clements Library dated 1669. Karpinski, *Bibliography of the Printed Maps of Michigan*, 13.) <Tarontorai>, however, is a distortion of the Huron name for Michilimackinac. This toponym is found in Potier's work in the form <Taontooraį>. See Potier, "Elementa grammaticae huronicae," *Huron* 3,155, Potier manuscripts, ASJCF; also see Toupin, *Les écrits de Pierre Potier*, 163. This is phonemic *teyõntará·ye*, from morphophonemic |te-k-õtar-ake|, dualic–third person singular neuter agent–"lake"–"be in number," meaning "two lakes." Analysis by Blair Rudes. In addition, Bressani's 1657 map titled "Nouae Franciae Deliniatio," a copy of Sanson's from the previous year, has the curious <Gatsitagve> to indicate the land south of Lake Huron. See Verner and Stuart-Stubbs, *Northpart of America*, 29. This term is in Chafe, *Seneca Morphology and Dictionary*, 81: Chafe's *kastẽʔkõʔh* refers today to Versailles, New York, as well as to Wolf Run, a section of the Allegheny Reservation. But generically speaking, the word means "in the cliff(s)," from |ka-stẽR-akõ·h|, third person singular agent–"cliff"–internal locative. This is clearly Seneca because of the presence of the root *-stẽR-* "cliff," which occurs only in Proto–Lake Iroquoian in the form **čtẽhr-*, "cliff, rock." The *R* is a morphophonemic symbol. Seneca lost original PI **r* but only with a complex variety of outcomes. I am indebted to Blair Rudes for this linguistic analysis.

2. For discussion of the map "Novvelle France," see Heidenreich, "Analysis of the 17th Century Map," 67–111; Steckley, "Early Map,'" 26–27; and Campeau, *Monumenta Novæ Franciæ*, 35–66.

3. For Nicollet's destination, see Michael McCafferty, "Where Did Jean Nicollet Meet the Winnebago in 1634? A Critique of Robert L. Hall's 'Rethinking Jean Nicollet's Route to the Ho-Chunks in 1634,'" *Ontario History* 96, no. 2 (Autumn

2004): 170–82. Because of editorial errors in the printed addition, see the on-line publication at http://www.ontariohistoricalsociety.ca/ohistory.asp (accessed January 5, 2006). Paul Ragueneau, a Jesuit missionary living with the Huron north of Lake Erie between 1645 and 1649, was the first European to *discuss* Lake Michigan. His report from 1647–48, in which the lake is distinctly described for the first time, also reflects geographic data supplied to the Jesuits by Nicollet. See Thwaites, *Jesuit Relations* 33:149–51; Campeau, "Route commerciale," 35.

4. Allouez first went to the West on 7 August 1665 and established a mission at Chaquamegon on the southern shore of Lake Superior known as La Mission du St.-Esprit. See Campeau, "Route commerciale," 21–49. "Chaquamegon" is Ojibwa *žaagawaamikaang*, from the verb *žaagawaamikaa*, where the initial *žaagaw-* is "oval, extended shape," *-aamik* is "bottom of a body of water," and *-aa* is the stative aspect marker. I am indebted to John Nichols for this analysis. Personal communication, November 29, 2003. See also "jagawamika There [*sic*] is a long shallow place in the lake, where the waves break [Il y a une batture longue]" in Baraga, *Dictionary of the Otchipwe Language* 1:163–64.

5. The translation of the French map's title is "Tracy or Upper Lake with the dependencies of the Mission of the Holy Spirit." Marquette was at La Mission du St.-Esprit in 1668 with Father Louis Nicholas. He was also there in 1669. See Hamilton, *Marquette's Explorations*, 16. The original Allouez-Marquette map is reproduced in Campeau, "Cartes relatives," 44.

6. For a thorough examination of this chart's patrimony, see Campeau, "Cartes relatives," 43–47. For a published *copy* of "Lac Tracy ou Supérieur avec les dépendences de la mission du Saint Esprit," see Tucker, *Indian Villages*, pl. I. The Allouez-Marquette map does, however, leave something to be desired—a precise delineation of the coasts of that part of Lake Michigan it portrays. A close examination reveals that the priests based their depiction of its western coastline south of Gills Rock and the Door Peninsula, as well as that of its eastern coastline below Michilimackinac, on Indian reports and/or their own speculations rather than on direct observation. Still, these two men provided information about Lake Michigan in far greater detail than any European had up to 1669, offering the first good picture of the lake's distinctive shape and its astronomical size. No Frenchman, at least as far as history tells us, traveled the length of either of Lake Michigan's shorelines before 1673. In that year, while returning from their famous Mississippi expedition, Marquette, Jolliet, and their French companions paddled two canoes along the lake's western shoreline from the mouth of the Chicago River to the Sturgeon Bay portage bisecting the Door Peninsula. For evidence of the Mississippi explorers' portage to Sturgeon Bay, see Beschefer and Franquelin, "La Carte de la Manitoumie," BNF. This is the prototype of the chart engraved by Liébaux for Melchisédech Thévenot, *Recueil de voyages de Mr Thévenot*. Thévenot's Manitoumie-based map also shows this portage. The map is reproduced in Karpinski, *Bibliography of the Printed Maps of Michigan*, 18. The excellent depiction of the lower Illinois River on Marquette's map clearly indicates

that the French party ascended the Illinois and did not return to the Peoria on the Des Moines River and then travel cross-country to the Illinois, as some have thought. Marquette, ["Carte du Missisipi"], ASJCF. Marquette's chart is the first European map to give a hint of the future shapes of Indiana and Illinois.

7. Thwaites, *Jesuit Relations* 54:221.

8. Note that de Gallinée's depiction of Lake Superior, Green Bay, and Michilimackinac was obviously a borrowing from the Marquette-Allouez map.

9. Thwaites, *Jesuit Relations* 54:255. For de Gallinée's remarks on this point, see Margry, *Découvertes* 1:165. Although the original map by de Gallinée is lost, there are two extant copies: "Carte du Canada et des terres decouverte [*sic*] vers le lac d'Erie," BNF; and "Carte Du Pays Que M. M. Dollier Et De Galinée Missionaires de St. Sulpice Ont Parcouru Dressée par le Même Mr De Galinée," reproduced in Faillon, *Histoire de la Colonie française,* vol. 3; see also Cumming, *Exploration of North America,* 33; and Gravier, *Carte des Grands Lac,* insert.

10. For example, around the time La Salle was locating his Mississippi delta along the northeastern coast of Mexico, Hennepin, in 1683, was situating the headwaters of the St. Joseph River of Lake Michigan in what is now southern Tennessee—they actually rise in southeastern Michigan. By 1704, he had imagined them to be in what is now southern Indiana. See Louis Hennepin, "Carte De La Nouvelle France," 1684, reproduced in Karpinski, *Bibliography of the Printed Maps of Michigan,* 19; Louis Hennepin, "Carte d'un tres grand Pais," 1697, in Karpinski, *Bibliography of the Printed Maps of Michigan,* 25. Curiously, on this chart Lake Erie extends farther south than Chesapeake Bay! The dearth of geographical knowledge about the interior of the continent among the British in the late 1600s is manifest on R. Daniel, "A Map of Ye English Empire in Ye Continent of America," 1679–90, Karpinski, *Bibliography of the Printed Maps of Michigan,* 17. The British emissary George Croghan, an Indian trader on the cutting edge of English knowledge of the Ohio Valley, expressed amazement in 1765 during his captivity on the Wabash at the lush vegetation of the surrounding lands, since disinformation filtering into the English colonies from Québec had led British colonists to believe that the area was a desert wasteland. See Cumming, *Exploration of North America,* 78.

11. Margry, *Découvertes* 1:159–60. For de Gallinée's journal, see ibid. 1:112–66. Unfortunately, a manuscript spelling of this place-name in either Allouez's or de Gallinée's hand does not exist, and we must therefore rely on the published forms.

12. Michelson, "Phonetic shifts," 135. Note original PA **meʔθe-*. But **θ* went to **š* before **i*.

13. *ontare ils appellent ainsi tous les Lacs a L'exception du Lac superieur qu'ils nomment ok8ateeňeňhe* (ontare they call in this manner all the Lakes with the exception of Lac Superior, which they call ok8ateeňeňhe). Potier, *Huron 3*, 156, ASJCF. The Huron name for Lake Superior is *okwatexẽxẽ́heʔ*, which is morphophonemic |yo-at-kw-atek-ẽ-kẽheʔ| third person singular neuter patient–reciprocal–dummy

noun–"build a fire"–stative aspect–decisive. The term means "(something) burned there once, it once burned." Blair Rudes, personal communication, December 21, 2001.

14. Jean-Baptiste Louis Franquelin, "Nouvelle Decouverte de Plusieurs Nations," 1675, reproduced in Tucker, *Indian Villages*, pl. IV. For an in-depth examination of the Jolliet-inspired maps, see Campeau, "Cartes relatives." Jolliet had Franquelin draw three maps very soon after the former's return to Québec. See Campeau, "Route commerciale," 45. Jolliet's place-name is no doubt the same one that the French government engineer Randin used for his map dated to between 1674 and 1681. See Hugues Randin, "Carte de l'Amerique Septentrionale," reproduced in Tucker, *Indian Villages*, pl. VI. For a discussion of Randin himself, see Tucker, *Indian Villages*, 3.

15. Melchisédech Thévenot, "Carte de la decouverte faite l'an 1673 dans l'Amérique Septentrionale," 1681, in Thévenot, *Recueil des Voyages de Mr Thevenot*. Reproduced in Karpinski, *Bibliography of the Printed Maps of Michigan*, 18. (See note 6 above.) The Manitoumie's *Lac des Michiganis* is an unusual French-Algonquian amalgam that literally means "Lake of the Michiganis." This informative historical oddity demonstrates that the person who drew the map, Dablon's Québec-based Jesuit assistant Thierry Beschefer, did not know the original meaning of the Native American hydronym. His use of the French plural possessive form *des Michiganis* shows he thought *Michiganis* was the name of a tribe, probably the Michigamea. This map actually appears in two original forms, both drawn by Father Beschefer in Québec. See Campeau, "Cartes relatives," 82.

16. Marco Vincenzo Coronelli, "Partie Occidentale du Canada," 1688, reproduced in Karpinski, *Bibliography of the Printed Maps of Michigan*, 22; also Marco Vincenzo Coronelli, "America Settentionale," 1688, reproduced in Tucker, *Indian Villages*, pls. IX and X.

17. See Jean-Baptiste Louis Franquelin, "Carte de l'Amérique Septentrionalle," 1688, reproduced in Tucker, *Indian Villages*, pl. XIA; also see "Anonymous Map of the Five Indian Nations," reproduced in Brown, *Early Maps*, pl. 6.

18. Bacqueville de la Potherie, citing Nicolas Perrot, said the lake itself was known as <Mécheygan>. See Perrot's account, "History of the Savage People Who Are Allies of New France," in Blair, *Indian Tribes of the Upper Mississippi* 1:302–3. Perrot was originally a soldier in the famous Carignan-Salières regiment in 1668, twenty-five years of age at the time. <Méchingan> is supposedly the name the Potawatomi used for their village at or near the Great Lake in the vicinity of Green Bay. See Kellogg, *French Regime*, 95–96; also see Thwaites, *Jesuit Relations* 44:245. For the Potawatomi here, see also the important study by Ronald J. Mason in its entirety: Mason, *Rock Island*.

19. Guillaume Deslisle, "Carte De La Louisane," 1718, reproduced in Tucker, *Indian Villages*, pl. XV; Vaugondy, "Amérique Septentrionale," 1750, AGS, reproduced in Karpinski, *Bibliography of the Printed Maps of Michigan*, 97.

20. PA *ke?cikamyi* is in Bloomfield, "Algonquian," 118. Historical attestations for the Miami-Illinois cognate include <kitchigami8i> glossed *grand lac* (big lake), in Illinois-French dictionary, 225; and in Le Boullenger, French-Illinois dictionary, 108, 160; <kitchi-kâmé>, in Volney, "Tableau du Climat," 470; and <kĭ́čĭkámĭ>, in Dunn, Miami file card dictionary, ISL. Also for *grand lac*, Le Boullenger has <metchagami8i>. Le Boullenger, French-Illinois dictionary, 108.

21. Gatschet, "Notes on Miami-Illinois," FN/748. See also <nekáwikamiû'ngi>, ibid., FN/569. I am indebted to Daryl Baldwin for the latter term. Personal communication, August 23, 2003.

22. A work in progress by this author will include a discussion of the two French portages from the St. Joseph to the Kankakee, La Salle's original one and the more commonly known one.

23. Champlain, ["La Nouvelle France"].

24. Campeau, "Route commerciale," 41. For the names of the soldiers in this regiment, see Laforest, "Carignan Regiment." Also see Laforest, "Carignan Regiment," on line at http://www.geocities.com/Heartland/Estates/5255/list1.html (accessed December 9, 1999). The apparent indication of the St. Joseph River on Sanson's map from 1656 could represent hearsay that reached Québec via the explorer Pierre-Esprit Radisson.

25. Franquelin, ["La Carte de la Colbertie ou des Griffons"], 1674, NL. This chart is also known as "Jolliet's Lost Map"—although it was never lost, simply misidentified. For an in-depth examination of this map see Campeau, "Cartes relatives," 54–64. The St. Joseph River is also depicted on Franquelin, "Nouuelle Decouverte de Plusieurs Nations."

26. Margry, *Découvertes* 1:455. The French passage reads "où le vent l'obligea de mettre pied à terre."

27. The *Jesuit Relations* note that during this trip Largillier and Porteret carried the ailing missionary in their arms like a baby from canoe to land and back again. For Marquette's journey from the Kaskaskia village to Lake Michigan, see Thwaites, *Jesuit Relations* 59:190–93; also see Margry, *Découvertes* 3:610; and Hamilton, *Marquette's Explorations*, 219. The passage from the *Jesuit Relations* cited above states specifically that, to reach Lake Michigan, Marquette took an unknown route. He had already been over the Chicago portage twice.

28. For Marquette's death, see Hamilton, *Marquette's Explorations*, 220. Hamilton's work contains a very useful chronology of Marquette's life and an excellent list of historical sources related to the missionary-explorer. However, his treatment of Marquette's Mississippi voyage narration, like those of Steck and Delanglez before him, is flawed. For the proper analysis, see Campeau, "Regards critiques."

29. Margry, *Découvertes* 1:459.

30. For an excellent guide to La Salle's travels in the West, see Delanglez, "La Salle Expedition of 1682," 278–305.

31. Often cited by historians and archaeologists, the term <Atchatchakangouen> simply represents the Ojibwa cognate of Miami-Illinois *čečaahkwaki*, "sandhill cranes" (sg. *čečaahkwa*). The Miami-Illinois phonemic form appears in Costa, "Miami-Illinois Animal Names," 21. <Atchatchakangouen> contains a common miscopy—the final "n"is actually the original miswritten animate plural marker *-k*.

32. The French place-name shows up on maps made by La Salle's chosen cartographers, but not in early Jesuit documents. See Coronelli, "Partie Occidental du Canada," 1688. Bauxar suggests that traders at Green Bay convinced the *čečaahkwaki*, Mascouten, and Wea to settle on the St. Joseph River in 1679 to prevent La Salle from setting up his own business in the area. See Bauxar, "History of the Illinois Area," 597. Although, as the Canadian historian Gérard Malchelosse asserted, there is nothing that proves Dablon and Allouez went to live on the Saint Joseph before 1679, Allouez was surely in residence there shortly thereafter. However, he did not set up camp at La Salle's small depot at the mouth of the river but established his own center about thirty miles upstream near a Miami village. The firmest date for the establishment of a Jesuit mission on the St. Joseph is 1684, the year when Allouez was surely there. Land for the mission was officially accorded to the Jesuits on October 1, 1686. Though La Salle's departure from the Illinois Country stage induced the Jesuits to return there, the Jesuit missionary Claude Aveneau did not arrive on the St. Joseph until 1690. The following year the French began the construction there of Fort St.-Joseph. See Malchelosse, "Poste de la Rivière Saint-Joseph," 140. It should be noted that the English language ethnonym "Miami" derives from the Miami-Illinois singular noun *myaamia* (and the older *myaameewa*; pl. *myaamiaki*, older *myaameewaki*). This term, which was the object of several unsuccessful attempts at analyses in the twentieth century, simply means "downriver person." Unlike its usage in late history and today's world, this name would obviously have not been an original self-designation created by the tribe. Furthermore, the stream on which the Miami were the "downriver folks" is a matter of conjecture. The Miami's traditional cultural link to the St. Joseph River, which figures in the Miami origin story, would be a likely candidate for a precontact location of this people, and the source of the name. But if "Miami" is a later Ojibwa invention, from the time of the Miami's stay in Wisconsin during the seventeenth century, it could refer to their well-known location on the upper Fox River. At the same time, some other, unidentified river could be the source of this tribal designation. Barring a serendipitous archival event, it is unlikely that we will ever know exactly where the Miami were living at the time they became known as *myaameewaki*. But their name does indicate that they were once living downstream from another Algonquian group, the party ostensibly responsible for creating this tribe name. "Miami" analysis by David Pentland 1997 per personal communication from David Costa, 5 January 1998; phonemic forms in Costa, "Miami-Illinois Tribe Names," 50–51. Compare Ojibwa-Ottawa *omaamii* (sg.), "Miami"; Nipissing and

Manwaki *maamiing*, "downstream" as well as *omaamiiwininiwag*, "Algonquins, downstream people"; and Cree *maamihk*, "downstream." See also the PA initial *mya·-, "downstream," in Hewson, *Computer-Generated Dictionary*, no. 2037. The year 1640 marks the first mention of the Miami, when Le Jeune's *relation* refers to them by their Huron name, <Attochingochoronon>. Thwaites, *Jesuit Relations* 18:233. In 1658, they were identified by the Ojibwa term <Oumamik> (see 44:246). Whereas the French first mentioned the Illinois in 1640, contact between the French and the Miami is only *inferred* for 1654 during Radisson's supposed visit, since he did not mention them in his memoirs. The French considered the Miami to be culturally and linguistically identical to the Illinois.

33. Strangely enough, Franquelin's map from 1681, which reflects La Salle's experience in the land at the southern end of Lake Michigan, does not show the St. Joseph River, although it does indicate that the Miami were living in that area. Franquelin, "Carte contenant Une Part du Canada," 1681, SBH. (A copy of this map is in the Karpinski Collection, NL.) I assume this was simply an oversight on Franquelin's part. The mapmaker had a large family to feed and never enough money with which to do so since Louis XIV consistently failed to reimburse him adequately for his cartographic services. Moreover, Franquelin was an *artist*; he was primarily preoccupied with presenting the Sun King with beautiful charts. In this light, he would have been an easily distracted fellow. Furthermore, La Salle would not have proofread the 1681 map as he had already left Québec before Franquelin completed it and sent it to France. For an excellent treatment of the life of the much-abused Franquelin, see Delanglez, "Franquelin, Mapmaker," 29–74. The first cartographic rendering of the St. Joseph River's modern name, naturally of French origin, appears to be on Guillaume Delisle's map of 1718, where we see *Rivière de St. Joseph*. Guillaume Delisle, "Carte de la Louisiane," 1718. Allouez coined this hydronym. Lucien Campeau, personal communication, August 27, 1999. The same missionary had already named Lake Michigan *le lac de St. Joseph* by 1676. See Thwaites, *Jesuit Relations* 60:152. For an excellent synopsis of the Cadillac-inspired debacle at Detroit, see White, *Middle Ground*, 82–90. For information on the Miami's departure from the St. Joseph Valley, see Malchelosse, "Poste de la Rivière Saint-Joseph," especially 146–47. It was during this general time frame that various Miami groups decided to move to the headwaters of the Maumee River, the site of their eighteenth-century villages. See Bauxar, "History of the Illinois Area," 600.

34. Apparently, the tribe's name first came from the pen of the explorer Radisson in the late 1650s, although it was improperly reproduced as <Pontonatemick>, where the original handwritten "u" was taken for "n." See Adams, *The Explorations of Pierre Esprit Radisson*, 89; also see Scull, *Voyages of Peter Esprit Radisson*, 148. It also appeared in the *Jesuit Relations* of 1642–43 as <Pouteatami>. See Thwaites, *Jesuit Relations* 23:225. Thereafter, it is found in Dreuillètes's *relation* of 1657–58 as <Oupouteouatamik> (Thwaites, *Jesuit Relations* 44:247) and in the *relation* of Menard to Lallement from June 2, 1661, as the misprinted <Oupoutesa-

tamis> (Thwaites, *Jesuit Relations* 46:143). All of these forms mentioned here are Ojibweyan and plural. Contrary to popular belief, the foregoing terms and the Potawatomi's self-designation *potewatmi* have nothing to do with "people of the place of fire." In fact, the tribal designation *potewatmi* has no known derivation. However, the early French term *les Gens du Feu*, "the people of the fire," indeed represents a translation of the *Iroquoian* name not only for the Potawatomi but also for all Algonquians living in the general area of the Lower Peninsula of Michigan in protohistoric times, including the Sauk, Fox, Kickapoo, and the Mascouten. See Baerreis, Wheeler-Voegelin, and Wycoco-Moore, "Identity of the Mascouten," 172–78; Goddard, "Historical and Philological Evidence," 131; and Clifton, "Potawatomi," 15:741–42. This Iroquoian designation was later applied to the Mascouten specifically. The Iroquoian ethnonym in question, written <ątsistaeęronnon> by the French, is *xačistaẽxehró˙nõʔ*, the constituents of which are |ka-čist-(a)yẽ-ke-hronõʔ|, "it"–"fire"–"lay"–external locative–populative. In standard English this expression would be "people of the place where there is fire." I am indebted to Blair Rudes for this linguistic analysis. The name probably refers to the bison hunting practices of the lower Great Lakes Algonquian peoples who would intentionally set prairie fires both to create "parklands" supporting vegetation that would attract the animals and to drive them in the hunt.

35. Clifton, "Potawatomi," 725. However, the Potawatomi's own subsequent pattern of occupancy of the St. Joseph watershed for the next century resembled more or less the earlier Miami residency. See Joutel, *Joutel's Journal*, 127–28. In fact, by 1745, most Potawatomi, choosing a path that some of their fellow tribal members had taken fifty years earlier, had begun moving out of the St. Joseph Valley and down into the Wabash watershed. Hence, by 1810, only one band of Potawatomi was still living on the St. Joseph River, while a second was on the Elkhart River, a third on the Kankakee River, and a fourth on the Wabash River itself. But by 1825, and before their ultimate dispersal from Indiana Territory, all the major villages of the Potawatomi were again located in the St. Joseph Valley as the tribe continued to move farther and farther north, away from American encroachment. The treaty with the United States in 1827 was a decisive moment in the tribe's history. For various locations and movements of the Potawatomi, see Draper and Thwaites, *Collections of the State Historical Society* 17:249, 251; O'Callaghan, *Documents Relative to the Colonial History of the State of New York* 10:84; Michigan Pioneer and Historical Society, *Collections and Researches* 10:453. For additional general information on the Potawatomi, see Bauxar, "History of the Illinois Area," 600; and Clifton, "Potawatomi," 726–27, 736–37. For a comprehensive account of Potawatomi locations within the present state of Indiana, see Baerreis, "Great Lakes Project."

36. Hough, "Indian Names."

37. Dunn, *True Indian Stories*, 302; also Dunn, *Indiana and the Indianans* 1:95.

38. I am indebted to Ives Goddard for this linguistic analysis. Compare Ojibwa *zaagiing* as well as Menominee *sa˙ke˙wew*. The long *ee* of the Miami II verb stem

saakiiwee- represents a derivational anomaly peculiar to Miami. Special thanks to Dave Costa, Phil Lesourd, and John O'Meara, who participated with gusto in the analysis of this place-name. Gatschet has <sākiwäki> and <sakiwéki>. Gatschet, "Notes on Miami-Illinois."

39. Dunn, *Indiana and the Indianans*, 95. The Illinois-French dictionary translates <saki8a8iki> as *la fourche ou embouchure* (the fork or confluence). Illinois-French dictionary, 521. This is phonemic *saakiiwaawiki*. Le Boullenger's French-Illinois dictionary has <sak8ei8nghi>, <saki8eki>, <saki8o8iki>, the latter term glossed *a l'entrée de la rivière* (at the entrance of the river) and *L'endroit où se partage la fourche* (the place where the fork splits). Le Boullenger, French-Illinois dictionary, 160. For an Eastern Algonquian language cognate, Zeisberger has Delaware <sákwīk> "the mouth of a river." Horsford, *Zeisberger's Indian Dictionary*, no. 127.

40. Dunn, *True Indian Stories*, 302.

41. Dunn, ms. 47, ISL.

42. Historically, the Potawatomi noun would have been *sagi* ~ *zagi*. Compare Old Ojibwa *saagi*, "outlet." See also Potawatomi *zagǰewen*, "outlet of a river," where *-wen*, is a nominalizing suffix. The l of <Sawkwawksilbuck> is a miscopy.

43. Toupin, *Les écrits de Pierre Potier*, 163, 165. There is an umlaut over the *n* in the spelling on page 163.

44. Ibid., 167.

45. Blair Rudes, personal communication, September 9, 2002.

46. In Huron-Wyandot, Proto–Northern Iroquoian *y* dropped and a following **o* became [u]. Between a vowel and *r*, *h* becomes lengthening of the preceding vowel. Blair Rudes, personal communication, May 12, 2000.

47. Thwaites, *Jesuit Relations* 66:279.

48. The spelling <Maskobeeninonk>, from 1828, is in Robertson and Ricker, *John Tipton Papers* 2:22. Tanner, *Atlas of Great Lakes Indian History*, 134–35. Dunn has the same spelling. Dunn, ms. 47, ISL.

49. <Sanbawodonek> is from John Warren (Potawatomi) via Tricia O'Connor, personal communication, July 19, 2001. I am indebted to these individuals for this place-name.

50. René Paul, "Compiled from the best authorities," 1815, reproduced in Tucker, *Indian Villages*, pl. XL; John Melish, 1818, "Map of Illinois," reproduced in Tucker, *Indian Villages*, pl. XLVI. Dana's "Chanin" is the same French term slightly disfigured. See Dana, "Geographical sketches," in Lindley, *Indiana as Seen by Early Travelers*, 214.

51. Phonemic spelling provided by Laura Buszard-Welcher, personal communication, December 22, 1996.

52. Dunn, *True Indian Stories*, 308; Dunn, *Indiana and the Indianans* 1:96. Guernsey's map has <meehwasebeweh>. Guernsey, "Indiana."

53. On an anonymous, untitled French map from the eighteenth century at the Newberry Library, Trail Creek is called *R. aux Iroquois* (Iroquois River), file

number SHB B4044-15, NB. In the seventeenth century there was also a stream in southern Michigan with the same name. See Potier, "Chemin de St Jos au Detroit," *Gazettes*, 180, Potier manuscripts, ASJCF. In the early American history of La Porte County we also find "Lake Dishmaugh," an anglicized *lac du Chemin*. Dunn mentioned this body of water. See Dunn, *True Indian Stories*, 6.

54. Kappler, *Indian Affairs* 2:44; Harrison to Secretary of War, October 13, 1812, Harrison to Secretary of War, October 26, 1812, and Harrison to Campbell, November 25, 1812, all in Esarey, *Messages and Letters of William Henry Harrison* 2:174, 190, 231; also Vogel, *Indian Names of Michigan*, 61.

55. Hough, "Indian Names"; Guernsey has <Wahbememe>. Guernsey, "Indiana."

56. "Elks-heart" is in Smith, *Greene Ville to Fallen Timbers*, 314. "Elksheart" appears on a map by Thomas Forsyth (drawn by M. Guiol), "Survey of the Country South West of Lake Huron," 1812, reproduced in Tucker, *Indian Villages*, pl. XXXVIII; Thomas Forsyth, ["Chart of the Country Southwest of Lake Huron"], 1812, reproduced in Tucker, *Indian Villages*, pl. XXXVII. The natural geographic perspective of Forsyth's maps was from Detroit, where he was born and reared. For *Coeur de Cerf* in the French records, see Krauskopf, "French in Indiana," 289, 367. I am indebted to Robert Vézina for the scientific identification of the elk.

57. Gatschet, "Notes on Miami-Illinois," FN/1189, per Daryl Baldwin, personal communication, June 9, 2000.

58. There is also an undocumented recording of this stream's name: <Mishiwatekisipiwi>. Here, however, an original "h" in the fifth syllable was rewritten incorrectly as "k," an example of one of the most commonly occurring copy errors. This presumed Miami-Illinois variant of the place-name exhibits the "elk" initial *mihšiiwee-*, and would probably be *mihšiiweeteehi siipiiwi*. Even though the <Mishiwatekisipiwi> spelling appears in McPherson's book on local place-name folklore and is, sadly, unreferenced, it is no doubt a genuine recording. Given its relatively modern and non-French orthography, it has the markings of an unattested transcription by Dunn. See McPherson, *Indian Names in Indiana*, 18.

59. Dunn, *True Indian Stories*, 264; Dunn, *Indiana and the Indianans* 1:112. A very curious early cartographic indication of the portage between the Elkhart River and the Eel River is evidenced on Jean-Baptiste Franquelin, "Carte de l'Amerique Septent.[le]." A copy of this map, incorrectly dated to 1687, is in Cumming, *Exploration of North America*, 153. This portage appears cartographically before any Frenchman had actually seen it.

60. Phonemic spelling by Laura Buszard-Welcher. The term also referred to a Potawatomi village site at the mouth of the Elkhart River. See Guernsey, "Indiana."

61. Dunn, Miami file card dictionary, ISL.

62. Late prehistoric pots identified with the Kaskaskia and known as Danner ware are nearly identical to a type in the western Lake Erie basin in late prehistoric times known as Fort Meigs Appliqué. See Stothers, "Late Woodland Models," 194–211, 207ff.

63. Although the origin of this place-name has been ascribed to the Potawatomi, the Potawatomi settled in this area long after the place-name was first recorded. For the Potawatomi on the Elkhart River, see Tanner, *Atlas of Great Lakes Indian History*, 134–35; also see Tipton's records in Robertson and Riker, *John Tipton Papers* 24:505–6, 597–98, 25:234–36. The Potawatomi were associated with the name "elk heart" by 1779. See *Petit Coeur de Cerf* in Draper and Thwaites, *Collections of the State Historical Society* 28:398.

64. Dunn, *True Indian Stories*, 286; Dunn, *Indiana and the Indianans*, 92.

65. See Illinois-French dictionary, 296. The French translation for <mis-s8ac8aki8i> is *bois, forest seichee par le feu, ou peut estre autrement, bois mort* (woods, forest dried out by fire, or perhaps otherwise, dead wood[s]). For a discussion of the authorship of the Illinois-French dictionary, see Michael McCafferty, "Latest Miami-Illinois Dictionary," 279–85. Note that in this article an editor's error misidentified the handwriting at the bottom of page 280. It should read "[Illinois-French dictionary], Watkinson Library, Hartford, Conn."

66. Costa, Miami-Illinois dictionary.

67. I am indebted to Ives Goddard for the Proto-Algonquian reconstruction. Personal communication, January 17, 2006.

68. Guernsey, "Indiana."

69. Kilver, *History of Lima Township*, 3; also Guernsey, "Indiana"; Hough, "Indian Names."

70. The final *a* of this name is the proximate singular animate noun marker used in the creation of personal names.

71. See "Treaty with the Miami, 1840," in Kappler, *Indian Affairs* 2:533. See chapter 5, note 27, for further discussion of multiethnic villages in the eighteenth and early nineteenth century.

72. Moore, *Calumet Region*, 9–14. For an excellent historic portrayal of the old Grand Calumet and Little Calumet Rivers, see Thomas Hutchins, "A New Map of the Western Parts of Virginia," 1778, reproduced in Tucker, *Indian Villages*, pl. XXIX. Hutchins notes that the portage between the Grand Calumet and the Little Calumet was only thirty yards long.

73. See *La Riviere de Kinouickomy* in the handwritten copy of "De Gannes Memoir," in Newberry Library, Chicago, Ayer MS. 293, vol. 3. For an accessible published version, see Pease and Werner, *The French Foundation*, 392. For Delliette, see Esarey, "On the Conflation of Tonty and Delliette," 8–10.

74. See chapter 2 for a discussion of the mishearing of [o] for Miami-Illinois [θ] on the part of historic French speakers.

75. See *neekawikamisiipi*, "sand-water-river" in chapter 7.

76. See the Ojibwa cognate *-kinokam*, "long-water," as in the hydronym *kaakinokamaak saakaiʔkan*, "where there is a long lake," in Hartley, "Preliminary Observations," 32. Baraga cites the cognate place-name <Kinogami> for Cree. Baraga, *Dictionary of the Otchipwe Language* 1:299. Cree has **kinokamaaw* (adapted from

Farie's Plains Cree dictionary entry <kinoókamaw>: Faries, *Dictionary of the Cree Language*, 280. Also compare the Potawatomi place-name *génogmeyak* for Long Lake in Wisconsin, a place-name evincing initial change from *gnogmeyak*. For forms with initial *kinw-* in Miami-Illinois, see <kin8acat8i>, glossed *bois long, arbre haut* (long wood, tall tree); <kin8ikitsita>, translated *grande queüe, d'un oyseau 8g coq d'nde* (large tail, of a bird, such as a turkey); <kin8ara8eta>, glossed *grand queue de beste; grand corps: d'un coffre, d'homme bien fait* (large tail of an animal; large body: of a trunk, of a well-formed man); also <kin8i8areta>, translated *grand corps, d'un coffre, d'un homme bien fait*; <kin8ira8ata>, translated *grand ours* (big bear); <kin8apicat8i>, glossed *longue ceinture, lien, corde* (long belt, tie, cord). Illinois-French dictionary, 204. La Salle's <Kinogaming> is on Franquelin, "Carte de la Louisiane," 1684, BNF.

77. Anonymous, untitled eighteenth-century French map, SHB B4044-15, AGS.

78. Jedidiah Morse, "A Map of the Northern and Middle United States," 1792, IHS; J. Stockdale, "A Map of the Northern and Middle States," 1792, AGS.

79. Sydney Hall, "United States," 1828 (IHS); Hough, "Indian Names"; 66 Indian Place-Name File Cards," IHS. If *Calumet* is an eponymous river name, it is possible that it represents a translation from an earlier Eastern Algonquian personal name, since the use of "pipe" (i.e, *Calumet*) as a personal name in Algonquian is not uncommon.

80. Forsyth, "Survey of the Country South West of Lake Huron"; Forsyth, ["Chart of the Country Southwest of Lake Huron"]; René Paul, "Compiled from the best authorities," 1815; Robertson and Riker, *John Tipton Papers* 1:266, 269; 140. This author has not yet found any evidence indicating the French ever applied the term "calumet," their name for the long-stemmed Native American pipe, to the Calumet River. The name's first historical appearance seems to be on Tipton's map: John Tipton, "A Map Showing the Fort Wayne Indian Agency in Indiana," 1824, reproduced in Tucker, *Indian Villages*, pl. XLIX.

81. See Dunn, ms. 47, ISL. See also Gatschet's <kínungi>, in Costa, Miami-Illinois dictionary; and Dunn's <kĭnóngĭ>, in Dunn, Miami file card dictionary, ISL. Guernsey, who borrowed <Kennomkia> for his map, said it signified "deep water." Guernsey, "Indiana."

82. Margry, *Découvertes* 2:58.

Chapter 2: ‹8AB8SKIG8›, *Ouabachi* and Beyond

1. Jacques Largillier, Pierre Moreau, Jean Tiberge, Jean Plattier, and a seventh Frenchman who remains unidentified. See Hamilton, *Marquette's Explorations*, 117. The notion that the trader Pierre Porteret took part in this voyage, though a possibility, is an inference unsupported by contemporary sources. See Cholenec's remarks in De Rochemonteix, *Les Lettres Jésuites* 3:607. It is clear from all accounts that the Frenchmen were the only people on the trip. No Indian guides accompanied them beyond the Fox River–Wisconsin River portage. Marquette was born

in Laon, northeastern France, on June 1, 1637. He turned thirty-six in the course of the Mississippi voyage. Jolliet, born at Beauport, four miles northeast of Old Québec City, on or a few hours before September 21, 1645, the date of his baptism, was twenty-seven going on twenty-eight at the time of the great expedition. See Delanglez, *Life and Voyages of Louis Jolliet*, 1.

2. Marquette, ["Carte du Missisipi"], ASJCF. This is reproduced in Tucker, *Indian Villages*, pl. V. The Marquette map is an exquisite piece of early cartography in that it is a statement of bare facts. It shows only what the explorer saw or already knew. It even marks with minute horizontal lines the location of rapids in the Mississippi River. The Mississippi birch bark canoe journey started at St. Ignace at Michilimackinac, proceeded to Green Bay, and ascended the Fox River to the Miami-Mascouten town near present-day Berlin, Wisconsin. There the Frenchmen enjoined the services of two Miami men who led them to the Fox River–Wisconsin River portage, at which point the French party was left to its own devices. Marquette called the Wisconsin River <Mesk8sing>. This is Old Miami-Illinois [meeskohsinki], "it lies red," composed of the old "red" initial *meeskw-*, the II verb final *-ihsin*, "lie" and *-ki*, the dependent II verb suffix. The optional contraction of *meeskw-* and *-ihsin* to [meeskohsin-] is supported by Gatschet's recording <Tchínk8sanwi> for [čeenkohsinwi], "it lies-noisy," the Miami-Illinois name for a stream in Oklahoma, as well as by other recordings by Gatschet. See Gatschet, "Notes on Miami-Illinois," FN/17. For an in-depth examination of the Wisconsin River's Miami name, see Michael McCafferty, "On Wisconsin: The Derivation and Referent of an Old Puzzle in American Placenames," *Onoma* 38 (2003): 39–56. For clarity's sake I have retained the form of Marquette's <8AB8SKIG8> in the manner that he penned it himself—with capital letters. Since the Ohio does not enter the Mississippi directly from the east, and the French party did not ascend the Ohio, Marquette must have gotten the information about the general location of the Ohio River from Indians.

3. See <8ab8kig8>, in Thwaites, *Jesuit Relations* 59:144.

4. Campeau, "Regards critiques," 35–42. The place-name appears without an s in the form <8ab8kig8> in not only the hand-copied but also the published versions of Marquette's narration of the voyage. See Thwaites, *Jesuit Relations* 59:144–45. This alternate spelling not only implies that some other Jesuits were aware of this place-name, but it also appears to confirm my *sk/hk* analysis of the K of Marquette's spelling, as the sound *sk* in Miami-Illinois was in the process of shifting to *hk* during the late seventeenth century—and the French would have, characteristically, written a simple "k" for *hk*. The Franquelin-Jolliet map of 1675 has <8ab8skig8>. Franquelin, "Nouvelle Decouverte de Plusieurs Nations," 1675, reproduced in Thwaites, *Jesuit Relations* 59:86; also Tucker, *Indian Villages*, pl. IV. Both Thierry Beschefer, the scribe responsible for the three copies of Marquette's narration of the Mississippi voyage now housed in Vanves, France, at the Archives de la province de Paris de la Compagnie de Jésus (Fonds Brotier, vols. 158, 159, known formerly as "Canada-

4") as well as Antoine Dalmas, responsible for a transcription of the narration that remained in Québec, recast Marquette's original spelling of this hydronym to <8ab8kig8>. In fact, in the document archived in Québec, Dalmas's original "s" has been *rubbed out*. See "Recit Des Voyages," *Recueil* 296, ASJCF.

5. Reuben Thwaites, the English-speaking editor of the *Jesuit Relations*, drove the term deeper into the realm of the unrecognizable with his weird, hyphenated, and modestly anglicized "Wabous-quigou," a rehash of Franquelin's <Ouabouski-quou> from the latter's map of 1681. See Thwaites, *Jesuit Relations* 59:296; and Jean-Baptiste Louis Franquelin, "Partie de l'Amerique Septentrionale," 1681, SHB B4040-4, NB.

6. Jolliet lost Marquette's other original map in the St. Louis rapids near Montreal in July 1674, when his canoe upset on his return to Québec. This was surely a disappointing, indeed, tragic, moment in Jolliet's young life. He lost not only the notes and map he and Marquette had made of their Mississippi voyage but also two friends, one of whom was a Pawnee boy. This accident occurred at Côte Saint-Sulpice, dubbed "La Chine" (China), a site that had until only a short time before belonged to La Salle, Jolliet's rival.

7. See Delanglez, "Récit des voyages," 222; also Thwaites, *Jesuit Relations* 54:186. Marquette stated, "For this topic we collected all the information that we could from the Indians who frequented those places and we even traced with their help a map of all this new country; we had marked there upon the river on which we would be traveling, the names of the peoples and of the places through which we would have to pass." Thwaites, *Jesuit Relations* 59:90–93. Note that the map discussed in this passage is not Marquette's holograph map. See also Hamilton, *Marquette's Explorations*, 161. For the Illinois boy, see Thwaites, *Jesuit Relations* 54:186–87. For the Illinois visiting Chaquamegon, see Thwaites, *Jesuit Relations* 54:184–85.

8. Bauxar, "History of the Illinois Area," 15:599. This town had three thousand inhabitants in 1670. See Thwaites, *Jesuit Relations* 55:199–201.

9. Margry, *Découvertes* 1:555. Since Marquette did not speak Mascouten but did speak Miami-Illinois, two Miami men were chosen to serve as guides to the Fox River–Wisconsin River portage. Marquette had both a strong academic background and particular expertise in Algonquian. In France, he was a highly educated scholar, an experienced college teacher perfectly fluent in Latin. In North America, in order to fulfill his passion to become a missionary, a path for which the Jesuit order *required* mastery of native languages, he became a fervent and successful student of Algonquian. Marquette began his language studies—beginning with Montagnais—on the very day he arrived at Québec from France, September 20, 1666. He then went on to study Ojibwa at Trois Rivières under the master Jesuit linguist Gabriel Druillètes. Finally, in 1669, while at the St. Ignace mission at the Straits of Mackinac, as mentioned in the text, he was fortunate to have for some two and a half years as his personal Miami-Illinois tutor an Illinois boy who was a slave among the Ottawa. In fact, by the time Marquette descended the Mississippi

in 1673, he was already adept in six native tongues. For Marquette's arrival in Québec and his early studies of Algonquian, see Hamilton, *Marquette's Explorations*, 218. For Marquette's learning Illinois, see Thwaites, *Jesuit Relations* 54:186. For his knowledge of several Indian languages, see Thwaites, *Jesuit Relations* 59:153. When Marquette and Jolliet stumbled upon the Peoria living on the Des Moines River during the Mississippi voyage, they were able to approach them to within a few meters without being detected. At the last moment, deciding that it was safer to announce their arrival, they did so in a loud voice. It must have been not only a great shock but also quite a delight for the Peoria to see Marquette and Jolliet—and one of the two even spoke their language!

10. In 1984, waterline surveyors working north of Wayland in Clark County, northeastern Missouri, came upon the remains of a large contact-era Indian village. Located near the Des Moines River not far from Keokuk, Iowa, this site has since been identified as the historically famous Miami-Illinois–speaking village of the Peoria visited by the French explorers Marquette and Jolliet in the last week of June 1673 during their epic voyage through the middle Mississippi Valley. Doubt about what western tributary of the Mississippi was home to the Peoria when they met Marquette and Jolliet pervaded the scholarly world in the last century. In the late 1940s this quandary culminated in the belief the tribe had been living on the Iowa River. See Delanglez, "Récit des voyages," 235; also see Weld, "Joliet and Marquette in Iowa," 16. However, not only do the Native American and French items recovered from the Clark County site, which include European trade beads and a Jesuit ring, support the notion that the Marquette-Jolliet Peoria village was located on the Des Moines River, the cartographic evidence demonstrates unequivocally that this historically famous locale was on the Des Moines. For the Peoria village, see Grantham, "Illinois Village," 1–20. The place-name "Missouri" first appears on Marquette's map of the Mississippi in the form <8EMESS8RIT>, an ethnonym referring to a Siouan language–speaking population. Marquette's term is the Miami-Illinois participle *weemeehsoorita*, "one who has a canoe," from |wi-mihs-oor-i-t-a| third person possessive prefix–"wood"–"watercraft"–inanimate noun suffix–third person animate intransitive participle marker–third person animate intransitive participle ending. For Marquette's discovery of the Peoria near the Mississippi, see Thwaites, *Jesuit Relations* 20:112–15. For French knowledge before the voyage that the Peoria were living on the Mississippi, see Thwaites, *Jesuit Relations* 58:42–43. For a discussion of the primary and secondary documents related to this trip, see Campeau, "Regards critiques," 21–60.

11. The ethnonym "Michigamea" is from Miami-Illinois *meehčaakamia*, "great-water person," which consists of *meehč-*, "great, big," the "water" final *-aakami-*, and the animate gender marker *-a*. The likely referent for "Michigamea" is the Ohio River. The Dhegiha Siouans referred to this tribe as <8arakia>. See Illinois-French dictionary, 373. This term is not analyzable in Siouan. Robert Rankin, personal communication, December 16, 2000. The word <8arakia> seems to be a borrow-

ing into Siouan from Old Miami-Illinois *waarahkia*, "cave/ravine country person." This analysis is supported by the placement of the Michigamea in the cave and ravine country of southern Illinois on Franquelin's map of 1697. See *Ancien pays des Matsagami* (Former land of the Michigamea) for the area near the confluence of the Ohio and the Wabash on Jean-Baptiste Louis Franquelin, "Cours du grand fleuve Missisipi," 1697, reproduced in Wood, *Atlas of Early Maps of the American Midwest: Part II*, pl. III.

12. Illinois-French dictionary, 363, 362; Pinet, French/Miami-Illinois dictionary. It should be noted that in the records for Miami-Illinois from the mid-1800s and thereafter voiced obstruents are for the most part lacking in nonnasal environments. Attributing this spelling to a mishearing by Frenchmen of [b] for unaspirated *p* does not appear to meet critical muster since Miami-Illinois *p* and French *p* are identical in that both are not aspirated. Although Miami-Illinois does not exhibit systematic voicing of consonants except in the environment of a nasal consonant (in other words, *p* does not automatically go to [b] in a context such as *waap-*), there may have been in this language free variation of [p] and [b] as intervocalic allophones of *p*, at least in the word for "white." The word *waapanwa* literally means "he is the dawn." For Miami-Illinois *waapikanahteewi*, Goddard says, "This is a … rule that is also found in Meskwaki and Kickapoo. Postmedial *-e·* + a 'heat' final replaces *-e·* with *-a* (Voorhis in IJAL 49:79). Actually, since the II has *-ahte·* here, I would say that synchronically the finals take the variant shape with PA **aʔC* instead of **-eC*, and the postmedial drops completely. Cf. Mesk. *pahki·kwasowa* AI, 'his eyes are bothered by smoke,' *pahki·kwahte·wi* II. This rule produces apparent cases of PA **CyaC*." Per David Costa, personal communication, October, 10, 2005.

13. Marquette's longer familiarity with Montagnais, a related Canadian Algonquian language to the northeast, which has *sk*, may have predisposed him to write the Ohio River's Miami-Illinois name with an [s] sound. For an in-depth discussion of the *sk/hk* phenomenon in Miami-Illinois, see Costa, *Miami-Illinois Language*, 83–87.

14. Phonemic *ahsahkwa*. See Costa, "Miami-Illinois Animal Names," 23.

15. Marquette, ["Carte du Mississippi"], ASJCF.

16. Marquette, "Récit du second voyage," *Recueil* 296, ASJCF.

17. Temple, *Indian Villages*, 19. <Chachag8essi8> is in Thwaites, *Jesuit Relations* 49:166–67, 175. See <chachach8essi8a>, glossed *petit serpent marqueté* (little snake strewn/marked with spots), in Illinois-French dictionary, 106.

18. Le Boullenger, French-Illinois dictionary, 92, 41.

19. Take, for example, *Chicagou* from <Chikag8> in Potier, "Chemin, par terre, de S jos: aux 8ia" and "avril S. joseph," *Gazettes*, 166b, Potier manuscripts, ASJCF. The hydronym component in question is *šikaakwa*, "wild leek." See Michael McCafferty, "A Fresh Look at the Place Name Chicago," *Journal of the Illinois State Historical Society* 96, no. 2 (2003): 116–29; also Michael McCafferty, "Additional Notes on the Place Name Chicago," *Journal* 20, no. 2 (Spring 2004): 8–11; and Michael

McCafferty, "Revisiting Chicago (Reader Response)," *Journal of the Illinois State Historical Society* 98, no. 1–2 (Spring–Summer 2005): 82–98. The *šikaakwa* analysis, fully supported by the French records, is also confirmed by the first Englishman to visit the area, in 1710, who spelled the stream's name <Chigaquea>. See Raymond Phineas Stearns, "Joseph Kellogg's Observations on Senex's Map of North America (1710)," *Mississippi Valley Historical Review* 23, no. 3 (December 1936): 345–54. This same report is available on line at http://www.theamericansurveyor.com/PDF/TheAmericanSurveyor-CompassAndChain-March-April2004.pdf (accessed January 25, 2006).

20. De Rochemonteix, "Le Récit et Relations inédites," *Les Lettres Jésuites* 3:19n4.

21. Le Boullenger, French-Illinois dictionary, 35. Phonemic form in Costa, 1998, Miami-Illinois dictionary.

22. See "De Gannes Memoir," Ayer Manuscript 293, vol. 3, NL, reproduced in Pease and Werner, *French Foundation*, 392.

23. Volney, "Tableau du Climat," 472. Volney's "xk" is a beautiful, solid recording of a Miami-Illinois preaspirated consonant. This Miami leader was known to English speakers as Little Turtle. Trowbridge, *Meearmeear Traditions*, 11. Trowbridge also wrote o for *a* in the Miami-Illinois name for the White River's west fork, *waapikami(i)ki* as <Waupeekomēēkee>, and in the Miami-Illinois ethnonym Wea, *waayaahtanwaki* (pl.) as <Wuyautōnoakee>. Trowbridge, *Meearmeear Traditions*, 11.

24. From PA **wa·paxkehkwa*. See Hewson, *Computer-generated Dictionary*, no. 3446. Cognate forms of this term include Cree *waapaskihk* and Ojibwa *waapakik*, which in these languages today signify "tin kettle." In Marquette's time, Illinois *ahkihkwa* meant both "clay pot" (Fr. *pot de terre*) and "drum" (Fr. *tambour*). See <akic8a> in Illinois-French dictionary, 21, 409, 427; *ahkihkwi* meant "pot, cauldron" (Fr. *chaudiere, chauderon*). See <akic8i>, in Illinois-French dictionary, 21. These forms are composed of the noun initial *ahkihkw-*, plus either *-a*, the singular animate gender suffix, or *-i*, the singular inanimate gender noun suffix. Note, however, that in late Miami-Illinois, *ahkihkwa* meant "drum" while *ahkihkwi* signified "pot, kettle." Algonquians used the term "white" to describe "limestone." See the discussion of Silver Creek in chapter 11. The late-seventeenth-century map by Raffeix marks the Falls of the Ohio. However, this information is based solely on Iroquois intelligence, not on direct observation by the French. Pierre Raffeix, 1688, "Parties les plus occidentales," reproduced in Kaufman, *Mapping of the Great Lakes*, 82–83; for a related note, see Margry, *Découvertes* 1:116. A similar hydrological phenomenon would be the source of the Québec hydronym *Rivière Chaudière*. See *Noms de Lieu du Québec*, 127. Although Shawnee might be considered a source for <8AB8SKIG8>, there is no solid evidence that either Marquette or Jolliet ever met a Shawnee Indian. Father Marquette met some Mosopelea on the east bank of the Mississippi south of the Ohio while descending the river in 1673. This is understood by combining the

relevant information in his narration and on his map. See Marquette, ["Carte du Mississippi"], and Thwaites, *Jesuit Relations* 59:145–48; also Campeau, "Cartes relatives," 53; Alford, "Unrecognized Father Marquette Letter," 679; and Delanglez, "First Establishment of the Faith," 210. Marquette's Mosopelea could have been Shawnee speakers. See also discussion of "Mosopelea" and the Shawnee in chapter 3.

25. For an excellent image of these "pots" at the Falls of the Ohio, see Fields, *Indiana Impressions*, 41.

26. Thwaites, *Early Western Travels* 1:137n.; Dunn, "Names of the Ohio River," 169; Delanglez, "Jolliet Lost Map,"113. See also Delanglez, *Life and Voyages of Louis Jolliet*, 111; Schwartz and Ehrenberg, *Mapping of America*, 126.

27. Costa, "Miami-Illinois Animal Names," 27.

28. For an examination of La Salle's virulent antipathy toward the Jesuits and the problems that it engendered, see Campeau, "Mémoires d'Allet," 27–59.

29. Lucien Campeau, personal communication, August 24, 1999.

30. See Delanglez, "Cartography of the Mississippi," 257.

31. Margry, *Découvertes* 2:244–45; see also La Salle's letter from Fort Frontenac, August 22, 1682, in ibid. 2:212–62.

32. Claude Bernou and M. Peronel, "Carte de l'Amérique Septentrionale," 1682, reproduced in Tucker, *Indian Villages*, pl. VIII.

33. De Gallinée, an objective firsthand witness, clearly states that La Salle did not know how to speak or understand Iroquois in the least. Margry, *Découvertes* 1:117. Another unusual fact about this voyage was de Gallinée's hiring of a Dutchman who did know how to speak an Iroquoian language but who scarcely knew a word of French! The party—or linguistic circus—left Montreal in July, spent a mild winter on the north shore of Lake Erie, then got caught in an extremely wintry early spring that nearly killed the explorers as they attempted to make their way up to Sault Ste. Marie. Finally, upon arriving at their destination, they stayed only three days and then turned around and headed back to Montreal, this time via the Ottawa River. See Margry, *Découvertes* 1:112–66.

34. Margry, *Découvertes* 1:526. The word <8i8ilamet>, also written <Ouiouilamet>, was the son of a chief from a village at Brookfield (Quahaug) near Boston. He served as La Salle's first translator in the Illinois Country.

35. See La Salle letter from Fort Frontenac, August 22, 1682, in Margry, *Découvertes* 2:245. Analysis of <Gastacha> by Blair Rudes, personal communication, June 21, 2001.

36. This term is morphophonemic |waʔ-ka-stahR-aʔ| factual mode–third singular neuter agent–"be not there"–punctual aspect, meaning "it's not there, it wasn't there." Blair Rudes, personal communication, April 21, 1998. See <Gastahron, Ch. rons, re, ronne>, glossed *ne trouver pas ce qu'on cherche* (to not find what one is looking for); Gaiatastahron, R., translated *ne pas trouver quelqu'un* (to not find someone); <Garish8astahron, Ch.>, glossed *ne pas trouver l'affaire, la nouvelle* (to not find the matter, the new one)," in Bruyas, *Radices verborum iroquaeorum*, 101.

37. Campeau, "Memoirs d'Allet," 33.

38. Margry, *Découvertes* 2:244–45.

39. Franquelin, "Carte de la Louisiane," 1684, BNF; Marco Vincenzo Coronelli, "Colle Nuoue Scoperte," 1688, reproduced in Tucker, *Indian Villages*, pl. X. Coronelli also has the river named <Aramoni>.

40. Of course, traders would have had to make their way *up* the Vermillion River.

41. Franquelin, "Carte de la Louisiane," 1684, BNF.

42. Careless French scribes were unaware of and often overlooked the final -é, for *e~i*, of the earliest French spelling, with obvious results.

43. Thwaites, *Jesuit Relations* 65:106–7. Author's translation. Parenthetical remarks and italics added by the author. By "country of the Oumiamis," Gravier is referring to the St. Joseph and Kankakee watersheds. The transitional English form "Wabache" appeared in the late 1700s. See Faden, "The United States of North America," 1783, AGS. The form "Ouabachee" for phonetic [wabaši] on Coxe's map of the Ohio Valley is the best English version that exists for the Native name of this river, which came through French. Coxe, "A map of Carolana," 1720, reproduced in Brown, *Early Maps*, 11. Modern English places the stress on the first syllable: [wɔ́bæš].

44. "La Riviere de ouabache dont Je vient de parler, ou sont une partie des Miamis Etablis est une tres belle Riviere, aussy tous Les sauvages l'appellent de mesme, je ne sçay ou elle prend sa Source, mais je sçay que de chez Les Iroquois il n'y a pas Loing pour s'y rendre, elle coure toujours au Sud oüest, se decharge dans Le Mississipi a soixante Lieuës de l'embouchure de celle des Illinois elle est plus Large que le Mississipi." "De Gannes Memoir," in Pease and Werner, *French Foundation*, 393–94. I have modified the original English translation for the better. For Sabrevois de Bleury, see "Memoir on the Indians of Canada," in Draper and Thwaites, *Collections of the State Historical Society* 16:364–65, 376. For Darby, see Lindley, *Indiana as Seen by Early Travelers*, 192; Dunn, "Mission to the Ouabache," 308; Delanglez, "Tonti Letters," 229 nn. 37 and 230. See also Thwaites, *Early Western Travels* 1:149: "Oubache … empties into the Mississippi."

45. The American government emissary, George Croghan, a reliable firsthand witness, stated that the Wabash at the confluence in the eighteenth century was nearly *three hundred yards wide*. The British military officer Thomas Hutchins, another reliable firsthand witness, recorded the same width of the Wabash at the Ohio confluence in his "Journal from Fort Pitt to the Mouth of the Ohio in the Year 1768," a distance that the local traveler George Imlay reiterated in 1793. Other early English-speaking visitors to the area provided similar data. In 1816, David Thomas said the river was four hundred yards wide at the mouth, three hundred at Vincennes, and two hundred at Terre Haute, an observation reconfirmed by David Baillie Warden in 1819. For Croghan, see Thwaites, *Early Western Travels* 1:137 n.; for Hutchins, see Lindley, *Indiana as Seen by Early Travelers*, 7; for Imlay,

see Lindley, *Indiana as Seen by Early Travelers*, 9; for Thomas, see Lindley, *Indiana as Seen by Early Travelers*, 113; for Warden, see Lindley, *Indiana as Seen by Early Travelers*, 221n.

46. I am indebted to archaeologist Cheryl Ann Munson for the description of the mouth of the Wabash.

47. In this word, the Miami-Illinois *-aahši(i)* is a reflex of Proto-Algonquian **a˙ʔθe˙*-, "shine," albeit an unexpected one. See Hewson, *Computer-generated Dictionary*, no. 0277. Compare also Massachusett <wampashauk> translated to English "brasse" [*sic*]. David Costa, personal communication March 12, 2004. Also, note that PA **wa˙ʔθe˙wi* goes to Miami-Illinois *waahseewi*, "it is light, it is dawn."

48. Le Boullenger, French-Illinois dictionary, 161, 176. The analysis for this terms is *mihkw-*, "red," *-aahši(i)*, "shine," and *-ki*, the third-person II suffix; *kiipihkatwi* is "metal"; Illinois-French dictionary, 216, 215. Compare Miami-Illinois *-itee* and PA **-ete˙*, "by heat." The reader should note that in all of the above historical French recordings the glyph 8 represents *w*. The metal-related terms presented here relate to blacksmithing.

49. Hough, "Indian Names."

50. Dunn, "Names of the Ohio River," 169. See chapter 5's discussion of <Kekionga> and chapter 7's discussion of "Mississinewa" for an explanation of the final orthographic -a of Hough's spelling.

51. Dunn's forms are from Costa, Miami-Illinois dictionary. In these Gatschet recordings, "x" as well as the symbol "ͨ" mark preaspiration. Gatschet also used h to mark preaspiration.

52. Dunn, *Indiana and the Indianans* 1:96; also Dunn, *True Indian Stories*, 312; and Shaver, *Compendium of Paleozoic Rock-Unit Stratigraphy*, 163. A worthy project for the people of Indiana would be to restore the stone bed of the river to its original whiteness.

53. Hartley, "Preliminary Observations," 31.

54. Dehart, *Past and Present in Tippecanoe County* 1:120; Illinois-French dictionary, 361. The word *waapaahši(i)ki* is simply the conjunct (dependent) form of the verb *waapaahši(i)-* also seen here in the independent order, written <8abachi8i>, for *waapaahši(i)wi*. Note that since the French language characteristically stresses the final syllable of any word with more than one syllable, it was natural that *Ouabachi*, the French place-name for the Wabash, ended where it did, as that syllable is precisely where the Miami-Illinois term from which it derives has its strong syllable: Miami-Illinois [waabaahš*í(i)*ki] and French [wabaší].

55. See, for example, Hamell, "Long-Tail," 258–88.

56. Bernou-Peronel, "Carte de l'Amérique Septentrionale," 1682; Franquelin, "Carte de la Louisiane," 1684, reproduced in Lauvrière, *Histoire de la Louisiane Française*, frontispiece; Minet, "Carte de la Louisiane," 1685, reproduced in Tucker, *Indian Villages*, pl. VII.

57. Delanglez, "Calendar of Lasalle Travels," 300, 303–4.

58. Griffin, *Fort Ancient Aspect*, 27. For the belief that La Salle was a reliable source of Ohio Valley data, see Wheeler-Voegelin, "Ethnohistorical Report," 37–38.

59. Delanglez, "Cartography of the Mississippi," 36–37.

60. Margry, *Découvertes* 2:196.

61. Franquelin, "Carte de La Louisiane," BNF. The same term appears on another, untitled chart by Franquelin from the same year: Jean-Baptiste Louis Franquelin, untitled map, 1684, BNF.

62. Minet, "Carte de La Louisiane," 1685.

63. Callender, "Fox," 646. See La Salle reference to the Outagame in Margry, *Découvertes* 1:116. See also <Ouagoussak> in Jean de Lamberville's *relation* of 1672–73, in Thwaites, *Jesuit Relations* 58:41.

64. Kenton, *Indians of North America* 1:247; Thwaites, *Jesuit Relations* 54:206; Thwaites, *Jesuit Relations* 58:41.

65. See Stothers, "Michigan Owasco and Iroquois Co-Tradition"; also see Stothers, "Late Woodland Models."

66. Beckwith, "Indian Names," 39.

67. Lewis Evans, "A General Map of the Middle British Colonies," 1766. A detail of this map is reproduced in Brown, *Early Maps*, 41.

Chapter 3: ‹Ohio›, *Ouabachi* and Beyond

1. Chafe, *Seneca Morphology and Dictionary*, 59; Delanglez, "Calendar of La Salle's Travels," 281–82; Campeau, "Route commerciale," 46. Although La Salle applied to have the site of his fief near Montreal named Saint-Sulpice, local Frenchmen had already dubbed it "la Chine" (China) to mock La Salle's quest to find a route to China across North America and/or his unrequited aspirations as a young Jesuit neophyte for going to China.

2. [Jean Bourdon], ca. 1646, no title, SHM, *Receuil* 67, no. 44. This map is reproduced and discussed in the interesting article by Heindenreich, "Analysis of the 17th Century Map," 78.

3. Blair Rudes, personal communication, January 11, 1998. The verb |-iyo-| also appears in the place-name "Ontar*io*."

4. See La Salle's statement: "une grande riviere que les sauvages appeloient Ohio et les autres Mississipi" (a great river that the Indians called Ohio and the others Mississippi), in Margry, *Découvertes* 1:436; also Rémy de Courcelles's statement from ca. 1669: "une grande rivière que les Iroquois appellent Ohio et les Outaouas Mississipy" (a great river that the Iroquois call Ohio and the Ottawa Mississippi). Margry, *Découvertes* 1:181, 1:114. See also de Gallinée's remarks on the Iroquoian hydrological conception for the Ohio River, in Delanglez, *Life and Voyages of Louis Jolliet*, 41.

5. Wallace Chafe, personal communication, November 10, 2004.

6. Margry, *Découvertes* 1:116.

7. See Frontenac to Colbert, November 13, 1673, in *Rapport de l'Archiviste*, 36; Also Margry, *Découvertes* 1:243.

8. Margry, *Découvertes* 1:330.

9. Franquelin, "Carte contenant Une Part du Canada," 1681, NL; also Jean-Baptiste-Louis Franquelin, "Partie de L'Amerique Septentrio[nale] depuis 27 iusques 44 degrez de latt. & depuis 268 degrez de longitude jusqu'a 300 prenant le premier meridian aux Isles Açores," 1681, BHM. Photocopy in author's possession; also Franquelin, "Cette Carte est une des quatre parties," 1681, BHM.

10. It was only after the Wabash became an avenue for French trade in the second decade of the eighteenth century that the French acquired a second perspective on the heartland.

11. Thwaites, *Jesuit Relations* 65:106–7; Roy, *Sieur de Vincennes Identified*, 87; Cumming, *Exploration of North America*, 156. In 1701, the governor of Louisiana, De Sauvole de la Villantray, described a trip made by two Frenchmen named Bellefeuille and Soton to Charlestown (South Carolina) via the "Wabash," meaning the Ohio. Rowland and Sanders, *Mississippi Provincial Archives* 2:14–15. Henri de Joutel, another Frenchman who spent time in the West, referred to the Ohio River as <Abach>, which of course is a distorted "Ouabache." For Joutel's map with <Abache>, see Gaither, *Fatal River*, map opposite page 260.

12. The name *le petit 8abache* for the Wabash as it is conceived today is in the document titled "etablissement dependant du Mississipi" in *Gazettes*, 182, Potier manuscripts, ASJCF. The journal composed by the French traveler Vaugine de Nuisement on his Mississippi voyage of 1752 clearly refers to *le petit Ouabache* as the Wabash we know today in contrast to *le grand Ouabache*, which for de Nuisement was the lower Ohio below the Ohio-Wabash confluence. See Canac-Marquis and Rézeau, *Journal de Vaugine de Nuisement*, 32. However, *le petit Ouabache* was also applied to a western tributary of the southern Wabash located in southeastern Illinois known today in English as the Little Wabash River. Why the latter stream picked up this name is unknown. See the itinerary "Chem: du Poste aux Illinois Par terre," *Gazettes*, 181, Potier manuscripts, ASJCF. An in-depth study of Potier's Illinois Country itineraries is currently being prepared by this author.

13. Louis de la Porte de Louvigny, "Carte du Fleuue Missisipi," 1697, reproduced in Tucker, *Indian Villages*, pl. XII.

14. Delangley, "Tonti Letters," 229. What is surprising, however, is that on one of his maps Le Boullenger, a French Jesuit among the Kaskaskia, wrote *Oio* for the Ohio below the confluence with the Wabash. Anonymous [*sic*], post-1719, reproduced in Tucker, *Indian Villages*, pl. XVIII. My analysis of this chart and that of Tucker's plate no. XIX indicate both are in Le Boullenger's handwriting.

15. The only exception among the Delislian maps that this author has been able to find is an early draft by Claude Delisle based on Le Sueur's data. Claude Delisle, "Carte de la Riviere de Mississippi sur les memoires de Mr le Sueur," 1702. Here *R.*

d'Ouabach refers to the Ohio River. See Wood, *Atlas of Early Maps of the American Midwest: Part II*, 2–4 and pl. 4.

16. Margry, *Découvertes* 5:403–4. See note by Pierre Le Moyne in Alvord, *Illinois Country*, 654; Minet, "Carte De La Louisiane," 1685, reproduced in Tucker, *Indian Villages*, pl. VII. La Salle's general, overarching set of geographical fantasies set a skewed tenor for cartography in the last quarter of the seventeenth century. They were a persistent lot, holding firm until Le Moyne's Mississippi expedition of 1700. See Delanglez, "Cartography of the Mississippi," 257; anonymous, post-1719, in Tucker, *Indian Villages*, pl. XIX.

17. Claude Delisle, 1702, "Carte de la Riviere de Mississippi sur les memoires de Mr. le Sueur."

18. Tucker, *Indian Villages*, pl. XIX.

19. Gabriel Marest [and Jean Mermet], "Cours des Riv. d'ouabache et Missouri," 1700, reproduced in Wood, *Atlas of Early Maps: Part II*, pl. III. For an examination of Marest's and Mermet's handwriting, see McCafferty, "Latest Miami-Illinois Dictionary," 275–78.

20. Even though France would have to abandon its claim to North America in little over a decade, a French spelling of the Seneca name for the Ohio River in the form <oyo> was engraved on lead plates designed to bear witness to French claims to the river, and these were deposited deep in its banks by Pierre-Joseph Céleron de Blainville during the first official French trip down the Ohio in 1749. If nothing else, the lead plates are certainly an unalloyed symbol of the unbending intention of the name "Ohio" to endure. A photograph of one of these very legible plates appears in Steele, *Guerillas and Grenadiers*, 54. The original is at the Virginia Historical Society, Richmond. The form <oyo> represents a French pronunciation of French orthographic *Ohio*.

21. Guernsey, "Indiana."

22. For Johnston, see Howe, "Vocabularies of the Shawanoese and Wyandott," 594.

23. Blair Rudes, personal communication, April 24, 2002.

24. The language known as "Huron-Wyandot" refers specifically to the tongue preserved by Potier, who used earlier French-recorded documents outlining the Huron language and added to them his later related Wyandot material.

25. Hough, "Indian Names"; De La Hunt, *Perry County/A History*, 7.

26. Howe, "Vocabularies of the Shawanoese and Wyandott," 594.

27. Blair Rudes, personal communication, August 12, 1997.

28. *Huron* 3, 448, Potier manuscripts, ASJCF. The symbol "˛" is pronounced [x]. In Potier, sequences such as aia, phonemic *aya*, are distinguished from those written with <ą̨a>, which is phonemic *axa*. But in the Wyandot language recorded in the 1900s, both sequences merged to *aya*. Blair Rudes, personal communication, September 9, 2002.

29. See Reichal, in *Narration of the Mission of the United Brethren*, 548. David Zeisberger, another Moravian, also wrote the Northern Unami form of this hydronym: <Kithánne>. See Horsford, *Zeisberger's Indian Dictionary*, no. 091; he also recorded the locative noun <Kithánnink> (nos. 118 and 160). Rementer recorded the form <kithane> in the late 1900s in Oklahoma. James Rementer, personal communication, September 11, 2000. Munsee phonemic form by Ives Goddard, personal communication, March 17, 2000. The modern expression in Munsee for "big-river" is the nominal form *kihtsi˙pəw*, from *kiht-*, "big," and *si˙pəw*, "river." See O'Meara, *Delaware-English/English-Delaware Dictionary*, 90.

30. Ives Goddard, personal communication, June 13, 2006. That the Unami names for the Ohio River and the Mississippi River are the same may suggest that the Unami adopted and/or shared the Iroquoian hydrological conception of the unified Ohio-Mississippi.

31. Franquelin, "Carte de La Louisiane," 1684, reproduced in Thwaites, *Jesuit Relations*, vol. 63, frontispiece.

32. Wheeler-Voegelin, "Ethnohistory of Indian Use and Occupation in Ohio and Indiana Prior to 1795," in Tanner and Voegelin, *Indians of Ohio and Indiana Prior to 1795* 1:44.

33. Thwaites, *Jesuit Relations* 4:188.

34. Precisely when Miami-Illinois *r* shifted to *l* has not been determined, but it had not occurred in Illinois, apparently, by the time Le Boullenger created his dictionary, which was after 1719. The shift, however, was complete at least in the Miami dialect spoken by Little Turtle in 1797, when it was recorded by Volney.

35. Margry, *Découvertes* 2:41.

36. Pinet, French/Miami-Illinois dictionary, 118. See also in Illinois-French dictionary <nitapiramina mons8 nipinghigi>, translated *nous faisons jetter a l'eau un chevreuil* (we have a deer thrown into the water), 45; <nic8irass8amina m8ns8>, glossed *nous navons pu tuer de chev* (we did not succeed in killing any deer), 135; <nikiskichim8ra m8ns8>, glossed *jay fait jeter le chevreuil a l'eau le suivant de pres* (I had the deer thrown into the water, following it from nearby), 221; <nimens8ma m8ns8>, translated *japorte un chevreuil toute entier* (I carry a whole deer), 270; <metic8nassintchi m8ns8>, translated *viande de chevreuil attendrie pour avoir este gardee* (deer meat tenderized on account of having been stored), 279; <pess8ats8i m8ns8>, glossed *mettons le feu a la prairie pour faire fuyr le chev et le tuer* (let's set the prairie on fire to flush the deer and kill it), 461; <nipih8ra m8ns8>, translated *si jen trouve un [chevreuil]* (if I find one [a deer]), 468. Also see Le Boullenger, French-Illinois dictionary, 41.

37. For an in-depth discussion of prenasalized sibilants in Miami-Illinois, see Costa, *Miami-Illinois Language*, 78–79.

38. Minet, "Carte de La Louisiane."

39. Costa, *Miami-Illinois Language*, 162–63.

40. Gatschet, "Notes on Miami-Illinois"; Dunn, Miami file card dictionary, ISL. Phonemic spellings are from Costa, Miami-Illinois dictionary.

41. Volney, "Tableau du Climat," 467–76.

42. Franquelin, "Nouuelle Decouverte de Plusieurs Nations," 1675, reproduced in Tucker, *Indian Villages*, pl. IV; Randin, "Carte de L'Amerique Septentrionale."

43. Marquette met some Mosopelea at that point. See Campeau, "Cartes relatives," 53; also see Alford, "Unrecognized Father Marquette Letter," 679; and Delanglez, "First Establishment of the Faith," 210.

44. Wheeler-Voegelin, "Ethnohistory of Indian Use," 46–52.

45. For Shawnee clans, see Callender, "Shawnee," in Sturtevant, *Handbook of North American Indians* 15:626–27. The <Honniasontkeronon>, another protohistoric middle Ohio Valley tribe mentioned by La Salle, could in some way have been associated with the Mosopelea. This ethnonym is |o-hnyaʔs-ut-ke-hronõʔ| third person neuter singular patientive–"neck"–"possess"–external locative–populative, meaning "people of the (place of the) gorget." Linguistic analysis by Blair Rudes. Wheeler-Voegelin's "People of the crook-necked squash" is incorrect. Wheeler-Voegelin, "Ethnohistory of Indian Use," 52. The cartographer Franquelin left off the Iroquoian populative suffix *-hrónõʔ* when he spelled this tribal designation <Oniassontké>. See Franquelin, "Carte de La Louisiane," BNF.

46. Gatschet, "Notes on Miami-Illinois."

47. Hough, "Indian Names." I am indebted to David Costa for supplying the Shawnee phonemic form. Although there is no telling just how old the Shawnee hydronym is, it is fair to say that it could date to late prehistoric times.

48. The "Turkey River" name for the Ohio is also noted by Morse in 1812, who mentions a prairie by the name of <Pilkawa> situated near the Ohio River in Clark County within the present city of Jeffersonville. Morse, *American Universal Geography*, 451. However, the -k- of Morse's term is a miscopied -l-, as this toponym would have originally been written *Pillawa, representing either the Miami-Illinois or Shawnee term for "turkey."

49. See H. D. Pursell, "A Map of the United States," 1785, reproduced in Karpinski, *Bibliography of the Printed Maps of Michigan*, 66; also John Fitch, "A Map of the north west parts of the United States of America," 1785, in Karpinski, *Bibliography of the Printed Maps of Michigan*, 65. Note that the final -a of "Pelisipia" is classical Latin, not Algonquian.

50. Thwaites, *Jesuit Relations* 65:106–7. While Gravier was the first to record the hydronym, the ethnonym <Akansea> itself was first penned by Jacques Marquette. It appears on his map of the Mississippi from 1673–74. Marquette, ["Carte du Mississippi"], ASJCF.

51. Marest [and Mermet], "Cours des Riv. d'ouabache et Missouri," 1700.

52. See letter from Henri de Tonti to Alphonse de Tonti, March 4, 1700, in Delanglez, "Tonti Letters," 230. Tonti wrote <Akanceasipi>. He lived a long time among Illinois speakers.

53. [Guillaume Delisle], "Carte du Mexique et De La Floride des Terres Angloises," 1703, reproduced in Tucker, *Indian Villages*, pl. XIII. Delanglez said that the creation of the Delisle maps of 1700 and 1703 has been incorrectly attributed to Guillaume Delisle. See Delanglez, "Source of the Delisle Map of America," 276–79.

54. Dunn, "Names of the Ohio River," 170.

55. Historically, pecan trees were common up the Wabash between the Ohio confluence and Busseron Creek. See Thomas, *Travels through the Western Country*, in Lindley, *Indiana as Seen by Early Travelers*, 42. Today the proverbial lone tree in the middle of a farmer's field in extreme southwestern Indiana is typically a pecan.

56. For "pecan," Dunn wrote <kanzänzäminĭ>. Dunn, Miami file card dictionary, ISL. Le Boullenger has <acansipacane> for *akaanseepakaani* (sg.). Le Boullenger, French-Illinois dictionary, 125. Dunn has <akansapäkana> for *akaansa pakaana* (pl.). Dunn, Miami file card dictionary, ISL. Gatschet has <ká^{n}za pakani> for *kaansa pakaani* (sg.). Gatschet, "Notes on Miami-Illinois." Related forms in other Algonquian languages include Shawnee *kaaθeemi*, "pecan," which was borrowed into Unami in the form *ká·se·m*, where short intervocalic *s* points to a loan. *ká·se·m* was naturalized by some speakers of Unami to *ká·nse·m*. Ives Goddard, personal communication, June 12, 2005. See also the study of the etymologies of "Kansa" and "Akansea" in *Handbook of North American Indians*, ed. William C. Sturtevant (Washington, D.C.: Smithsonian Institution Press, 2001), vol. 13. pt. 1, pp. 462, 474–75, 512.

57. Robert Rankin, personal communication, June 4, 1999. Muriel Wright stated, "Early French explorers referred to the Quapaw as the *Akansea*, from which came the name of the Arkansas River. The name *Akansea*, found in some French records as *Akansa*, signifies 'South Wind People.' ... The name *Akansa* is also found in early records applied to the closely related Kansa or Kaw." Wright, *Guide to the Indian Tribes*, 218–19. Though there is no truth to the statement that the term means "south wind people," this idea could be a remnant of something quite ancient as the Kaw tribe itself perpetuates this story. Robert Rankin, personal communication, August 4, 1999.

58. Illinois-French dictionary, 373. Cognate terms in other Algonquian languages include Unami *ká·nsiya*, "Kansa," and Meskwaki (Fox) *akaasa*, "Kansa, Kaw." I am indebted to Ives Goddard for these forms.

59. <Kanzänzäpiwi> is in Dunn, *Indiana and the Indianans* 1:94; <Kánzäzäpĭungĭ> is in Dunn, ms. 47, ISL. The same progression of nasalization through a word can be seen in <mensensac8a> for underlying *misesaahkwa*, "horsefly" (*Tabanidae*). Illinois-French dictionary, 270. Phonemic spelling in Costa, *Miami-Illinois Language*, 60.

60. Voegelin, *Shawnee Stems* 8:299; also "'nehotáatcimó yeecimeʔtcipiyaaci caawanwa hoháayo hotci kaaθeewiθiipi hómawi hót·a," in Voegelin's field notes, "Walum Olum Song III: Migrations," no. 108, American Philosophical Society,

Philadelphia. My thanks to David Costa for calling my attention to this. Compare Shawnee *hokahpeewiθiipi*, "Arkansas River" (lit. "Quapaw River," from *hokahpa*, "Quapaw"), and *homaskoowiθiipi*, "Verdigris River" (lit. "Muskogee River," from Shawnee *homasko*, "Creek, Muskogee").

61. Costa, "Miami-Illinois Tribe Names," 35.

62. "It is called by the Illinois and by the Oumiamis the River of the Akansea, because the Akansea formerly dwelt on it." Gravier, in Thwaites, *Jesuit Relations* 65:105. See also "River Acansea" for the Ohio River in the account by the New Englander Joseph Kellogg of his trip to the West in 1710, in Stearns, "Joseph Kellogg's Observations on Senex's Map of North America (1710)," 354.

Chapter 4: The Kankakee and Its Affluents

1. The explorers first saw the river *in terms of its ancient hydrology*, that is, at the Mississippi, in the last week of September 1673.

2. Marquette, ["Carte du Missisipi"], ASJCF; Franquelin, "Nouvelle Decouverte de Plusieurs Nations," 1675, reproduced in Thwaites, *Jesuit Relations* 59:86; also Tucker, *Indian Villages*, pl. IV.

3. Delanglez, "Calendar of La Salle's Travels," 293–304.

4. Margry, *Découvertes* 2:128.

5. Ibid 2:174.

6. Ibid. 2:245. French *la rivière des Illinois* comes from Miami-Wea <in8ka asipi8mi>. Pinet, French/Miami-Illinois dictionary, 537. Pinet's translation is *riviere des ilinois*. The native language term is literally "Illinois his/her-river." The word <asipi8mi> is Miami-Illinois *asiipiomi*, "his/her river." For <in8ca>, see note 7 below.

7. Ibid. 2:170. Henri de Tonti agrees when he states "after going up the River of the Miami [i.e., the St. Joseph River] about twenty-seven leagues, and having no one who could guide us in order to find a portage that led to the River of the Illinois [i.e., the Kankakee]" (*après avoir monté la rivière des Miamis environ vingt-sept lieues, et n'ayant personne qui peust nous guider pour trouver un portage qui va a la rivière des Islinois*). Ibid. 1:581. The tribal designation "Illinois" was pronounced [ilinwé] ~ [ilinwɛ́] by the early French. See "illinouest" in Bibliothèque et Archives nationales du Québec, fonds Ramezay (P345): A, Lemoine dit Moniére, Journal no. 1, p. 1. Robert Vézina, personal communication, October 30, 2007; and, from 1640, <Erinioua>. Thwaites, *Jesuit Relations* 18:231. The name derives from an Ojibwa name for these people. However, this tribe name had to have gone into Ojibwa from Miami *ilenweewa*, "he/she speaks in a regular way," as this was, in all likelihood, a descriptive term originally employed by the Miami, who also "spoke in a regular way," that is, who spoke *the same language* as the Illinois. For other ideas about this ethnonym, see Costa, "Miami-Illinois Tribe Names," 46–47. Note that *ilenweewa* is not the term the Illinois used for themselves. The Illinois Indians' self-designation was <in8ca> (sg.), a name of unknown meaning and equally elusive phonological

shape. Included under the umbrella term *Les Illinois* at contact were the Cahokia, Chepoussa, Coiracoentanon, Espeminkia, Kaskaskia, Peoria, (Ta)Maroa, Michigamea, Moingouena, Tapouaro—and the Miami, Wea, and Piankashaw, among others. See Thwaites, *Jesuit Relations* 55:199, 201.

8. Ibid. 1:463.

9. Ibid. 2:174.

10. Ibid. 2:128.

11. Ibid. 2:174.

12. Ibid. 2:135.

13. Ibid. 2:248.

14. Pease and Werner, *French Foundation*, 393–94. This very interesting document by Pierre-Charles Delliette, with an English translation, is also available online at http://www.gbl.indiana.edu/archives/miamis3/M82-99_46j.html (accessed April 18, 1999).

15. Claude Delisle, "L'Amerique Septentrionale," 1700, reproduced in Karpinski, *Bibliography of the Printed Maps of Michigan*, 27; Claude Delisle, "Carte du Canada," 1703, reproduced in Karpinski, *Bibliography of the Printed Maps of Michigan*, 28; also Claude Delisle, "Carte Du Mexique," 1703, reproduction in the Edward E. Ayer Collection, NL, reproduced in Tucker, *Indian Villages*, pl. XIII; also Cumming, *Exploration of North America*, 155; Louis Armand de Lom D'Arce, "Carte Generale du Canada," 1703, reproduced in Verner and Stuart-Stubbs, *Northpart of America*.

16. Titled "avril S. joseph," *Gazettes*, 166b, Potier manuscripts, ASJCF. Moments before the traveler reaches the Mississippi, the itinerary states, "Le tiatiki coule et courre est" (The Tiatiki flows and runs east). La Salle was born November 21, 1643, and died March 19, 1687; Potier was born April 21, 1708, and died July 16, 1781.

17. See, for example, Margry, *Découvertes* 2:246, 266, and 247–48, respectively.

18. Ibid. 2:174; Claude Bernou and M. Peronel, "Carte de l'Amérique Septentrionale," 1682, reproduced in Tucker, *Indian Villages*, pl. VIII.

19. Pierre-François-Xavier de Charlevoix and Jacques-Nicolas Bellin, "Carte des Lacs du Canada," 1744, in Karpinski, *Bibliography of the Printed Maps of Michigan*, 43; Charlevoix-Bellin, "Partie Occidentale de la Nouvelle France," 1745, in Karpinski, *Bibliography of the Printed Maps of Michigan*, 44. Bellin was a French naval engineer. Vaugondy, "Amérique Septentrionale," 1750, AGS, and reproduced in Karpinski, *Bibliography of the Printed Maps of Michigan*, 97. See also <Teakiki> on the anonymous French government map titled "Forts Français et anglais sur l'Ohio en 1755," reproduced in Trudel, *Collection de Cartes Anciennes*, pl. 67; and an official French map bearing the same spelling for the river's name: Anonymous, 1757, "Carte de la Floride," AGS.

20. Like the malformed and misinformed *Ouabouskigou*, *Teatiki* is seen even in modern historical scholarship. See Malchelosse, "La Salle et le Fort Saint-Joseph des Miamis," 91–92. For the only decent spelling of this hydronym penned by Potier,

see *portage du teakiki* in "Chemin, par terre, de S jos: aux 8ia," *Gazettes*, 180, Potier manuscripts, ASJCF.

21. Thwaites, *Jesuit Relations* 66:348; Charlevoix visited the St. Joseph from August 6 to September 17, 1721. Malchelosse, "Poste de la Rivière St-Joseph," 148.

22. Thwaites, *Jesuit Relations*; see also Charlevoix, *Journal of a Voyage to North America* 2:171.

23. Dunn, ms. 47, ISL.

24. Margry, *Découvertes* 2:170.

25. See Faulkner, "Late Prehistoric Occupation of Northwest Indiana." Parts of the original wetlands have been restored, particularly at the Grand Marsh Lake County Park, in the Beaver Lake area, and in the English Lake area. Richard Schmal, personal communication, February 17, 2004.

26. Ibid., 26.

27. Margry, *Découvertes* 1:464.

28. Ibid. 2:247. Author's translation. An excellent view of the old Kankakee marsh as La Salle would have seen it is portrayed in the painting titled *Approaching Storm*, by Clarence Ball, reproduced in Bartlett and Lyon, *La Salle in the Valley of the St. Joseph*. I tried unsuccessfully to locate the original.

29. See <teïahan8i>, glossed *en plain air, qui n'a aucun abri, cabane au milieu d'une prairie* (outdoors, in the open, that has no shelter, a house in the middle of the prairie); <teïatapate8i, teïa8ate8i>, glossed *exposé a la veüe de tous* (exposed to everyone's view); <teïateheta>, translated *qui decouvre son Coeur* (one who reveals his heart); <teïa8e>, an adverb, glossed *a decouvert, en public* (in the open, in public), all in Illinois-French dictionary, 567. The combination of the final *-ahki*, "land, country" plus independent and dependent verb suffixes, the latter as we see in <Téakiki>, is discussed in the Illinois-French dictionary: "*-aki8i est une terminaison qui marque la situation, ou la difference des terres, -akiki pour le subjonctif*" (-akiwi is an ending that marks the situation of or the difference between land, -akiki for the subjunctive). Ibid., 567. What is referred to as the conjunct (dependent) II verb suffix *-ki* is, more precisely, the conjunct (dependent) II peripheral suffix *-k* and the verb ending *-i*. I am indebted to David Pentland for our discussion concerning the vowel length of the first syllable of *teeyaa-* of this place-name.

30. René Paul, "A Map Exhibiting the Territorial limits of several Nations," 1816, reproduced in Tucker, *Indian Villages*, pl. XLI.

31. Hyacinthe Lasselle Papers, ISL.

32. See excerpt of La Mothe's letter from April 24, 1782, in Baerreis, *Indians of Northeastern Illinois*, 136. A Guillaume Dagnaux known as "Lamotte" was in the company of Delatour at the Miami post in the 1700s. See Krauskopf, "French in Indiana," 104. A Guillaume de Lamothe was on his way to the Miami from Québec with brothers and associates in 1726. Krauskopf, "French in Indiana," 126. For Pierre-Guillaume Lamothe, *dit* Guillaume Lamothe, see http//:www.usinternet.com/users/dfnels/lamothe.htm (accessed May 25, 2003).

33. See Charlevoix, "Journal d'un Voyage," in Bartlett, *La Salle in the Valley of the St. Joseph*, 115; also Thwaites, *Jesuit Relations* 66:348. Guernsey's translation of Charlevoix's *Kiakiki* to Potawatomi "swamp land" is wrong on two counts: The word is not Potawatomi and it does not mean "swamp land" in any known Indian language. Guernsey, "Indiana"; Dunn's assumption that "Tĕ́hyakkĭkĭ" was Potawatomi and his belief that its translation was "swamp country" are also both in error. Dunn, *Indiana and the Indianans* 1:88.

34. Once imperfect pronunciations of native words were generated and once they were adopted by the French, then written, copied and recopied, correct native or near-native pronunciations were rarely seen, despite the continuous and very considerable contact between Frenchmen and Indians.

35. Lasselle Papers, "Licenses granted by the governor to Indian traders," 1802, doc. no. 566.

36. Charlevoix, "Journal d'un Voyage," in Bartlett, *La Salle in the Valley of the St. Joseph*, 115.

37. Ninian Edwards, "Illinois River leaving Peoria to go to Chicago," 1812, reproduced in Tucker, *Indian Villages*, pl. XXXV.

38. Thomas Forsyth, ["Chart of the Country Southwest of Lake Huron"], 1812, in ibid., pl. XXXVII. Note also "Kankekee" on Tipton's chart from 1824: "A Map Showing the Fort Wayne Indian Agency," reproduced in Tucker, *Indian Villages*, pl. XLIX. Tipton was obviously uncertain or unconcerned about the spelling of this term. Both "Kankiki" and "Kinkiki" appear in an abstract of trading licenses which he prepared in 1828. See Robertson and Riker, *Tipton Papers* 2:90. Paul's chart (see note 30 above) was designed by a French-speaking American for the American government. On his map there is no indication as to where the Kankakee ends. The name "Illinois River" appears only near the confluence of the Mississippi.

39. American mapmakers often borrowed <Theakiki> from old French maps after 1800. See, for example, <Tiakiki> on the anonymously created map known as "Region south and west of Chicago and Fort Dearborn," ca. 1811, reproduced in Tucker, *Indian Villages*, pl. XXXVI. At the same time, the term became rare in French cartography. In rounding out this study of La Salle's place-name, I should add the following curiosity. The -akee of "Kankakee" was considered by previous scholars to represent *-ahki*, "land." However, the -akee of "Kankakee" actually represents the *-iki* of *teeyaahkiki*; it is the garbled segment of "Kankakee" spelled -nka- that distortedly represents Miami-Illinois *-ahki*.

40. Thwaites, *Jesuit Relations* 66:287.

41. See Guillaume Delisle, "Carte de La Louisiane," 1718, reproduced in Tucker, *Indian Villages*, pl. XV; also Cumming, *Exploration of North America*, 156.

42. Anonymous, "A Map of the Countrey of the Five Nations," 1730, reproduced in Brown, *Early Maps*, pl. 13; D'Anville, "Canada Louisiane & Terres Angloises," 1755, AGS. One of the "Boulton-revised" copies of the same chart is housed at the Indiana Historical Society; L. Fielding, "A Map of the United States," 1785, AGS.

43. See Dunn, *True Indian Stories*, 267. The -a- of <Huakiki> is either a miscopied original -e-, or else Marest heard *æ*, as in English "sat," for Illinois *ee* and therefore wrote a. This is not unexpected, however, since the pronunciation of the Miami-Illinois vowel could range from a rather mid high front vowel sound as in English "bait" to a mid low front vowel as in "bet," and even extend into the range of a rather low front vowel sound as in "bat."

44. Verbs are a common form of place-names in Miami-Illinois, as they are in other Algonquian languages.

45. Note that in the Miami-Illinois language, as elsewhere in Algonquian, a noun ending in a vowel plus *-wa*, such as *mahweewa*, drops the *-w-* (and the following animate noun suffix *-a*) when it becomes an initial. For example, PA **pele·wa*, "partridge" plus **anyikwa*, "squirrel" gives **pele·nyikwa*, "flying squirrel," not ***pele·wa·nyikwa*. In like manner, in the Miami-Illinois language, "it is wolf country" is *mahweehkiki*, not ***mahweewaahkiki*. Thus the initial allomorph of "wolf" in Miami-Illinois is *mahwee-*, as seen in Miami *mahweeyaakwi*, "eastern wahoo."

46. See <mitec8abinti> translated *corde de l'arc* (bowstring) in Illinois-French dictionary, 298; and <tékwapindi> in Gatschet, "Notes on Miami-Illinois." For a thorough discussion of this phonological phenomenon, see Costa, *Miami-Illinois Language*, 56–58. Even in Miami-Illinois terms in which initial *m* plus a short vowel was retained, this syllable could still pass right by the untrained ears of a nonnative speaker of the language. This explains how, in part, the Miami-Illinois personal name *mahkookima*, "Bear Chief" became the Indiana place-name "Kokomo." Just as in the case of <Huakiki>, the first person to record "Kokomo" did not notice the initial *ma-*. I am indebted to Carl Leiter of Kokomo for providing the interest and the variant historical spellings that made the analysis of "Kokomo" possible.

47. Margry, *Découvertes* 2:172; Faulkner, "Late Prehistoric Occupation of Northwest Indiana," 51. LeMoine Marks, a Miami man from Indiana, mentioned in an interview an old fur buyer who said the Kankakee marsh was once full of wolves. Stewart Rafert, personal communication, August 31, 2001. Also, "A friend of mine showed me a hide he said was from a black wolf caught along the Kankakee. My dad's hunting friend, in the 1920s, had two Russian wolf hounds, complete with the marks from fighting wolves." Richard Schmal, personal communication, February 17, 2004.

48. See Brasser, "Mahican," 211.

49. Thwaites, *Jesuit Relations* 66:348.

50. Margry, *Découvertes* 2:174.

51. Ibid. 2:127.

52. Margry, *Découvertes* 2:175; Bauxar, "History of the Illinois Area," 595.

53. For Iroquois escape routes, see Margry, *Découvertes* 1:527. For Trail Creek, see the anonymous French map, file number SHB B4044-15, NL.

54. See Bauxar, "History of the Illinois Area," 594. Kellogg says the first attack on the Illinois occurred in 1653. Kellogg, *Early Narratives*, 98. For the invasion of 1678,

see Thwaites, *Jesuit Relations* 60:167. For the invasion of 1680, see "Relation de La Salle," in Margry, *Découvertes* 2:175. For the invasions of 1683 and 1685, see Tonti's Memoir in Baerreis, "Anthropological Report," 50; Bauxar, "History of the Illinois Area," 595; and Temple, *Indian Villages*, 23.

55. Potier noted a village of Mascouten at this site in the mid-1700s. See "Chemin de S. joseph aux illinois par Le tiatiki," *Gazettes*, 171, Potier manuscripts, ASJCF. It was here that Tonti saved the lives of some Iroquois in this vicinity in 1682 while returning to Michilimackinac from the 1682 descent of the Mississippi. See Delanglez, "La Salle Expedition of 1682," 35.

56. Bernou-Peronel, "Carte de l'Amérique Septentrionale"; Franquelin, "Carte de La Louisiane," 1684, reproduced in Thwaites, *Jesuit Relations*, vol. 63, frontispiece.

57. Margry, *Découvertes* 2:174.

58. Franquelin, "Carte de l'Amerique Septent.[le]," 1684. A copy of this map, incorrectly dated 1687, is reproduced in Cumming, *Exploration of North America*, 153. This French hydronym is seen again on Franquelin's 1688 map, "Carte de l'Amérique Septentrionalle," reproduced in Tucker, *Indian Villages*, pls. XIA and XIB.

59. <Pickamik>: Hiram W. Beckwith, "Indian Names of Water Courses," 41; <Pickamink>: John Tipton, ["Map Showing the Fort Wayne Indiana Agency in Indiana"], 1824; <Pecamink>: Robertson and Riker, *Tipton Papers* 1:256. <Pickamik>, <Pickamink>, <Pickemink>: Robertson and Riker, *Tipton Papers* 1:258; <Pecamink>, <Pekamink>: *History of Jasper County*, 8–9; <Pinkamink>: Hough, "Indian Names"; <Pickamick>: Guernsey, "Indiana"; <päkamik> in Costa, Miami-Illinois dictionary. This place-name is related to the Old Potawatomi name for the Missouri River, spelled historically <Pikitin>. See Lance, "Origin and Meaning of Missouri," 284. This hydronym would be composed of the "mud" initial *_pik-_ and the II final *-_itən_, "flow."

60. Miami-Illinois phonemic spelling by David Costa, personal communication, June 10, 1996. Coincidentally, the Miami-Illinois name for the Kankakee is the same as the Miami-Illinois name attested by Gatschet for the Missouri River: <päkámiki> and <päkámikisipíwi>, phonemic *peekami(i)ki (siipiiwi)*. Compare Old Illinois <pekitan8i>, glossed *eau bourbeuse* (muddy water), in Illinois-French dictionary, 450. This verb is *piikihtanwi*, "it mud-flows," although the historical recording seems to indicate the ablauted initial *peek-*. Contrary to what some have said, there is no basis for thinking that any of the recordings listed above includes a Potawatomi term for "beaver," even though in Potawatomi the word for "beaver" happens to be *mək*. Hiram Beckwith was the first to publish the incorrect "beaver" translation for this place-name, which has persisted in various publications over the years. See Beckwith, "Indian Names," 41. For the muddiness of the Iroquois River, see http://www.indianaoutfitters.com/iroquois_river.html (accessed September 23, 2005).

61. See *La Rive jaune (ossa sip)*, in "Chemin de S. joseph aux illinois par Le tiatiki," *Gazettes*, 171, Potier manuscripts, ASJCF.

62. Ibid.

63. The term *oonsaa-* can combine with noun stems, as for example in *oonsaan-ikwa*, literally "yellow squirrel, brown squirrel" for English "fox squirrel" (*Sciurus niger*). See <8nsanic8a> in Pinet, French/Miami-Illinois dictionary, 69.

64. Dunn in Costa, Miami-Illinois dictionary. The third *a* of *oonsaalamoon-akami(i)ki* is unexpected and seems to represent assimilation to the following *a*, just as in *meehčakaminki* ("at the great water") instead of the ungrammatical ***meehčikaminki*. The phonetic realization is [óonzaalamóonakamíiki], although the length of the penultimate vowel in the phonemic form is unknown.

65. Robertson and Riker, *Tipton Papers* 2:22, 31–32. Phonemic spelling by Laura Buszard-Welcher, personal communication, May 4, 1997.

66. Dunn, *True Indian Stories*, 320; Dunn, *Indiana and the Indianans* 1:97. Hough's map's <Wethogan> is noteworthy in that the "water" final, written -gan, could have suffered the same fate as that of the hydronym "Michi*gan*." Hough, "Indian Names."

67. Paul Voorhis, personal communication, August 1, 1998. Father Claude-Jean Allouez noted between 1669 and 1671 that the Kickapoo spoke the same language as the Mascouten. See "*les Kikabou, & les Kitchigamich, qui parlent même langue que les Machkouteng*" (the Kickapoo and the Kitchgamich, who speak the same language as the Mascouten), in Thwaites, *Jesuit Relations* 54:232.

68. See Tanner, *Atlas of Great Lakes Indian History*, 134–35.

69. See Robertson and Riker, *Tipton Papers* 3:246, 312–13, 391, 686–87, 690, 713–14.

70. Dunn, *True Indian Stories*, 235; Kappler, *Indian Affairs* 2:369.

71. Guernsey, "Indiana."

72. Ibid.

73. For a relatively good general but incomplete map of presettlement vegetation in Indiana, see Lindsey, *Natural Features of Indiana*, 51.

74. See Ball, *Northwest Indiana*, 65.

75. Hough, "Indian Names"; Dunn, ms. 47, ISL.

76. Margy, *Découvertes* 4:597.

77. "Chemin de S. joseph aux Illinois," *Gazettes*, 171, Potier manuscripts, ASJCF.

78. See, for example, Guillaume Delisle, "Carte de La Louisiane," 1718. Regarding the spelling of the family name of these cartographers, *The Dictionary of Canadian Biography*, upon researching this topic twenty years, decided on the "Delisle" spelling. Ed Dahl, personal communication, September 20, 1997. The reader should not confuse Indiana's Potato Creek with the Macoupin River, tributary of the Illinois River, which was also named after cow lily, or spatterdock.

79. "Chemin, par terre, de S jos: aux 8ia- de 60 L.," *Gazettes*, 171, Potier manuscripts, ASJCF.

80. "De Gannes Memoir," in Pease and Werner, *French Foundation* 23:345. Notably, in the same line of his memoir, Delliette, believing that he was remembering the seeds of *Nuphar*, actually wrote about the seeds of another edible aquatic

plant, probably *Nelumbo lutea*, as the description he offers of his seed pods fits the description of those of *Nelumbo lutea*. The latter plant was commonly cut and dried by historic Native Americans.

81. I am indebted to Duane Esarey for the identification of *macopine*.

82. See Feest, *Indians and a Changing Frontier*, 187.

83. Margry, *Découvertes* 2:173–74.

84. The Jesuit missionary Jean-Baptiste Antoine-Robert Le Boullenger, who spent decades among the Illinois and would have known the plant well, described it as a "*grosse racine dans leau*" (big root in the water). Le Boullenger, French-Illinois dictionary, 113. The Pinet dictionary has both <macopiniki> and <mic8piniki>: Pinet, French/Miami-Illinois dictionary, 169, 343. The Illinois-French dictionary has <mic8pena>, <mic8peniki> (pl.) and <mic8piniki> (pl.), defined as *macopin, grosses racines* (macopin, big roots). See Illinois-French dictionary, 288. Dunn wrote <micoupena> for the singular. Dunn, *Indiana and the Indianans* 1:76. Dunn incorrectly identified this plant as the white water lily (*Nymphaea tuberosa*) (1:76); Faulkner likewise. See Faulkner, *Late Prehistoric Occupation of Northwest Indiana*, 299. According to metrical principles in Miami-Illinois, the *e* of the independent animate noun *ahpena* shifts to *i* in *mahkohpina* and *mihkohpina*. This explains the orthographic *i* in the French recording *macopine(s)*.

85. Siebert, "Resurrecting Virginia Algonquian from the Dead," 413. One of the most colorful events in the history of the Kankakee has to be the invasion of the area by Spain in the winter of 1781. French militia from Spanish St. Louis traipsed up the Kankakee to burn Fort St.-Joseph near present-day Niles, Michigan, and overcome the British soldiers who were stationed there. See Balard, *Old Fort St. Joseph*, 47; Blanchard, *History of the Discovery*, 164; McDermott, *Old Cahokia*, 31, 32, 200; and Malchelosse, "Poste de la Rivière Saint-Joseph," 182.

Chapter 5: Trails to ‹Kekionga›

1. Letter from Capt. James Riley to the *Philadelphia Union*, November 24, 1819, in Lindley, *Indiana as Seen by Early Travelers*, 241. Parenthetical remarks added by this author. River lengths are from Simmons, *Rivers of Indiana*, 67, 46, respectively.

2. Champlain, ["La Nouvelle France"]; Champlain, "Carte de la Nouvelle France," 1632, reproduced in Karpinski, *Bibliography of the Printed Maps of Michigan*, 5. For earlier Champlain maps, see Champlain, "Carte Geographique De La Nouuelle Franse," 1612, reproduced in Laverdière, *Oeuvres de Champlain*, tome III; in Armstrong, *Samuel de Champlain*, 174–75; also in Verner and Stuart-Stubbs, *Northpart of America*, 21; Champlain's chart from 1615 is reproduced in Armstrong, *Samuel de Champlain*, opposite p. 160; Champlain, ["La Nouvelle France"].

3. Lucien Campeau, personal communication, December 29, 1998. For Brûlé, see Campeau, "Route commerciale," 21–49. For Lake Erie and Brûlé, see Campeau, "Découverte du Lac Érié," 24, 29, 36–37; and Thwaites, *Jesuit Relations* 21:188–92.

For early historical Lake Erie, see Delanglez, *Life and Voyages of Louis Jolliet*, 8; and Margry, *Découvertes* 1:112–66.

4. Steckley, "Early Map," 17–29; and Thwaites, *Jesuit Relations* 21:191. The lake's Iroquoian name, originally transcribed by the French as <Érié>, has often been taken to signify "cat." Indeed, the French did call the Erie tribe *la nation du chat,* literally "the nation of the cat." Many have incorrectly assumed that the "cat" was the bobcat. See, for example, Heidenreich, "Analysis of the 17th Century Map," 100. However, the mammal in question is the raccoon.

5. Wright, "The People of the Panther—A Long Erie Tale," 47–118; Gravier, *Carte des Grands Lacs*, 16. For precontact abundance of fruit trees in the area of southern Lake Erie, see also Thwaites, *Jesuit Relations* 42:178. This linguistic analysis is premised on the belief that the term is from a Huron-like language where the Proto–Northern Iroquoian external locative **-ke* shows up in Huron as *-xe*. This place-name represents a case similar to Shawnee **(hah)θenaamiisi(iθiipi)* and Miami-Illinois *ahsenaamiši siipiiwi*, both signifying "sugar maple tree river," names for two of Indiana's Sugar Creeks. In each instance, local aboriginal peoples were so impressed by the abundance of a plant species in an ecological niche that they naturally used the name of the plant to designate water nearby, such as a stream running through it.

6. Margry, *Découvertes* 1:112–66. Adrien Jolliet traversed the north coast of Lake Erie since, theoretically at least, the Iroquois had been pacified. But after La Salle incited the Iroquois in the early 1680s, the French were again denied this route. See Campeau, "Route commerciale," 43; Talon to Colbert, August 29, 1670, in *Rapport de l'archiviste*, 117. De Gallinée, Dollier de Casson, and their entourage first saw Lake Erie right after running into Adrien Jolliet, near today's Hamilton, Ontario. The former then descended the Grand River to its mouth and traversed the north shore of Lake Erie west to Long Point, where they spent a mild winter but encountered ferocious early spring storms on their historic voyage to Sault Ste. Marie. See Margry, *Découvertes* 1:143–47ff. De Gallinée and Dollier de Casson wintered on the right bank of the Black River, near the mouth of Lynn River, also known as Patterson Creek, near Port Dover, Ontario, before continuing in the spring towards Lake Huron and finally Sault Ste. Marie. See Malchelosse, "La Salle et Le Fort Saint-Joseph des Miamis," 86.

7. Franquelin, "Carte de la descouverte du Sr Jolliet," 1674. Original at the Service français de l'Hydrographie et de la Marine, BSH B4044-37. Photocopy in the author's possession.

8. Original in the Bibliothèque Service Hydrographique, Paris, B4044-49. Reproduced in Marcel, *Reproduction de cartes*, pl. 27.

9. Margry, *Découvertes* 2:139, 244. The French were no doubt aware of the Maumee at this time.

10. Blair Rudes, personal communication, February 28, 2006. The early French commonly wrote ti for Iroquoian *tey* before a vowel. The preservation of the *-kt-*

cluster (Proto-Iroquoian **kt* went to *hk* in Huron and Wyandot) would make this a Seneca term, which is expected given La Salle's known interaction with the Seneca.

11. See Stothers, "Late Woodland Models"; and Steckley, "Early Map," 17–29 (map on 26–27); and Stothers, "Michigan Owasco and the Iroquois Co-Tradition," 5–41.

12. The Bernou-Peronel chart of ca. 1682 is an impressive embodiment of La Salle's ability to guess in matters geographic, for here the Ohio River is shown to flow within 30 miles of Lake Erie. But at its closest point the river comes only to within 80 miles of the shores of the Great Lake, and the two are typically at least 160 miles apart. Claude Bernou and M. Peronel, "Carte de l'Amérique Septentrionale," ca. 1682, reproduced in Tucker, *Indian Villages*, pl. VIII.

13. Drawn from La Salle's personal large map, now lost. At the same time Franquelin's chart from 1688 shows a portage from the St. Joseph to the Wabash via what appears to involve the Elkhart and Eel Rivers. Franquelin, "Carte de l'Amérique Septentrionalle," 1688, reproduced in Tucker, *Indian Villages*, pls. XIA and XIB; Marco Vincenzo Coronelli, "Colle Nuoue Scoperte," reproduced in Tucker, *Indian Villages*, pl. X; also in Buisseret, *Mapping the French Empire*, 20; Minet, "Carte de La Louisiane," 1685, reproduced in Tucker, *Indian Villages*, pl. VII. It is known that La Salle tinkered with geographical data for personal reasons. For instance, he portrayed the lower Mississippi River as veering off wildly into what is now western Arkansas and Texas. In fact, he ended up locating the delta of the river for all intents and purposes along the northeastern coastline of Mexico. This could not have been an honest mistake for someone who had descended the river. For appraisals by modern historians of La Salle's cartographic shenanigans, see Delanglez, "Cartography of the Mississippi," 34–38; also Campeau, "Route commerciale," 49.

14. Louis de la Porte de Louvigny, "Carte du Fleuue Missisipi," 1697, reproduced in Tucker, *Indian Villages*, pl. XIV.

15. See Cumming, *Exploration of North America*, 53.

16. Author's translation. Parentheses added. De Bonnécamps, "Carte d'un voyage," 1749. Original at the Service historique de la Marine, Paris. Photocopy in author's possession. See also the anonymous French map from the mid-eighteenth century titled "Carte de La Nouvelle Angleterre Nouvelle Yorc," AGS, which reads "sources de l'Oyo peu connues" (little-known sources of the Ohio). For La Salle's ignorance of the land south of Lake Erie, see Delanglez, *Some La Salle Journeys*, 35–37.

17. Nicolas de Fer, "Le Canada, ou Nouvelle France," 1705, reproduced in Karpinski, *Bibliography of the Printed Maps of Michigan*, 33. This chart also indicates the portage to the Wabash. The Delisle chart of 1718 reiterates this information. Guillaume Delisle, "Carte de la Louisiane," 1718, reproduced in Buisseret, *Mapping the French Empire*, 24.

18. Malchelosse, "Poste de la Rivière Saint-Joseph," 139–86, especially 146–47. For Bissot's excursion to the Maumee in 1711 and 1712, see the Cadillac Papers, in Michigan Pioneer and Historical Society, *Collections and Researches* 33:551; for the Miami near the Maumee in 1707, see 33:338.

19. For the movement of the Miami to the headwaters of the Maumee, see Cadillac Papers, in Michigan Pioneer and Historical Society, *Collections and Researches* 33:338, and Malchelosse, "Poste de la Rivière Saint-Joseph," 147. For the Miami wanting the French to escort them to the Maumee, see the "Archives nationales de France: Colonies," v. C11A31:83–87; C1132:71, 213–213, ANQ; and Vaudreuil's correspondence in *Rapport de l'Archiviste*, 454–55. Jean-Baptiste Bissot de Vincennes had gone to the St. Joseph in 1696 to replace Le Gardeur de Courtemanche. See Malchelosse, "Poste de la Rivière St-Joseph," 146.

20. Delisle, "Carte de la Louisiane."

21. The signatories to the historically important peace treaty of 1701 are in "Archives nationales de France: Colonies," v. C11A19, f. 41.

22. Anson, *Miami Indians*, 29; Rafert, *Miami Indians of Indiana*, 27, 29. In 1721, the Miami noted that hunting was good near their new home at the headwaters of the Maumee. See Krauskopf, "French in Indiana," 93.

23. Bernou-Peronel, "Carte de l'Amérique Septentrionale."

24. Some Miami were still on the St. Joseph in 1715. See Krauskopf, "French in Indiana," 47.

25. Marco Vincenzo Coronelli, 1688, "America Settentrionale," reproduced in Tucker, *Indian Villages*, pls. IX, X. For the first sighting of the Maumee by the French, see "Archives nationales de France: Colonies," v. C11/A33, 124–25.

26. Beckwith says the portage from the Maumee and the head of the Little River started directly at Fort Wayne. Beckwith, *History of Vigo and Parke Counties, Indiana*, 22. The knowledge of a portage linking the Maumee River to the Wabash appearing as early as 1688 on Coronelli's La Salle–based chart came from geographical data obtained from Indians. The French came to know the Maumee River as *la rivière du Portage* (the Portage River). See map by Le Page de Pratz, reproduced in Cumming, *Exploration of North America*, 161. Additional discussion of the portage to the Wabash appears in chapter 7. The English version of this particular French place-name persisted into the nineteenth century.

27. Although they originally established themselves at what was to become the interface between the French and the British, most of the Miami proper, accompanied by other Algonquians, took a step over that line and established a town even farther east in territory frequented by English traders. This, the most famous of the British-oriented Indian towns, was known in English as Pickawillany, a name that derives from Shawnee *pkiiwileni*, "Miami." I am indebted to Dave Costa for the phonemic spelling of this term. See also the historical spelling of the plural form of this ethnonym <Peekeeweeleneekëë> in Trowbridge, *Shawnee Traditions*, 66. Pickawillany was located near the confluence of the Great Miami River and Loramie Creek, near modern Piqua, Ohio. It was under the direction of the Maumee Miami leader *meemeehšikia*, whose name literally means "big head" but is also the term in Miami-Illinois for "dragonfly." This chief was known to the French as la Demoiselle (pronounced [ladwɛzɛ́l] in New World French, a term which literally

means "the Lady" but is also a French term for "dragonfly" (*Libellula*). The name of a Piankashaw man from the following generation known to the French as La Grosse Tête (The Big Head) is a translation of the same Miami-Illinois term and suggests that *meemeehšikia* was a relatively common name among Miami-Illinois speakers. See Temple, *Indian Villages*, 79. Though La Demoiselle did not play a direct role in Indiana place-names, he was the father of *mihšihkinaahkwa*, known to the French as La Tortue (The Turtle), who became the namesake of several Wabash tributaries. The reader should not confuse La Tortue, however, with the celebrated Miami leader known in English as Little Turtle, who also bore the name *mihšihkinaahkwa*. Another of these multiethnic Indian towns, this one located at the confluence of the Great Miami and Ohio Rivers, was under the leadership of a Miami known in French as Le Baril (The Barrel). For a lucid, informed discussion of these Indian "republics," see White, *Middle Ground*, 186–240, 510. It was during the Ohio Valley days of La Demoiselle and Le Baril that the current names of the Great Miami River of Ohio and Indiana and the Little Miami River of Ohio were conceived. As noted in chapter 11, only the English, and the Shawnee in translated form, used the hydronym "Great Miami River."

28. Krauskopf, "French in Indiana," 94–95. Krauskopf shows a list of soldiers stationed at this fort in 1722 (104). The first priest on the Wabash was the Jesuit Jean-Charles Guymonneau, also written Guimeneau, who received a permit in May 1725 from the Marquis de Vaudreuil to go to the Miami and *Ouiatanon* with a *frère donné* and two canoes. He arrived in 1726 (119).

29. "Archives nationales de France: Colonies," v. C11A44, f. 366–67. Bissot père was forty-eight at the time of his death. His son took over temporary command at the age of eighteen. Krauskopf, "French in Indiana," 84. Fort des Miamis appeared cartographically in 1745. See D'Anville, "Amérique Septentrionale," 1745, reproduced in Karpinski, *Bibliography of the Printed Maps of Michigan*, 45.

30. Malchelosse, "La Salle et le fort Saint-Joseph des Miamis," 95–103. See *R. des Miamis* for the Maumee on Charlevoix-Bellin, "Partie Occidentale De La Nouvelle France," 1745, in Karpinski, *Bibliography of the Printed Maps of Michigan*, 44. Krauskopf notes that the Frenchmen Joseph Magdelaine, known as La Douceur, Jean Richard, Pierre Roy, and Nicolas Ladouceur were in the earliest days the men involved in the business of being translators, both at the *Fort des Miamis* and at *les Ouiatanons*. Roy holds a particular distinction in this respect—he could neither read nor write. Krauskopf also notes that the French stock in trade was cosmetics (vermilion) and liquor.

31. The commonly occurring variant <Kikakon> also is seen in many historic French documents and was even used by the French envoy Céleron in speaking to La Demoiselle in 1749. See Roy, *Sieur de Vincennes Identified*, 75; also Margry, *Découvertes* 6:716, 721–23. The English spelling of this place-name is "Kishkakon."

32. The French said the word <Kiskakon> meant "cut-tail" and was a reference to the bear. See Thwaites, *Jesuit Relations* 33:273.

33. There were two other totem subgroups of the Ottawa—the Sinago, or "Black Squirrel," and the Sable (French for "sand"), and possibly a fourth group whose name is toponymic in nature—<Nassauakueton>, referring to the "fork" (of a river). See Feest and Feest, "Ottawa," 776.

34. Pro-English Ottawa arrived on the Maumee in the 1740s and 1750s. See Hanna, *Wilderness Trail* 1:333–34; O'Callaghan, *Documents Relative to the Colonial History of the State of New York* 9:1072, 10:163, 608; and Draper and Thwaites, *Collections of the State Historical Society* 16:290, 17:367–72.

35. See "De Gannes Memoir," in Pease and Werner, *French Foundation*, 392. The *kiiškakkamikaa* form provided by the Ojibweyanist Chuck Fiero, personal communication, March 23, 2006.

36. Letter from Riley to the *Philadelphia Union*. Winter wrote that "Ft. Wayne … stood high upon the banks of the river." See Feest, *Indians and a Changing Frontier*, 192.

37. Brice, *History of Ft. Wayne*, 23.

38. Dunn, *True Indian Stories* 1:89.

39. Phonemic spellings in Costa, Miami-Illinois dictionary.

40. The English-language toponym "Kettle Town" is in General Wayne's officer's journal from that campaign. See Smith, *Greene Ville to Fallen Timbers*, 277.

41. Phonemic spelling in Costa, Miami-Illinois dictionary.

42. "A Sketch Taken in the Month of Novr 1778, H. Duvernet, 2nd Lt. R.R.A.," PAC. This report also tells of the great difficulty in ascending the Maumee because of its challenging rapids.

43. Bliss, *Diary of David Zeisberger*, 200.

44. Heckewelder, *Narrative of the Mission of the United Brethren*, 397; Beckwith, *History of Vigo and Parke Counties*, 172–73.

45. See the de Gallinée map in Gravier, *Cartes des Grands Lacs*; Volney, "Tableau du Climat," 470, 472.

46. Even George Washington, apparently, wrote the Algonquian vowel in this manner. Witness the last vowel of his <Pikkavilinua> for Shawnee *pkiiweleni*, "Miami," that is, Pickawillany, the name of the town of La Demoiselle discussed in note 27 above. See [Anonymous], "Map of the western parts of the colony of Virginia," 1754, reproduced in Brown, *Early Maps*, pl. 19. Brown's notes concerning this map indicate that it was based on George Washington's excursion west begun in 1753.

47. George Winter Papers, file 69.86.344, TCHS. Also Feest, *Indians and a Changing Frontier*, 193; Hough, "Indian Names." Of course, English speakers also transcribed Algonquian *i(i)* as e, our "alphabet E."

48. Gatschet, "Notes on Miami-Illinois." Dunn has a good albeit ambiguous <kíkīúngĭ> in Dunn, *Indiana and the Indianans*, 89, but also a misinformed <Kekióongi> in Dunn, *True Indian Stories*, 18. In <Kekionga> and <Kegaiogue>, the "g" (the third dorso–velar obstruent in this term, alongside the two k's) stands for

phonemic *k*. In this case, according to the rule in Miami-Illinois that governs the voicing of an obstruent following a nasal, *k* is pronounced as [g]. In fact, the written "g" following a nasalized syllable in <Kekionga> was my initial wake-up call, as it suggested this particular term could be Miami and warranted consideration from that perspective. The occurrence of a final vowel in the segment -onga, even though it was strangely shaped when viewed through a Miami-Illinois lens, was the second call.

49. As Cayton has pointed out, this battle, rather insignificant in its own right, directly led to an Indian retreat to the then British-held fort at the headwaters of the Maumee. Here the Indians suffered a far greater humiliation than they had in the battle itself—the British refused to lend them the helping hand that they had expected. *That* was the most historically important event of the day. In this connection, history should remember General Wayne less as a warrior of the Old Northwest than as a statesman who orchestrated the Treaty of Greene Ville in 1795, which opened up south-central Ohio to American settlement. See Cayton, *Frontier Indiana*, 163.

50. Smith, *Greene Ville to Fallen Timbers*, 282, 286, 310.

51. Cayton, *Frontier Indiana*, 163–64. The Delaware were in the St. Mary's and St. Joseph Valleys about 1789.

52. See Ferguson, "White River Indiana Delawares," 47.

53. The Miami name *alaamhsenwa* for Wayne may have developed from the Miami's confusing the sounds of the English terms "Wayne" and "wind." Wayne certainly did not move like the wind. He suffered from gout during his campaign against the Indians and had to be carried by his men. The Miami name for Wayne comes from Daryl Baldwin, personal communication, December 17, 2001.

54. Goddard, "Delaware," 225; Munsee spelling by John O'Meara, personal communication, December 29, 1998. The Delaware were living on the east bank of the St. Joseph River of northeastern Indiana in 1785. Two more groups arrived on the St. Mary's in 1787, and some Shawnee were on the Maumee in 1788 and 1790. See Rafert, *Miami Indians*, 38. For an examination of the Delaware in Indiana, see chapters 6 and 9. In modern Unami *khíkˑay* means "old person," especially "old woman"; in modern Munsee *kíhkay* means "chief." Ives Goddard, personal communication, June 3, 2002.

55. Phonemic form from David Costa, personal communication, July 13, 1994.

56. See Fraser, *Huron Manuscripts*, 154; *Huron* 3, 156, Potier manuscripts, ASJCF. Potier also mentions the Huron name for the Miami people <θochiengootr8nnon> "people of the crane." His "θ" represents phonemic *th*, not *θ*. *Huron* 3, 155, Potier manuscripts, ASJCF; see also <tochingootr8nnon>, translated "Miamis" (156). The underlying form of the toponym is |th-yo-hsinkoʔt-ke| contrastive–third person singular neuter patient–"crane"–external locative. The Huron reflex of the Proto–Northern Iroquoian locative [-ke] is *-xe*, which was normally written "ę" by the French. However, when *-xe* immediately follows *t*, the resulting cluster appears as *hk* (although the *h* does not typically show up in the historic records since it is not

a sound in French). In the term for the Miami town, the locative suffix and the last consonant of the root overlap: *-t* + *-xe* becomes *-hke*. In other words, after a root ending in *t*, as in the case of *thohšinkóhke(h)*, the underlying *-tke* cluster shifts to *-hke*, which Potier would write simply as -ke. At the same time *-nk-* is realized as phonetic [ng], and initial *th-* is aspirated [t]. Epenthetic *h* may or may not have been the final sound in this term, although all word-final short vowels in the Lake Iroquoian languages are followed by epenthetic *h*. I am indebted to Blair Rudes for this linguistic analysis. Personal communication, March 20, 1998.

57. Dunn, *True Indian Stories*, 275.

58. John Tipton, ["Map Showing the Fort Wayne Indiana Agency in Indiana"], 1824, reproduced in Tucker, *Indian Villages*, pl. XLIX. For Ottawa *(o)maamii*, "Miami," spelled <mamí>, see Gatschet's fieldnotes on the Oklahoma dialect of Ottawa. I am indebted to David Costa for supplying this historical attestation.

59. David Pentland, personal communication, August 26, 2005. John Nichols observes, "From Ojibwe dialects I have seen much variation even within communities and from repetition to repetition by individuals. Some people like compounds where the prior members look like words and others like tighter compounds that have prior members that look like stems or have connectives. Both are 'right' they tell me." John Nichols, personal communication, February 11, 2006.

60. Bliss, *Diary of David Zeisberger*, 44; Smith, *Greene Ville to Fallen Timbers*, 269, 271–73; Samuel Lewis, "A Map of the United States," 1795, reproduced in Karpinski, *Bibliography of the Printed Maps of Michigan*, 72, under the heading "Mathew Carey, 1795." This chart originally appeared in Carey's *American Atlas*.

61. For the Maumee River, Beckwith has <Ottawasepoie>, a spelling which actually has a Kickapoo flavor but could be just a miscopy. Beckwith, "Indian Names," 39. John Johnston wrote the same hydronym in the form <Ottawasepe> and attributed it to the Shawnee. Howe, "Vocabularies of the Shawanoese and Wyandott," 594. However, Johnston's spelling does not look like a Shawnee place-name. In fact, it is not clear what language this term is supposed to represent. It appears to be a hybrid expression composed of terms from different Algonquian languages that together signify "Ottawa River." The "s" of -sepe, "river" in this and other Shawnee hydronyms recorded by Johnston is curious. In light of contemporaneous recordings of Shawnee by Thomas Ridout that evince the sound *θ*, one must conclude that the change from *s* to *θ* had just occurred—or was perhaps occurring on a different timetable across Shawnee dialects. Thus in *Old* Shawnee the name of Indiana's Salt Creek would have been **nepipemiisiipi*. See chapter 9 for Salt Creek.

62. Antoine-François Tardieu, 1789, "Compagnies De l'Ohio et de La Scioto," reproduced in Smith, *Mapping of Ohio*, 128, pl. III. The author of this map was originally thought to be Pierre-François Tardieu.

63. The French used, for example, *Aux-Pez* (pronounced [opé]) for *Aux Pe8are8as* (at the Peoria), *Aux-Ca8x* (pronounced [okaú]) for *Aux Ca8kias* (at the

Cahokia), *Aux-Mis* (pronounced [omí]) for *Aux Miamis* (at the Miami), and *Aux-Cas* (pronounced [oká]) for *Aux Cascaskias* (at the Kaskaskia). In October 1790, Harmar wrote *Au-Mi*. See Josiah Harmar Papers. See also <Omie> in "Treaty with the Wyandot, etc., 1789," in Kappler, *Indian Affairs* 1:21.

64. Howe, "Vocabularies of the Shawanoese and Wyandott," 594. For John Johnston, see Esarey, *Messages and Letters of William Henry Harrison* 1:123; also Cayton, *Frontier Indiana*, 232, 240, 248, 250; Beckwith, "Indian Names." Guernsey also used this place-name and indiscriminately attributed it to the Shawnee. Guernsey, "Indiana."

65. Blair Rudes, personal communication, June 14, 1997. The morpheme |-hrɛ̃ʔn-|, "rock" occurs only in Wyandot, Huron, and Tuscarora.

66. Duvernet called the rock "Roche de bout" and said it was "a large mass of rock." Duvernet, "Sketch Taken in the Month of Novr 1778." George Winter drew the rock, the surrounding waters, and nearby island in the 1880s. See his sketches in Feest, *Indians and a Changing Frontier*, 197.

67. Daryl Baldwin, personal communication, 6/21/99.

68. The name "Roche de Bout" even appears in English sources, such as the Wayne officer's journal: Smith, *Greene Ville to Fallen Timbers*, 262, 274, 276.

69. Gatschet, "Notes on Miami-Illinois," FN/1584.

70. See <totontaraton> in "etablissement [*sic*] dependant du Mississipi," *Gazettes*, 155, Potier manuscripts, ASJCF. In late prehistory the Mascouten are thought to have lived along the western shores of Lake Erie as members of what archaeologists term the Sandusky Tradition (ca. A.D. 1250–1650). See Stothers, "Late Woodland Models," 194–211, especially 207ff. Later, during part of the second half of the seventeenth century, before the Mascouten came into Indiana, the Miami and the Mascouten, war refugees, shared a town on the upper Fox River near present-day Berlin, Wisconsin. See Wood, "Mascouten Village," 167–74; also Jones, "Site of the Mascoutin Village," 175–82.

71. I am indebted to Blair Rudes for this Iroquoian linguistic analysis.

72. Dunn, *True Indian Stories*, 303; Guernsey, "Indiana." The earliest historical Miami-Illinois form for "sturgeon" had initial *n*.

73. Dunn, *Indiana and the Indianans* 1:59. Dunn also wrote the noun <mamä́wa>, where ä stands for *ee*. Dunn, Miami file card dictionary, ISL.

74. I am indebted to the ichthyologist Vadim Birstein for the information about the lake sturgeon. Personal communication, January 1, 1999.

75. See Thwaites, *Early Western Travels* 1:151; "Journal de Voyage," 156, Potier manuscripts, ASJCF.

76. John Johns(t)on, in *Archaeologia, Americana* 1:292, 298; Howe, "Vocabularies of the Shawanoese and Wyandott," 594; Dunn, *True Indian Stories*, 303; and Dunn, *Indiana and the Indianans*, 95; Beckwith, "Indian Names," 66. I am indebted to Ives Goddard for offering his ideas about this place name.

77. For Shawnee in the Kekionga area, see *Papers in Illinois History* 7:316–17; also Meek, "Harmar's Expedition" 20:92. Hay says that Shawnee groups that settled near the Miami town in the late 1700s were the *čalakaaθa* and *pekowi*. Hay, "Narrative of Life on the Old Frontier," 257–59. It appears the Shawnee first settled three leagues (about nine miles) above the fork of the Wabash. See Krauskopf, "French in Indiana," 239. Some Shawnee were also at Vincennes and along the west fork of the White River. The French first mentioned the Shawnee in 1648 by an Ojibweyan plural form, <Ouchaouanag>. Thwaites, *Jesuit Relations* 33:151. The historical movements of the Shawnee are far too complex to examine in this volume. For a good introduction to this topic see Callender, "Shawnee," 622–35. The name of the Scioto River comes from Huron-Wyandot. Pierre Potier writes this hydronym in the form <s8gñióto> ~ <s8gnioóto> accompanied by the description *R. vers la source* (R[iver] toward the source), linking it to <D'8tsand8ske> with the description *on fait portage pour y entrer* (a portage is made in order to enter it). Fraser, *Huron Manuscripts*, 155. The latter term is the origin of the name Sandusky and signifies "place of the spring(s)." Rudes suggests the etymology for "Scioto" contains the verb root *-hnyo-*, "row a boat." A cognate term can be found in Chafe, *Seneca Morphology and Dictionary*, no. 632. In addition, the hydronym in question appears to contain the causative/instrumental suffix *-ht-*. Potier gives a derived form <ąndi8chra> *cajeu … tout ce qui sert a traverser une riviere* (raft … anything that serves for crossing a river). Fraser, *Huron Manuscripts*, 440. This would come from *|ka-hnyo-ht-hsr-aʔ| third person singular neuter agent–"row a boat"–causative–nominalizer–noun suffix. Therefore, "Scioto" probably comes from *|č-yo-hnyo-ht-o-˙ | repetitive–third singular neuter patient–"row a boat"-causative–"be in water"–stative, which would mean "canoe (or other watercraft) in water." The Huron phonemic form for the name would be **sohnyóhto˙*. The place-name was probably originally a toponym that was generalized by the Huron or by the French to name the entire river. The structure of this hydronym, that is, "something-in-water" is common in Iroquoian, seen, for example, in the place-names "Toronto" and "Oswego." Linguistic analysis by Blair Rudes, personal communication, January 23, 2006.

78. Hough, "Indian Names"; Guernsey, "Indiana."

79. Dunn, *True Indian Stories*, 302; Dunn, *Indiana and the Indianans* 1:95.

80. Smith, *Greene Ville to Fallen Timbers*, 316.

81. I am indebted to Robert Vézina for this idea.

82. Dunn, *True Indian Stories*, 256; Dunn, *Indiana and the Indianans*, 87. Note that Dunn's accent mark indicates stress.

83. Laura Buszard-Welcher, personal communication, December 23, 1996.

84. Young, 1836, "Map of the United States."

85. Keating, *Narrative of an Expedition* 1:85. Guernsey places the town at the confluence of Cedar Creek and the St. Joseph River.

86. Beckwith, *History of Vigo and Parke Counties*, 147.

Chapter 6: The White River and the People from the Dawn

1. Franquelin, "Carte de La Louisiane," 1684, reproduced in Thwaites, *Jesuit Relations*, vol. 63, frontispiece. <Oiapikaming> also appears on an undated, untitled Franquelin map: Jean-Baptiste Louis Franquelin, Ge DD2987-8695//2987-8802, NL.

2. Franquelin, "Carte de l'Amérique Septentrionalle," 1688, reproduced in Tucker, *Indian Villages*, pls. XIA and XIB; also Franquelin, "Carte de l'Amerique Septent.[le]," 1684, reproduced in Cumming, *Exploration of North America*, 153.

3. Trowbridge, *Meearmeear Traditions*, 11; Dunn, *True Indian Stories*, 65; Dunn, *Indiana and the Indianans* 1:97. The Marquis de Vaudreuil located an Illinois Indian village on the White River in the mid-1700s. Temple, *Indian Villages*, 46. Temple cites letters from Vaudreuil from August 8 and October 10, 1751. Temple calls their village a "republic" and says that the inhabitants were friends of the English.

4. Gatschet, "Notes on Miami-Illinois," FN/744. See also <8abigami8i>, translated *liqueur blanche, lait* (white liquid, milk), the independent II form of this verb in Illinois-French dictionary, 363. A long vowel for the penultimate syllable of Miami-Illinois *waapikami(i)ki* is suggested by Meskwaki *kehčikamiiwi*, "big-water." I am indebted to Daryl Baldwin for pointing out *peehkonteekinki*. Personal communication, January 17, 2006. As noted in the discussion of "Wabash," place-names in the form of verbs are very common in the Algonquian place-name tradition.

5. An idea difficult to believe, but one that appears in Miami oral tradition, is that the river got its name from some section of it where the water had taken on a cloudy or milky-white appearance because of salt springs. See Trowbridge, *Meearmeear Traditions*, 11. Thomas did say salts springs made the water of Lick Creek "pale whitish blue, like a mixture of milk and water." He even suggested that this is the origin of the names for the White, Whitewater, and Blue rivers of Indiana. Thomas, *Travels through the western country*, 61.

6. Goddard, "Delaware," 213.

7. Ibid., 235–37. The first or one of the first uses of "Unami" as a tribal designation in modern historical discussions is in Thompson, *Sons of the Wilderness*, 37. In Munsee the apostrophe indicates vowel deletion by virtue of syncope. For example, *mən'si·w* would originally have been **mənVsi·w*, where *V* is a vowel. Since an inherited nasal plus an obstruent cluster causes the obstruent in Delaware to be voiced, nonhomorganic consonant clusters such as *ns* are pronounced [nz]. However, if a secondary nasal plus an obstruent cluster is the result of deletion of an intervening vowel (syncope), the obstruent will not be voiced. Hence, phonemic *n's* is pronounced [ns], not [nz].

8. Ferguson, "White River Indiana Delawares," 47; also, Thompson, *Sons of the Wilderness*, 42.

9. An excellent description of the Delaware Indians, with maps showing the locations of the various Delaware groups throughout their history, appears in Goddard, "Delaware," 213–39.

10. Hildreth, *Pioneer History*, 168.

11. I am indebted to Ives Goddard for the phonemic spelling of Buckongehelas. Contrary to what Dunn said, the name does not mean "Breaker to Pieces." Dunn, *Indiana and the Indianans*, 86; it signifies "one who goes directly." James Rementer, personal communication, March 4, 1999. For Buckongehelas, see Beckwith, *History of Vigo and Parke Counties*, 135; also White, *Middle Ground*, 436ff. For the search for the location of this the easternmost Delaware town on the White River, see McCord, *Ghosts of the Delaware*, 14. For the gloss "White Grave," see Gipson, *Moravian Indian Mission on White River*, 604; and Thompson, *Sons of the Wilderness*, 42. For a fine description of the White River Moravians, see Cayton, *Frontier Indiana*, 196–97. Strangely enough, recent archaeological surveys were unable to locate *any* remains of the early-nineteenth-century Delaware towns on the upper West Fork of the White River. Unfortunately, in the case of the home of *pahkančíhəla·s*, the primary sources do not even indicate its precise location.

12. Phonemic spellings by Goddard, personal communication, June 3, 2002. See also Goddard, *Delaware Verbal Morphology*, 129.

13. The phonemic spellings are from Dave Costa's notes from Ives Goddard. The Klammerform idea is from Goddard, personal communication, June 3, 2002. An example of a Klammerform in German is the word for "Sunday evening," *Sonnabend*, which is literally "Sun-evening." ***Sonntagabend*, literally "sun-day-evening," does not exist. If Luckenbach's translation is correct, to what did "White Grave River" refer? To the impressive clusters of riverside earthworks and mounds at Mound State Park near Anderson and/or to those at Newcastle? Such a notion, while attractive, is speculative.

14. Krauskopf, "French in Indiana," 273. The Unami name for the White River of Missouri is *ɔ́·p·e·k-sí·p·u*, "that which is a white river." See Afable and Beeler, "Place-Names," 193. This hydronym is not attested for Indiana's White River–West Fork. French "Maison blanche" as a name for the White River may be a translation of a French mishearing of **waapikaani*, presumably "white tent" for Miami-Illinois *waapikami*, "white water." See *masaanikaani*, "tent." Historical support for the Delaware place-name meaning simply "that which is a white house" based on an earlier French name is found in the known interaction between French traders and early Delaware Indian immigrants in the Ohio country.

15. Dunn wrote <Wahpih[illegible]ni>. Dunn, *True Indian Stories*, 65.

16. Ives Goddard, personal communication, May 23, 1996. The park in Bloomington, Indiana, known as "Wapehani," received its name from Ross Lockridge. See the *Bloomington (Ind.) Herald-Times*, February 6, 1960, sec. 2. This name is not an acronym created by local boy scouts as some have thought.

17. Lucy Blalock, personal communication, via James Rementer, May 4, 1997. Blalock, who helped with some of the questions that I had about Indiana's Unami place-names, died February 11, 2000, in Quapaw, Oklahoma. She was born June 14, 1905, in Alluwe, Oklahoma. She was a member of the First United Methodist Church of Quapaw and the Native American Church. Her Indian name was Ahkoupouaquah (Early Dawn Woman), and she was of the Wolf clan (Tukseet). Blalock was a full-blooded Delaware Indian and a fluent native speaker of Unami. Her parents were George Parks (Turkey clan) and Nancy (Wilson) Parks (Wolf clan). I am indebted to James Rementer for this biographical information.

18. Hough, "Indian Names"; Dunn, *True Indian Stories*, 286. Dunn's <útĕnĭnk> is very curious in that it demonstrates that he did not redraft Hough's original spelling, for he obviously recognized the -au- of Hough's <Outaunink> was a miscopy. However, there is no evidence that Dunn consulted with the Delaware to get his Delaware language pronunciations. Therefore, he probably added the accent marks, using as a basis his knowledge of Algonquian in general, his knowledge of Miami-Illinois in particular, and perhaps to some degree the English pronunciations of some Delaware terms. For the Southern Unami locative noun form, pronounced [-ŋg], see Goddard, "Pidgin Delaware," 93n.127. The phonemic Munsee form is from Goddard, personal communication, June 3, 2002. This term is cognate with Potawatomi *odanəg* seen in chapters 1 and 5.

19. Gipson, *The Moravian Indian Mission on White River*, 643, 56. Dunn, *True Indian Stories*, 253; Dunn, *Indiana and the Indianans* 1:86.

20. See Southern Unami *-mə́·nši* in Goddard, "Delaware," 228. In Munsee, "chestnut" is *wa·pi·m*. See Goddard, "Pidgin Delaware," 54; in Unami it is *ɔ·pi·m* (Goddard, "Pidgin Delaware," 54). For the *-ə* of *-ənk* realized as phonetic [i], see Goddard, *Delaware Verbal Morphology*, xii.

21. Gipson, *Moravian Indian Mission on White River*, 643.

22. Phonemic spelling in Goddard, "Pidgin Delaware," 79. It is not known if the occurrence of *énta*, "where" was idiomatic or not for Delaware place-names. Ives Goddard, personal communication, June 5, 2005.

23. Guernsey, "Indiana."

24. Horsford, *Zeisberger's Indian Dictionary*, no. 143. Zeisberger collected his data ca. 1760. The information that Pipe was Unami comes from James Rementer, personal communication, June 21, 1998, based on his conversation with William Hunter, the former Pennsylvania state historian. White notes that Pipe belonged to the Wolf phratry. White, *Middle Ground*, 436. For Captain Pipe, see also Thompson, *Sons of the Wilderness*, 24–29. The phonemic spelling for Southern Unami *hupɔ́·k·an* is in Goddard, "Pidgin Delaware," 79. Here, the historical spelling oa stands for phonemic *ɔ́·*. This Native name is no doubt Unami since it also evinces an expected metathesis in its initial syllable. Moreover, it is definitely not a Munsee term as that language does not even have a word for "pipe" that is cognate with the

Unami form—and if it did, it would be ***opwa·kan*, which would bear only a faint resemblance to the historically recorded spelling of Captain Pipe's Indian name.

25. Unami *pak·ánke*, "seven(teen?)-year locust." Custaloga seems to be from Oneida *kastóla·ke*, the term for the single-feathered headdress of chiefs. The Oneida term was provided by Blair Rudes. However, it could also be Mohawk *kahstaró·kwa·*, "necklace of big beads." Gunther Michelson, personal communication, August 19, 2000.

26. Pipe's earlier name was <Kanieschaquanohill>. Nora Thompson Dean, the well-known twentieth-century Unami speaker and author of books and tapes of her native language, recognized this name and pronounced it [kukiškɔ́nohel] (this form is not marked for consonant or vowel length). She noted that the name's Native form was "strange." James Rementer, personal communication, April 10, 1998. For an enlightened, comprehensive examination of *this* Pipe's role in history, see White, *Middle Ground*, 359ff. Note that there were two other historical Captain Pipes. One lived at Sandusky and was Trowbridge's language consultant in 1824. James Rementer, personal communication, December 17, 2000. His name appears on a treaty from 1814. See Kappler, *Indian Affairs* 2:106. A third Captain Pipe, whose Indian name was written <Tauhaugeeacaupouye>, was also a leader of the Sandusky Delaware. James Rementer, personal communication, December 17, 2000.

27. Hough, "Indian Names."

28. Killbuck should not be confused with the more famous *pahkančíhəla·s*, whose name, as noted, is commonly spelled Buckongehelas in English. Although English speakers simplified Buckongehelas's name to "Buck," they occasionally also called him "Killbuck." But *pahkančíhəla·s*, signatory to the Treaty of Greeneville in 1795, died between the spring and midsummer of 1805, while <Wenavakhenon>, popularly known as Killbuck, from whom Duck [*sic*] Creek got its name, was still dealing with the U.S. government in 1814. For Killbuck, see the "Treaty with the Delaware, 1809" and "Treaty with the Wyandot, 1814," in Kappler, *Indian Affairs* 2:102, 106.

29. <Wenavakhenon> is in Esarey, *Messages and Letters of William Henry Harrison* 1:303–4. Phonemic spelling and analysis by Gunther Michelson.

30. Gunther Michelson, personal communication, August 19, 2000.

31. Chamberlain, *Indiana Gazetteer*, 220; Dunn, *True Indian Stories*, 264. Phonemic form by Goddard, personal communication, June 3, 2002.

32. Dunn, *True Indian Stories*, 264; Dunn, *Indiana and the Indianans* 1:88. For the height of the falls, see Harden, *History of Madison County*, 309. Dunn published a nice old photograph of these falls. See Dunn, *True Indian Stories*, 207. I nearly went over these falls backward in a canoe in a swift current when I was twelve years old.

33. Illinois-French dictionary, 556.

34. Gatschet, "Notes on Miami-Illinois," FN/7 and FN/14.

35. See Robertson and Riker, *John Tipton Papers* 1:202.

36. Chamberlain, *Indiana Gazetteer*, 213.

37. Dunn, *True Indian Stories*, 261–62.

38. Unami phonemic forms by Goddard, personal communication, June 3, 2002. Compare *xínkwi-šínk˙e˙*, "it is a big timber."

39. Guernsey, "Indiana."

40. Brinton and Anthony, *A Lenape-English Dictionary*, 71. If genuine, this place-name would have had the prenoun **wa˙p˙i-* in Northern Unami and could have had the form **wapi-* in Southern Unami, depending on whether "static" words existed in Southern Unami. Goddard, personal communication, June 3, 2002. The precise phonological shape of the Unami term for "salt lick" is not known since it disappeared from the modern language. Ives Goddard, personal communication, March 6, 1996. However, the first two vowels of the term are probably long. Ives Goddard, personal communication, June 25, 2001.

41. See Horsford, *Zeisberger's Indian Dictionary*, no. 2114; also Heckewelder, *Narrative of the Mission of the United Brethren*, 35. Heckewelder glossed the term "Deer's Lick; a place where salty, or brackish water issues out of the earth."

42. James Rementer, personal communication, June 21, 1998. When we look down the White River and back into time, the Indian man known in English as Big Fire, who had a rather famous village near Gosport in Owen County, was not Shawnee, as Guernsey's map indicates, but was in fact Delaware. See Tanner, *Atlas of Great Lakes Indian History*, 98–99. Tanner supports Wilson's earlier statement that correctly notes this village belonged to the Delaware. See Wilson, *Early Trails and Surveys*, 14. However, there were Shawnee villages on the lower White River–West Fork in 1788 and 1789, as also noted by Tanner. See Tanner, *Atlas of Great Lakes Indian History*, 92. There was, however, reluctance on the part of a great many Shawnee to settle in the Wabash Valley in the late eighteenth century. Indications are that they were on an extended collision course with the Piankashaw and the Wea.

43. Guernsey, "Indiana."

44. Note that this term can have various allomorphs depending on the preceding phonological context: *-áhəne˙*, *-háne˙*, or *-hɔ́ne˙*. Ives Goddard, personal communications, March 17, 2000, August 24, 2000, and June 3, 2002.

45. Horsford, *Zeisberger's Indian Dictionary*, nos. 020, 063.

46. James Rementer, personal communication, March 21, 1997. However, Dean did say that people in her younger days sometimes used it as a term for "peanut." This cultivated plant would, of course, not be the referent for a historical Native name for Beanblossom Creek.

47. See Unami *hák˙i*, "earth" in Goddard, "Pigdin Delaware," 66. Delaware phonemic forms in the analysis of this place-name are from Goddard, personal communications, March 17, 2000, and June 3, 2002.

48. Guernsey, "Indiana."

49. Hough, "Indian Names."

50. McPherson, *Indian Names in Indiana*, 4. Unfortunately, McPherson's book, which has been widely distributed, abounds in linguistic and ethnographic errors at every turn.

51. Although the evidence, despite its obvious problems, seems to indicate a native origin for the name Beanblossom Creek, there is a curious note in Colonel John Ketcham's reminiscences from 1812. Ketcham contended that General John Tipton had named Beanblossom Creek after an American soldier whose last name was Bean Blossom. See Esarey, *Harrison Messages and Letters* 2:279. I have been unable to find any evidence to substantiate this claim. This could simply be an early American folk etymology. Ketcham also stated that Tipton and a Colonel Beam, with approximately twenty men, while scouting the west fork of White River, crossed a tributary of Bean Blossom Creek. The horses of fellow riders Jack Storm and John Ketcham got mired in the mud. Tipton and/or his men then jokingly named the creek "Jack Defeat's Creek" because of this incident (2:279). This stream, located in northwestern Monroe County, Indiana, still bears this name, whose origin is often a topic of discussion among local folklore enthusiasts.

52. George Winter Papers, file 69.86.344, TCHA; see also Feest, *Indians and a Changing Frontier*, 163.

53. See Max Griffith's web site on the history of Shakamak State Park at http://www.geocities.com/the_town_historian/ShakP1.html (accessed July 14, 2002). The Kickapoo phonemic form for "eel" is from Voorhis, *Kickapoo Vocabulary*, 171.

Chapter 7: The Northern Wabash Valley

1. "Chemin des Mis aux 8ias," in *Gazettes*, 181, Potier manuscripts, ASJCF; Barnhart, *Henry Hamilton and George Rogers Clark*, 116. For use of the Little Wabash, see Krauskopf, "French in Indiana," 91. Regarding the length of the local portage(s), a nine-mile carry is described in 1778 by Hutchins. See Lindley, *Indiana as Seen by Early Travelers*, 7. Also, in 1778 British soldier H. Duvernet said the carry was six to nine miles in length, depending on the availability of water. Duvernet, "Sketch taken in the Month of Novr. 1778," PAC.

2. One of the earliest cartographic pieces of evidence for the Maumee-Wabash portage(s) is on the map by De Fer, 1702, "Le Canada, ou Nouvelle France," reproduced in Karpinski, *Bibliography of the Printed Maps of Michigan*, 33. This remarkably early date, nearly ten years before the French arrived at the headwaters of the Maumee, represents Indian intelligence, though it may reflect a report by a *coureur de bois* whose name and story have not survived. The map by Jean-Louis Baptiste Franquelin from 1688 titled "Carte de l'Amérique Septentrionalle" shows the portage from the St. Joseph to the Wabash via what appears to be the Elkhart and Eel Rivers. See Tucker, *Indian Villages*, pls. XIA and XIB.

3. See "Chemin des Mis aux 8ias," in *Gazettes*, 181, Potier manuscripts, ASJCF. The "volets" mentioned in this account are the leaves of water lilies (Fr. *nénuphar*),

genus *Nuphar*. The term was also used by the French in former times for plants of the genus *Nymphæa* (Fr. *nymphées*). I am indebted to Robert Vézina for these botanical identifications. Personal communications, April 29, 2002 and June 10, 2002.

4. See Cox, *Geological Survey of Indiana 1875*, 117. Beckwith stated that Little River rose in a marsh seven miles southwest of Fort Wayne. Beckwith, *History of Fountain County*, 103. The old bed of Little River was as broad as the Wabash at the southeast corner of Huntington County. See *Geological Survey of Indiana 1875*, 130.

5. Samuel Lewis, "A Map of the United States," 1795, reproduced in Karpinski, *Bibliography of the Printed Maps of Michigan*, 72. The reader may have noted that many English-language place-names in Indiana made their first appearance in history about 1795. This was a result of the American victory at the Battle of Fallen Timbers and the consequent loss of land and power by local Native groups. The French hydronym *Petite Rivière* is in Krauskopf, "French in Indiana," 91. For *petite rivière* and *rivière du Portage* surviving in English translation into the first part of the nineteenth century, see Riker, "Two Accounts of the Upper Wabash Country," 385. *Petite* is a relative expression in light of the stream's paramount commercial importance. On a map from 1796, this little watercourse was one of only twelve recorded for the entire expanse of the land now known as Indiana. See Mathew Carey and Samuel Lewis, "A Map of the United States," 1796, reproduced in Karpinski, *Bibliography of the Printed Maps of Michigan*, 192.

6. Dunn, *True Indian Stories* 1:90.

7. See the root <p8a8i> glossed *marque de foiblesse* (indication of weakness) in Illinois-French dictionary, 482.

8. The river's name in English maintained a French spelling into the nineteenth century. See "river A Bouette" in "Treaty with the Miami 1818," in Kappler, *Indian Affairs* 2:172. See also Riker, "Two Accounts of the Upper Wabash Country," 385.

9. "Chemin des Mis aux 8ias," in *Gazettes*, 181, Potier manuscripts, ASJCF.

10. See also Capt. James Riley's letter to the *Philadelphia Union*, November 24, 1819, in Lindley, *Indiana as Seen by Early Travelers*, 242. I have been unable to locate "Fiatro" in the Canadian archives. However, the family name Filiatreau is written "Fiatro" at http://homepages.rootsweb.com/~afgs/F2dit-etc.html (accessed December 1, 2001). The name is associated with early historical Detroit. A Jean and a Jacques Filiatreault, associates of Henri de Tonti, were at Fort St.-Louis in 1686. Suzanne Sommerville, personal communication, May 29, 2004.

11. *Boîte* does not translate to "minnows" as Dunn thought. See Dunn, *True Indian Stories*, 253; also Dunn, *Indiana and the Indianans* 1:86.

12. Dunn, *Indiana and the Indianans* 1:86; Dunn, ms. 47, ISL. Dunn, *True Indian Stories*, 253. The reader is reminded that Dunn's ä generally stands for *ee* . Impressionistically speaking, Miami-Illinois *ee* sounds like the vowel in "fell" or "fail," and even the sound written a in "fallow," but not like the vowel in "wheel," which is represented in linguistics by the symbol *i*, not ee. The Miami-Illinois expression

for a sandy creek, *neekawihtanki*, "it sand-flows," demonstrates that *neekaw-* is a Miami-Illinois initial.

13. The bedrock underlying this particular chert is known as Liston Creek limestone. The outcrop does not extend up the Little Wabash River. This chert was an important regional lithic resource in use since Paleo-Indian times. Don Cochran, personal communication, June 26, 2000. As an independent noun Miami-Illinois *ahki*, phonetic [ahkí], means "field." However, the original Proto-Algonquian sense of "land" and "country" applies to the Miami-Illinois final *-ahk*.

14. Illinois-to-French dictionary, 397. For the Illinois making flint knives as late as 1694, see Father Claude Chauchetière's notes to his brother Villemarie in Kenton, *Indians of North America* 2:326. The Illinois language of the early 1700s certainly had the term for "stone knife." See <pimitakinasseni> and <asseni pimitakinghi> glossed *couteau de Pierre* (Stone knife) in Le Boullenger, French-Illinois dictionary, 52, 140. However, by the early 1700s local Indians had effectively abandoned their millennia-old chert technology. White offers an interesting report on the gradual replacement of stone-age technology, including numerous sources. See White, *Middle Ground*, 134.

15. Dunn, ms. 47, ISL; Dunn, *True Indian Stories*, 42, 265; Dunn, *Indiana and the Indianans*, 89. The phonemic spelling *wiipica*, where *c* stands for *č*, is in Costa, Miami-Illinois dictionary.

16. Goddard, "Contraction in Fox (Meskwaki)," 222–23. Central Algonquian cognates include Ojibwa *ozaanaman*.

17. "Chemin des Mis aux 8ias," in *Gazettes*, 181, Potier manuscripts, ASJCF. In a future publication, I intend to explain the authorship of this itinerary and discuss the dating of the document.

18. Dunn, *True Indian Stories*, 303; Dunn, *Indiana and the Indianans* 1:95.

19. "Treaty with the Miami, 1818," in Kappler, *Indian Affairs* 2:172. John Scott, "Map of Indiana," 1826, AGS; Tipton, June 1827, in Robertson and Riker, *John Tipton Papers* 1:743; James Young, "Indiana Tourists Pocket Map," 1835; S. Morrison, "Indiana," 1835; "Treaty with the Miami, 1838," in Kappler, *Indian Affairs* 2:522; J. H. Young, "The Tourist's Pocket Map of the State of Indiana," 1852; "Treaty with the Miami, 1834," in Kappler, *Indian Affairs* 2:425; Tipton, ["Map Showing the Fort Wayne Indian Agency in Indiana"], 1824, reproduced in Tucker, *Indian Villages*, pl. XLIX.

20. For Le Gros, see Rafert, *Miami Indians of Indiana*, 40, 77, 86, 92, 94.

21. Plant names were used by the Miami-Illinois–speaking tribes to name streams. Consider, for example, the place-name "Chicago River." Historically, the waterway known as "Chicago," which represents a Miami-Illinois term for the wild leek (*Allium tricoccum*), bracketed the south branch of the Chicago River and the canal emptying into Lake Michigan, whose waters came from a little lake just to the southwest, *plus* the waters that flowed in the opposite direction out of that little lake toward the Des Plaines River, *plus* the waters of the Des Plaines River from that

point down to the confluence of the Kankakee. See McCafferty, "Fresh Look at the Place Name Chicago," 116–29; McCafferty, "Additional Notes on the Place Name Chicago," 8–11; and McCafferty, "Revisiting Chicago (Reader Reponse)," 84.

22. "Treaty with the Miami, 1818," in Kappler, *Indian Affairs* 2:172; Riker, "Two Accounts of the Upper Wabash Country," 386; Dunn, *Indiana and the Indianans* 1:86. Note again that Dunn's ä represents phonemic *ee*. Compare Miami-Illinois *eečipoonkweeta*, "one who has a wrinkled face" and Cree *očipayiiw*, "it shrinks; it shrivels."

23. It is not impossible that the "snapping turtle egg" element of <atchepongga-wawee seepe> is a "snapping turtle egg" initial. However, a thorough examination of the various initials that *waaw-*, "egg" can form does not seem to support this hypothesis. The analysis of this place-name could also be **eečipaankwaawiisiipi*, "snapping turtle egg river," composed of the "snapping turtle" initial *eečipaankw-*, the noun stem *waaw-*, "egg," a relic derivational noun + noun connector *-i-*, the same hydronymic "river" final *-(i)siip*, and the singular inanimate noun marker *-i*. Evidence for an ancient derivational connector in the form of **-ii-* may be seen in Le Boullenger's unexpected <miaramec8i> translated *riv. de maramec* (catfish river, Meramec River), which would be phonemic **myaarameekwii-*. Le Boullenger, French-Illinois dictionary, 23.

24. The term "cold water" itself was recorded by Dunn as <tak̆inggamĭ>, "cold water." Dunn, Miami file card dictionary, ISL; Gatschet has <taxkingámi>, where "x" indicates preaspiration: Gatschet, "Notes on Miami-Illinois," FN/2483. Compare Shawnee *tkikami* and Ojibwa *dakigami*. The "cold water" etymology of the Miami-Illinois term for "spring" makes perfect sense, given the remarkable difference in temperature between river water and spring water on a hot summer day.

25. Dunn, *True Indian Stories*, 312; Dunn, *Indiana and the Indianans* 1:96. The ah of Dunn's first spelling indicates *a*. There was a deer lick southeast of Wabash, Indiana, known to the Miami as *waalantaakaninki*, "at the deer lick," literally, "at the hole-made-by-mouth thing." See <waladakáningi> in Gatschet, "Notes on Miami-Illinois," FN/748; he says, "name of a bygone Indian (Wea?) settlement southeast of Wabashtown, Wabash County, Indiana." The word *waalantaakani* is *waal-*, "hole in the ground" + *-antam-* the transitive inanimate "by mouth" final + *-aakan*, "instrument," + *-inki*, the locative suffix. Costa notes that the term evinces a regular dropping of *-am-* before *-aakan*. David Costa, personal communication, January 29, 2006.

26. Ball, *Journals and Indian Paintings of George Winter*, 163. Feest, *Indians and a Changing Frontier*, 112.

27. Hough, "Indian Names."

28. Dunn, ms. 47, ISL; Dunn, *Indiana and the Indianans* 1:92; Dunn, *True Indian Stories*, 283. To round out the historical forms of this hydronym, Gatschet has <nematchĭssinwe>. Gatschet, "Notes on Miami-Illinois." In the case of the name <Shepaconah>, the final -ah of the traditional spelling is another example of the

animate gender marker noted above. Miami-Illinois inanimate noun stems take the animate suffix *-a* when they form personal names.

29. Dunn, *Indiana and the Indianans* 1:92.

30. Compare Shawnee *lemat-*, "down" as in *lemačšinwa*, "he lies on an incline, sloping downward," in Voegelin, *Shawnee Stems* 9:351; also Fox *nemat-* as in *nemat-oowa*, "he set it upright," in Goddard, "Primary and Secondary Stem Derivation," 456.

31. Dunn, ms. 47, ISL.

32. *Indiana Canoeing Guide*, 48. The Mississinewa also had waterfalls, for example, the Liston Glen Falls.

33. See Krauskopf, "French in Indiana," 272.

34. Hutchins, "New Map," 1778. See also White, *Middle Ground*, 275. <Massissinoui> also occurs in a letter in French from July 22, 1786, from Lorimier to Jamy and in a document from 1802 titled "Licenses granted by the governor to Indian traders." Lasselle Papers, docs. 224 and 566, ISL.

35. Dunn, *True Indian Stories*, 284.

36. Esarey, *Messages and Letters of William Henry Harrison* 1:142, 147, 364, 424.

37. Ibid. 1:432, 478–79; René Paul, "Compiled from the best authorities," 1815, reproduced in Tucker, *Indian Villages*, pl. XL; Paul, "A Map Exhibiting the Territorial Limits," 1816, in Tucker, *Indian Villages*, pl. XLI; Morse, *Report to the Secretary of War*, 109.

38. Esarey, *Messages and Letters* 1:40.

39. Beckwith, *History of Vigo and Parke Counties*, 124.

40. Shaver, *Compendium of Paleozoic Rock-Unit Stratigraphy*, 93. The Miami know these rocks as *aašipehkwa waalaaliči*. There is also a culturally important site for the Miami, once located four miles upstream from Peoria at a red bridge but now under the waters of the Mississinewa reservoir, known as [aašipehkwa weenšhkwapiči].

41. Dunn, *Indiana and the Indianans* 1:94; Dunn, *True Indian Stories*, 297.

42. Gatschet, notes on Miami.

43. Phonemic spelling in Costa, Miami-Illinois dictionary.

44. Dunn, *Indiana and the Indianans* 1:94. The parenthetical *(a)* of *(ah)pwaakana*, "pipe" indicates that this unstressed, short-vowel syllable evidenced in the earliest recordings of Miami-Illinois disappeared from the speech of late historic Miami-Illinois.

45. Gatschet, "Notes on Miami-Illinois," FN/17.

46. "Chemin des Mis aux 8ias," in *Gazettes*, 181, Potier manuscripts, ASJCF.

47. Robert Vézina, personal communication, August 25, 2005.

48. See Hutchins, "New Map," 1778.

49. By 1824, however, the stream's name had become the semantically ambiguous "Pipe River," a designation that applied for at least eleven additional years. Then, by 1876, the stream had become "Pipe Creek." See A. Anderson, "An Accurate Map,"

1796, reproduced in Karpinski, *Bibliography of the Printed Maps of Michigan*, 76; Young, "Indiana Tourist's Pocket Map," 1835. Historically, the French term *rivière* meant both "river" and "creek." In terms of the three European languages, German, English and French, German is by far the most liberal in using capital letters, English is a distant second, while French is by far the most conservative.

50. Hough, "Indian Names." For François Godfroy and his family, see Rafert, *Miami Indians of Indiana*, 81, 98–100, 120, 134.

51. See <Pa Lon Swa> on the "Treaty with the Wea, 1820," in Kappler, *Indian Affairs* 2:190. Another example of this same replacement of *p* for *f* is in the English borrowing "coffee," which in Miami-Illinois is pronounced [káahpi].

52. Generally speaking, in terms of Miami-Illinois, one finds *r* if the records come from the seventeenth century and into the eighteenth century and *l* after that.

53. Dunn, *True Indian Stories*, 272; Dunn, *Indiana and the Indianans*, 90; Gatschet, "Notes on Miami-Illinois," FN/17. It should be noted that in southeastern Miami County, south of Deer Creek and approximately five miles northwest of the headwaters of this stream is a small town known today as Wawpecong. This toponym derives from a Miami-Illinois name for the area in and around Wawpecong which no doubt contained the Miami-Illinois noun *waapakaan-*, "hickory nut." However, Gatschet's recording of this place-name in the form <Wapípakan-shikongi>, ostensibly meaning "hickory nut tree land," is not good Miami-Illinois either grammatically or morphologically speaking. It seems to be an example of a native speaker's creating a "forced" and unusually literal translation when asked to translate English "hickory nut tree land."

54. [Anonymous], "Map of the States of Indiana and Ohio with Part of Michigan Territory," 1832, AGS.

55. Franquelin, "Carte de La Louisiane," 1684, reproduced in Thwaites, *Jesuit Relations*, vol. 63, frontispiece. This chart is a copy of a copy of La Salle's large map. See Delanglez, "Franquelin, Mapmaker," 59–60; Minet, "Carte De La Louisiane," 1685, reproduced in Tucker, *Indian Villages*, pl. VII; Franquelin, "Carte de l'Amerique Septent.^{le}," 1684, BHM. A copy of this map, dated 1687, is reproduced in Cumming, *Exploration of North America*, 153.

56. "Chemin de Mis aux 8ias," 181.

57. At a deeper morphological level, Miami-Illinois *kineepikw-*, "snake" is *kinee-*, "long" and *-apikw*, "rope, string," from PA **-a·py-*, "cordage." See Goddard, "Primary and Secondary Stem Derivation," 453.

58. Dunn, *True Indian Stories*, 263; Dunn, *Indiana and the Indianans* 1:88; Riker, "Two Accounts of the Upper Wabash Country," 386; Gatschet attested the noun <kinepikumékwa>. Gatschet, "Notes on Miami-Illinois." There is a commonly written spelling of this hydronym in the form "Kenapocomoco," which appeared first in the writings of Otho Winger in the early 1900s but even persists today. This is both an oversimplification and a pidginization of the Miami-Illinois word. See Winger, *Last of the Miamis*, 7; and Karst, "Eel River," 42.

59. Beckwith, *History of Fountain County*, 242.

60. George Winter Papers, file 69.86.344, TCHS; see also Feest, *Indians and a Changing Frontier*, 163; Horsford, *Zeisberger's Indian Dictionary*, no. 064.

61. Unami *-í·i* is a particle final that attaches to pronouns, coming from *-i·wi* in Moravian sources. In modern Munsee it takes the form *-i·*. It is important to not confuse this particle final with the proximate inanimate singular PA **-i*, which does not show up on nouns in the Eastern Algonquian languages. Ives Goddard, personal communication, March 28, 2005. Although Delaware terms for "eel" are commonly glossed "straight fish" in the historical literature, this is a mistaken translation. The word *šɔ·x·ame·k·w*, "eel" is composed of the initial *šɔ·x·-*, "slippery" and *-ame·kw*, the "fish" final. See Zeisberger's <Scháchamēk>. The phonemic spelling for Southern Unami "eel" is in Goddard, "Pidgin Delaware," 52. See also Brinton and Anthony, *A Lenape-English Dictionary*, 125. Brinton and Anthony stated that the term means "straight fish," while also noting that it comes from <w'schachamek>. This statement indicates that the initial does not mean "straight," for they correctly gloss their own Munsee term <Wschacheu>, "slippery; smooth, glossy." The Unami form is derivable by metathesis from the Proto-Delaware term that resembles the Munsee term: *wsh-* went to *shw(a·)-*, and then *w(a·)-* rounded to *ɔ-*.

62. Gatschet, "Notes on Miami-Illinois," FN/748, FN/17; Dunn, *Indiana and the Indianans* 1:91; Gatschet, "Notes on Miami"; Le Boullenger, French-Illinois dictionary, 160. Winter painted a picture of the confluence of the Wabash near the confluence of the Eel River. See Feest, *Indians and a Changing Frontier*, 152.

63. Le Boullenger, French-Illinois dictionary, 160. The *-e-* of the Miami-Illinois term is an anomaly.

64. Ball, *Journals and Indian Paintings*, 73; and Feest, *Indians and a Changing Frontier*, 162. Potawatomi *zibiwe* is cognate with Ottawa *ziibiiwenh*, "stream, creek." The latter form is in Rhodes, *Ojibwa-Chippewa-Ottawa Dictionary*, 404. See the discussion of the Potawatomi noun + noun connector in chapter 5's treatment of the Maumee River.

65. Daryl Baldwin, personal communication, July 12, 1998.

66. I am indebted to Dave Costa for the morphological analysis and phonemic spelling.

67. For an excellent discussion of where the Underwater Panther dwells, see Hamell, "Long-Tail," especially 258.

68. Dunn, *Indiana and the Indianans* 1:88; Dunn, *True Indian Stories*, 260; Gatschet, "Notes on Miami-Illinois."

69. Gatschet, "Notes on Miami-Illinois."

70. This is a regular morphophonemic process whereby nouns ending in *-ia* take the locative in the form *-ionki*. The *-o-* of the locative suffix *-onki* we see here is triggered by the *-w-* in the term for "fawn" in the older language, which was *apeehsiwa*. See Costa, *The Miami-Illinois Language*, 182.

71. Dunn, *True Indian Stories*, 260.

72. Tyson, *A Mission to the Indians*, 68.

73. Hough, "Indian Names."

74. Kewanna sat for his portrait for the painter George Winter before being displaced to Kansas in 1837. See Ball, *Journals and Indian Paintings*, pl. VIII; also in Feest, *Indians and a Changing Frontier*, pl. 34.

75. Paint Creek rises in southwestern Cass County and flows generally west to meet Deer Creek in central Carroll County. The elemental nature, the unusual shape, and the early occurrence of this hydronym in history suggest that it is of Native origin, perhaps Miami-Illinois **alamooni siipiiwi*, "paint river, red ocher river, vermilion river." See Owen, *Geological Reconnaissance*, 82.

76. Hough, "Indian Names."

77. Kappler, *Indian Affairs* 2:369; Robertson and Riker, *Tipton Papers* 1:393n.15. This simple note is very informative. For Winter's portrait of Misquabuck, see Feest, *Indians and a Changing Frontier*, 68; see also Royse, *Standard History of Kosciusko County* 1:50. The phonemic spelling of this man's name is from Laura Buszard-Welcher, personal communication, August 12, 2000.

78. Dunn, *True Indian Stories*, 259; Dunn, *Indiana and the Indianans* 1:87.

79. For Winter's notes on his travels in the Lake Manitou area, see *Indians and a Changing Frontier*, 124. Winter gave the translation of this Potawatomi hydronym as "Spirit Lake."

80. Dunn, *Indiana and the Indianans*, 65. For an excellent treatise on the Underwater Panther, see Hamell, "Long-Tail," 258–88.

81. Robertson and Riker, *Tipton Papers* 1:803, 814; 2:10, 90.

82. "Chemin, par terre, de S jos aux 8ia," *Gazettes*, 180, Potier manuscripts, ASJCF.

83. This hydronym is on Thomas Forsyth, ["Chart of the Country Southwest of Lake Huron"], 1812, reproduced in Tucker, *Indian Villages*, pl. XXXVII. Forsyth would have known about this stream given his vast experience in the area between 1800 and the outbreak of the War of 1812, which found him in St. Louis as the subagent of the Indian Department for the Illinois district. Forsyth's map also mentions a fifteen-mile portage between Yellow River and the Tippecanoe as well as a six-mile portage between the Iroquois and Big Monon Creek. "Old Woman's River" is also on the map by Paul, "Compiled from the best authorities," 1815, in ibid., pl. XL.

84. Dillingham discusses a Kickapoo female leader active in 1791. Dillingham, "Oklahoma Kickapoo," 140–41.

85. See Temple, *Indian Villages*, 163–65.

86. Hutchins, "Courses of the Ohio River taken by Lt. T. Hutchins anno 1766."

87. Franquelin, "Carte de La Louisiane," 1684.

88. See <kitepic8n8a> glossed *espece de grosse carpe* in Pinet, French/Miami-Illinois dictionary, 474; <kitepicon8a> is glossed *Carpe* in Le Boullenger, French-Illinois Dictionary, 34; and <kitepic8n8a> glossed *espece de grosse carpe* (a kind of big carp) in Illinois-French dictionary, 228. It is important to note that the lack of

this initial syllable in the place-name "Tippecanoe" is a nonnative feature, that is, not an aspect of Miami-Illinois phonology. However, these spellings do support the notion that the first vowel of *kiteepihkwana* is short. The second vowel of Miami-Illinois <kitepicon8a> is probably long, since it matches the -ä- in the spelling of the Potawatomi form. Based on internal evidence, a reasonable assessment would not make the Potawatomi vowel the short *ə* sound. The third vowel in this Miami-Illinois etymon must be short since it deletes in the modern language, giving the observable *pk* cluster. Costa notes that the second k has to be preaspirated *hk*, while calling attention to the fact that at the same time there is no evidence indicating that the *p* is also preaspirated, that is, *hp*. David Costa, personal communication, February 5, 1997. Then, while the Jesuit missionary sources in Illinois suggest *-oo-* in the fourth syllable of this word, only *-wa(a)-* is attested for the historically recorded Miami-Wea forms in Indiana. However, this variation between contracted and noncontracted forms simply represents dialectal differences. Finally, the length on the fourth vowel is unknowable, while, clearly, the last syllable can be both *-na* and *-nwa*, again representing minor differences of a dialectal or even idiolectal nature.

89. Margry, *Découvertes* 4:597.

90. "Chemin de S. joseph aux Illinois," *Gazettes*, 171, Potier manuscripts, ASJCF.

91. "Chemin, par terre, de S jos aux 8ias," 180, ASJCF.

92. See <Quitepiconnae> in Jablow, *Indians of Illinois and Indiana* 2:136. Tipton's letter to Cass from October 19, 1827, spells Gamelin's name <Antwine Gamlin>, an excellent—and delightful—English rendition of the New World French pronunciation of this man's name, with a diphthongized last-syllable vowel inherent in the New World French pronunciation of this name.

93. Esarey, *Messages and Letters* 1:429.

94. Tipton, ["Map Showing the Fort Wayne Indian Agency in Indiana"], 1824.

95. Paul, 1815, "Compiled from the best authorities." If it had been a long vowel, it would not have dropped.

96. Dunn, *True Indian Stories*, 307. If Dunn actually got this form from a native speaker of Miami, he did not correctly hear the final syllable of the Miami word.

97. Ibid.; Dunn, *Indiana and the Indianans* 1:96.

98. "Chemin des Mis aux 8ias," in *Gazettes*, 181, Potier manuscripts, ASJCF; Dunn, ms. 47, ISL.

99. Robertson and Riker, *Tipton Papers* 2:28. Tipton's interesting survey of the Wabash Islands appears on 27–30. A map from the early nineteenth century has the unusual spelling <Tippecanin>: Samuel Lewis, "United States," 1804, reproduced in Karpinski, *Bibliography of the Printed Maps of Michigan*, 81.

100. Dunn, *True Indian Stories*, 270; Dunn, *Indiana and the Indianans* 1:90.

101. Abraham Bradley Jr., "Map of the United States," 1804, AGS.

102. William Henry Harrison referred to the stream as "Wildcat Paunch Creek." Snelling to Harrison, in Esarey, *Messages and Letters* 1:644. In Richardville's time, some Wyandot Indians, supporters of the Shawnee Prophet, also lived on Wild-

cat Creek. Their village located at the mouth of this stream is mentioned in the treaty between the U.S. government and the Miami in 1818, and was the site of another treaty negotiated between these same parties in 1828. See Wilson, *Early Trails and Surveys*, 89; in 1817, Samuel R. Brown noted that "ten or twelve families" of "Hurons" were living southeast of Ouiatanon. See Lindley, *Indiana as Seen by Early Travelers*, 164; for similar information, see "Treaty with the Miami, 1818" and "Treaty with the Miami, 1828," in Kappler, *Indian Affairs* 2:173, 287. Another location for the Wyandot is indicated on an anonymous map of Indiana from the mid-nineteenth century where their village is depicted as close to what is now Burlington, Indiana. Anonymous, "Treaty Lines," ca. 1844, AGS. See also the reference to the history of Ervin Township, Howard County, in Brelsford, *Indians of Montgomery County, Indiana*, 171. Furthermore, the crossroads known today as Wyandot, Indiana, located on the south branch of Wildcat Creek, preserves in memory these late-arriving Iroquoian-speaking residents. However, the name of this stream in the Wyandot language was apparently not recorded. In addition to Wyandot, there were also some Winnebago living on Wildcat Creek. Dehart notes a Winnebago village near the mouth of Wildcat Creek. Dehart, *Past and Present of Tippecanoe County, Indiana* 1:31. According to Brown, the Winnebago had "forty-five to fifty houses, several . . . fifty feet long" on the Wildcat "seven miles east of the Prophet's town." This would have been a village of the early 1800s comprised of followers of Tecumseh and the Prophet. See Brown, *Western Gazeteer*, 64.

103. Dunn, ms. 47, ISL; Dunn, *True Indian Stories*, 111; Dunn, *Indiana and the Indianans* 1:94; Gatschet, "Notes on Miami-Illinois," FN/17; Hough, "Indian Names."

104. Richardville lived from 1761 to 1841. See Rafert, *Miami Indians*, 48ff.; also Cayton, *Frontier Indiana*, 53ff.; Esarey, *Messages and Letters* 1:240.

105. See "Chemin des Mis aux 8ias," in *Gazettes*, 181, Potier manuscripts, ASJCF. This is the same designation that later appears on Paul's map, a chart based on information provided by the famous St. Louis trader Auguste Chouteau. Paul, "Compiled from the best authorities," 1815.

106. Ibid., 181.

107. Recorded Old Illinois forms are <michipinchi8a>, <aramipichia>, <arimipichia>, <akimarenia>, and <8ic8epichia>. Illinois-French dictionary, 286, 51, 59, 21, 389, respectively. In the late historical Miami-Illinois language the Underwater Panther was called *lenipinšia*, phonetic [lenipinžia] "ordinary bobcat, original bobcat, real bobcat." Old Illinois has <8ic8egami8i>, translated *anse de riviere, enfoncement* (river cove, recess), in Illinois-French dictionary, 389.

Chapter 8: The Southern Wabash Valley

1. The forms <peïanghichi8a>, <peïanghichia>, <peïanghichata>, translated *oreilles dechirées* (torn ears) are in Illinois-French dictionary, 450. Phonemic spellings *peeyankihšiiwa* and *peeyankihšia* are from Costa, Miami-Illinois dictionary.

Sabrevois, likely basing his report on the findings of others, considered the Piankashaw a subgroup of the Wea. See Krauskopf, "French in Indiana," 81.

2. Thwaites, *Jesuit Relations* 58:23.

3. Krauskopf, "French in Indiana," 70–79. Picoté was sent to Indiana by the Marquis de Vaudreuil, the governor general of Canada.

4. Pease and Werner, *French Foundations*, 392–93; "Archives nationales de France: Colonies," *Recueil* C11A, v. 19, f. 338, ANQ; Louis de la Porte de Louvigny, "Carte du Fleuue Missisipi," 1697, reproduced in Tucker, *Indian Villages*, plate XIV. This map is also reproduced in Brown, *Early Maps*, 7.

5. O'Hair, Index Glossary of Indiana Indian Names; Hough, "Indian Names." Dunn's opinion was that the ultimate source of the Wea village's name was the Miami-Illinois term for "whirlpool, eddy," his <wawíatánwi>, phonemic *waawiaahtanwi.* See Dunn, *Indiana and the Indianans* 1:94. See also <8iatahan8i> in Illinois-French dictionary, 387. The Shawnee cognate *waawiyawhtanwi* is typically glossed "(water) circles around." There is an interesting note in John Melish's journal about *les Ouiatanon*: he found whirlpools there in 1822. See Melish, *Geographical Description of the United States*, 270. However, since the Wea had this tribe name long before they moved to the Wabash for the first time near the beginning of the eighteenth century, the villages near Lafayette were probably not the original eponymous site for the Wea. Dunn also provided a locative form <waiatanongici>, phonemic *waayaahtanonkiši*, "toward the Wea place" ("Wea" [sg.] + "at" + "toward"). Phonemic spelling in Costa, Miami-Illinois dictionary. The historic English language form <Wawiaghta> by William Johnson in 1763 is an example of the *waawiaahtanonki* form of the place-name. See Libby, "Anthropological Report on the Piankashaw Indians," 1:57.

6. Michelson, "Notes on Peoria," NAA; also Dunn, Notes on Miami, ISL.

7. The names Big Shawnee Creek and Shawnee Prairie commemorate the arrival in the area of the Shawnee leader Martin Chartier in June 1745 from Lower Shawnee Town on the Ohio (at the Scioto River). He lived in the area until the spring of 1748. See Wheeler-Voegelin, "Ethnohistorical Report on the Indian Use and Occupancy in Ohio and Indiana Prior to 1795," in Tanner and Voeglin, *Indians of Ohio and Indiana Prior to 1795* 1:151; also *Collections of the Illinois State Historical Library* 29:67–70. See also "Archives nationales de France: Colonies," *Recueil* C11A, v. 19, f. 338, ANQ.

8. In 1818, Flint Creek was the location of a reserve belonging to the Potawatomi leader whose name was written <Perig>. See "Treaty with the Potawatomi, 1818," in Kappler, *Indian Affairs* 2:169. For Black Rock, see Beckwith, *History of Vigo and Parke Counties*, 240.

9. Don Cochran, personal communication, July 10, 2000.

10. Don Cochran, personal communication, October 29, 2001. For Miami-Illinois *paraani* of Tutelo origin, see Rankin, "On Some Ohio Valley Siouan and Illinois Algonquian Words," 544–47.

11. See *Riviere a la Tortue* in William McMurray, (1784), "The United States according to the definitive Treaty of Peace signed at Paris Sept. 3rd. 1783," Photocopy (1960), no. 3705. Library of Congress, Washington, D.C. Photocopy in author's possession.

12. La Tortue appears in many historical accounts; for example, see Krauskopf, "French in Indiana," 302, and Beckwith, *History of Vigo and Parke Counties*, 222. For his movements following the death of his father, La Demoiselle, see Temple, *Indian Villages*, 76. See the numerous references to a Miami and not a Piankashaw origin for La Demoiselle in Krauskopf, "French in Indiana," 263ff.

13. Beckwith, *History of Vigo and Parke Counties*, 222. Note, however, that the painted terrapin is not a big turtle. Indeed, the original referent for this Miami-Illinois word may have been the very similar-looking map turtle (*Trachemys scripta elegans*), which can grow to an enormous size.

14. Hutchins, "New Map," 1778. This particular Turtle Creek was in fact a natural demarcation between the Carolinian forests lying generally south and east across the continent and the prairies stretching to the north and west.

15. Beckwith, "Indian Names," 40.

16. Laura Buszard-Welcher, personal communication, August 12, 2000.

17. Dehart, *Past and Present of Tippecanoe County* 1:42; Hutchins, "New Map," 1778; Brown, *Western Gazetteer*, 140.

18. See Milton Smith, "Map of Indiana showing the Railroads & Townships," 1858, AGS.

19. Beckwith, "Indian Names," 40. This initial comes from the Proto-Algonquian noun stem **meçkw-*, "blood." See Goddard, "Primary and Secondary Stem Derivation," 452. In this case, we see an initial which, like others, is derived from a noun stem with no change in form.

20. Potawatomi were living at the mouth of Big Pine Creek on the Wabash by 1810. See Tanner, *Atlas of Great Lakes Indian History*, 98–99; also, in Warren County along the Wabash at the confluence of Kickapoo Creek, see Tanner, *Atlas of Great Lakes Indian History*, 80, 85, 88, 93; and "Treaty with the Potawatomi, 1818," in Kappler, *Indian Affairs* 2:168–69. For the Potawatomi on the Wabash below Ouiatanon, see Whickcar, "Potawatomi Reservations in Benton, Fountain, Warren and Tippecanoe Counties," 5–8.

21. Hough, "Indian Names." See also *History of Vermillion County*, 191.

22. An observation by Croghan on June 22, 1765, in Cumming, *Exploration of North America*, 78; also Beckwith, *History of Vigo and Parke Counties*, 219. For George Croghan, see Cayton, *Frontier Indiana*, 26–44.

23. See the 1675 Jolliet-directed map by Jean-Baptiste-Louis Franquelin, "Nouuelle Decouverte de Plusieurs Nations," reproduced in Tucker, *Indian Villages*, pl. IV. According to Jolliet himself, local red ocher was of a particularly high quality compared to French hematite.

24. Margry, *Découvertes* 2:124; Claude Bernou and M. Peronel, "Carte de l'Amérique Septentrionale," 1682, reproduced in Tucker, *Indian Villages*, pl. VIII; Marco Vincenzo Coronelli, "Partie Occidentale du Canada," 1688, reproduced in Karpinski, *Bibliography of the Printed Maps of Michigan*, 22; also Marco Vincenzo Coronelli, "America Settentionale," 1688, reproduced in Tucker, *Indian Villages*, pls. IX and X; also Karpinski, *Bibliography of the Printed Maps of Michigan*, 22; Guillaume Delisle, "Carte du Mexique et de La Floride," 1703, has <Ouramani>. See Tucker, *Indian Villages*, pl. XIII. This is the 1745 edition of the 1703 map. Original in the Edward E. Ayer Collection, NL. Delisle's 1703 map is also reproduced in Karpinski, *Bibliography of the Printed Maps of Michigan*, 28; and Buisseret, *Mapping the French Empire in North America*, 60.

25. Here, "grand" was used by the French to distinguish the Vermillion River from *le petit vermillon jaune* (the Little Yellow Vermillion), a small stream nearby. See "Chem: des 8ias au Poste," in *Gazettes*, 181, Potier manuscripts, ASJCF. Also compare "Vermillion Jaune," in use sometime after 1788, for the larger waterway, in Cutler and Le Raye, "Topographical Description of the Indiana Territory," 38.

26. For the Piankashaw being more numerous than the Wea, see *Mississippi Provincial Archives* 2:61–62; also Krauskopf, *Ouiatanon Documents*, 168; and Libby, "Anthropological Report on the Piankashaw Indians," 1:18. The Piankashaw village near the mouth of the Vermillion River was known by the French as *Mercata*. Costa suggests this term represents the initial component meaning "black" of an incompletely recorded composite Native American place-name. David Costa, personal communication, December 9, 2005.

27. Beckwith says that the Miami proper called the Vermillion River "Piankashaw (River)." Beckwith, *History of Vigo and Parke Counties*, 103; also Beckwith, "Indian Names," 41. He probably heard this name from Mary Ann Baptiste. If Beckwith's information is correct, this eponymous Miami dialect place-name would probably have been *originally* in Old Miami-Illinois **peeyankihšiiwa asiipiomi*, "Piankashaw his-river." Reconstruction based on <in8ca sipi8mi>, literally "Inoca-his river" and translated *riviere des Illinois* (River of the Illinois), in Pinet, French/Miami-Illinois dictionary, 537; also Le Boullenger, French-Illinois dictionary, 160. If authentic, **peeyankihšiiwa asiipiomi* would date to the very early 1700s, to the arrival of the Piankashaw at the mouth of the Vermillion River after the Algonquian diaspora of the seventeenth century.

28. Toupin, *Les écrits de Pierre Potier*, 165.

29. Blair Rudes, personal communication, December 16, 2000. Linguistic analysis done with the help of Blair Rudes.

30. Fraser, *Huron Manuscripts*, 451. The first ą of Potier's <ąnnod8> and <ąnnodok8a> sports a backwards cedilla, which stands for a subscript Greek iota. This was a symbol used by the Jesuits to represent the palato-velar fricative *x*, which became phonetic [y] in Huron-Wyandot.

31. Beckwith, *History of Montgomery County*, 10.

32. Dunn, *Indiana and the Indianans* 1:47.

33. The term for sugar maple tree applied as a name to this Wabash tributary occurs in the Illinois-French dictionary as <assenaminghi>, where "gh" is a miswritten "g," "g" being one of the French orthographic symbols for ž. See Illinois-French dictionary, 71.

34. For PA **aʔsena·minsya*, see Aubin, *Proto-Algonquian Dictionary*, 12. Proto-Algonquian speakers likely created this particular name for the tree since, in their earlier, more northerly homeland, the sugar maple was an important hardwood species among a virtual sea of softwoods—pine, fur, spruce, hemlock, cedar, yew, birch, and poplar. Next to these sorts of woods, maples would have proven to be outstandingly dense—"as hard as a rock." The second term for maple tree in Miami-Illinois is *ahsenaamišaahkwi*, literally "stone-tree tree."

35. <Pungosecone> bears the impressionistic, lyrical translation "water of many sugar trees" in Beckwith, *History of Parke and Vermillion Counties*, 125. Beadle noted that the Piankashaw were most numerous on Sugar Creek and upper Raccoon Creek. Beadle, *History of Parke County*, 5. The oblique gloss "sugar tree" for <Pungosecone> is in Beckwith, *History of Vigo and Parke Counties, Indiana*, 125.

36. The Peoria term was recorded by the linguist Charles Hockett in the 1930s. See [pɑŋgósi*k*à*ʔα*ni], in Hockett, "Notes on Peoria and Miami," 39. To mark voicelessness Hockett used small dots in his published report, whereas he actually used underlining in his notes (here rendered as italics). Hockett's ʔ is an unexpected glottal stop. He also indicated that the two [i]'s and the third [ɑ] were voiceless (i.e., whispered). Note that in Miami-Illinois nonpreaspirated *k* is voiced following a nasalized syllable. Curiously, Hockett actually used the symbol "ɑ" for schwa (ə). This sound does not occur in other recordings of the Miami-Illinois language across time, and one can only speculate that its appearance in the speech of Hockett's Peoria represents influence from English in his Miami-Illinois–speaking informants. Interestingly, this unexpected vowel is also reflected in Beckwith's spelling, where "u" stands for schwa. Truman Michelson also recorded the Peoria term for "sugar" in the "Story of Fox and Wolf" from George Finley in the form <pᴀñgő̂sikᴀni>. David Costa, personal communication, June 23, 2007.

37. See Beckwith, *History of Vigo and Parke Counties*, 125. On the eastern Kansas reservation Mary Ann Baptiste's husband, known as "Batticy" Baptiste the Peoria (d. September 13, 1878, in Baxter Springs, Kansas), was the head of a regeneration movement directed toward acculturation. See Beckwith Papers, File SC 98 2/3, ISHL; also Morgan, *Indian Journals, 1859–1862*, 40–42. Baptiste was Morgan's consultant for the kinship survey he conducted in Kansas in 1859. See Morgan, *Systems of Consanguinity*. For Baptiste, see also Beckwith, *History of Vigo and Parke Counties*, 134–35. Mary Ann Dagenais's remarriage is noted in the Beckwith Papers. Playing the role of the devil's advocate, I can also imagine that Beckwith himself could have created the Miami-Illinois name for Sugar Creek by naïvely asking Mrs. Baptiste for the Miami-Illinois word for "sugar." She then would have told him the correct

Peoria pronunciation, and voilà—<Pungosecone>, an "Indian" place-name. If this scenario is true, it would represent but one of the disquieting vagaries of American Indian place-name studies. For the Wea form of this term, see <pυxgosυkυne> in *The Wea Primer*, where υ indicates phonemic *a*.

38. Brelsford, *Indians of Montgomery County*, 4.

39. Cox and Collett, "Geological Map of Montgomery County," 1875, reproduced in Brelsford, *Indians of Montgomery County*, 28–29.

40. For an in-depth discussion of aboriginal maple syrup and sugar production, see Munson, "Still More on the Antiquity of Maple Sugar and Syrup," 159–70. <Pungosecone>, I hasten to add, has nothing to do with "ashes at the head of the river," a fanciful yet broadly popularized translation of this Indian hydronym. This erroneous gloss seems to involve a confusion of *pankoo-*, the first two syllables of *pankoosaakani*, with *pinkwi*, "ashes," and of the last syllable *-aakani*, "instrument" with *-(i)kami*, "water."

41. Gibson and Vigo to Harrison, in Esarey, *Messages and Letters* 1:141–42. According to Cayton, Vigo was a Spanish soldier. Cayton, *Frontier Indiana*, 58. For French *Érablière*, see Brown, *Western Gazeteer*, 140. For the early English language name of this stream, see "Sugartree Creek" in "Treaty with the Miami, 1828," in Kappler, *Indian Affairs* 2:286. Sugar Creek, already rich in native nomenclature, attests yet another putative American Indian name that Hough wrote as <Keankiksepe>. Unfortunately, this word is not analyzable aside from the -sepe spelling, which is "river." Although it is not a historically attested local place-name, *θiiθepaahkwi θiipoohi*, "maple tree river" could be the name that local Kickapoo applied to this creek. Paul Voorhis, personal communication, September 6, 1998. The Kickapoo frequented the Sugar Creek Valley throughout the 1700s, but especially after 1791, and would have had a name for it.

42. A historically famous Wea man with ties to Sugar Creek was known in English as "Stone Digger" and "Stone-Eater" or "The One That Eats Stones." *See History of Parke and Vermillion Counties*, 50. Dunn gave this man's name as <Sănḗmăgŏnga>. Dunn, *True Indian Stories*, 106. He also wrote it <Sanemamitch>, which he translated to "stone eater," and <sanemahhongah>, glossed "stone digger." Daryl Baldwin, personal communication, July 10, 2000. The latter spelling, but glossed "Stone Eater," is present in the "Treaty with the Wyandot, 1814," in Kappler, *Indian Affairs* 2:107. The initial segment <Sane-> of these recordings ostensibly represents the Miami-Illinois inanimate noun *(a)hseni*, "stone"; the second part of <Sanemamitch> appears to contain the morpheme "eat," with initial syllable reduplication: *maamiič-* ~ *meemiič-*, giving *(ah)seni maamiičika*, "he continuously eats (the/a) stone." <sanemahhongah> is *(a)hseni maahanki*, "he shovels stone," where the -ah of the historical recording is an "alphabet A." This man was a Wea leader after the abandonment of Ouiatanon near present-day Lafayette, a contemporary of the famous Miami chieftain Pacanne, a partisan of Tecumseh, and a participant

in the battle of Tippecanoe. He was also a signatory to an armistice concluded in Detroit on 14 October 1813, where he gave his name as <Newa Shosa>. See Esarey, *Messages and Letters of William Henry Harrison* 2:578. Stone-Eater was killed by another Wea in 1822. See Beckwith Papers, Illinois State Historical Library. An early historic Wea reservation, established in 1818, was located near the mouth of Sugar Creek. Esarey, *Messages and Letters of William Henry Harrison* 2:580, 686 and 645; also "Treaty with the Wea," in Kappler, *Indian Affairs* 2:169.

43. Dunn, *Indiana and the Indianans* 1:96. Dunn's j represents phonetic [ž]. The place-name would not refer to the cockleburr (*Xanthium strumarium*). This was known in Miami as *sakinteepwa*.

44. Tipton, ["Map Showing the Fort Wayne Indian Agency in Indiana"], 1824.

45. The generic *form* of this place-name is attested by the Illinois-French dictionary as <aca8iaki8nghi>. See Illinois-French dictionary, 574. The older form of "thorn" was *akaawia*, with short initial *a*. Dunn glossed <Kawiakĭungĭ>, his own version of this particular hydronym, as "place of thorns." Normally, this would be an acceptable albeit loose translation, but in this particular case it is unacceptable since it was based on an incorrect grammatical understanding that he had. One of Dunn's unpublished manuscripts outlines this: "Kahwēŏ́kkyoong, place of thorns, from kahwēŏ́k, thorns, and the terminal locative." Dunn, ms. 47, ISL. However, as noted in chapter 7, Miami-Illinois does not allow plural nouns to combine with the locative noun suffix whose basic form is *-enki*; only singular nouns can do this. So even though *kaawiaki*, as Dunn stated, means "thorns," and this term sounds somewhat like *kaawiahki*, "thorn land," these two Miami-Illinois words are not homophones. The words *kaawiaki* and *kaawiahki* are contrastive in Miami-Illinois, distinguished by the presence of *k* in the former term and that of preaspirated *hk* in the latter. Although this difference is perhaps baffling to English speakers, the two words are as phonologically and semantically distinctive in Miami-Illinois as "cat" and "catfish" are in English. Notably, an apparently unimportant sound in one language can be vitally important in another. The major primary records of the Miami-Illinois language show that, among the European recorders, the *h* of preaspirated consonants often went in one ear and out the other.

46. See *Combination Atlas of Boone County, Indiana.*

47. The painter George Winter has a sketch of Flowers' grave. See Feest, *Indians and a Changing Frontier*, pl. 49. A brief sketch of this man's life is in Robertson and Riker, *The John Tipton Papers* 1:313, note 23. His name also appears as <Ngotakaupwa> in the "Treaty with the Miami, 1826" and in the "Treaty with the Miami, 1828," in Kappler, *Indian Affairs* 2:279, 287. See also note from early June 1825 in Robertson and Riker, *Tipton Papers* 1:465–66. Little Squirrel's Miami-Illinois name is commonly written <Neconzah> ~ <Neconsaw> and insufficiently translated to "Squirrel" in the literature.

48. Hough, "Indian Names."

49. The forms this name has taken include the commendable "Kawiaski," and the distorted "Keewasakee," and "Kawaskaski." I am indebted to Dave McCafferty for these variant spellings for *kaawiahki.*

50. The word <äsepánasipiwĭ> is in Dunn, *Indiana and the Indianans* 1:95.

51. See Cayton, *Frontier Indiana*, 22–25.

52. Gatschet, "Notes on Miami-Illinois," 747.

53. <Pishewaw>, in Beckwith, the *History of Vigo and Parke County, Indiana*, 7.

54. <Passheweha> in Temple, *Indian Villages*, 163. I am indebted to Paul Voorhis for the phonemic form of this name and for other Kickapoo etyma in this volume. In modern Kickapoo, this term is *pesiia.* The map by Jacques-Nicolas Bellin, "Partie Occidentale du Canada, Contenant les Lacs Ontario, Huron, Erie, et Lac Superieur," ca. 1755–57, shows the Mascouten residing up the right bank of the Vermillion not far from the confluence, and Kickapoo below the Vermillion on the west side of the Wabash. Reproduced in Wood, *Atlas of Early Maps*, pl. VII. The various village locations of the Mascouten and the Kickapoo in the Wabash Valley have not been adequately investigated.

55. "Chem: des 8ias au Poste," in *Gazettes*, 181, Potier manuscripts, ASJCF.

56. Hutchins, "New Map," 1778; Morse's map from 1798 locates "Du Chat R." above "Brouette River," the latter being modern-day Brouilletts Creek, a western tributary of the Wabash that rises in eastern Illinois and enters the Wabash just south of the Vigo county line. See the reduced reproduction of this map in Karpinski, *Bibliography of the Printed Maps of Michigan*, 78.

57. This man's name is also memorialized on a French itinerary for the trip between Vincennes and the Illinois Indian villages near the confluence of the Illinois River and the Mississippi, where we find *La Prairie du chat* (The Prairie of the raccoon). See "Chem: du Poste aux illinois," *Gazettes*, 181, Potier manuscripts, ASJCF.

58. "Chem: des 8ias au Poste," in *Gazettes*, 181, Potier manuscripts, ASJCF; Cox, "Indiana Department of Geology and Natural Resources Annual Report."

59. Beckwith, *History of Vigo and Parke Counties*, 31–32.

60. Phonemic spelling in Costa, Miami-Illinois dictionary.

61. The majority of the Wea left the Lafayette area and moved to what the French called *la terre haute* (the high land) in 1791, though some had arrived in the area to live with resident Kickapoo and Piankashaw as early as 1786.

62. See Beckwith, *History of Vigo and Parke Counties*, 31–32; Dunn, "Mission to the Ouabache," 326; and Helman, *Archaeological Survey of Vigo County*, 18–22. When the Wea began moving down the Wabash, French *les petits ouyas* referred to the first Wea village established at Terre Haute, as opposed to *les grands ouyas*, which was still located near present-day Lafayette. In time the latter village relocated to Terre Haute and was identified by the French in the same way. Tanner has Upper Wea and Lower Wea for the names of these two villages. See Tanner, *Atlas of Great Lakes Indian History*, 98–99. Lower Wea Town was also known in English as Old Orchard Town. See Dunn, *True Indian Stories*, 132. Although this name

might have been originally Wea, I have been unable to locate a Miami-Illinois form for it in the literature. Gookins said that the orchard, probably planted by Frenchmen, was located south of the Vandalia railroad tracks on the banks of the Wabash. See Gookins, *History of Vigo County Indiana*, 65.

63. See Roy, *Sieur de Vincennes Identified*, 100–105; also Krauskopf, "French in Indiana," 190.

64. See Margry, *Découvertes* 4:630; Krauskopf, "French in Indiana," 159ff.; and Michigan Pioneer and Historical Society, *Collections and Researches* 34:110.

65. See Krauskopf, "French in Indiana," 75.

66. Dunn, ms. 47, ISL. Note the loss of short *i* according to stress rules outlined in Costa, *Miami-Illinois Language*, 103; Trowbridge, *Meearmeear Traditions*, 11.

67. Phonemic spelling in Costa, Miami-Illinois dictionary.

68. Dunn, ms. 47, ISL.

69. See "a town of the Piankeshaw Indians, called Cippecaughke," in Thomas, *Travels through the Western Country*, in Lindley, *Indiana as Seen by Early Travelers*, 101. Hough, "Indian Names."

70. Dehart, *Past and Present of Tippecanoe County* 1:33.

71. In France, on January 30, 1731, Jean-Fréderic Phélypeaux, the count de Maurepas (1701–1781), for twenty-six years secretary of the navy and thirty-four secretary of the royal household of Louis XV, devised the plan for a French fort at Vincennes. See Dunn, "Mission to the Ouabache," 296. However, the exact date of its construction is a matter of disagreement. Krauskopf states that the fort was constructed during the winter of 1732–33 and shows that it was completed by March 1733. See Krauskopf, "French in Indiana," 159. Others believe the date was 1732. See Barnhart and Riker, *Indiana to 1816*, 80. Cayton says the Piankashaw finally abandoned Vincennes in the fall of 1788. Some went to the Vermillion, while others went west. Cayton, *Frontier Indiana*, 141.

72. "Chem: du Poste au grand 8abache," *Gazettes*, 181, Potier manuscripts, ASJCF. *Le Poste* was the term the French applied to Vincennes; *grand 8abache* refers to the Ohio River. See the discussion of "Wabash" in chapter 2.

73. See "Registre de la mission huronne du Détroit," in Toupin, *Les écrits de Pierre Potier*, 246.

74. Stewart, *American Place Names*, 361. See also note 54 above.

75. Dunn, *True Indian Stories*, 297; Dunn, *Indiana and the Indianans* 1:94. Note, however, that Father Le Boullenger baptized the infant son of one Marthe Pad8ca in the early eighteenth century. See Eschmann, "Kaskaskia Church Records," in *Transactions of the Illinois State Historical Society*, IX (1904). Also, Alvord notes a leader of the Cahokias in 1777 named Patoka. Alvord, *Kaskaskia Records, 1778–1790*, 39.

76. Josiah Harmar, Harmar Papers, William C. Clements Library, University of Michigan. Microfilm copy at the Glenn Black Laboratory of Archaeology, Indiana University, Bloomington, Indiana. For the spelling "Potoka," see the maps by W. Barker, "N.W. Territory," 1796, reproduced in Karpinksi, *Bibliography of the*

Printed Maps of Michigan, 74; and Pinkerton and T. Hebert, “United States of America Southern Part,” 1816, AGS. This spelling also occurs in the early 1800s. See Thomas, _Travels through the Western Country_, 113, 128. For the spelling “Petoka,” see the excerpt from Brown in _The Western Gazetteer_, 138, 165. For the spelling “Pataka,” see Collett, “Map of Crawford Co., Indiana,” 1878, Indiana University Map Library, Bloomington.

77. Margaret Johnson’s history of Patoka suggests that the name might be of Shawnee origin. See http://www.luciefield.net/patokahist.html (accessed December 12, 2000). However, I have been unable to analyze the term for Shawnee. The trader and Indian agent John Johnston wrote <Potakasepe> as the name for the Sandusky River, translating it “rapid river” and attributing it to the Shawnee. See Howe, “Vocabularies of the Shawanoese and Wyandott,” 594. It is not impossible that Johnston’s term is in some way cognate with Ojibwa _baawitig_, “rapids in a river.”

78. O’Meara, _Delaware-English/English-Delaware Dictionary_, 239.

79. Thomas refers to these falls. See Thomas, _Travels through the Western Country_, 129.

Chapter 9: The Driftwood and Its Branches

1. For “north and south forks” for the White rivers of Indiana, see Morse and Morse, _New Universal Atlas of the World_; also John Tipton, [“Map Showing the Fort Wayne Indian Agency”], 1824, reproduced in Tucker, _Indian Villages_, pl. XLIX. The all-time champion among “fork”-related place-names in the United States seems to be the “East Fork North Fork North Fork American River.” Roger L. Payne, personal communication, December 17, 2001. Note the lack of “of.”

2. Lockridge, “Indian Names of Indiana Streams,” 215–16.

3. Kappler, _Indian Affairs_ 2:82. Tipton noted the same designation. See Robertson and Riker, _John Tipton Papers_ 1:91.

4. Vawter, _Indiana Gazette_, 240.

5. _History of Johnson County_, 292.

6. <Óngwahsahkah> is in Dunn, ms. 47, ISL; see also Dunn, _True Indian Stories_, 261. The reformulated <Óngwasaka> appears in Dunn’s _Indiana and the Indianans_ 1:88; <óngwasákwa> is in Dunn’s notes from 1910 on file at the National Anthropological Archives. Even though his translation is correct, Dunn’s spellings are distorted. As noted, the biggest problem is his initial O-. Phonemic initial short _o-_ does not exist in Miami-Illinois and long _oo-_ would be highly unlikely in the Miami-Illinois word for “driftwood,” as the initial vowel in cognate Algonquian forms for this term is short _a_. Compare Cree _akwaahonaahtik_, “stick of driftwood.” The Proto-Algonquian root appears to be _*akwa·-_. Observe, for example, Ojibwa _angwaasag_ (Ojibwa form provided by David Costa), and Southern Unami _*ankɔ́həna·kw_ (Southern Unami form provided by Ives Goddard); Shawnee <hagwanthaku> glossed “piece of driftwood,” an unusual plural form of presumed

singular **hagwanθakwi*, is in Gatschet, "Vocabularies, Texts, Notes: Shawnee, Potawatomi, Chippewa," NAA. Short *a* is typically lost in word-initial position in middle to late historical Miami-Illinois. Therefore, if the first vowel had been short *a* in Miami-Illinois, one would expect to find historical forms for "driftwood" resembling *Gwasakwa, which does not happen. In this light, the initial vowel of this Miami-Illinois term for "driftwood" must be long *aa*. The long *aa*- in the Miami-Illinois term for "driftwood" would, however, be an anomaly within Algonquian. The Miami-Illinois term contains a final in the form *-sakw*, cognate with Objiwa *-sag(w)-*, "processed wood," as in Ojibwa *angwaasag*, "driftwood." See also Illinois <ang8atahan8i>, glossed *amas de bois flottant, bois ramassé par les eaux* (a pile of floating wood, wood gathered by the waters). The Illinois-French dictionary says the initial <ang8> ~ <ang8e> means "collection," "assembly," or the "process or act of assembling" (Fr. *assemblage*). Illinois-French dictionary, 29.

7. Phonemic spelling by David Costa, personal communication, June 7, 1994.

8. Libby, "Anthropological Report on the Piankashaw Indians."

9. For Delaware on the Big Miami River, see Krauskopf, "French in Indiana," 370–71; for Delaware in southeastern Indiana by 1770, see Ferguson, "White River Indiana Delawares," 47–48. There is also reason to believe that the watershed of White River–East Fork was actually a *refuge* in the late 1700s and early 1800s for Delaware, Shawnee, and other indigenous peoples. Unfortunately, owing to the area's isolated character, there seems to be scant ethnohistorical documentation available that is particularly relevant to this study.

10. Esarey, *Messages and Letters of William Henry Harrison* 2:274.

11. Hypothetical phonemic form provided by Ives Goddard, personal communication, April 1, 2002. See chapter 6 for a discussion of Unami *-í·i-*.

12. David Thomas, *Travels through the Western Country*, 62.

13. J. H. Young, "Map of the United States," 1836, AGS; see also [Anonymous], "Map of Washington County, Indiana," 1860, AGS.

14. *Indiana Canoeing Guide*, 27. Interestingly enough, the greater valley of the White River–East Fork is only about one hundred miles long as the crow flies.

15. Guernsey, "Indiana." In Southern Unami the sugar maple tree is *ahsəna·mə́·nši*. Ives Goddard, personal communication, April 2, 2002.

16. See Horsford, *Zeisberger's Indian Dictionary*, nos. 120 and 187.

17. Hough, "Indian Names." The phonemic spelling for "sugar maple tree" in Shawnee is adapted from the historically recorded version of the term in the form <thenomeysee> translated "the sugar tree" by Thomas Rideout, explorer and captive among the Shawnee in 1788. See Edgar, *Ten Years in Upper Canada*, 377.

18. Brelsford, *Indians of Montgomery County*, 156. It seems the Shawnee first appear in the historical record with the French spelling <Ouchaouanag>. See Thwaites, *Jesuit Relations* 33:151. This is a northern Algonquian plural form of the self-designation *šaawanwaki*, "south people." The initial Ou- of the earliest recording essentially represents an Algonquian ethnonymic prefix.

19. Tanner, *Atlas of Great Lakes Indian History*, 92. Ferguson, "White River Indiana Delawares," 46. See also Krauskopf, "French in Indiana," 217ff.

20. Big Shawnee Creek, a name for a waterway in Tippecanoe and Fountain Counties and no doubt a translation of an old French place-name, marks an earlier Shawnee presence in Indiana. For more on this place-name, see chapter 7.

21. Dunn, *True Indian Stories*, 304. See Horsford, *Zeisberger's Indian Dictionary*, no. 134.

22. The reader should remember that Delaware *x* is a velar fricative and is not the sound represented by the English letter "x" as in "fix," where "x" represents [ks].

23. The term "flat rock" for the name of this stream is in Robertson and Riker, *Tipton Papers* 1:92; <Puchkachsin> is on Guernsey, "Indiana."

24. *History of Rush County*, 281.

25. Guernsey, "Indiana."

26. Lucy Blalock, personal communication per James Rementer, March 15, 1997.

27. See <Ahanhokqui> glossed "descending from, sprung from" in Brinton and Anthony, *Lenape-English Dictionary*, 14. Waterfalls composed of dolomite once overlain with shale are found on the Fall Fork of Clifty Creek, south of Hartsville.

28. Robertson and Riker, *Tipton Papers* 1:9.

29. Hough, "Indian Names."

30. I am indebted to Ives Gooddard for this phonemic spelling. See also *lé·kaw*, "sand," in Goddard, "Historical Phonology of Munsee," 21.

31. Robertson and Riker, *Tipton Papers* 1:92.

32. Such sand deposits are also found in the valley of the East Fork of the White River in general. See "An Investigation of Late Woodland Period Settlement in the East Fort White River Valley, Indiana," at http://www.gbl.indiana.edu/abstracts.90/Redmond_90.html (accessed May 17, 1999); also E. Cox, *Geological Survey of Indiana 1875*; and Robertson and Riker, *Tipton Papers* 1:92.

33. This hydronym is spelled in various ways throughout history. See "Wyalosing" on Milton Smith, "Map of Indiana Showing the Railroads & Townships," 1858, AGS; also J. H. Colton, "Map of the State of Indiana," 1856, AGS.

34. Dunn cited Heckewelder for his spelling. Dunn, *Indiana and the Indianans* 1:97; Dunn, *True Indian Stories*, 319; Bliss, *Diary of David Zeisberger*, xv.

35. In this term morphophonemic |-səs-| of "old man" was realized phonetically as [-ss-]. I am indebted to Ives Goddard for the phonemic form of this term. I am also indebted to John O'Meara for his help in sorting out this place-name. Note that in modern Munsee the initial *m-*, as in the term for "old man," deletes when not preceded by a prefix. The [w] after the *x* is due to labialization after *x*. *hiló·s·əs*, "old man" is the Southern Unami cognate. See Goddard, "Pidgin Delaware," 47. Rementer notes that *hiló·s·əs* was the term for "old man" used by the Unami at the time they were in Indiana. James Rementer, personal communication, February 3, 1998. In the Delaware locative final *-Vnk* (where *-V-* indicates a vowel), the consonant cluster is realized phonetically as [-ŋg].

36. Dunn, *True Indian Stories*, 156, 287. Dunn, *Indiana and the Indianans* 1:93. Dunn said the earlier spelling comes from *Indiana House Journal 1820–1821*, p. 54.

37. Dunn, *True Indian Stories*, 287; Horsford, *Zeisberger's Indian Dictionary*, no. 019; Brinton and Anthony, *Lenape-English Dictionary*, 86.

38. Ives Goddard, personal communication, June 12, 2002.

39. Robertson and Riker, *Tipton Papers* 1:91.

40. See Goddard, "Historical Phonology of Munsee," 23.

41. Hough, "Indian Names." See the 1836 <Muskakituck> on Young, "Map of the United States"; Chamberlain, *Indiana Gazetteer*, 329.

42. Dunn's citation reads, "Laws of 1815, page 4"; see also Dunn, ms. 47, ISL. For this basic spelling, see John Melish's map of 1817, reproduced in Finley, *New American Atlas*; also H. S. Tanner, "United States of America," 1829, AGS; Fenner Sears & Co, "Map of the States of Indiana and Ohio with Part of Michigan Territory," ca. 1830, AGS; Young, "Map of the United States"; J. H. Hinton and Simpkin and Marshall, "Map of the State of Indiana," 1842, IUGL; and Colton and Co., ["United States of America"], AGS.

43. See Young, "Map of the United States." On his map, the term designated the White River–East Fork below its confluence with the Muscatatuck, and was the name for the river *all the way to present-day Bedford.* "Stream flowing through swampy land," Guernsey's intriguing yet poetically licensed translation of the river's name, supports the "swamp river" analysis, although I am hesitant to trust Guernsey for reasons noted elsewhere.

44. Colton "Map of the State of Indiana."

45. Dunn, ms. 47, ISL.

46. Cheryl A. Munson, personal communication, January 25, 2001. Noel Justice, personal communication, December 4, 2000.

47. Southern Unami phonemic form from Goddard, personal communication, June 3, 2002.

48. Hough, "Indian Names." The Delaware terms for "otter" literally mean "long-beaver."

49. Around the turn of the nineteenth century there was also a local Kickapoo leader named Otter, who theoretically could be the source of the middle Wabash Valley place-name. See "Treaty with the Kickapoo, 1815," in Kappler, *Indian Affairs* 2:117. See <Ketatäha> and <Kitatäa>, presumably for Kickapoo *ketateeha* and *ketatea*, respectively, in Jones, *Kickapoo Tales*, 42. This animal name is not attested in modern Kickapoo. For the Delaware at Vincennes, see Staab, "Hypolite Bolon *Père et Fils.*"

50. See http://www.shawnee-traditions.com/Names-16.html (accessed December 2, 2006).

51. See *namé·s*, "fish" in Goddard, "Historical Phonology of Munsee," 26. The phonetic realization of this term comes from James Rementer, personal communication, November 18, 1996. The reader should note that *sh* here represents

the sounds *s* + *h* as in English "les*s h*ot" and not the sound represented by sh in English "she."

52. See Zeisberger's "fish" in Horsford, *Zeisberger's Indian Dictionary*, no. 2075. Phonemic form of the participle provided by Goddard, personal communication, June 3, 2002. It is not impossible that Guernsey's spelling could also represent a genuine Munsee hydronym in the form **namè·sháne·w*, "fish river," composed of the Munsee term for "fish," *namé·s*, and the Munsee noun final *-háne·w*, "river." This is, however, my own speculation, as is the Unami verb form **namè·sháne·*.

53. Guernsey, "Indiana."

54. Note that this term is a verb. Also compare the modern Munsee cognate *wá·sə̆lew*.

55. Horsford, *Zeisberger's Indian Dictionary*, no. 028.

56. Guernsey, "Indiana"; <Nīskassīsku> is in Horsford, *Zeisberger's Indian Dictionary*, no. 056. Compare Northern Unami <assisku> [ahsí·sku], "mud, clay," in Goddard, "Pidgin Delaware," 54. The twentieth-century Southern Unami cognate for "mud" is *sí·sku*, Goddard, "Pidgin Delaware," 54. See also Munsee *así·skəw*, written "asíiskuw," in O'Meara, *Delaware-English/English-Delaware Dictionary*, 40. Compare Munsee *ni·skpó·ši·š*, written "niiskpóoshiish," meaning "dirty cat." O'Meara, *Delaware-English/English-Delaware Dictionary*, 197.

57. See Williams and Justice, "Interim Report of the Archaeological Survey of Brown County." Jack Weddle, personal communication, December 19, 2000. This large salt lick is located on the north bank of the north fork of Salt Creek approximately one and a half miles north-northeast of Belmont, Indiana, and almost due south of the dam at Yellowwood Lake.

58. Bailey places the salt lick at Township 9, Range 2, Section 31. Bailey, *Brown County*, 45.

59. Hough, "Indian Names."

60. See Voegelin, *Shawnee Stems* 9:375.

61. Howe, "Vocabularies of the Shawanoese and Wyandott," 594.

62. Phonemic spelling by Goddard, personal communication, June 3, 2002. The translation is mine. If genuine, this place-name is clearly not Munsee since the Munsee language has a different term for beaver: *amóxkw*. See O'Meara and Delaware Nation Council, *Delaware-English/English-Delaware Dictionary*, 35. Participles in Unami should, but do not always, undergo initial change, which would shift the schwa sound *ə* in the first syllable of the simplex noun form of the term for "beaver" to long *e·* in the "beaver" initial occurring within the participle "that which is a beaver river," which would then be **te·ma·kwe·háne·k*. I am grateful to Ives Goddard for pointing out initial change here.

63. <Tommaqua> is in a letter to Harrison from four Delaware leaders, September 9, 1808, in Esarey, *Messages and Letters* 2:303–4. "Treaty with the Delaware, 1804," in Kappler, *Indian Affairs* 2:71; "Treaty with the Delawares, 1805," in Kappler, *Indian Affairs* 2:81. See also "The Beaver" in "Treaty with the Delawares, 1809,"

and "Captain Beaver" in the "Treaty with the Wyandot, 1815," both in Kappler, *Indian Affairs* 2:102, 119. See also White, *Middle Ground*, 244, 249. White notes the famous eighteenth-century Unami leader <Tamaqua> was of the Turkey phratry, ca. 1756. He died in 1769. This particular *təma·kwe* is too early to be the source of Indiana's place-name. But White's information is important, for it indicates this was a personal name among the Unami. See also Goddard, "Delaware," 15:223. Unami *təma·kwe* is from *təm-*, "cut" and *-a·kw*, "wood."

64. Guernsey, "Indiana."

65. The name of the Orange County town on Lick Creek known today as Paoli has been attributed to the Miami-Illinois language. See Dunn, ms. 47, ISL. In fact, it very closely resembles Southern Unami *pe·yɔ́·le*, the Unami name for the Peoria. It appears, however, to derive from the given name of Pasquale Paoli Ash, the son of North Carolina governor Samuel Ash, who actually never lived in Orange County. The Carolina boy received his name in honor of Pasquale Paoli, a Corsican patriot born in 1725. See *History of Orange County*, 9.

66. Ferguson, "White River Indiana Delawares," 47n13.

67. Guernsey, "Indiana."

68. The term **le·x·awí·tank* provided by Ives Goddard, personal communications, August 21, 2000, and June 3, 2002.

Chapter 10: The Heart of the North Country

1. "Chemin, par terre, de S jos aux 8ia," in *Gazettes*, 180, Potier manuscripts, ASJCF. Hutchins's map shows this trail, but not in an accurate fashion: Hutchins, "New Map,"1778.

2. Lake Wawasee, though larger and essentially natural, is actually the result of the artificial union of smaller lakes.

3. "Chemin, par terre, de S jos aux 8ia," in *Gazettes*, 180, Potier manuscripts, ASJCF.

4. *Indiana Document Journal*, 1835, Doc. No. 8; George Winter Papers, file 69.86.344, TCHA; also Feest, *Indians and a Changing Frontier*, 51, 194–95; and Ball, *Journals and Indian Paintings of George Winter*, 76, 107. In 1858, the name appeared in the form <Muxincukkee>, an apparent spin-off of one of Winter's spellings. See Smith, "Map of Indiana," AGS.

5. Dunn, *Indiana and the Indianans* 1:91; Dunn Papers, ISL.

6. Illinois-French dictionary, 243.

7. McDonald, *Twentieth Century History of Marshall County* 1:92.

8. Ibid. Guernsey has <Kopenuckeonbes>. Guernsey, "Indiana." Phonemic spelling provided by Laura Buszard-Welcher, personal communication, December 22, 1997.

9. Guernsey, "Indiana."

10. Analysis and translation by the author: *nbəs* is phonetic [mbəs].

11. Beckwith, "Indian Names," 41.

12. Guernsey, "Indiana"; Hiestand, *Archaeological Report of Newton County*, 7–8.

13. Smith, "Map of Indiana," AGS.

14. Laura-Buszard-Welcher, personal communication, December 22, 1997.

15. Potawatomi phonemic spelling provided by Richard Rhodes, personal communication, March 3, 2006. I have replaced the traditional final *-k* of his spellings with modern *-g*.

16. See "Treaty with the Potawatomi, 1832" and "Treaty with the Potawatomi, 1834," in Kappler, *Indian Affairs* 2:374, 431.

17. Dunn, *True Indian Stories*, 305. Dunn, *Indiana and the Indianans* 1:95.

18. Potawatomi phonemic spelling provided by Laura Buszard-Welcher, personal communication, December 23, 1997.

19. See *Illustrated Historical Atlas of Indiana*.

20. "Treaty with the Miami, 1826," in Kappler, *Indian Affairs* 2:279–80.

21. See Royse, *Standard History of Kosciusko County* 1:49. Here the name <Waw-waesse> applied to Nine Mile Lake. The Miami man *waawiyasita* was also known as Wabee, whence Wabee Lake, also in Kosciusko County, got its name (49, 57). He was the brother of <Papakeecha>, that is, *papahkiča*, "flat tail," commonly known as "Flatbelly"(57). In 1830, *waawiyasita* was living at the southeast corner of this lake (49). See also Robertson and Riker, *John Tipton Papers* 2:438.

22. Ibid. 1:476, 478, 776, 794; 2:186, 384.

23. Dunn, *True Indian Stories*, 314.

Chapter 11: Indiana's Ohio River Tributaries

1. "Kentucky" is from Northern Iroquoian, for example, Mohawk *kẽ́hta˙ke* and Seneca *kẽhtaʔkeh*, "at the prairie." See Wright, "People of the Panther," 67.

2. See Thwaites, *Early Western Travels* 1:136. For the location of historical Delaware and Shawnee in southwest Indiana, see *History of Warrick, Spencer and Perry Counties*, 250–51. A historic Indian village was located at the headwaters of Little Pigeon Creek. See Wilson, *Early Trails and Surveys*, 40.

3. See Shawnee <Shimeameesepe>, in Howe, "Vocabularies of the Shawanoese and Wyandott Languages," 594. See also "Big Miami River" in Gage, "Draft of the Ohio from an Indian Account."

4. See the anonymous French maps referenced SHB B4044-21, 1749; SHB B4044B87; and SHB B4040-13, in AGS. See also Margry, *Découvertes* 6:666–726. *Rivière des Miamis* is an early French name for the Fox River of Wisconsin, since that is where the Miami were living when the French first met them. See Jean-Baptiste D'Anville, ["Lake Superior and the Upper Mississippi River"], early eighteenth century, reproduced in Tucker, *Indian Villages*, pl. III.

5. Thwaites, *Jesuit Relations* 69:184–85. Eighteenth-century English speakers used their own hydronym "Great Miami River" as well as the French name for the

stream. *La rivière à la Roche* occurs in English as "Rocky River" on various British maps. See, for example, Patten's map from 1752 and Mitchell's famous chart from 1755, wherein the watercourse is said to be "full of falls." [John Patten], ["A map of the Ohio country"], 1752, reproduced in Brown, *Early Maps*, 16; John Mitchell, "A map of the British and French domains in North America," 1755, reproduced in Brown, *Early Maps*, 25.

6. Lewis Evans, "A General Map of the Middle British Colonies in America," 1758, AGS.

7. Trowbridge gives <Usaanëë sëëpee> for a stream near Pickawillany. This spelling stands for Miami-Illinois *ahsenisiipi*, "stone river" and refers to the Great Miami River, whose headwaters are located near this historically famous site. See Trowbridge, *Meearmeear Traditions*, 11. Note that the -ss- of <Assereniet> represents preaspirated *hs*. One typically sees in historical texts the doubling of a consonant as a representation of an original preaspirated consonant.

8. Jacques Nicolas Bellin, "Carte de la Louisiane," 1744, reproduced in Charlevoix, *Journal of a Voyage to North America*, vol. 1; also, Jacques-Nicolas Bellin, "Partie Occidentale du Canada," ca. 1750, reproduced in Buisseret, *Mapping the French Empire in North America*, 48. Bellin's 1764 map has "Assenissipi ou R. a la Roche" for the Rock River of Wisconsin. Jacques-Nicolas Bellin, "Carte des Cinq Grands Lacs du Canada," 1764, in Buisseret, *Mapping the French Empire in North America*, 50. See also Joseph-Pierre de Bonnécamps's map archived at the Service Historique de la Marine, Paris. Photocopy in the author's possession.

9. Scott, *Indiana Gazeteer*.

10. Hough, "Indian Names."

11. The others are <Shehaconnah> for *šiipaakana* and <Chihkahwekay> for *čiipihkahki*.

12. See <wabiskĭū nipéu> in Vogel, *Indian Names on Wisconsin's Map*, 131; also Bloomfield, *Menomini Lexicon*, 158, 266.

13. Guernsey, "Indiana."

14. The Munsee cognate would be *wa˙pahsə́nənk*, which is not a good match for the historical recording here.

15. See Southern Unami *ahsən* in Goddard, "Pidgin Delaware," 47; also Goddard, personal communication, June 3, 2002.

16. See Shaver et al., *Compendium of Paleozoic Rock-Unit Stratigraphy*, 144.

17. For the Portersville bison crossing in southern Daviess County, see Meyers, *Daviess County Indiana History*, 20. For more on this trail, the reader can visit the Eiteljorg Museum of the American Indian and Western Art in Indianapolis. There on permanent display is a map with data on the Great Buffalo Trace that was gathered by Michael McCafferty.

18. Wilson also noted that the original bison trails were said to be in general twelve to twenty feet wide. The reader may also enjoy the many interesting descriptions of this bison-carved road in Wilson's *Early Indiana Trails and Surveys* and

in Thornbrough's and Wilson's *Buffalo Trace.* See also Harold Allison, "Nature Trails," *Bloomington (Ind.) Herald-Times*, February 28, 1999.

19. Wilson, *Early Trails and Surveys*, 21. For an impressive local salt lick, see Heckewelder, "Narrative of John Heckewelder's Journey to the Wabash in 1792," 173–74.

20. See Illinois-French dictionary, 172, 95; the earlier Pinet dictionary has <irenans8ikana8i>. Pinet, French/Miami-Illinois dictionary, 69.

Glossary

affricate. A consonant released with friction, produced by combining a stop consonant and a homorganic fricative, for example, *t* + *š* > *č*, the sound written ch in English "chat."

Algonquian. A North American language family comprised of dozens of languages, including several spoken historically in Indiana. Important for this study are Miami-Illinois, Kickapoo, Munsee, Shawnee, Ottawa, Unami, and Potawatomi.

allophone. One or more possible phonetic realizations of a particular phoneme. For example, English *p* has two allophones: a plosive syllable-initial [p^1] as in "pick" and a nonplosive syllable-final [p^2] as in "stop."

back-formation. A presumed native language form constructed on the basis of a European language form.

devoicing. The pronunciation of a voiced sound without vibration of the vocal cords, for example, "news" pronounced [nus] rather than [nuz]. Here *z* undergoes devoicing to [s].

epenthesis. The insertion of a sound into a word, for example, English "sherbet" pronounced [šərbə*r*t] instead of [šərbət], or "warmth" pronounced [warmpθ] instead of [warmθ].

eponym. A place-name derived from a personal name, for example, McCormick's Creek, Lafayette, Squirrel Creek.

ethnonym. A proper name of a people or ethnic group, for example, *potewatmi,* the term meaning "Potawatomi" in Potawatomi.

final. In a composite Algonquian word, the segment that occurs at the end of a term before the inflectional markers, for example, in Miami-Illinois, the segment *-iinkwee*, "face, eyes, corn" of *peehkiinkweewi*, "(it is) nice corn" (Fr. *beau bled*).

(frère) donné. French for "(a) given (brother)." A French layman who dedicated himself to the service of a missionary priest.

fricative. A consonant produced by air moving through a narrow passage with audible friction, for example, [f], [s], [z].

hagionym. A place-name that has a religious content.

hydrology. The study of the flow and distribution of water.

hydronym. The proper name of a body of water, for example, Fall Creek, Lake Erie.

Illinois. A grouping of dialects of the Miami-Illinois language spoken by the Peoria, Kaskaskia, Tamaroa, Cahokia, Michigamea, and other related groups.

initial. In a composite Algonquian word, the segment that occurs at the beginning, for example, Miami-Illinois *pim-*, "across, past, crosswise, sideways, this way and that," as in *pimiteewi*, "it burns past" (the term represented by the historical place-name <Pimitéoui> in Illinois).

Iroquoian. A North American language family comprised of the following languages: Laurentian (Stadaconan), Cayuga, Mohawk, Oneida, Onondaga, Seneca, Susquehannock, Huron-Wyandot, Nottoway, Neutral, Tuscarora, and Cherokee. In this book Seneca and Huron-Wyandot are particularly important.

Les pays d'en Haut (The Upper Countries). This designation, pronounced [lepeídãó], was used by the French in the seventeenth and eighteenth centuries for that part of North America which lay up both the Ottawa and St. Lawrence Rivers, referring in particular to the area west of Lake Ontario and north of the Ohio River. It included present-day Indiana, Illinois, Michigan, and Wisconsin.

Le pays des Illinois (The Country of the Illinois). In the late 1600s and through the mid-1700s, this French term, pronounced [ləpeídezilinwɛ́], referred to the area where the Illinois Indians lived, essentially from the Wabash River west to the Illinois River, including the Kankakee watershed.

locative. Referring to location, for example, the Miami-Illinois locative suffix *-ionki*, "at, in, on" as in *wiipičahkionki*, a locative noun meaning "in the flint land."

medial. In an Algonquian word, the segment that occurs in the middle of the term, that is, after the initial and before the final and the inflectional suffixes, as in *-aahši-*, "shine" in *waapaahšiteewi*, "it shines white because of heat."

metathesis. The transposition of sounds, as in [pərfər] for [prəfər] ("prefer"), or [rilətər] for [riəltər] ("realtor").

Miami. A dialect of the Miami-Illinois language spoken by the Miami, Wea, Piankashaw, and related groups.

Miami-Illinois. A language spoken historically in Indiana, Illinois, and adjoining states by the Miami, Wea, Piankashaw, Pepicokia, Mengakonkia, Kilatika, Peoria, Kaskaskia, Tamaroa, Cahokia, Michigamea, and other related bands.

morpheme. The smallest meaningful unit of a language. The English term "words" is composed of two morphemes: "word" and -s, the plural marker.

morphology. The study of word formation; the form of a word itself.

morphophonemic spelling. The underlying form of a morpheme or a set of morphemes, irrespective of the different surface forms that they may take. Any given morpheme is always spelled in a consistent manner although it may be pronounced in different ways according to the influence of its phonological environment.

obstruent. A consonant produced with complete or partial obstruction of the air flow from the lungs through the mouth or nose, for example, *t, c, hš.*

obviative. A grammatical category in Algonquian languages involving two non-coreferential third-person animate nouns in the same clause, whereby one is marked grammatically in a special way for obviation. For example, in Algonquian, in a statement such as "The fox saw the bear," the term for "bear" would be marked for obviation.

odonym. The proper name of a trail, a street, a highway, and so on. Examples include the Great Buffalo Trace, Interstate 74.

Old Miami-Illinois. The Miami-Illinois language recorded by the Jesuits in the late seventeenth and early eighteenth centuries at Chicago and elsewhere in the Illinois and middle Mississippi Valleys.

Old Potawatomi. The Potawatomi language spoken in the eighteenth and early nineteenth centuries and before.

onomastic. Of or related to the study of names.

onomastics. The study of names.

phone. A sound, with no commitment to structural interpretation.

phoneme. The abstract, fundamental sound unit of a language consisting generally of a class of related sounds known as allophones. See *allophone.*

phonemicization. The underlying form of a sound or word. For example, the historically recorded Miami-Illinois <m8ns8>, meaning "deer" (Fr. *chevreuil*), is phonemic *mooswa.*

phonetic spelling. The linguistic spelling of a word or sound according to how it is pronounced, for example, [moonswa] for underlying phonemic *mooswa.*

phonetics. The science that analyzes the sounds of a language as they are produced.

phonological. Related to the sounds of a language.

phonology. The analysis of the sounds of a language according to their function and structural relationship.

preaspirated consonant. An obstruent preceded by *h,* that is, a short period of voicelessness just before the articulation of the consonant, for example, *hk, hs, ht.*

reflex. A term or part of a term in a language that derives from the ancestral language, for example, Miami-Illinois *mihsoor-,* "wood-boat" from PA **mehθweθ-*. (PA reconstruction in Ives Goodard, "Heckewelder's 1792 Vocabulary from Ohio: A Possible Attestation of Mascouten," in *Papers of the 34th Algonquian Conference,* ed. H. C. Wolfart, 165-92 [Winnipeg: University of Manitoba Press, 2003].)

sibilant. A fricative or affricate consonant, for example, *s* or *č.*

Siouan. A North American language family comprised of the following languages— Crow, Hidatsa, Dakotan, Dhegiha, Chiwere, Winnebago, Tutelo, Ofo, and Biloxi. Dhegiha, which includes the dialects Kansa (Kaw), Omaha-Ponca, Osage and Quapaw, is the Siouan language that relates to the study of Indiana's native place-names.

stop consonant. A sound produced by a blockage of the air, for example, *p* and *d*. Like all consonants, stop consonants are classified according to their points of articulation. Examples include bilabials such as *b* and *m*, palatals such as *č* and *š*, and dorso-velars such as *k* and *g*.

toponym. The name of a place.

voicing. The pronunciation of a sound accompanied by a vibration of the vocal cords, for example, the voicing of *t* results in [d] and the voicing of *s* in [z].

Bibliography

Manuscript Materials

INDIANA UNIVERSITY GEOGRAPHY LIBRARY, BLOOMINGTON, INDIANA

Anonymous. "Map of the States of Indiana, Ohio, with Part of the Michigan Territory." 1858.

Collett, John. "Map of Crawford Co. Indiana." 1878.

Hinton, J. H., and Simpkin and Marshall. "Map of the States of Indiana, Ohio, with Part of the Michigan Territory." 1842.

THE NEWBERRY LIBRARY, CHICAGO, ILLINOIS

Champlain, Samuel de. "Carte de la Nouvelle France." Graff 642. 1632.

D'Abbéville, Nicholas Sanson. "Le Canada, ou Nouvelle France, &c." Map. 1656.

Delisle, Guillaume. "Carte de La Louisiane." 1718. Edward E. Ayer Collection.

Franquelin, Jean-Baptiste Louis. "Carte contenant Une Part du Canada & les terres qui S'estendent depuis 44 jusqu'a 61 de lattitude et de longitude, depuis a 46 jusqu'a 297." 1681.

———. ["La Carte de la Colbertie ou des Griffons."] 1674. Photostat copy in the Karpinski Collection. SHB B4044-37.

———. No title. N.d. Ge DD2987-8695//2987-8802.

SBH, B 4040-4. Copy in Karpinski Collection.

INDIANA STATE LIBRARY, INDIANAPOLIS

Dunn, Jacob P. Ms. file 47.

———. Miami file card dictionary.

———. Notes on Miami.

Lasselle, Hyacinthe. Papers.

INDIANA HISTORICAL SOCIETY, INDIANAPOLIS

Hall, Sydney. "United States." Map. 1828.
"Indian Place-Name File Cards." Manuscript.
Morse, Jedidiah. "A Map of the Northern and Middle United States." 1792.

TIPPECANOE COUNTY HISTORICAL ASSOCIATION, LAFAYETTE, INDIANA

Winter, George. Papers.

AMERICAN GEOGRAPHICAL SOCIETY, MILWAUKEE, WISCONSIN

Anonymous. French map. No title. Eighteenth century. SHB B4044-15.
———. "Map of the States of Indiana and Ohio with Part of Michigan Territory." Fenner Sears & Co. AGS 831-B-[1832].
———. "Map of Washington County, Indiana. AD 1860." AGS 831-B-1860.
———. "Treaty Lines." AGS 831-E-[1844].
[Bellin, Jacques Nicolas]. "Carte de la Floride, de la Louisiane et Pays Voisins Par M.B., Ing. de la Marine." AGS 800-A-1757.
[———]. "Carte de La Nouvelle Angleterre Nouvelle Yorc." AGS 800-B-1757.
Bourguignon d'Anville, Jean-Baptiste. "Canada Louisiane & Terres Angloises." AGS RARE AT. 050 A-[1743-1776 d'Anville].
Bradley, Abraham, Jr. "Map of the United States, Exhibiting the Post-roads, the Situations, Connexions & Distances of the Post Offices, Stage Roads, Counties & Principal Rivers." AGS Rare 800-A-1804.
Colton, J. H. "Map of the State of Indiana." AGS Y-131-a. 1856.
———. ["United States of America."] AGS Y-131. 1856.
Evans, Lewis. "A General Map of the Middle British Colonies in America." AGS 800-a-B-1758.
Faden, William. "The United States of North America with the British and Spanish Territories." AGS RARE 800-B-1783.
[Fielding, John]. "A Map of the United States as Settled by the Peace of 1783." AGS 800-a-B-1785.
Fielding, L. "A Map of the United States as Settled by the Peace of 1783." AGS 800-a-B-1785.
Pinkerton, and T. Hebert. "United States of America Southern Part." AGS Rare 800-A-1816.
Russell, T. Map of North America. No title. AGS 800-A-1795.
Smith, Milton. "Map of Indiana Showing the Railroads & Townships." AGS 831-D-1858.
Stockdale, John. "A Map of the Northern and Middle States Comprehending the Western Territory and the British Dominions in North America." AGS 800-A-1792.
Tanner, H. S. "United States of America." AGS RARE 800-B-1829.

Vaugondy, Robert de. "Amérique Septentrionale, dressée par les Relations les plus modernes des Voyageurs & Navigateurs et divisée suivant les différentes possessions des Européens." AGS Rare A.T. 050 A-1757.

ARCHIVES NATIONALES DU QUÉBEC, MONTREAL

"Archives nationales de France: Colonies (narratives)." Photostats of handwritten copies.

PUBLIC ARCHIVES OF CANADA, OTTAWA, ONTARIO

"The Sketch taken in the Month of Novr. 1778 H. Duvernet, 2d Lt, R.R.A." Map file no. NMC 0011835 HI 1210, "Maumee 1778."

ARCHIVES DE LA BIBLIOTHÈQUE NATIONALE DE FRANCE, PARIS

Beschefer Thierry, and Jean-Baptiste Louis Franquelin. "La Carte de la Manitoumie." That is, ["Manitoumie I"] or "Carte de la nouvelle découverte que les R.R. Pères Jésuites ont fait en l'année 1672 et continuée par le R. P. Marquette en l'année 1673."1678. Département des Cartes et Plans. *Recueil* Ge C 5014.

Franquelin, Jean-Baptiste Louis. "Carte de la Louisiane En l'Amerique jusqu'au Golfe de Mexique, ou sont decris les Pays que le Sieur de la Salle a decouverts dans un grand continent compris depuis 50. degr., de l'Elevation du Pole jusques a 25, les annees 1679.80.81.82." 1684. *Recueil* Ge DD 2987, no. 8782.

———. "Carte de la nouvelle découverte que les R.R. Pères Jésuites ont fait en l'année 1672 et continuée par le R. P. Marquette en l'année 1673." ["La Carte de la Manitoumie."] *Recueil* Ge C 5014.

[Franquelin, Jean-Baptiste Louis]. Map of North America. No title. 1684. *Recueil* Ge DD2987-8695//2987-8802.

Gallinée, René-François Bréhant de. "Carte du Canada et des terres decouverte [*sic*] vers le lac d'Erie." *Recueil* GeDD 2989, no. 8662-1670.

BIBLIOTHÈQUE HISTORIQUE CENTRALE DE LA MARINE, CHÂTEAU DE VINCENNES, FRANCE

Franquelin, Jean-Baptiste. "Carte de l'Amerique Septent.[le] entre 27 et 64 degrés de lattitude & environ 250 & 340 de longitude ou est compris les pays de … Par Jean Baptiste Louis Franquelin; dessignée et Écrite par F. de la Croix." 1684. *Recueil* 66, no. 8-11.

———. "Cette Carte est une des quatre parties de la description generale du Canada et des terres qui s'estendent depuis 27 degrez jusqu'a 61 de lattitude Septentrionale, et depuis 246 degrez jusqu'a 338 de 1681, par Jean Louis Franquelin." 1681. SHB, B4040-2.

ARCHIVES DE LA SOCIÉTÉ DE JÉSUS CANADA FRANÇAIS, ST-JÉRÔME, QUÉBEC

Marquette, Jacques. [Carte du Mississippi.] 1673-74. *Recueil* 196.

———. "Recit Des Voyages et Des Découvertes Du P. Iacques Marquette De la Compagnie de Jesus En l'annee 1673. Et aux Suiuantes." Edited by Pierre Dablon. *Recueil* 296.

———. "Récit du second voyage que le Pere Jacques Marquette a fait aux Ilinois, pr. y portee la foy, et la glorieuse mort du mesme Pere dans les trauaux." *Recueil* 296.

Pinet, Pierre-François. French–Miami-Illinois dictionary. 1696-1702.

Potier, Pierre-Philippe. Potier manuscripts.

Illinois State Historical Library, Springfield

Beckwith, Hiram W. Papers.

Unpublished Materials

[Largiller, Jacques]. Illinois-French dictionary. Post-1700. Watkinson Library, Trinity College, Hartford, Conn.

Costa, David J. Miami-Illinois dictionary, ca. 1992.

Dillingham, Betty Ann (Wilder). "The Oklahoma Kickapoo." Ph.D. diss., University of Michigan, 1963.

Faulkner, Charles H. "The Late Prehistoric Occupation of Northwest Indiana: A Study of the Upper Mississippian Cultures of the Kankakee Valley." Ph.D. diss., Indiana University, 1970.

Ferguson, Roger James. "The White River Indiana Delawares: An Ethnohistoric Synthesis, 1795-1867." Ph.D. diss., Ball State University, 1972.

Gage, Thomas. "A Draft of the Ohio from an Indian Account." Ca. 1755. Thomas Gage Papers, American Series, William L. Clements Library, University of Michigan, Ann Arbor. Microfilm copy at Glenn Black Laboratory of Archaeology, Bloomington, Ind.

Gatschet, Albert. "Notes on Miami-Illinois." Ca. 1885-1902. National Anthropological Archives, Washington, D.C. Copies courtesy of David Costa and Daryl Baldwin.

———. "Vocabularies, Texts, Notes: Shawnee, Potawatomi, Chippewa." Manuscript 68. 1878-93. National Anthropological Archives, Washington, D.C. Copy courtesy of David Costa.

Harmar, Josiah. Papers. William C. Clements Library, University of Michigan. Microfilm copy at the Glenn Black Laboratory of Archaeology, Indiana University, Bloomington.

Krauskopf, Frances. "The French in Indiana, 1700-1760: A Political History." Ph.D. diss., Indiana University, 1953.

Le Boullenger, Jean-Baptiste Antoine-Robert. French-Illinois dictionary. Post-1719. John Carter Brown Library, Providence, R.I.

McMurray, William. "The United States according to the definitive Treaty of Peace signed at Paris Sept. 3rd. 1783." 1784. Original map in Library of Congress, Washington, D.C. Photocopy in author's possession.

Michelson, Truman. "Notes on Peoria." 1916. National Anthropological Archives, Washington, D.C. Copy courtesy of David Costa.

O'Hair, Mary C. Index Glossary of Indiana Indian Names. Ca. 1960. Wabash County Historical Society, Wabash, Ind. Photocopy in author's possession.

Wisconsin Native American Language Project. Records, 1973-1976. University of Wisconsin–Madison Manuscript Collection 20, Madison.

Special Published Maps

Guernsey, E. Y. "Indiana: The Influence of the Indian upon Its History—with Indian and French Names for Natural and Cultural Locations." 1932. Department of Natural Resources, State of Indiana, Publication No. 122. Indianapolis: Department of Natural Resources, 1933.

Hough, Daniel. "Indian Names of Lakes, Rivers, Towns, Forts of Indiana." Before 1880. In Hiram W. Beckwith, "Indian Names of Water Courses in the State of Indiana." Indiana Department of Geology and Natural History, *Twelfth Annual Report*, 39-43, map opposite 42. Indianapolis: William B. Buford, 1883.

Books and Articles

Alford, Clarence W. *The Illinois Country 1673-1818*. Springfield: Illinois Centennial Commission, 1920.

———. *Kaskaskia Records, 1778-1790*. Springfield: Trustees of the Illinois State Historical Library, 1909.

———. "An Unrecognized Father Marquette Letter." *American Historical Review* 25 (1920): 676-80.

Allison, Harold. "Nature Trails." *Bloomington (Ind.) Herald-Times*, February 28, 1999.

American States Papers 1789-1809. 10 vols. Washington, D.C.: Gales and Seaton, 1832-61.

Anson, Bert. *The Miami Indians*. Norman: University of Oklahoma Press, 1970.

Armstrong, Joe C. W. *Samuel de Champlain*. Québec: Les Éditions de L'Homme, 1988.

Arthur T., ed. *The Explorations of Pierre Esprit Radisson*. Minneapolis: Ross & Haines, 1961.

Aubin, George F. *A Proto-Algonquian Dictionary*. Ottawa: National Museums of Canada, 1975.

Baerreis, David A., Erminie Wheeler-Voegelin, and Remedio Wycoco-Moore. *Indians of Northeastern Illinois*. New York: Garland, 1974.

Bailey, Dorothy B. *Brown County, Indiana: History and Families, 1836-1990*. Paducah, Ky.: Turner Publishing, 1991.

Ball, Cable G. *The Journals and Indian Paintings of George Winter, 1837-1839*. Indianapolis: Indiana Historical Society, 1948.

Ball, T. H. *Northwest Indiana from 1800-1900*. Crown Point, Ind.: T. H. Ball, 1900.

Ballard, Ralph. *Old Fort St. Joseph*. Niles, Mich.: Niles Printing, 1949.

Baraga, Friedrich. A *Dictionary of the Otchipwe Language, Explained in English*. New ed. 2 vols. Montreal: Beauchemin et Valois, 1878-80. Reprint, Minneapolis: Ross and Haines, 1966.

Barnhart, John D. *Henry Hamilton and George Rogers Clark in the American Revolution*. Crawfordsville: R. E. Banta, 1951.

Barnhart, John D., and Dorothy L. Riker. *Indiana to 1816: The Colonial Period*. Indianapolis: Indiana Historical Society, 1971.

Bartlett, Charles H., and Richard H. Lyon. *La Salle in the Valley of the St. Joseph*. South Bend, Ind.: South Bend Tribune Printing, 1899.

Bauxar, J. Joseph. "History of the Illinois Area." In *Handbook of North American Indians*, vol. 15, ed. William C. Sturtevant, 594-601. Washington, D.C.: Smithsonian Institution Press, 1978.

Beadle, J. H. *History of Parke County*. Knightstown, Ind.: J. H. Beadle, 1880.

Beckwith, Hiram W. *History of Fountain County*. Chicago: H. H. Hill and N. Iddings, 1881.

———. *History of Montgomery County*. Chicago: Hill & Iddings, 1881.

———. *History of Parke and Vermillion Counties*. Chicago: Knight & Leonard, 1879.

———. *History of Vigo and Parke Counties, Indiana*. Chicago: H. H. Hill and N. Iddings, 1879.

———. *The Illinois and Indiana Indians*. Chicago: Fergus, 1884.

———. "Indian Names of Water Courses in the State of Indiana." Indiana Department of Geology and Natural History, *Twelfth Annual Report*, 39-43. Indianapolis: William B. Buford, 1883.

Berthrong, Donald J. "Indians of North Central and Northeastern Indiana." In *American Indian Ethnohistory*, ed. David Agee Horr. Garland series vol. 18. New York: Garland, 1974.

Black, Glenn A. *The Angel Site: An Archaeological, Historical and Ethnological Study*. 2 vols. Indianapolis: Indiana Historical Society, 1967.

Blair, Emma H., ed. *The Indian Tribes of the Upper Mississippi Valley and Region of the Great Lakes*. Cleveland: Arthur C. Clarke, 1911-12.

Blanchard, Rufus. *History of the Discovery and Conquests of the Northwest, with the History of Chicago*. Wheaton, Ill.: R. Blanchard, 1879.

Bliss, Eugene F., ed. *Diary of David Zeisberger*. Cincinnati: Robert Clarke, 1885.

Bloomfield, Leonard. "Algonquian." In *Linguistic Structures of Native America*. Vol. 6 of *Viking Fund Publications in Anthropology*, ed. Osgood Cornelius, 85-129. New York: Viking Fund, 1946.

———. *Menomini Lexicon*. Milwaukee: Milwaukee Public Museum, 1975.

———. "On the Sound System of Central Algonquian." *Language* 1 (March 1925): 130-56.

———. "The Word-Stems of Central Algonquian." In *Festschrift Meinhof*, 393-402. Hamburg: Kommissionverlag von Friederichsen, 1927.

Boomhower, Ray E. *Jacob Piatt Dunn: A Life in History and Politics, 1855-1924*. Indianapolis: Indiana Historical Society, 1997.

Brasser, T. J. "Mahican." In *Handbook of North American Indians*, ed. William C. Sturtevant, 15:198-212. Washington, D.C.: Smithsonian Institution Press, 1978.

Brelsford, Bridgie Brill. *Indians of Montgomery County, Indiana*. Crawfordsville, Ind.: Montgomery County Historical Society, 1985.

Brinton, Daniel G., and Albert Seqaqkind Anthony. *A Lenape-English Dictionary*. Philadelphia: Historical Society of Pennsylvania, 1889.

Brose, David S., C. Wesley Cowans, and Robert C. Mainfort Jr., eds. *Societies in Eclipse, Archaeology of the Eastern Woodland Indians, A.D. 1400-1700*. Washington and London: Smithsonian Institution Press, 2001.

Brown, James A., and Patricia J. O'Brien, eds. *At the Edge of Prehistory: Huber Phase Archaeology in the Chicago Area*. Springfield, Ill.: Department of Transportation, 1990.

Brown, James A., and R. F. Sasso. "Prelude to History on the Eastern Prairies." In *Societies in Eclipse: Archaeology of the Eastern Woodland Indians, A.D. 1400-1700*, ed. D. S. Brose, C. W. Cowan and R. C. J. Mainfort, 205-28. Washington, D.C.: Smithsonian Institution Press, 2001.

Brown, Lloyd Arnold. *Early Maps of the Ohio Valley*. Pittsburgh: University of Pittsburgh Press, 1959.

Bruyas, Jacques. *Radices verborum iroquaeorum*. Reprint. New York: AMS Press, 1970.

Buisseret, David. *Mapping the French Empire in North America*. Chicago: Newberry Library, 1991.

Callaghan, Edmund B., ed. *Documents Relative to the Colonial History of the State of New York; Procured in Holland, England and France, by John R. Brodhead*. New York: Parsons and Weed, 1853-87.

Callender, Charles. "Fox." In *Handbook of North American Indians*, ed. William C. Sturtevant, 15:636-47. Washington, D.C.: Smithsonian Institution Press, 1978.

———. "Shawnee." In *Handbook of North American Indians*, ed. William C. Sturtevant, 15:622-35. Washington, D.C.: Smithsonian Institution, 1978.

Campeau, Lucien. "Les Cartes relatives à la découverte du Mississipi par le P. Jacques Marquette et Louis Jolliet." *Les Cahiers des Dix* 47 (1992): 41-90.

———. "La découverte du Lac Érié." *Les Cahiers des Dix* 44 (1989): 21-37.

———. "Les mémoires d'Allet rendus à leur auteur." *Les Cahiers des Dix* 43 (1983): 27-59.

———. *Monumenta Novæ Franciæ*. "Les grandes épreuves." Québec: Éditions Bellarmin, 1989.

———. "Regards critiques sur la *Narration* du P. Jacques Marquette." *Les Cahiers des Dix* 46 (1991): 21-60.

———. "La Route commerciale de l'Ouest au dix-septième siècle." *Les Cahiers des Dix* 29 (1994): 22-49.

Canac-Marquis, Steve, and Pierre Rézeau, eds. *Journal de Vaugine de Nuisement*. Québec: Les Presses de l'Université Laval, 2005.

Cayton, Andrew R. L. *Frontier Indiana*. Bloomington: Indiana University Press, 1996.

Chafe, Wallace L. *Seneca Morphology and Dictionary*. No. 4 of *Smithsonian Contributions to Anthropology*. Washington, D.C.: Smithsonian Institution Press, 1967.

Chamberlain, E., ed. *The Indiana Gazetteer; or Topographical Dictionary of the State of Indiana*. 3rd ed. Indianapolis: E. Chamberlain, 1849.

Charlevoix, Pierre François-Xavier de. *Journal of a Voyage to North America*. 2 vols. Chicago: Caxton Club, 1923.

Clifton, James A. "Potawatomi." In *Handbook of North American Indians*, ed. William C. Sturtevant, 17:725-742. Washington, D.C.: Smithsonian Institution Press, 1978.

Collections of the Illinois Historical Library. Springfield: Trustees of the Illinois State Historical Library.

Collett, John. *Indiana Department of Geology and Natural History, Twelfth Annual Report*. Indianapolis: Wm. B. Buford, 1883.

Combination Atlas of Boone County, Indiana. Chicago: Kingman Bros., 1878.

Combination Atlas of Howard County, Indiana. Chicago: Kingman Bros., 1877. Reprint, Knightstown, Ind.: Bookmark, 1976.

Costa, David J. "The Historical Phonology of Miami-Illinois Consonants." *International Journal of American Linguistics* 57, no. 3 (July 1991): 365-93.

———. "Miami-Illinois Animal Names." *Algonquian and Iroquoian Linguistics* 17, no. 3 (1992): 19-44.

———. *The Miami-Illinois Language*. Lincoln: University of Nebraska Press, 2003.

———. "Miami-Illinois Tribe Names." *Proceedings of the Thirty-first Algonquian Conference*, ed. John Nichols, 30-53. Winnipeg: University of Manitoba, 2000.

Cox, E. T. *Geological Survey of Indiana 1875*. Indianapolis: Sentinel, 1876.

———. "Indiana Department of Geology and Natural Resources Annual Report, Maps." Indianapolis: Indiana Department of Natural Resources, 1869.

Crist, L. M. *History of Boone County, Indiana*. Indianapolis: A. W. Bowen, n.d.

Cumming, W. P., S. E. Hillier, D. B. Quinn, and G. Williams. *The Exploration of North America 1630-1776*. New York: G. P. Putnam's Sons, 1974.

Cutler, Jervis, and Charles Le Raye. *A Topographical Description of the State of Ohio, Indiana Territory, and Louisiana*. Reprint. New York: Arno Press, 1971.

Day, Gordon M. "Place-Names as Ethnographic Data." In *Actes du Huitième Congrès des Algonquinistes*, ed. William Cowan, 26-31. Ottawa: Carleton University, 1977.

Dehart, R. P. *Past and Present in Tippecanoe County, Indiana.* 2 vols. Indianapolis: B. F. Bowen, 1909.

De La Hunt, Thomas James. *Perry County/A History.* Indianapolis: W. K. Stewart, 1916.

Delanglez, Jean. "A Calendar of Lasalle Travels 1643-1683." *Mid-America* 22, no. 4 (1940): 278-305.

———. "Cartography of the Mississippi." *Mid-America* 30 (1948): 257-84; 31 (1949): 29-52.

———. "First Establishment of the Faith in New France, Chapters XXI-XXV." *Mid-America* 30, no. 3 (1948): 187-214.

———. "Franquelin, Mapmaker."*Mid-America* 25, no. 1 (1943): 29-74.

———. "The Jolliet Lost Map of the Mississippi." *Mid-America* 28, no. 2 (1946): 67-144.

———. "The La Salle Expedition of 1682." *Mid-America* 22, no. 1 (1940): 3-53.

———. *Life and Voyages of Louis Jolliet (1645-1700).* Chicago: Institute of Jesuit History, 1948.

———. "Marquette's Autograph Map of the Mississippi River." *Mid-America* 27 (1945): 30-53.

———. "The "Récit des voyages et des découvertes du Père Jacques Marquette." *Mid-America* 28, no. 3 & 4 (1946): 173-94, 211-58.

———. *Some La Salle Journeys.* Chicago: Institute of Jesuit History, 1938.

———. "The Source of the Delisle Map of America, 1703." *Mid-America* 25, no. 4 (1943): 275-98.

———. "Tonti Letters." *Mid-America* 21, no. 3 (1939): 209-38.

De Montigny, Dumont. *Mémoires historiques sur la Louisiane.* Paris, 1753.

De Rochemonteix, Camille. *Les Jésuites et la Nouvelle-France au XVIIe Siècle, d'après Beaucoup de Documents Inédits.* 3 vols. Paris: Macon, Photat Frères, 1895-96.

De Vorsey, Louis. *Keys to the Encounter: A Library of Congress Resource Guide for the Study of the Age of Discovery.* Washington, D.C.: Library of Congress, 1992.

Draper, Lyman C., and Reuben G. Thwaites, eds. *Collections of the State Historical Society of Wisconsin.* 21 vols. Madison: Society, 1855-1911.

Dunbar, Rowland, and Albert G. Sanders. *Mississippi Provincial Archives.* 5 vols. Jackson: Press of the Mississippi Department of Archives and History, 1927-84.

Dunn, Jacob P. *Indiana and the Indianans: A History of Aboriginal Territorial Indiana and the Century of Statehood.* 5 vols. Chicago: American Historical Society, 1919.

———. "Mission to the Ouabache." *Indiana Historical Society Publications* 3 (1902): 254-330.

———. "Names of the Ohio River." *Indiana Magazine of History* 7 (December 1912): 166-70.

———. *True Indian Stories: With Glossary of Indiana Indian Names*. Indianapolis: Sentinel Printing, 1909.

Edgar, Matilda, ed. *Ten Years in Upper Canada in Peace and War, 1805-1815: The Ridout Letters*. London: T. Fisher Unwin, 1891.

Esarey, Duane. "On the Conflation of Tonty and Delliette Careers in Illinois Country History." *Le Journal* (Center for French Colonial Studies) 21, no. 1 (Winter 2005): 8-10.

Esarey, Duane, and Lawrence A. Conrad. "The Bold Counselor Phase." *Wisconsin Archaeologist* 79, no. 2 (1998): 38-61.

Esarey, Logan, ed. *Messages and Letters of William Henry Harrison*. 2 vols. Indianapolis: Indiana Historical Commission, 1922.

Eschmann, C. J., ed. "Kaskaskia Church Records." *Transactions of the Illinois State Historical Society* 9 (1904): 394-413.

Faillon, Étienne-Michel. *Histoire de la Colonie Française en Canada*. 3 vols. Paris, 1865-66.

Faries, Richard., ed. *A Dictionary of the Cree Language as Spoken by the Indians in the Provinces of Quebec, Ontario, Manitoba, Saskatchewan and Alberta*. Toronto: General Synod of the Church of England in Canada, 1938.

Feest, Christian F. *Indians and a Changing Frontier: The Art of George Winter*. Indianapolis: Indiana Historical Society, 1993.

Feest, Johanna E., and Christian F. "Ottawa." In *Handbook of North American Indians*, ed. William C. Sturtevant, 15:772-786. Washington, D.C.: Smithsonian Institution Press, 1978.

Field, Richard. *Indiana Impressions*. Helena: Far Country Press, 2005.

Finley, Anthony, publ. *A New American Atlas*. Philadelphia, 1826.

Fraser, Alexander. *Huron Manuscripts from Rev. Pierre Potier's Collection*. Report of the Bureau of Archives for the Province of Ontario 15. Toronto: C. W. James, 1920.

Gaither, Frances A. *The Fatal River*. New York: Henry Holt, 1931.

Gipson, Lawrence H., ed. *The Moravian Indian Mission on White River: Diaries and Letters, May 5, 1799 to November 12, 1806*. Indiana Historical Collections 23. Indianapolis: Indiana Historical Commission, 1938.

Goddard, Ives. "Contraction in Fox (Meskwaki)." In *Papers of the 32nd Algonquian Conference*, ed. John Nichols, 164-239. Winnipeg: University of Manitoba, 2001.

———. "Delaware." In *Handbook of North American Indians*, ed. William C. Sturtevant, 15:213-39. Washington, D.C.: Smithsonian Institution Press, 1978.

———. *Delaware Verbal Morphology: A Description and Comparative Study*. New York: Garland, 1979.

———. "Heckewelder's 1792 Vocabulary from Ohio: A Possible Attestation of Mascouten." In *Papers of the 34th Algonquian Conference*, ed. H. C. Wolfhart, 165-92. Winnipeg: University of Manitoba, 2003.

———. "Historical and Philological Evidence Regarding the Identification of the Mascouten." *Ethnohistory* 19, no.2 (1972): 123-34.

———. "The Historical Phonology of Munsee." *International Journal of American Linguistics* 48, no. 1 (1982): 16-48.

———. *Leonard Bloomfield's Fox Lexicon*, Algonquian and Iroquoian Linguistics *Memoir* 12. Winnipeg: University of Manitoba Press, 1994.

———. "Pidgin Delaware." In *Contact Languages: A Wider Perspective*, ed. Sarah G. Thomason, 43-98. Amsterdam: John Benjamins, 1996.

———. "Primary and Secondary Stem Derivation in Algonquian." *International Journal of American Linguistics* 56 (1990): 449-83.

———. "The West-to-East Cline in Algonquian Dialectology." In *Papers of the Twenty-fifth Algonquian Conference*, ed. William Cowan, 187-211. Ottawa: Carlton University, 1994.

Gookins, S. B. *History of Vigo County Indiana*. Chicago: H. H. Hill and N. I. Iddings, 1880.

Grantham, Larry. "The Illinois Village of the Marquette and Jolliet Voyage of 1673." *Missouri Archaeologist* 54 (1993): 1-20.

Gravier, Gabriel. *Carte des Grands Lacs de l'Amérique du Nord: Dressée en 1670 par Bréhan de Gallinée, missionnaire sulpicien*. Rouen: E. Cagniard, 1895.

Habig, Marion A. *The Franciscan Père Marquette: A Critical Biography of Father Zénobe Membré, O.F.M, La Salle's Chaplain and Mississippi Companion 1645 (ca)-1689*. Franciscan Studies no. 13. New York: Joseph F. Wagner, 1934.

Hamell, George R. "Long-Tail: The Panther in Huron-Wyandot and Seneca Myth, Ritual, and Material Culture." In *Icons of Power: Feline Symbolism in the Americas*, ed. Nicholas J. Saunders, 258-91. London: Routledge, 1998.

Hamilton, Raphael N. *Marquette's Explorations: The Narratives Reexamined*. Madison: University of Wisconsin Press, 1970.

Hanna, C. A. *The Wilderness Trail*. 2 vols. New York: G. P. Putnam's Sons, 1910-11.

Harden, Samuel. *History of Madison County, Indiana*. Markleville, Ind., 1874.

Hartley, Alan H. "Preliminary Observations in Ojibwa Place-Names." In *Papers of the Twelfth Algonquian Conference*, ed. William Cowan, 31-38. Ottawa: Carleton University, 1981.

Hay, Henry. "A Narrative of Life on the Old Frontier." *Proceedings of the State Historical Society of Wisconsin* 62:208-61. Madison: Society, 1915.

Heckewelder, John G. E. "Narrative of John Heckewelder's Journey to the Wabash in 1792." *Pennsylvania Magazine of History and Biography* 12 (1888): 34-54, 165-84.

———. *Narrative of the Mission of the United Brethren among the Delaware and Mohegan Indians, from Its Commencement in the Year 1740, to the Close of the Year 1808*. Philadelphia: McCarty and Davis, 1820.

Heidenreich, Conrad. "An Analysis of the 17th Century Map 'Nouvelle France.'" *Cartographica* 25 (3): 67-111.

Helman, Vernon Rueben. *Archaeological Survey of Vigo County.* Indianapolis: Indiana Historical Bureau, 1952.

Hewson, John. *A Computer-Generated Dictionary of Proto-Algonquian.* Canadian Museum of Civilization, Mercury Series. Canadian Ethnology Service *Paper* 125. Hull, 1993.

Hicks, Ronald, ed. *Native American Cultures in Indiana: Proceedings of the First Minnetrista Council for Great Lakes Native American Studies.* Muncie, Ind.: Minnetrista Cultural Center and Ball State University, 1992.

Hiestand, Joseph S. *An Archaeological Report of Newton County, Indiana.* Indianapolis: Indiana Historical Bureau, 1951.

History of Jasper County, Indiana. Rensselaer, Ind.: Jasper-Newton Counties Genealogical Society, 1985.

History of Johnson County, Indiana. Chicago: Brant & Fuller, 1888.

History of Orange County. Paducah, Ky.: Turner Publishing, 1992.

History of Parke and Vermillion Counties, Indiana. Indianapolis: B. F. Bower, 1913.

History of Rush County, Indiana. Chicago: Brant and Fuller, 1888.

History of Vermillion County. Chicago: Lewis Publishing, 1888.

History of Warrick, Spencer and Perry Counties Indiana. Chicago: Goodspeed, 1885.

Hockett, Charles. "Notes on Peoria & Miami." *Algonquian and Iroquoian Linguistics* 10, no. 4 (1985): 29-41.

Horsford, Eben Norton, ed. *Zeisberger's Indian Dictionary; English, German, Iroquois—The Onondaga and Algonquin—The Delaware.* Cambridge, Mass.: John Wilson, 1887.

Howe, Henry. "Vocabularies of the Shawanoese and Wyandott Languages, Etc." In *Historical Collections of Ohio,* 3:278-83. Cincinnati: Bradley & Anthony, 1848.

Hutchins, Thomas. *The Courses of the Ohio River Taken by Lt. T. Hutchins Anno 1766, and Two Accompanying Maps.* Cincinnati: History and Philosophical Society of Ohio, 1942.

Illustrated Historical Atlas of Indiana. Baskin, Forster, 1876.

Indiana Canoeing Guide. Indianapolis: Indiana Department of Natural Resources, 1987.

Jablow, Joseph. *Indians of Illinois and Indiana.* New York: Garland Press, 1974.

Jones, Arthur Edward. "The Site of the Mascoutin Village." In *Proceedings of the State Historical Society of Wisconsin* 54:175-82. Madison: Democrat Printing, 1907.

Jones, William. *Kickapoo Tales.* American Ethnology Society *Publications* 9. New York: Society, 1915.

Joutel, Henri. *Joutel's Journal of La Salle's Last Voyage, 1684-7. New Edition with Historical and Biographical Introduction, Annotations and Index by Henry Reed*

Stiles. To Which Is Added a Bibliography of the Discovery of the Mississippi, by Appleton P.C. Griffin. Albany: J. McDonough, 1906.

Justice, Noel D. *Stone Age Spear and Arrow Points of the Midcontinental and Eastern United States.* Bloomington: Indiana University Press, 1987.

Kappler, Charles J., ed. *Indian Affairs: Laws and Treaties.* 2d ed., 2 vols. Washington, D.C.: GPO, 1904.

Kari, James, and James A. Fall, eds. *Shem Pete's Alaska: The Territory of the Upper Cook Inlet Dena'ina.* Fairbanks: Alaska Native Language Center, University of Alaska, 1987.

Karpinski, Louis C., comp. *Bibliography of the Printed Maps of Michigan, 1804-1880: With a Series of Over One Hundred Reproductions of Maps Constituting an Historical Atlas of the Great Lakes and Michigan, by Louis C. Karpinski; Including Discussions of Michigan Maps and Map-makers by William Lee Jenks.* Lansing: Michigan Historical Commission, 1931.

Karst, Frederick. "The Eel River." *Outdoor Indiana* 70, no. 4 (July-August 2005): 36-47.

Kaufman, Kevin. *The Mapping of the Great Lakes in the Seventeenth Century: Twenty-two Maps from the George S. and Nancy B. Parker Collection.* Providence, R.I.: John Carter Brown Library, 1989.

Kellogg, Louise Phelps. *Early Narratives of the Northwest, 1634-1699.* Vol. 16, *Original Narratives of Early American History.* New York: Charles Scribner's Sons, 1917.

———. *The French Regime in Wisconsin and the Northwest.* Madison: State Historical Society of Wisconsin, 1925.

Kenton, Edna Kenton. *The Indians of North America.* 2 vols. New York: Harcourt, Brace, 1927.

Kilver, M. D., ed. *A History of Lima Township, La Grange County, Indiana.* Howe, Ind.: Lions Club, 1976.

Knight, Robert, and Lucius H. Zeuch. *The Location of the Chicago Portage Route of the Seventeenth Century.* Chicago: Chicago Historical Society, 1928.

Krauskopf, Frances. *Ouiatanon Documents.* Indianapolis: Indiana Historical Society, 1955.

Lance, Donald M. "The Origin and Meaning of Missouri." *Names* 47 (1999): 281-90.

Langlois, Michel. *Carignan-Salière, 1665–1668.* Drummondville, Québec: Maison des Ancêtres, 2004.

Lauvrière, Émile. *Histoire de la Louisiane Française, 1673-1939.* Baton Rouge: Louisiana State University Press, 1940.

Laverdière, C.-H. *Oeuvres de Champlain.* 2nd ed. Québec: Geo.-E. Desbarats, 1870.

Le Clerq, Chrétien. *The First Establishment of the Faith in New France.* 2 vols. [Paris, 1691.] Translation by John G. Shea. Reprint, New York: J. G. Shea, 1881.

Les Noms de Lieu du Québec. Sainte-Foy: Les Publications du Québec, 1996.

Lindley, Harlow, ed. *Indiana as Seen by Early Travelers*. Indianapolis: Indiana Historical Commission, 1916.

Lindsey, Alton A., ed. *Natural Features of Indiana*. Reprint. Indianapolis: Indiana Academy of Sciences, 1970.

Lockridge, Ross F. "Indian Names of Indiana Streams." *Indiana Teacher* (April 1945): 215-16.

Longfellow, Henry Wadsworth. *Hiawatha: The Courtship of Miles Standish; and Other Poems*. London: Oxford University Press, 1925.

Lounsbury, Floyd G. "Iroquoian Linguistics." In *Handbook of North American Indians*, ed. William C. Sturtevant, 15:334-43. Washington, D.C.: Smithsonian Institution Press, 1978.

———. *Iroquois Place-Names in the Champlain Valley*. Albany: University of the State of New York, State Education Department, 1960. Reprinted from the Report of the New York–Vermont Interstate Commerce Commission on the Lake Champlain Basin, 1960, Legislative Document 9:23-66.

Malchelosse, Gérard. "La Salle et le fort Saint-Joseph des Miamis." *Les Cahiers des Dix* 22 (1957): 83-103.

———. "Le Poste de la Rivière St-Joseph (Michigan)." *Les Cahiers des Dix* 23 (1958): 139-86.

The Mapping of the Great Lakes in the Seventeenth Century: Twenty-two Maps from the George S. and Nancy B. Parker Collection. Introduction and Commentary by Kevin Kaufman. Providence, R.I.: John Carter Brown Library, 1989.

Margry, Pierre, ed. *Découvertes et Établissements des Français dans L'ouest et dans le Sud de l'Amérique Septentrionale 1614-1754, Mémoires et Documents Inédits Recueillis et Publiés par Pierre Margry*. 6 vols. Reprint. New York: AMS Press, 1974.

Mason, Ronald J. *Rock Island, Historical Indian Archaeology in the Northern Lake Michigan Basin*. MCJA Special Paper No. 6. Kent, Ohio: Kent State University Press, 1986.

McCafferty, Michael. "Additional Notes on the Place Name Chicago." *Le Journal* 20, no. 2 (Spring 2004): 8-11.

———. "A Fresh Look at the Place Name Chicago." *Journal of the Illinois State Historical Society* 96, no. 2 (2003): 116-29.

———. "The Latest Miami-Illinois Dictionary and Its Author." In *Papers of the Thirty-Sixth Algonquian Conference*, ed. H. C. Wolfhart, 271-86. Winnipeg: University of Manitoba Press, 2005.

———. "On the Birthday and Etymology of the Place Name Missouri." *Names* 51, no. 2 (June 2003): 31-45.

———. "Revisiting Chicago" (Reader Response). *Journal of the Illinois State Historical Society* 98, nos. 1-2 (Spring-Summer 2005): 82-98.

———. "Wabash, Its Meaning and History." In *Proceedings of the Thirty-first Algonquian Conference*, ed. John Nichols, 225-28. Winnipeg: University of Manitoba Press, 2002.

McCord, Beth. *The Ghosts of the Delaware: An Archaeological Study of Delaware Settlement Along the White River, Indiana*. Report of Investigation 62. Muncie, Ind.: Archaeological Resources Management Service, Ball State University, 2002.

McDermott, J. F., ed. *Old Cahokia: A Narrative and Documents Illustrating the First Century of Its History*. St. Louis: St. Louis Historical Documents Foundation, 1949.

McDonald, Daniel. *A Twentieth Century History of Marshall County Indiana*. 2 vols. Chicago: Lewis, 1908.

McPherson, Alan. *Indian Names in Indiana*. Monticello, Ind.: Blasted Works, 1994.

Meek, Basil. "Harmar's Expedition." *Ohio Archaeological and Historical Publications*. Multiple vols. Columbus: Fred J. Heer, 1911.

Melançon, Arthur. *Liste des Missionaires Jesuites/Nouvelle-France et Louisiane 1611-1800*. Montreal: Collège Sainte-Marie, 1929.

Meyers, Rex L. *Daviess County Indiana History*. Paducah, Ky.: Turner Publishing Co., 1988.

Michigan Pioneer and Historical Society. *Collections and Researches*. 40 vols. Lansing, Mich.: Society, 1877-1929.

Mississippi Provincial Archives, French Dominion. Jackson: Press of the Mississippi Department of Archives and History, 1927-84.

Moore, Powell A. *The Calumet Region*. Indianapolis: Indiana Historical Bureau, 1959.

Morgan, Lewis Henry. *The Indian Journals, 1859-1862*. Edited by Leslie A. White. Cambridge: Harvard Press, 1959.

———. *Systems of Consanguinity and Affinity of the Human Family*. Smithsonian Contributions to Knowledge 17. Washington, D.C.: Smithsonian Institution, 1871.

Morse, Jedidiah. *The American Universal Geography*. Boston: J. T. Buckingham, 1812.

Morse, Jedidiah, and Sidney E. Morse. *A New Universal Atlas of the World*. New Haven, Conn.: Howe & Spalding, 1822.

Munson, Patrick J. "Still More on the Antiquity of Maple Sugar and Syrup in Aboriginal Eastern North America." *Journal of Ethnobiology* 9, no. 2 (1989): 159-70.

Nichols, John B., and Earl Nyholm. *A Concise Dictionary of Minnesota Ojibwe*. Minneapolis: University of Minnesota Press, 1995.

Olafson, Sigfus. "Gabriel Arthur and the Fort Ancient People." *West Virginia Archeologist* 12 (December 1960): 32-42.

O'Meara, John, and the Delaware Nation Council, Moravian of the Thames Band. *Delaware-English/English-Delaware Dictionary*. Toronto: University of Toronto Press, 1996.

Owen, David Dale. *A Geological Reconnaissance and Survey of the State of Indiana 1837 and 1838: Carroll County*. Department of Natural Resources, Geological Survey *Bulletin* 61. Bloomington: State of Indiana, 1987.

Rafert, Stewart. *The Miami Indians of Indiana: A Persistent People, 1654-1994*. Indianapolis: Indiana Historical Society, 1996.

Rapport de l'Archiviste de la Province de Québec. Québec: Redempti Paradis, 1929-44.

Rankin, Robert L. "On Some Ohio Valley Siouan and Illinois Algonquian Words for 'Eight.'" *International Journal of American Linguistics* 51:544-47.

Rhodes, Richard. *Eastern-Ojibwa-Chippewa-Ottawa Dictionary*. New York: Mouton, 1985.

Ricker, Dorothy, ed. "Two Accounts of the upper Wabash Country 1819-20." *Indiana Magazine of History* 37 (1941): 384-95.

Robertson, Nellie A., and Dorothy Ricker, eds. *The John Tipton Papers*. 3 vols. Indianapolis: Indiana Historical Bureau, 1942.

Roy, Pierre-Georges. *Sieur de Vincennes Identified*. Indiana Historical Society *Publications* 7, no. 1. Indianapolis: C. E. Pauley, 1918.

Royse, L. W. *A Standard History of Kosciusko County*. 2 vols. Chicago: Lewis Publishing, 1919.

Rudes, Blair A. "Iroquoian Vowels." *Anthropological Linguistics* 37, no. 1 (Spring 1995): 16-69.

Salts, Walter, comp. *Warren County, Indiana, and Its People*. Williamsport, Ind.: Warren County Historical Society, 1981.

Schoolcraft, Henry Rowe. *Archives of Aboriginal Knowledge. Containing All the Original Paper Laid before Congress Respecting the History, Antiquities, Language, Ethnology, Pictography, Rites, Superstitions, and Mythology, of the Indian Tribes of the United States, &c by Henry R. Schoolcraft*. 6 vols. Philadelphia: J. B. Lippincott, 1860.

Schwartz, Seymour I., and Ralph E. Ehrenberg. *The Mapping of America*. New York: Harry N. Abrams, 1980.

Scott, John. *The Indiana Gazeteer or Topographical Dictionary, 1826*. Reprint. Indiana Historical Society *Publication* 28, no. 1. Indianapolis: Indiana Historical Society, 1954.

Scull, Gideon D., ed. *Voyages of Peter Esprit Radisson*. Boston: Prince Society, 1885. Reprint, New York: P. Smith, 1943.

Shaver, Robert H., H. Curtis, Ann M. Burger, Donald D. Carr, John B. Droste, Donald L. Eggert, Henry H. Gray, Denver Harper, Nancy R. Hasenmueller, Walter A. Hasenmueller, Alan S. Horowitz, Harold C. Hutchinson, Brian Keith, Stanley

J. Keller, John B. Patton, Carl B. Rexroad, and Charles E. Wier. *Compendium of Paleozoic Rock-Unit Stratigraphy in Indiana: A Revision*. Department of Natural Resources Geological Survey *Bulletin* 59. Bloomington, Ind., 1986.

Siebert, Frank T., Jr. "The Original Home of the Proto-Algonquian People." In *Contributions to Anthropology: Linguistics I (Algonquian)*, 13-37. Anthropology Series 78. Ottawa: National Museum of Canada, 1967.

———. "Resurrecting Virginia Algonquian from the Dead: the Reconstituted and Historical Phonology of Powhatan." In *Studies in Southeastern Indian Languages*, ed. James M. Crawford, 285-453. Athens: University of Georgia Press, 1975.

Simmons, Richard S. *Rivers of Indiana*. Bloomington: Indiana University Press, 1985.

Smith, Dwight L., ed. *Greene Ville to Fallen Timbers: A Journal of the Wayne Campaign July 28-September 14, 1794*. Indianapolis: Indiana Historical Society, 1952.

Smith, Thomas H. *The Mapping of Ohio*. Kent, Ohio: Kent State University Press, 1977.

Staab, Rodney. "Hypolite Bolon *Père et Fils*: Interpreters to the Delawares." In *Proceedings of the Thirty-first Algonquian Conference*, ed. John Nichols, 381-401. Winnipeg: University of Manitoba.

The St. Clair Papers: The Life and Public Services of Arthur St. Clair. 2 vols. Cincinnati: R. Clarke, 1882.

Stearns, Raymond Phineas. "Joseph Kellogg's Observations on Senex's Map of North America." *Mississippi Valley Historical Review* 23, no. 3 (December 1936): 345-54.

Steckley, John. "The Early Map 'Nouvelle France': A Linguistic Analysis." *Ontario Archaeology* 51 (1990): 17-29.

Steele, I. K. *Guerillas and Grenadiers: The Struggle for Canada, 1689-1760*. Toronto: Ryerson Press, 1969.

Stewart, George R. *American Place Names*. New York: Oxford University Press, 1970.

Stothers, David M. "Late Woodland Models for Cultural Development in Southern Michigan." In *Retrieving Michigan's Buried Past: The Archaeology of the Great Lakes State*. Cranbrook Institute of Science *Bulletin* 64. Edited by John R. Halsey. Bloomfield Hills, Mich.: Cranbrook Institute of Science, 1999.

———. "The Michigan Owasco and Iroquois Co-Tradition: Late Woodland Conflict, Conquest, and Cultural Realignment in the Western and Lower Great Lakes." *Northeast Anthropology* 49 (1995): 5-41.

Swenson, John F. "Chicagoua/Chicago: The Origin, Meaning, and Etymology of a Place Name." *Illinois Historical Journal* 84 (1991): 235-48.

Tanner, Helen Hornbeck. *Atlas of Great Lakes Indian History*. Norman: Published for the Newberry Library by the University of Oklahoma Press, 1987.

Tanner, Helen Hornbeck, and Erminie Wheeler-Voegelin. *Indians of Ohio and Indiana, Prior to 1795*. New York: Garland Publishing, 1974.

Temple, Wayne. *Indian Villages of the Illinois Country: Historic Tribes*. Revised edition. Vol. 2, pt. 2. Springfield: Illinois State Museum, 1966.

Thévenot, Melchisédech. *Receuil de Voyages de Mr. Thévenot. Dédié au Roy*. Paris: Estienne Michallet, 1681.

Thompson, Charles N. *Sons of the Wilderness: John and William Conner*. Indianapolis: Indiana Historical Society, 1937.

Thwaites, Reuben Gold, ed. *Early Western Travels, 1748-1846*. 32 vols. Cleveland: Arthur H. Clark, 1904-7.

———. *Jesuit Relations and Allied Documents*. 73 vols. Cleveland: Burrows Brothers, 1896-1901.

Toupin, Robert. *Les écrits de Pierre Potier*. Ottawa: Les Presses de l'Université d'Ottawa, 1996.

Trowbridge, Charles C. *Meearmeear Traditions*. Vol. 7 of University of Michigan Museum of Anthropology, *Occasional Contributions*. Ann Arbor, 1938.

———. *Shawnee Traditions*. Ann Arbor: University of Michigan Press, 1939.

Trudel, Marcel. *Collection de Cartes Anciennes et modernes pour servir à l'étude de l'histoire de l'Amérique et du Canada*. Québec: Tremblay and Dion, 1948.

Trumbull, J. Hammond. *Natick Dictionary*. American Ethnology *Bulletin* 25. Washington, D.C.: Government Printing Office, 1903.

Tucker, Sarah Jones, comp. *Indian Villages of the Illinois Country*, Illinois State Museum Scientific Papers 2, pt. 1. Springfield, 1942.

Tyson, Martha E., ed. *A Mission to the Indians, from the Indian Committee of Baltimore Yearly Meeting, to Fort Wayne, in 1804; Written at the Time, by Gerard T. Hopkins; with an Appendix, Compiled in 1862*. Philadelphia: T. E. Zell, 1862.

Verner, Coolie, and Basil Stuart-Stubbs. *The Northpart of America*. Toronto: Academic Press Canada, Hunter Rose Company, 1979.

Voegelin, Carl F. "Delaware, an Eastern Algonquian Language." *Viking Fund Publications in Anthropology* 6 (1946): 130-57.

———. *Shawnee Stems and the Jacob Piatt Dunn Dictionary*, vol. 1, nos. 3 (63-108), 5 (135-167), 8 (289-341), 9 (345-406) and 10 (409-476) of *Prehistory Research Series*. Indianapolis: Indiana Historical Society, 1938-40.

Vogel, Virgil J. *Indian Names of Michigan*. Ann Arbor: University of Michigan Press, 1986.

———. *Indian Names on Wisconsin's Map*. Madison: University of Wisconsin Press, 1991.

Volney, Constantin F. C. "Tableau du Climat et du Sol ses États-Unis d'Amérique." Tome 4 of *Œuvres Complètes*. 2nd ed. Paris: Parmentier and Froment, 1825.

Voorhis, Paul. *Introduction to the Kickapoo Grammar*. Language Science *Monographs* 13. Bloomington: Indiana University Press, 1974.

———. *Kickapoo Vocabulary*. Algonquian and Iroquoian Linguistics *Memoirs* 6. Winnipeg: University of Manitoba Press, 1988.

Walthall, J. A., and T. E. Emerson, eds. *Calumet and Fleur-de-Lys: Archaeology of Indian and French Contact in the Midcontinent.* Washington, D.C.: Smithsonian Institution Press, 1992.

Warbus, Mark. *Another America: Native American Maps and the History of Our Land.* New York: St. Martin's Press, 1997.

The Wea Primer, Wev Mvs Kv Kv Ne, to Teach the Wea Language. Cherokee Nation: Mission Press, 1837.

Weld, Laenneas Gifford. "Joliet and Marquette in Iowa." *Iowa Journal of History and Politics* 1 (1903): 3-16.

Whickcar, J. Wesley. "The Potawatomi Reservations in Benton, Fountain, Warren and Tippecanoe Counties." In *Warren County, Indiana, and Its People,* ed. Walter Salts, 5-8. Williamsport, Ind.: Warren County Historical Society, 1981.

White, Richard. *The Middle Ground: Indians, Empires, and Republics in the Great Lakes Region, 1650-1815.* New York: Cambridge University Press, 1991.

Wilson, George R. *Early Trails and Surveys.* Indianapolis: C. E. Pauley, 1919.

Wilson, George R., and Gayle Thornbrough. *The Buffalo Trace.* Indianapolis: Indiana Historical Society, 1946.

Winger, Otho. *The Last of the Miamis.* North Manchester, Ind., 1935.

Wood, John J., Jr. "The Mascouten Village." In *Proceedings of the State Historical Society of Wisconsin* 54:167-174. Madison: Democrat Printing, 1907.

Wood, W. Raymond, comp. *An Atlas of Early Maps of the American Midwest: Part II.* Springfield: Illinois State Museum, 2001.

Wright, Muriel Wright. *Guide to the Indian Tribes of Oklahoma.* Norman: University of Oklahoma Press, 1951.

Wright, Roy A. "The People of the Panther—A Long Erie Tale." *Papers in Linguistics from the 1972 Conference on Iroquoian Research*, Mercury Series, Ethnology Division Paper 10. Ottawa: National Museums of Canada, National Museum of Man, 1974.

Young, James. "Indiana Tourists Pocket Map. 1835." Philadelphia: S. Augustus Mitchell, 1835.

———. "The Tourist's Pocket Map of the State of Indiana Exhibiting Its Internal Improvements Roads Distances &c." 1852. Philadelphia: S. Augustus Mitchell.

Internet Sites

American-French Genealogical Society. "French-Canadian Surnames." http://homepages.rootsweb.com/~afgs/F2dit-etc.html. Accessed November 17, 2002.

Baerreis, David A. "The Great Lakes Project; The Geographic Location of Potawatomi Bands: 1795-1846; with a consideration of the earlier habitat and migrations of the Potawatomi and other Indian occupations on lands ceded to the United States by the Potawatomi Indians." http://www.gbl.indiana.edu/Pot/Ptoc.html. Accessed December 1, 2000.

Du Val, Pierre. "Le Canada faict par le Sr. de Champlain, ou sont la Nouvelle France, la Nouvelle Angleterre, la Nouvelle Holande, La Nouvelle Svede, la Virginie &c. avec les nations voisines et autres terres nouvellement decouvertes / suivant les memoires de P. Du Val, geographe du Roy, a Paris en l'Isle du Palais, Avec privilege, 1664." Map. http://digital.library.mcgill.ca/pugsley/Pugsmaps06-10.htm. Accessed August 1, 1998.

Greene, Don. "Historic Shawnee Names of the 1700s." http://www.shawnee-traditions.com/Names-16.html. Accessed July 21, 2003.

Griffith, Max E. "History of Shakamak State Park 1926-1960." http://www.geocities.com/the_town_historian/ShakP1.html. Accessed July 14, 2002.

Indiana Outfitters. http://www.indianaoutfitters.com/iroquois_river.html. Accessed April 18, 2004.

Johnson, Margaret. "Patoka Oldest Town in Gibson County." http://www.luciefield.net/patokahist.html. Accessed December 12, 2000.

Kellogg, Joseph. http://www.theamericansurveyor.com/PDF/TheAmericanSurveyor-CompassAndChain-March-April2004.pdf. Accessed December 19, 2003.

La Forest, Thomas J. "The Carignan Regiment." http://www.geocities.com/Heartland/Estates/5255/list1.html. Accessed December 9, 1999.

Libby, Dorothy. "An Anthropological Report on the Piankashaw Indians, Dockett 99, 4 parts." http://www.gbl.indiana.edu/home/html. Accessed October 8, 1899.

Redmond, Brian G. "An Investigation of the Late Woodland Period Settlement in the East Fork White River Valley, Indiana." http://www.gbl.indiana.edu/abstracts/90/redmond_90.html. Accessed May 17, 1999.

Trade Goods. "Pierre-Guillaume Lamothe." http://www.usinternet.com/users/dfnels/lamothe.htm. Accessed May 25, 2003.

Williams, John M., and Noel D. Justice. "An Interim Report of the Archaeological Survey of Brown County." http://www.gbl.indiana.edu./abstracts/90/williams_90.html. Accessed July 7, 1998.

Index

MICHAEL MCCAFFERTY is an ethnolinguist who specializes in Algonquian languages and in the early historical Algonquian-French interface of the Illinois Country. He is a member of the faculty of the Department of Second Language Studies at Indiana University, where he was previously a visiting lecturer in Nahuatl.

The University of Illinois Press
is a founding member of the
Association of American University Presses.

Composed in 10.5/13 Adobe Minion
with Meta display
by BookComp, Inc.
for the University of Illinois Press
Manufactured by Sheridan Books, Inc.

University of Illinois Press
1325 South Oak Street
Champaign, IL 61820-6903
www.press.uillinois.edu